"*Teaching Children About Science* is a good resource for persons in both school and nonschool settings who are helping children learn science . . . much more functional than other activity-oriented books."

—*Curriculum Review*

"An excellent source of ideas presented in a simple, sound format. It belongs in the library of every science curriculum lab, school, and teacher . . . . Levenson's work could be the key to running an exciting, effective science program."

— *Science and Children*

"This author knows what scientific information children need and how that information is successfully transferred to the child . . . . She is involved in improving the quality of science instruction on a grand scale with this wonderful book."

—*Science Activities*

"Highly recommended."

—*Science Books & Films*

Children's Science Booklist (Education)

TEACHING CHILDREN ABOUT SCIENCE

Ideas and Activities Every Teacher and Parent Can Use

Elaine Levenson

Illustrations by Deborah A. Coulombe

Foreword by Mary Budd Rowe, Past-President
National Science Teachers Association

PRENTICE HALL PRESS

New York London Toronto Sydney Tokyo Singapore

I dedicate this book to my mother, to parents and teachers who feel insecure about teaching science subjects, to the young children they teach who ask, "why?" and "how come?" and to my own very special children, William and Emily, whose curiosity and thoughts helped inspire many of the ideas put forth in this book.

Prentice Hall Press
15 Columbus Circle
New York, New York 10023

Published in 1987 by Prentice Hall Press
A Division of Simon & Schuster, Inc.
Originally published by Prentice-Hall, Inc.

PRENTICE HALL PRESS and colophon are registered trademarks of Simon & Schuster Inc.

Library of Congress Cataloging-in-Publication Data

Levenson, Elaine.
Teaching children about science.

Bibliography: p. 210
Includes index.
1. Science—Study and teaching (Elementary)
2. Activity program in education. I. Title
II. Series
LB1585.L395 1985 372.3'5044 85-9583
ISBN 0-13-891730-2

Manufactured in the United States of America

10 9 8 7

CONTENTS

FOREWORD

One afternoon I went to a rural first grade classroom, invited by the young teacher who was doing the "career education" part of the curriculum in that district. The program called for a visiting scientist (me) to whom the children were to ask a set of questions about careers in science. They sat on tiny chairs in a semi-circle around me. Finally, in dutiful fashion the questions began. No children in first grade would ever have thought of them: "Do you have career satisfaction? How many years of training did you have? Are you satisfied with your job? Would you advise others to go into science?" There were ten questions. It took five minutes to answer them. Then we sat facing each other. I finally said, "Are there any questions you always wanted to ask a scientist? I can't promise to answer all of them—maybe there are no answers yet. We keep learning new things every day. What I can't answer I will try to find out by asking other scientists."

They sat for a moment in silence. Then the first hand went up and a small boy said, "Why is it that every time just before I start a fight, I sweat?" I answered that, and the next question was, "I watch preying mantises eat some leaves and he looks like it's good. But when I try chewing those leaves I get sick. Why is that?" Another asked, "Are we sort of a sack of blood? It seems like any place you get cut blood pours out. What good is that?" And so the questions came—for nearly two hours.

There is a great drive on the part of children to know, to get answers. They have to learn, however, that the way we explain things today may change tomorrow. New discoveries lead to new ways of thinking about the facts. In fact, as the children themselves mature their conceptions of the world and their ability to deal with abstraction expands, just as science does. We need to nurture the ability of children to ask questions and to seek answers; to compare competing ideas and to learn strategies for finding out which explanations are more likely. It is characteristic of scientists to ask questions, to continually challenge ideas. Children start life that way, but somewhere many of them appear to lose it. (Actually, we now know they go 'underground'; they get answers, sometimes from undesirable sources. The questions do not stop.)

Once during a trip to China I met a history teacher who was teaching science. He knew very little science and a great deal of history, but he preferred to teach the science because "They keep changing the version of history to be taught. But science doesn't change. You can count on it," he said wistfully.

He is wrong of course. Science is always changing. Someone challenges an interpretation; that prompts a basketful of questions, and these are usually followed by experiments meant to provide evidence which favors one of the competing interpretations. Our explanations are continually subject to new interpretations. Science thrives on argument, on resolving conflicting views through experiment and observation, on exploration and on asking questions.

That is one thing little children do with great gusto if anyone will listen—they ask questions!

This book provides three things to adults who work with young children: a large set of science activities that do not require any sophisticated equipment;

guidance about how to conduct the activities; some relevant science content to help answer questions.

Be careful in using the information provided. The temptation is to tell it all before its pertinence ever occurs to students. One second grader in a class I was visiting sat without doing anything during a science class, despite the fact that he had materials on his desk. When I asked him why, he shrugged, "What's the use. They don't care what I think or what we find out ourselves—just what they think. They always tell you what that is whether you believe it or not. I have lots of questions, but who cares?"

For very young children nothing is ordinary. Every thing is worthy of their attention. They have no hard and fast rules about priorities, about what is important and what is not. They have a million questions for anyone who will listen. Remember that about the questions; listen to their questions as you start to use this book. There is a host of simple activities and little explorations in this book that you can use to provide occasions for children to do some 'sciencing.' Warning: Do not turn these occasions into inquisitions. Let the questions come from the children. Answer them when you can; encourage them to find answers on occasion by asking other people; and help them plan activities that will produce both answers and more questions. If you do not know answers, do not worry about it. Let them help you find out.

Use this book as the valuable resource it is. Listen to the questions and the observations of children—that will show them you care. Besides, it's great fun. They do see the world in a different way. One young child gazed up at the contrail of a jet and said, "Look how that plane is scratching up the sky." She needed no comment, just someone to see it, too.

Enjoy using this book. Science ought to be fun, an adventure. More learning takes place when we are having fun, when we feel compelled to find out something or to make something work. Once while doing some science problem-solving activities with a small group of first graders, I asked if they wanted to come back for another session. One of them said, "I had a good time and I learned how to make that system work the way I wanted it to. But my mother didn't send me to school to have a good time. I'm supposed to get into Stanford and I have no time for fun in school." (First grade!) This mother did not understand that there is a close connection between what information a person has and how he learns it. We all know people who are virtually walking encyclopedias but who cannot seem to do anything with the information. The ability to solve problems is closely related to what you know and how you came to know it. Science is best learned through involvement, by talking over what happened, by arguing and experimenting until some satisfactory explanation emerges—and by holding on to ideas tentatively until something better comes along. Science is fun, and the bonus is that it is the most successful device we know of for developing language comprehension.

Mary Budd Rowe

PREFACE

To a young child the unexplainable is magic. Experiments and activities that help explain physical phenomena help children understand their environment better and help them to have a sense of mastery over it. Children should be encouraged to observe and to compare, to predict and test their ideas. They should be encouraged to repeat an experience or an activity several times to see if the results are always the same or if they vary. In learning about the process of inquiry, you can encourage children to question their results and to try varying their experiences or "experiments" to find out if their results change. You can encourage children to devise ways to measure, record, and arrange their findings in an orderly way, and to think in a logical way when they try to find answers or try to set up experiments.

When science ideas are presented to young children, the experiences need to be real, concrete, tangible experiences with real materials. The ideas and experiences need to be presented in a way that will allow children to feel a connection to them. Avoid presenting information, ideas, or activities in isolation. Try to tie them to a child's life so that the child will feel a desire to know. As adults we often become carried away with content and facts. Try to remember that it is more important for young children to be actively involved in science experiences than for them to learn all of the facts. They will learn and remember what they choose to and that for which they are ready.

My goal is that, through the activities in this book, children will see that learning about and understanding science is simply a matter of looking at the world a bit differently. Science is thinking about the world in terms of how and why. It is seeing relationships between common occurrences and looking for patterns in these common occurrences to help make the world make sense. Science helps young children learn to control their world and to develop a better understanding of natural and physical phenomena. It is exciting for young children to understand that some things are yet to be discovered and understood—and that someday, when they are older, they themselves may be the very ones who find the answers to today's mysteries.

Acknowledgments

I wish to acknowledge the following people for their assistance and help in the preparation of this book.

I am grateful to these people for editing and reviewing the content for scientific accuracy: David Feit, Eng., Sc.D., for reviewing Sound and Light; Jack Rosenthal, for reviewing Air, Water, and Weather; Richard Williamson, Ph.D., for reviewing Magnetism, Static Electricity, Rocks and Volcanoes; Gerald Snyder and Harry Baisden for being resources.

I am grateful to my special friends Estelle Feit, a terrific editor; Cherie Berg-Fett, a superb typist; Ellen Cromwell, Dorothy Goldman, Sandra Reeves, Lynn Oboler, Pam Trumble, Babs Savitt, June Chaudet and Renee Colner, inspirational and creative teachers from whom I learned much; to the staffs and students at Franklin Montessori School, Beth Shalom Learning Center, Har Shalom Nursery School, and Georgetown Hill Nursery School, Childcare Center; to Nat and

Georgia Kramer, Rose Marie Ciccone, Marilyn Klainberg, Jill Harrison-Bloom, Barbara Shapiro, and Fred Schneider, for being so supportive of me when I was in doubt; to Hillary Schneider and Barbara Jaeger, for their art work; to Linda Worden, Joan Bartlett, Lee Gillette, Nicole Amoyt, Joanne Cornish, "Bubbles" Blinder, and John Lincoln Jones, for inspiring me to write this book; to Jean Harlan, whom I have never met, but whose book greatly influenced me; and to Mary Kennan of Prentice-Hall, for accepting my proposal.

My greatest acknowledgment goes to my family for their patience, tolerance, and support. I am especially indebted to my ten-year-old daughter, Emily, from whom I have learned so much; to my thirteen-year-old son, William, who helped me organize my thoughts, who made suggestions for activities and materials, and who edited most of the chapters with me; and to my husband, Hal, for his special understanding in the latter stages of this project.

1
INTRODUCTION TO SCIENCE

How to Use This Book

At the beginning of each topic you will find *"Objectives,"* followed by *"General Background Information for Parents and Teachers"* about the science content and concepts.

The chapters are divided into several concepts for each science topic. The concepts are further broken down into numerous sequential activities. In the *"Activities and Procedures"* section of Chapters 3–13, you will find numbered sequential activities. They progress from simple concrete experiences to more complicated abstract ideas. It is suggested that this sequence be followed. The activities have been arranged to progress from simple ideas to more complicated ones in a sequential order. Try to present the activities in order, even if you skip some. Each numbered activity lists:

- materials needed
- a description of procedure for the activity
- suggested questions to ask
- suggested vocabulary to use when appropriate
- and when necessary, a list of *Fine Points to Discuss With Children* as to why the activity was done and the expected outcomes. (*Fine Points to Discuss With Children* will be of more use when working with older children.)

Each chapter ends with a bibliographic list called *"Further Resources,"* which has been separated into *"Suggested Books for Children"* and *"Resource Books for More Ideas."* Most of the suggested books for children tend to be books that have many pictures and that are easy to read.

An Important Note to Teachers and Parents About Using This Book

As you read this book you will notice many of the procedures have long explanations. These explanations to children have been included more for your benefit than for the children's. They are provided in the event that a child asks a question that you might not be able to answer. But, primarily, the explanations are included so that you, as adults, will understand the content of a procedure.

It is wise, if the children are intellectually able, to have them reason on their own and not to "tell them everything." Allow the children to come up with their own explanations whenever possible. Have children do the experiments or do research in age-appropriate reference books such as those listed in the bibliographies at the end of each chapter. Many of the explanations are included so that you, as an adult, will know whether a child is on the right track or needs to be guided to use more reason and systematic logic to solve a problem.

With older children or those who are able intellectually, show the materials and let the children devise ways to use them, rather than telling them how to use everything.

The content of science is a wonderful tool for helping children develop their reasoning and thinking skills. Reasoning is the fourth "R," along with reading, writing, and 'rithmetic. Help children develop themselves by allowing them the freedom to think problems out on their own and to test out their ideas.

To do many of the procedures in the book, you will need to assist many of the children, but remember not to overassist.

How to Teach Science

Young children (and those who have not been exposed to science) should learn about science through a multitude of hands-on experiences with real physical objects or models* or real things. The objects, ideas, and concepts presented should be placed in a meaningful context, so that a need is created within the child to want to know more. If a question or problem can be created, the experience becomes more relevant and significant to the child's life. The information learned from the experience is more likely to be remembered.

Many adults feel insecure about their knowledge of science and therefore are uncomfortable teaching content areas with which they feel a lack of familiarity. In reality, most adults understand much more than they give themselves credit for. The basic problem is that of not knowing how to organize the science knowledge they already possess.

Science is "everything" and "everywhere." Just zero in on what you already understand and know a little about, or choose something you are already interested in and want to know more about. As parents and early childhood educators, you have the freedom to choose what areas to study in science and what you want to expose your children to. You have the total world to choose from; the natural world, the physical world, the ancient world, and the universe. The study of most science subjects at the early stages is merely a matter of looking at the content in a methodological way and organizing the content into classes and subsets so that a meaningful context and relevance can be set up for the information.

Teaching by contrasts and similarities The easiest way to help children understand or learn something new is to expose them to sharp contrasts, so that differences will be obvious. Then they can try to find the similarities between objects that are different. For example, if you are looking at mammals, you might ask if the cat and the horse look alike: How are they different? How are they alike? How are their bodies like our bodies? How are they different? What special features do horses have in their anatomy that help them run faster than we can? What does a cat have on its feet that helps it climb a tree faster than we can, if we can at all? How do cats and horses stay warm? When we run, what part of our body starts to perspire first?

Teaching with a topic and a sequential plan in mind Avoid a flamboyant "magic-show" style, one that creates mystery and awe. For example—one day presenting magnets, the next day making a cloud appear in a glass, and the next day taking a flower apart. It is difficult to connect these three experiences. Instead, a more formal plan should be implemented. For example: Decide on a science unit you or the children would like to investigate, and then spend a week or two doing activities related to the topic being studied so that a relevant context for the experiences can be created and built upon.

Teaching systems for categorizing Help children develop a system for categorizing and classifying, so that they will be able to break down a large area of study into its smaller parts. Then create an order out of the chaos by grouping, sorting, matching, and positioning materials.

Teaching to discriminate among details Help children develop their ability to discriminate among details by looking for attributes held in common. Compare likenesses and differences of size, color, shape, texture, age, sound, smell, and if possible, taste.

Teaching by helping children think and make discoveries Ask children a lot of questions, rather than giving them information. Try to make them find the answers and think. Allow children the opportunity to feel, manipulate, and discover on their own, and then encourage them to share their thoughts. As an adult, help children make predictions, and help them design experiments to test out their hypotheses. Allow yourself and the children to make mistakes; then try to analyze the mistakes together. Stress the importance of testing something several times before drawing conclusions.

Teaching by using logic Science is logical. Categories and sets need to make sense. Things are included or excluded for reasons, and sometimes sets can overlap and form a union or intersection of two sets. For example: Animals can be categorized by two sets: those with backbones and those without backbones. An intersection can occur, however, between the two sets that consists of all animals with jointed legs. Allow children to form a classification system thought out by

**Models:* Models are representations of real things and can be much smaller or much larger than the objects' real-life size. A more detailed description of what is meant by models is presented in Chapter 2.

themselves. Question the child's logic. Ask, "Why is this included and why is that not included?" Ask if there is another way of sorting the items. "Can you make more piles or fewer piles that would make sense?" There is no right or wrong way as long as there is a logical reason for inclusion or exclusion. All categories are artificial and arbitrary.

Teaching abstract thinking skills by discussing familiar objects Discuss things around you that can be observed for likenesses and differences. For example:

- Are tables and chairs alike?

How are they alike?

How are they different?

- Are the floor and the ceiling alike?

How are they alike?

How are they different?

- Are people and flowers alike?

How are they alike?

How are they different?

Then progress to:

- What is like a pencil?
- What is like a ball?

How to Organize a Science Unit

When introducing a new unit, it is necessary to establish a context for the unit. Children understand new ideas better if they can relate them to a context. It also helps them remember what they learn. There are three basic approaches to organizing a science unit:

Moving from the familiar to the less familiar Children are familiar with their own bodies but are less familiar with the structure of other organisms. For example, if you decide to investigate trees, you might want to compare our human body to the tree's "body": Both we and trees are alive. Both we and trees become taller and wider as we grow. We have feet, trees have roots. We have skeletons; trees have trunks. We need to eat food and cannot make our own food; trees are able to make their own food. We have veins and tubes going through our bodies; trees also have veins and tubes going through their "bodies." Veins and tubes carry liquids. Liquids can flow.

Or you could compare our bodies to an insect's body: We both have eyes, jointed legs, and are able to walk. Our skeleton is on the inside of our body; the insect has an exoskeleton on the outside of its body. Most of us are unable to fly unless we take an airplane ride. We have senses in our ears and noses that an insect has on its antennae.

Another choice might be to compare our human body processes to that of an exploding volcano. If we hold our breath, we too will need to let the air (which is a form of gas) out of our body. Like a volcano we cannot hold it in. Eventually, our body will force air out, just as a volcano must ventilate its accumulated gases.

Moving from the beginning of a process to a result with a tangent or two Children are familiar with many things that are made from lumber, but they may not understand where the lumber comes from, or how something is constructed. For example, you might want to investigate how wooden boats are made, by examining the building process in detail. Trace a boat's origin from forest to log to mill to factory. Then go on a tangent and investigate the properties of wood, metals, and rocks. Try hammering a nail into wood, metal, and rock. Which is the easiest to penetrate? Which weighs the least and is the easiest to carry?

Or, take another tangent. Try to design a wooden boat that will float. Experiment with different designs. Add a sail. Find out if the sail can catch wind. Find out what kind of sail design is most efficient.

Or, you might want to find out where paper comes from by tracing its origin. As with boats, you might examine other kinds of materials from which books could be made, and determine which material is easiest to find, and lightest to carry. Also, which would be the easiest to inscribe or mark?

Arranging information in chronological order Children are familiar with life as it is today. They take it for granted that life has always existed as it does now. It is revealing and fun for children to think about how life might have been during cave-man times or to think about how electricity might have been discovered. It is possible to trace the steps in mankind's knowledge that eventually led to the discovery of electricity. It was not until the 1900's that electric companies came into existence. There was a long series of events, and much experimentation took place before electricity was harnessed. Many of those experiments can be duplicated. Especially easy are the Oersted and Faraday experiments dealing with electromagnetism.

In summation, there are many possibilities and ways to cover topics. The important thing is to design a cognitive structure that makes all the pieces of new information stick together. Moving from the familiar to the less familiar, following a process and/or a chronological order establishes a direction, a focus, and a relevancy, so that a context can be provided.

Skills to be Worked on and Developed Through Teaching Science

Observation skills Learning to use our five senses

Learning to classify Identifying, matching, sorting, naming, comparing, contrasting, grouping, and distinguishing likenesses and differences

Learning to measure Arranging objects in sequence by: length (shortest to longest); weight (lightest to heaviest); volume (least to greatest); chronologically (beginning to end); numerically (in ordinal order).

Learning to communicate By identifying, matching, sorting, naming, comparing, contrasting, grouping, and distinguishing likenesses and differences by verbalizing descriptions, asking questions, relating observations, and using words accurately

Learning to make predictions By developing skills of thinking systematically and logically about what might happen next, and beginning to think about planning ahead

Role of Parent or Teacher in Exposing Young Children to Beginning Science Experiences

We as adults can greatly influence children's interests. Most children have a vast untapped potential. It is our responsibility to tap that potential and to expose children's curiosity to new and stimulating topics and to help them organize their knowledge. Knowledge that is not categorized, sorted, and classified in some internal way is not helpful. The knowledge is out of reach. It is useless trivia, meaningless facts and unconnected thoughts, like the information on a television game show. The ability to generalize is based on our past experiences and the significance those experiences hold for us. If we can convey our enthusiasm about the topics we are interested in to our children, then we can arouse their curiosity and interest in those areas of science to which we expose them. Children's interests are acquired. If they are stimulated and exposed to "something," they become curious about the "something" and acquire an interest in it. It is easier for children to build future cognitive bridges* with ideas and topics with which they are familiar.

Try to see the world through a child's eyes, but try to add structure and organization to observations that are made. Children are experts at observing, but they lack analytical skills.

Our job as early-childhood educators is not to give an intense course in science, but rather to open doors and plant seeds of knowledge that will grow and will continue to excite children about the wonders of their environment. We want to encourage them to delve and be curious, to ask questions, to experiment, to learn and to integrate knowledge from their own experiences.

*Cognitive bridge: When two seemingly unrelated ideas fit together to form a broader concept. For example: A young child learns the names of the basic colors. Later the child learns that by mixing and combining two colors, he/she will form a new color with a new name. A cognitive bridge is built. The idea forms that materials can be mixed and combined to form new colors and/or new substances.

2
MODELS

Objectives

- For children to develop an awareness of what models are.
- For children to develop an understanding of how and why models are used.
- For children to become aware of what the words "science" and "observe" mean.
- For children to develop an awareness that some events continually reoccur in cyclical patterns in nature.
- For children to develop an awareness that living things have many parts to them and that each "part" is important to the "whole."
- For children to develop an awareness that objects and models can be arranged in an orderly way.
- For children to develop an awareness that objects and models can be sorted or classified into groups.

General Background Information for Parents and Teachers

Models are representations of real things. They can be much smaller or much larger than the object's real-life size. Scientists and engineers build models or replicas of large and small objects to see if the objects or "things" are constructed well. They test, study, and observe working models close up. Many of children's art projects are models they have constructed of real things in their world. Most toys are models of real things. Toy cars, trucks, houses, dolls, etc., are miniature models which represent reality. Many toys are models of the real things that children might not be allowed to touch and manipulate. For example, a child can "drive" a play truck, or play "parent" to a doll, "cook" dinner for the doll-house people, or "mow" the lawn with a model of a lawn mower.

The wonderful part about introducing and using the word "model" with children is that it helps train them to think abstractly. They can learn to picture something in their minds that they are familiar with without having to touch it. When children do have a model to look at and to touch, they can study and observe the model to compare it to reality. How is the model like the real thing? How is it different? For example:

Does a real fire truck have only two doors and six windows like the toy model?
(It depends on the model design of the real fire truck we are comparing it to.)

Does a real frog have four front toes as the rubber model shows?
(Yes.)

Do the little wooden people found inside of commercial toys look like real people? What part of them is missing?
(All of their joints are missing, including their arms, legs, fingers, and toes.)

Some models are much larger than reality, like rubber spiders and rubber insects. Their large size allows us to examine and observe things we might not have discovered if the creatures were moving or were too small to see. Some models are built in exact proportion to their real-life size, like silk flowers. A silk flower is a model representing reality. Usually it contains the stamen, pistil, calyx, stem, and leaves along with the flower petals, to make it look real. Pictures are also models. A picture of a flower or a house can be seen as a model of the flower or the house. The picture helps us visualize what something looks like when we cannot touch it. Likewise, a cross-section diagram is a model of reality. It is a model representing a splitting open of a surface. It allows us to use our imaginations, and gives us the ability to think abstractly. We can look at a model and imagine that it has been cut open. A globe is also a model. A map is a flat representation or "model" of a globe (or part of a globe). Maps are models of models. They are flat representations of a curved surface.

In the most general sense, practically anything that is not "real"* but a representation of something real can be called a model.

Definitions of Frequently Used Terms

Concept A concept is a general idea or understanding, derived from specific instances or occurrences.

It is important to try to establish the concept of what "model" means. *It is a goal to be worked on all year.* When children understand the concept of what a model is, they are free to develop their abstract thinking skills and to use their minds more effectively. They will not be constricted by needing concrete materials in order to think.

The concept of a model is a way of thinking about something. It allows children and adults to paint pictures in their minds of real things when the real things or objects are not available to touch.

Models in play When children use their imaginations in playing house, building with blocks, and sand construction, they are creating models of things they are thinking about. Art activities and play activities are chances for young children to role-play, act out, build or construct, "pretend" play, and manipulate reality. They provide an opportunity to discover a problem or create a challenge and to try to solve the problem or meet the challenge.

*"Real" in this sense means an object or thing that is tangible and three-dimensional, something which we are able to touch physically as a whole that is not a representation or model of "something" else.

Science Is the art of studying. It is also the study of observation, identification, description, experimental investigation, and theoretical explanation of those (observable) events. It is a methodological activity that attempts to answer and discover "why, when, and how" observable natural and physical events occur as they do.

The five senses Seeing, hearing, smelling, tasting, feeling. All five senses are located in our faces. Our senses help us make observations. (See Chapter 3 for activities which develop an awareness of our five senses.)

Cycle A phenomenon or event that repeats itself predictably.

Classification The systematic grouping of objects or organisms into categories based on shared characteristics or traits.

Attribute A quality or characteristic belonging to an object or thing. It is a distinctive feature which results in an object or thing belonging to a set or group.

Sort Grouping similar objects together.

Group The assembling of objects or things into a set.

The short lessons that follow represent a "model" of how to present a science idea or concept to young children. Each mini-lesson takes about five or ten minutes to present. The model lessons include the kinds of questions you might want to ask, the kinds of comparisons you might want to make to induce a child to want to inquire further on his/her own, and the kinds of explanations you might give to children about a particular topic.

The model lessons have been included in this chapter on models to set the tone and to be a "model" or an example of how to present ideas. The model lessons do not need to be followed. However, the tone of "acceptance" the lessons try to demonstrate does need to be followed. Please feel free to develop your own style. Do remember to have a direction or a focus. Your focus or direction could simply be to develop observation skills, to heighten awareness and curiosity, and to help children develop an inquiring attitude.

The experiences and information gained by the children from individual science units and from the activities described in the chapters are important. However, they are not nearly as important as nurturing children to develop a desire and a need to know more about natural and physical phenomena, so that they will develop a positive attitude toward inquiry.

Eight Model Lessons

Lesson One: Science

Objective For children to become aware of what the words "science" and "observe" mean.

Materials needed The word "Science."

Procedure Hold up the word "science."

Does anyone know what this word says?
(It says science.)*

Does anyone know what the word "science" means?
(*Explain:* The word science means the art of studying. It is a way of looking at everything around us that is living, nonliving, and not living now. It is also the study of how things work and why things happen.)

Are dinosaurs alive today?
(No.) *Explain:* Scientists study and observe everything. They study and observe things that were never alive, like rocks and sound. They study and observe things that are alive, like plants and animals. And they study and observe things that are no longer living, like dinosaurs and other things that have died. Scientists also study subjects such as: why shadows are formed, how to make jobs feel easier, and why volcanoes erupt. Scientists try to answer why, how, and when things happen. The first thing a scientist does is observe.

What does observe mean?
(To study carefully.)

What parts of our body do we use when we observe?
(Our eyes help us see. Our ears help us hear. Our nose helps us smell. Our skin helps us feel. Our tongue helps us taste.) *Explain:* We use our senses—eyes, ears, nose, skin, and tongue—to find out about things. Our senses help us observe. Sometimes we need to use all of our senses.

Conclusion (See Chapter 3, "The Five Senses," for activities and ideas of what to do with the children to make them aware of their five senses.)

Vocabulary Science; living; alive; nonliving; once living; observe.

Evaluation See if after this discussion, a child can name or point to something that is alive or was once alive and then to something that was never alive. Also, see if the children can point to a part of their body that helps them observe.

*In most cases, italic type indicates questions to ask children. Material in parentheses indicates a possible answer.

Lesson Two: Natural and Man-Made

Objective For children to develop an awareness that all materials and things can be classified.

Materials needed Assorted natural objects, such as: Seeds, leaves, flowers, rocks, soil, bark, feathers, and chicken bones; Assorted man-made objects, such as: Nails, bottle caps, paper, pencil, scissors, paper clips, and rubber bands.

Procedure 1
- Place all of the objects in a container and then spill the objects out onto the floor.
- Ask the children to find objects which grow on plants or can be found in the soil, and to place all of these objects in a pile.
- *Explain:* All of the objects in the pile are called natural things. The materials not in the pile are things people have made with the help of machines.

Procedure 2
Can you name something that is living?
(We are living.)

What is something that we can find on the ground outside that is not alive and never has been?
(A rock.)

Note: If children say "picnic table" or "chair" and the picnic table or chair are made out of wood, then explain to the class that the wood for the picnic table and the chair came from a tree. Even though the picnic table and the chair are not alive now, the materials they are made from were once alive. They have been made into a table and chair by people and machines. They are man-made. Tables and chairs are often made from natural materials but would not be found in nature unless people made them.

- Explain the difference between objects that are man-made and objects that are natural and found in nature.
- Ask the children to name on their own some things that are made by people and some other things that are natural or found in nature.

Conclusion Take a nature walk with the children so they can collect natural and man-made objects. Most man-made things that are found on a nature walk are called litter (bottle caps, paper, empty containers, nails, wire, etc.).

Vocabulary Nature; natural; man-made; machine-made; pile; litter.

Evaluation Show a child an object and ask the child to place it in the appropriate pile of man-made or natural objects. See if children can separate the pile of natural objects into things that are still alive now, things that are not alive now, and things that were never alive.

Lesson Three: Cycles

Objective For children to develop an awareness that some events continually reoccur in cyclical patterns in nature.

Materials needed Fresh flowers; dead flowers; full seed pods; one paper plate labeled "seeds"; one paper plate labeled "petals."

Procedure Bring fresh flowers to class. (Marigolds are easy to study. They grow in abundance.)

Are these flowers alive now?
(The children will probably say: "No, they have been picked and they can no longer grow.")

• Hold up some dead flowers.
• *Explain:* Even when flowers stay on a plant, they eventually die. They do not stay alive forever. If the flowers are not picked they may look pretty longer, but eventually the flowers will die.

Are these dead flowers really dead?
(The children will probably say, "Yes.") *Explain:* The flower has died, but it has produced seeds which are very much alive. The seeds can create whole new plants that will flower again. The new flowers from the new plants will create seeds all over again for new plants.

Why do plants grow flowers?
(To make seeds.)

Where do we look to find the seeds on a marigold flower?
(In the seed pod at the bottom of the petals.)

• Open up a seed pod.
• Pass out a petal with a seed attached to it to each child. *Explain:* The petal is the yellow part. The seed is the black part. Hold the petal with one hand and the seed with your other hand and pull.

What happens?
(The petal separates from the seed.)

• Set up two paper plates—one labeled "seeds" and one labeled "petals."
• Drop some seeds into the "seed" plate.
• Drop some petals into the "petal" plate.
• Then have the children drop their petals and their seeds into the appropriate paper plate.
• Have children check the placement and correct the placement of any misplaced seed or petal.

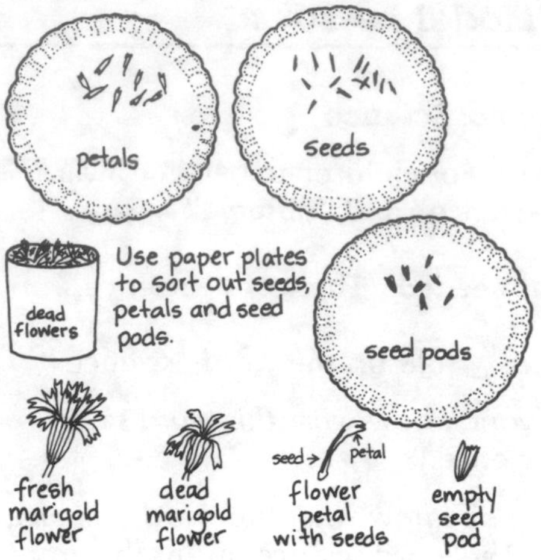

FINDING SEEDS IN FLOWERS

Are the seeds alive now?
(Yes.)

Are the petals alive now?
(No.)

• *Explain:* The plant grows flowers to make seeds so it can flower again next year. The seeds grow into new plants with flowers.
When events or things occur or happen in a pattern over and over again, it is called a cycle. A cycle is like a bicycle wheel: it goes around and around and has no beginning or end.

Do all of the flower seeds become plants?
(No.)

Why not, and what happens to them?
(Some seeds are eaten by small insects and birds, and some decay. Many animals eat plant seeds for food.)

Note: The topic of seeds can be expanded. Various edible nuts and seeds can be tasted: peanuts, almonds, sesame seeds, poppy seeds, caraway seeds, sunflower seeds, etc. The diets of animals like squirrels and other small rodents can be discussed to see the relationship and interdependence that exists between plants and animals for food, and seed dispersal of plants by animals.

Conclusion Have the children find other dead flowers in their yards or at school and open them up to look for the seeds.

Vocabulary Alive; dead; plant; seed(s); flowers; marigold; seed pod; petal; cycle.

Evaluation Show a child a dead flower. Ask the child if he/she can find a seed and separate it from the petal. Ask the child what is inside a dead flower.

Lesson Four: The Marigold Plant

Objective For children to develop an awareness that living things have many parts to them and that each "part" is important to the "whole."

Materials needed Marigolds with leaves, buds, flowers, and stems; Styrofoam tray labeled for flower parts (see diagram).

Procedure
- Examine the parts of a marigold plant.

Does it have leaves?
(Yes.)

Who can show me a leaf?
(Have child show and then tear a leaf off for the Styrofoam tray. Point to the stem. Break one off and add it to the labeled Styrofoam tray.)

Does anyone know what this long part underneath the flower is called?
(Stem.)

- Point to a bud. Break off and add to tray.
- *Explain:* This is a baby flower that has not opened yet. It is called a bud. When it blossoms, it will be a flower.
- Point to a smaller bud without a stem.
- *Explain:* This bud is so small it is hard to see.

Which of these buds do you think will open first?
(The larger one on the longer stem.)

Why?
(The larger bud has a longer stem and the petals look larger.)

What part of the plant is missing from this plant?
(The roots.)

DISSECTING A FLOWER

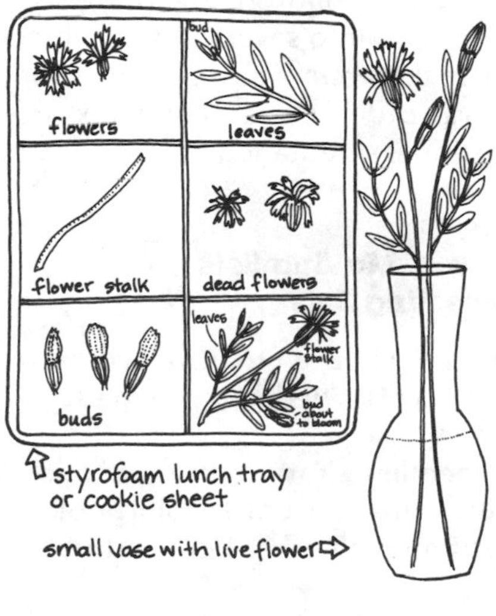

- *Explain:* The roots grow under the ground. If the plant had roots, and the roots were in the ground, it would still be growing.
- Finish adding appropriate parts of the marigold plant to the labeled Styrofoam tray. Discuss how each part of the plant is important to it.
- *Explain:* The leaves help make food for the plant, the stem helps the plant stand tall, the bud helps protect the baby flower until it is ready to bloom, the dried-out old flower contains a seed pod which holds new seeds to make new plants and food for animals. The roots help anchor the plant and help the plant get water.

Conclusion Have the children find other plants with flowers outside or inside and then name and point to the stem, buds, leaves, and flower of the plant.

Vocabulary Marigold plant; bud(s); stem(s); flower parts; leaf; large; small; dried; roots.

Evaluation If children are young and not very verbal, see if the child can point to the parts of the plant as you name them. If the child is older and has better verbal ability, see if the child can name the parts of the plant as you point to them, and/or see if the child can find a very tiny bud hidden in the leaves.

Lesson Five: Models

Objective For children to develop an awareness of what models are.

Materials needed Rubber frog, toy model car or truck; picture of a flower; real flower; silk flower.

Procedure
- *Explain:* Sometimes scientists use models to look at or study things.
- Display a model toy car or truck, rubber frog, and a picture of a flower.
- Hold up the toy truck.

Is this a real truck that we could ride in?
(No.) *Explain:* This is a model of a nonliving thing. We can count the windows, the tires, and the doors.

Do real trucks have four windows too?
(It depends on the truck, since trucks vary.) *Explain:* Some models are built exactly like the real thing. Some models are not very real looking.

- Hold up the rubber frog.

Is this frog real?
(Yes, it is a real* model of a frog.)

**Real* in this context means not make-believe—something tangible that we can touch and see.

Is this frog alive?
(No, it is the model of something that is alive.) *Explain:* The rubber frog is a model of a living thing.

- Hold up a picture of a flower.

Is this flower real?
(Yes, it is real, but it is a picture of a flower.) *Explain:* The picture is real. The flower in the picture is a model. The picture is a model of a real living thing.

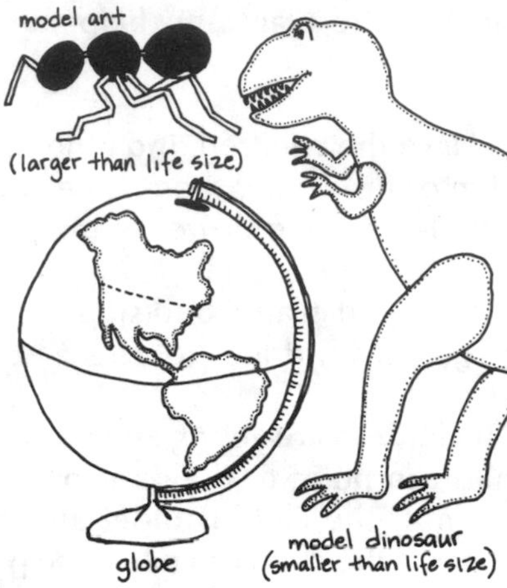

MODELS

Conclusion Have children draw a model of their favorite toy, their room, their house, their car, their family.

Vocabulary Model(s); exactly; compare; different; alike; real.

Evaluation See if the child can point to a picture or a model of "something" and then name what "it" is a model of. See if the children can find something that is not a model, but is "real," like a pair of scissors or a crayon.

Lesson Six: Sorting Objects into Sets

Objectives
1. For children to develop an awareness of how objects can be arranged in an orderly way.

2. For children to become aware of what it means to sort or classify objects and models into groups.

Materials needed About 15 assorted buttons; about 5 pencils of different lengths; some coins, 4 models of people, 4 models of cars; 6 fat crayons in assorted colors and lengths; 6 rocks and pebbles; 6 thin crayons in colors that match the fat crayons.

Procedure
- Fill a small box with the assorted materials.
- Spill out the assorted materials onto the floor.
- Explain to the children that there are sets of things in the big, messy pile, but it is hard to make sense of what is in the pile because everything is mixed together.
- Ask the children if they can find groups of "things" in the big pile that look alike and to name those "things." (Pencils, buttons, crayons, coins, toy cars, toy people, rocks, etc.)
- Ask the children to make a pile for each group of "things" they find. (There will be a set of pencils, a set of crayons, a set of rocks, etc.)
- After the big messy pile is separated into several sets of "things" that look alike, ask the children to arrange each set in an orderly way so that each set can be observed more closely. For example, pencils can be arranged from largest to shortest. Fat crayons can be color-matched to thin crayons. Toy cars can be lined up so that all the headlights are facing in the same direction and so they all have their wheels on the floor. The pebbles can be separated out from the rocks, etc.
- Discuss with children how sorting and order help us observe and find "things" more easily. Ask them to think about how food is organized into an order at the grocery store, books in a library, furniture in a house, clothes in dresser drawers.
- Discuss the man-made order of material things in general and why order is helpful for finding "things" quickly.

Conclusion Have the children sort a deck of playing cards into groups and subgroups; for example, reds and blacks, pictures and numbers, or matching sets of numbers or pictures into sets of four or into suits.

Vocabulary Order; mess; arrange; separate; alike; different; match; "line-up"; longest; shortest; rough; smooth; organize; sort; group; set.

Evaluation See if children can arrange a messy pile of assorted "things" into several sets of objects that have something in common. See if the sets of objects can be arranged in an order: by size, color, texture, and/or the same directional orientation.

Lesson Seven: Making Sets and Intersecting Sets

Objective For children to develop an awareness that objects can be classified and grouped.

Materials needed Yarn circles; a deck of marked picture cards (made from an old book or children's picture dictionary that has been cut up).

Procedure

• *Explain:* Scientists have divided the world into two large groups. One group is made up of all the things in the world that are alive . . . all the plants and animals. The other group of things is made up of all the things in the world that are not alive like rocks, mountains, and houses.

• Place two yarn loops into the shape of a circle. The loops should be different colors. Place one of the yarn circles so that it is intersecting the other circle.

• Show the children that there are three enclosed areas inside the circles. Point out the space in the middle. This space is a special area called an intersection. Both of the circles overlap and meet here. You might want to compare this meaning of intersection with a street intersection—the area in the middle of all the crosswalks where the streets join and blend together.

SORTING PICTURE CARDS

• Hold up a deck of adult-made marked picture cards which have symbols or a color code depicting pictures as being living, nonliving, or both on their nonpicture side.

Are these cards alive?
(No, they are nonliving.) *Explain:* Each card has a picture on it. The picture is a model of something real. It is a model of something living, nonliving, or both. For example:

Living	= A tree, flower, person, animal
Nonliving	= House, car, furniture
Both	= A house with a yard and flowers; a person wearing clothes.

• Show the children each picture and ask:

Is it a model of something living, nonliving, or both living and nonliving?

Where should we place pictures that are both?
(In the intersection space.)

• After the children have sorted the cards, explain how the symbol or color code helps you to know if you separated the cards the way they have been marked. The code is there to help you in case you do not feel sure of where to place a picture card. You can peek on the back. It is better to try to think first and then to look, or to wait until the end and to check all of the picture cards in the sets together.

Conclusion Have children make and mark a set of their own cards from magazine pictures or from old workbooks to show pictures that represent both living things and nonliving things.

Vocabulary Living; nonliving; both; group; divided; intersection; space; model; code; set.

Evaluation With a younger child, see if the child can sort out the deck of cards into "living" and "nonliving" sets. With an older child, see if he/she can sort the deck of cards out and form an intersection of sets.

Lesson Eight: Sets of Rocks and Pebbles

Objective For children to develop an awareness that objects can be classified and grouped.

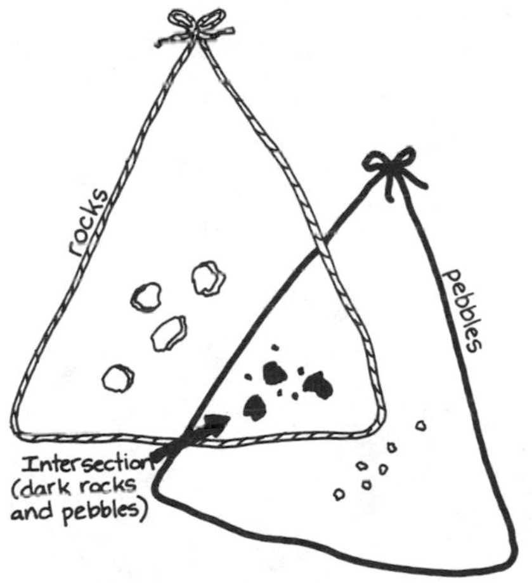

SETS OF ROCKS AND PEBBLES

Materials needed Rocks; pebbles; yarn circles.

Procedure

• *Explain:* We can place things that are alike into a group. When we put things together into groups that are alike we can observe them more closely and look for things that make the things that look alike look different from each other.

- Display some rocks and pebbles.

Do all of these rocks look alike?
(No.)

How are they different?
(Some are round and smooth, some are rough and sharp, some are very small, some are darker than others.)

Are they all rocks?
(Yes.)

Which ones can be called pebbles?
(The round smooth ones.)

Are all the pebbles rocks?
(Yes.)

Are all rocks pebbles?
(No.)

Explain: Pebbles are a special kind of rock. They are rocks that have been worn down by water or by rubbing to become smooth. Let's see if we can sort the pebbles from the rocks. We can place all of the pebbles into this yarn circle. We can place all of the rocks that are not pebbles into this other yarn circle.

Is there anything about the rocks and pebbles that makes them look alike?
(Some of the rocks and some of the pebbles are dark.)

Can we form an intersection to put all of the darker-colored rocks and pebbles together?
(Yes.)

Are all of the darker rocks the same color?
(Probably not. Some may be tinted yellow or brown or red; some may be striped or spotted. If you look closely enough, you will be able to see differences.)

- Ask the children to suggest other ways to sort the rocks into groups or sets. (Possible ways: large from small, broken from whole, speckled and striped from solids)

Conclusion Have the children group the rocks and pebbles and then have other children guess how the rocks and pebbles were grouped.

Vocabulary Rock; pebble; smooth; rough; round; sharp; light(er); dark(er); worn; striped; spotted; alike; different; broken; whole, group(s).

Evaluation With a younger child, see if he/she can form a group of rocks and a group of pebbles. With an older child, see if he/she can form those groups plus an intersection of rocks and pebbles that are the same color or speckled and striped.

3
THE FIVE SENSES

Objective

To help children develop a heightened awareness of their five senses and to improve their observation skills.

General Background Information for Parents and Teachers

As adults we are quite familiar with our ability to see, hear, smell, taste, and touch. We often take these abilities and skills for granted. We have learned how to integrate the knowledge and information gained from our senses. However, most children and many adults do not fully appreciate all of the information available to them through thoughtful and systematic use of their senses. If we use our senses fully and perceive all we can from them, they will communicate to us in a way that words do not.

If our senses are not fully developed, we can train ourselves and our children to become more observant. When we slow down from our usual pace and when we are patient about what we are observing, we begin to notice and observe "happenings" we were not aware of before. For example, if we play ball with our children in the park or jog with them along a path, we are absorbed in the physical activity of moving our body. We tend to notice our surroundings on a superficial level. However, when we walk slowly in the same park or on the same path with the purpose of observing, we begin to sense more "happenings." If we choose to stop and stay very still, we can use all of our senses. We can choose to concentrate on one sense at a time, or on many at once. Often our senses do not get used unless we concentrate on using them. If we are very still when we are outside, we can hear things that we cannot hear when we are moving. If we stop to touch "things," we can feel textures that we might not have been able to sense physically unless we stopped to touch the "things." We can smell aromas on our hands of objects we have touched or rubbed. We can even taste objects and spit out those things that might taste bitter.

Becoming fully aware of our five senses and the subtle differences that our senses can communicate to us helps us to develop the techniques of observing, comparing, matching, identifying, sorting, classifying, sequencing, and measuring. The development of these skills provides the framework for enjoying and understanding scientific phenomena, as well as enriching readiness activities in reading and math.

When children become more aware of these senses, they often enjoy hypothesizing or predicting, and testing their ideas. It gives them reasons for wanting to communicate and to investigate things they are curious about. The child acquires a feeling of mastery over his/her world when he/she is allowed and encouraged to study, observe, and investigate materials which are part of his/her everyday life.

The child's five senses can be stimulated by familiar items. Young children absorb experiences with their bodies. They are extremely egocentric. Experiences that can be felt by them or that can be related to their own bodies are experiences they internalize and remember. For example, the word "hot" has meaning when one is burned. If a child is burned, he/she will avoid things that are called "hot." "Hot" will become an abstract idea that he/she will understand without continuing to need the "hands-on" experience of being burned.

Young children learn through such experiences. The senses can be used as tools for enhancing these learning experiences. Not only will children be learning about their five senses; their heightened awareness of their senses will help them become more aware of the world around them.

It is easy to recall and name all of our sense organs. All of them are located on our face: eyes, see; ears, hear; nose, smells; tongue, tastes; and skin surfaces sense touch. Our face is crucial to our identity because it houses all these senses, and because it contains the features by which other people know us.

Our hands serve us as a second set of eyes and ears. Our fingers are very sensitive to touch. If our eyes are closed our fingers can become our "eyes." If we cannot hear, our fingers are able to sense sound vibrations. They can be trained to pick up vibrations caused by sound waves. Most of us do not need to train our fingers to read braille or to "hear" throats vibrate, but we are all capable of training and developing our fingers to become highly sensitive to the sensations felt by touch.

The list of activities that follows is only a partial list. It has been written to entice you into thinking of your own activities. Our senses are constantly bombarded by stimuli. The important idea is to become more aware of what our senses can do for us, and to develop our senses more fully so that we can all enjoy our surroundings and our lives to their fullest.

Activities and Procedures

I. Sound

1. Ring a Bell

Material A small brass bell.

Procedure Have a child sitting in a chair close his/her eyes and guess which direction the sound came from: up, down, behind, in front of, to the left, right, or middle.

Note: This activity helps reinforce positional and spatial terms.

2. Guessing Sounds

Materials Various objects, *i.e.*, coins, comb, ruler, rubber band, tinfoil.

Procedure Parent or teacher shows child various objects. Child closes his/her eyes. Parent or teacher drops one of the objects. Child tries to guess which object was dropped.

3. Tape Recorder

Material A tape recorder.

Procedure 1 Tape-record individual children's voices and familiar adult voices. See if the children can recognize each others' voices as well as their own voices.

Procedure 2 Tape-record sounds of familiar "things." For example: garbage truck, fire engine, dishwasher filling up, dog barking, telephone ringing, bird chirping, ball bouncing, airplane overhead, ice-cream truck, cricket chirping, door slamming, baby crying. Have child try to identify the sounds heard, and to decide whether the sound is made by something that is alive, or something that is not alive but mechanical or man-made.

Fine points to discuss with children

How are natural sounds different from mechanical sounds?

What are the qualities that make them different?

What kinds of sounds appear to last longer, and to be more monotonous?
(Sounds with little variety to them.)

When do sounds become monotonous and boring?
(When we can no longer "hear" them because they blend into everything else. We often do not hear traffic on a busy street, or a machine that is humming, or the motor in a car, because the sound is constant.)

What are the sounds we cannot hear?
(Quiet "happenings" in nature. See diagram on next page.)

Does the rainbow make a sound?

Does the sunrise make a sound?

Do butterflies make noise when they flutter?

Can we hear a bud opening up to blossom?

Can we hear clouds moving in the sky?

... a butterfly flying?
... a flower bloom?
... a snail slithering?
Can you hear?
... grass growing?
... clouds floating?
... the sun setting?

Can we hear an ant walk?

Why do animals make sounds?
(To communicate.)

What do animal sounds communicate to us?
(Hunger, fear, happiness, hurt, pain, warning.)

Why do cats purr?

Why do babies cry?

Why do dogs growl?

Why does a rattlesnake rattle its tail?

What are other animal sounds?

What does laughter mean?

What does a scream mean?

Note: For more activities on Sound, see Chapter 6, which gives a more detailed description of what sounds are and how sounds travel.

II. Sight and Touch

1. Describing

Materials Attribute set. A commercially prepared attribute set can be used, or you can prepare an attribute set yourself. If you make it yourself, it should consist of at least 12 pieces for touching and sorting.

Circles:	2 large circles, 2 small circles
Rectangles:	2 large rectangles, 2 small rectangles
Squares:	2 large squares, 2 small squares

One set of each of the two matching pieces should have a rough texture (sandpaper finish), and the other set of six pieces should have a smooth texture. All of the pieces in the set of 12 should be one color. Otherwise, color will become an attribute and more pieces will need to be added to the set. (If color is going to be an attribute then the set will consist of 18 pieces. Each set of shapes and sizes will have to be made in three different colors.)

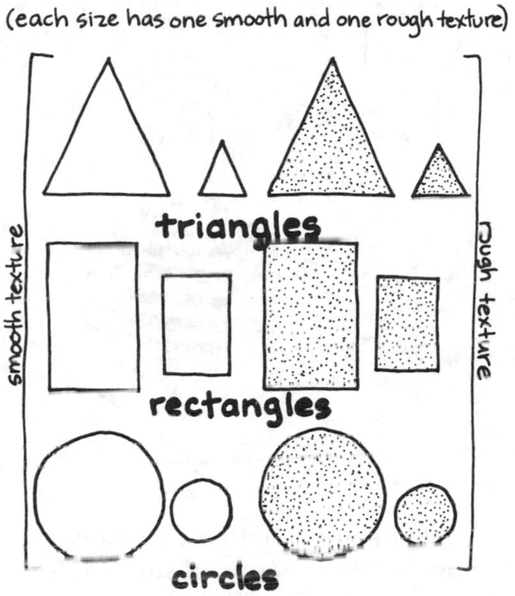
(each size has one smooth and one rough texture)
triangles
smooth texture
rough texture
rectangles
circles

ATTRIBUTE SET

Procedure Children play with the 12 pieces. They describe what piece they are touching. For example:
"I am holding a large, smooth circle."
"I am holding a small, rough square."
Note: This activity helps increase a child's verbal abilities and his/her ability to clarify and distinguish.

2. Sets

Materials Attribute set (refer to materials listed in II.1, the *Describing* section).

Procedure 1 Divide the 12 pieces into sets by shape, size, or texture.

Procedure 2 Try the same activity blindfolded.

3. Which Piece Is Missing?

Materials Attribute set (refer to materials listed in II.1, the *Describing* section).

Procedure Lay out all of the pieces to the Attribute set. Remove one piece from the set while the child has his/her eyes closed. Have child open his/her eyes and guess which piece of the set is missing.

4. Barefoot Touch

Materials A collection of materials such as sandpaper, cellophane, bath towel, jacks, chalkboard, chalk eraser, inflated balloon, animal cage, wet sponge, dry sponge, baseball, paintbrush.

Procedure Show the children the materials. Have a child remove his/her shoes and socks. Choose three items from the collection. Then have the child close his/her eyes. Let the child touch an object from the three objects chosen with his/her bare feet and then try to guess which object is being touched. Have the child describe how the object feels. Later, advance to not showing the child which three objects you will choose, as this will increase the difficulty of the activity.

5. Feeling Weight

Materials Three to five empty half-gallon milk cartons. Fill each of the cartons with a different amount of sand.

Procedure Have the children arrange the sand-filled milk cartons in order from the lightest in weight to the heaviest while blindfolded or with their eyes closed.

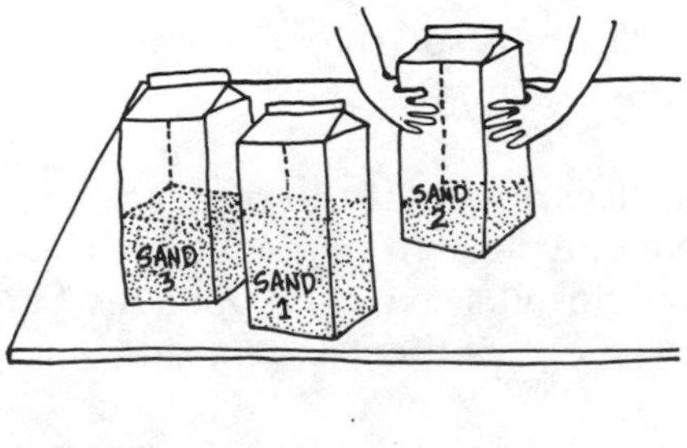

Note: This activity reinforces the need to have more than one object when comparing weights. An object cannot feel "heavier" or "lighter." In order to feel weight, we have to compare the object to something else.

6. Feeling Height

Materials Cut the top off empty half-gallon milk cartons to create three to five different heights.

Procedure Have the children arrange the cartons in order according to their height while blindfolded or with their eyes closed.

Note: This activity reinforces the need to have more than one object when comparing heights. An object cannot look "taller" or "shorter." In order for the object to look tall or short, it has to be compared to something else.

7. Feeling Temperature

Materials Arrange three water basins on a table together. Fill one basin half full with warm water, another basin half full with hot water, and the third basin half full of cold water. Place the basin filled with warm water between the other two basins.

Procedure Blindfold a child and have the child dip his/her hand into the hot, cold, and warm water. The child is to identify what the temperature of the water feels like. Take the blindfold off and place one hand in hot water and the other hand in cold water at the same time. After a minute, place both hands into the warm water. The warm water will feel cold to the hand that was in hot water and hot to the hand that was in cold water.

Note: This activity helps children understand the relative nature of temperature. Warm can feel both hot and cold. It depends on what our body temperature was before.

8. Mystery Box

Materials Make a "feely box" (call it a "mystery box") that you can "feel through" without peeking. Either hang a piece of cloth in front of a small open cardboard box, or cut out holes on the two sides of a small cardboard box.

Procedure Place an object inside the box. Children feel the object with their fingers and try to guess what the object is without peeking inside. Suggested items to hide in the box: a pencil, a shoelace, a ball of yarn, a seashell, a marble, a crayon.

9. Construction

Materials Mystery box or "feely box" and colored wooden blocks, each block shape a different color, *i.e.*, rectangle, green; square, red; cylinder, purple. Two of each block shape in matching colors.

Procedure One set of blocks is inside the feely box, and the other set is outside the box. The child constructs an "arrangement" of the blocks that are outside the box in an order. Then the child tries to reconstruct the same arrangement of the blocks with the blocks that are inside the feely box without peeking.

Note: This activity takes a certain level of skill on the part of our fingers, since our fingers have to "see" for us. The activity can be made more difficult by adding more wooden blocks, or by trying to duplicate pictures of block formations by only looking at a "picture" of the formation and not looking at three-dimensional blocks.

FEELY BOX

III. Smell

1. Spices

Materials An assortment of aromatic spices: mint, tarragon, onion, basil, parsley, thyme, marjoram, bay leaves, garlic. Paper napkins or cheesecloth to wrap the individual crushed spices. One whole leaf of each spice left uncrushed and unwrapped.

Procedure Children have to sniff and match the smell of the spice wrapped in cheesecloth to the smell of the unwrapped whole-leaf spice.

2. Mystery Box

Materials Mystery box (refer to Activity II.8, "Sight and Touch," in this chapter); a slice of fruit peel; crayons in the colors of fruit.

Procedure Hide a slice of fruit peel in the "mystery box." Have children sniff and try to identify what the odor is. (Suggestions of fruit peels to hide: lemon, orange, apple, banana, cantaloupe, watermelon.) Have the children draw a circle using the color of crayon that the fruit peel smells like:

Yellow	—banana, lemon
Red	—apple, watermelon
Orange	—orange, cantaloupe

Note: This coloring activity reinforces the names of colors and the names of common foods, and develops children's awareness of how color symbols can be used to represent ideas.

3. Flowers

Materials An assortment of fresh flowers: carnation, rose, marigold, dandelion, violet, zinnia, daisy. A flower identification guidebook, or flower and seed catalogue.

Procedure Smell all the flowers. Sort out which ones have an aroma and which ones have very little scent. Look through the flower identification guidebook. Match the real flowers to models of flowers in the book. Discuss how the model does not have the aroma that the real flower has.

Note: This activity reinforces the idea that books can be used as a reference aid for identifying specimens, and that books contain useful and interesting information.

4. Take a Nature Walk

Materials Gathering a variety of leaves, rocks, tree bark, and soil.

Procedure Take a walk. Gather things that smell. Compare the different aromas of leaves, tree bark, and soil odors. Which things smell earthy?

IV. Taste

1. Salt and Sugar

Materials Salt; sugar; two cups.

Procedure Pour some sugar into one cup and some salt into another cup. Discuss with your child the difficulty of telling the difference between these two "white powders." They both look alike. Ask what is an easy way to tell which is which? (By tasting them.)

2. Lemon Juice, Vinegar, and Water

Materials Lemon juice; vinegar; water; sugar.

Procedure Have the child taste each liquid. Discuss how each tastes. Add sugar and water to the lemon juice. Does the lemon juice still taste sour? Do sugar and water change the taste of the vinegar?

3. Skull and Crossbones

Materials A poison label with a skull and crossbones; ammonia.

Procedure Show the children the poison label. Discuss with them what it means, and why we should avoid ever tasting something from a bottle with this kind of label. Let the child take a whiff of ammonia to smell how bad poison would taste. Discuss how odors often tell us when something is dangerous to swallow.

Note: It is important to emphasize with children that it is not always smart to taste unknown things because they might be dangerous to us. If we taste something unknown and it tastes awful, it is wise to spit it out and not swallow it. Sometimes things taste awful, like cod liver oil, but they are good for us. It is okay to swallow something that tastes awful if we know what it is and know that it is not poisonous.

4. How We Taste

How We Taste!

Tongues have taste buds for tasting bitter, sour, sweet and salty things.

Materials A tongue chart showing where our taste buds are located.

Procedure Experiment tasting foods that are bitter, sweet, salty, and sour. Experiment touching different parts of our tongue as we taste the foods. Do foods taste different on different parts of our tongues? Does candy taste better on the front tip of our tongue than in the rear of our tongue near our throat?

5. Use Food Color

Materials Food color, mashed potatoes, rice.

Procedure Have the child taste the mashed potatoes and the rice. Then add blue food color to the rice and to the potatoes. Does the color affect the taste of the food?

Fine points to discuss with children

- Discuss how the color of the food we eat affects the way we think it will taste. *Can we taste the color?*
- Discuss how important it is to smell foods when we eat them. Smell enhances the taste of food. It is often difficult to distinguish taste from smell. Hold your nose while you taste a food! *Does the food taste as good as it does when you can smell the food as you taste it?*

Further Resources

Suggested Books for Children

Dewey Decimal Classification Numbers for the five senses are: 372.3, 516.22, 591.4, 612, and 641.1.

Brenner, Barbara, *Bodies.* New York: Dutton, 1973. (Photographs that tell a story. Shows how our body is like a machine.)

Froman, Robert, *Hot and Cold and In Between.* New York: Young Readers Press, 1971.

Hoban, Tana, *Circles, Triangles and Squares.* New York: Macmillan, 1974. (Black and white photographs of a city environment. The photos emphasize the shapes of things. There are no words, just photos. Good for a discussion about shapes we see around us and for the development of observation skills.)

Ogle, Lucille, *I Spy, A Picture Book of Objects in a Child's Home Environment.* New York: American Heritage Press, 1970. (A good preschool and kindergarten book. The book helps develop vocabulary and sight words. It sharpens observation skills and develops rudimentary schemes of classification.)

Schwartz, Julius, *Magnify and Out Why.* New York: McGraw-Hill, 1972. (Sketches stimulate ideas of things to look for and things to look at under a magnifying glass.)

Van Gelden, Richard, *Whose Nose Is This?* New York: Walker, 1974. (Good for development of observation skills. Great close-up photos of animal noses. Reader has to guess which animal the nose belongs to.)

Resource Books for More Ideas

Brown, Sam Ed, *One, Two, Buckle My Shoe, Math Activities for Young Children.* Mt. Rainier, Maryland: Gryphon House, 1982.

Cobb, Vicki, *Science Experiences You Can Eat.* New York: Lippincott, 1972. (Describes cooking experiences to develop the senses.)

Forte, Imogene, and Marjorie Frank, *Paddles and Wings and Grapevine Swings.* Nashville, Tennessee: Incentive Publications, 1982. (Things to do with nature's treasures.)

Frank, Marjorie, *I Can Make a Rainbow.* Nashville, Tennessee: Incentive Publications, 1976. (Describes art activities which help develop the senses.)

Furth, Hans G., and Harry Wach, *Thinking Goes to School: Piaget's Theory in Practice.* New York: Oxford University Press, 1975. (Describes thinking activities to make us more aware of our senses.)

Hibner, Dixie, and Liz Cromwell, *Explore and Create.* Livonia, Michigan: Partner Press, 1980. [Distributed by Gryphon House, Mt. Rainier, Maryland.] (Describes various activities which develop the senses.)

Knapp, Clifford, "Exploring the Outdoors with Young People," *Science and Children,* October, 1979.

Marzollo, Jean, and Janice Lloyd, *Learning Through Play.* New York: Harper and Row, 1972. (Describes play activities which help develop the five senses.)

McIntyre, Margaret, *Early Childhood and Science: A Collection of Articles. Reprinted from* Science and Children. Washington, D.C.: National Science Teachers Association, 1984. (Describes a multitude of science activities for younger children.)

Warren, Jean, *Learning Games.* Palo Alto, California: Monday Morning Books, 1983. (Describes activities to reinforce sorting, observing, and counting.)

Wilt, Joy, and Terre Watson, *Taste and Smell.* Waco, Texas: Creative Resources, 1978. (Describes activities related to taste and smell.)

Wolfgang, Charles H., et al., *Growing and Learning Through Play.* New York: Instructo/McGraw-Hill, 1981. (Describes play activities which help develop the five senses.)

4

MAGNETISM

Objectives

- For children to become aware that some magnets are man-made and others are found in nature.
- For children to become aware of how magnets behave toward each other and toward materials that are sensitive to magnetic force.
- For children to become aware that the strength of magnets varies.
- For children to become aware that magnets have invisible lines of force.
- For children to become aware that magnets have an invisible force field.
- For children to become aware that some metal materials can become temporary magnets.
- For children to become aware of how magnets can be made.
- For children to develop an understanding about the Laws of Magnetism: like poles repel; unlike poles attract.
- To help children develop an awareness of how magnets behave toward each other and toward materials that are sensitive to magnetic force.

General Background Information for Parents and Teachers

Magnetism The study of magnets and their effects.

Magnetic field The area around a magnet where a force can be detected.

Loadstone It is also spelled lodestone. It is a black rock that has magnetic properties. It is made from a mineral known as magnetite. (**The mineral form of black oxide, Fe_3O_4.) It is a natural magnet, found in nature. Loadstones made early sailing easier. They were used in compasses. Sailors no longer had to rely on the stars and the sun for navigating the seas.

Poles The ends of a magnet, where the magnetism is strongest.

North and south poles The poles are named for the direction a magnet would point if it were allowed to hang freely suspended from a string.

Repel This means to push away from; "like" poles repel.

Attract This means to pull together; "unlike" poles attract.

Permanent magnets Magnets that are man-made. They are made from steel or mixtures of iron, nickel, and cobalt.

Temporary magnets Magnets that do not keep their magnetic force. They have magnetic force only when they are in a strong magnetic field—for example, when a piece of metal such as a paper clip or a nail acts as a magnet to another piece of metal. The nail or paper clip will stay magnetic only as long as a

**Items marked by two asterisks indicate that the information is too abstract and too complicated for young children to understand or comprehend. It is included to enhance parent or teacher background only.

permanent magnet is near it. (**The magnetism is induced.)

Kinds of magnets and their poles Bar magnets have poles at each end. Horseshoe magnets are really bar magnets that have been bent. Circular magnets have their poles on the inside and outside perimeter of the circle.

Strong This is a relative term in relation to the ability of the magnet to lift or pull, attract or repel.

Weak See above explanation for strong. It refers to the strength of the magnet.

Iron A mineral that is affected by magnetism.

****What causes magnetism?** Magnetism is caused by electric charges that are moving. Moving electric current is inside a bar magnet. The electric charge is a constant part of the magnet. The electric current produces a magnetic field.

Iron molecules Not all molecules in an iron nail are lined up. They are randomly arranged. We can magnetize a nail by stroking it many times in one direction with a strong magnet. The stroking forces the randomly arranged iron molecules to align themselves in one direction.

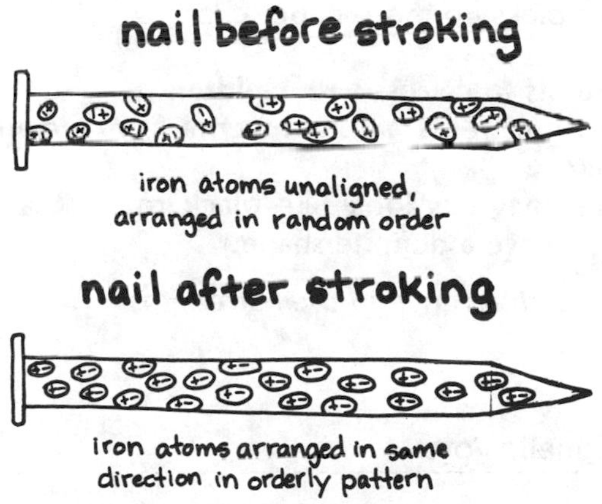

Man-made magnets can lose their magnetism. The atoms of iron molecules can become unaligned and go back to a random pattern. This can happen when a magnet is dropped, heated, or hit hard with a hammer. Therefore, it is *extremely important* to handle magnets with care: keep them away from heat, and do not drop them. If they are treated poorly, they will lose some of their magnetic properties.

****Dipoles** Atoms of iron molecules are sensitive to magnetic forces and are sometimes called dipoles because they contain two poles each and have divided poles. (The positive and negative sides are called poles.) Objects that are composed of many atomic dipoles (such as objects that contain iron, nickel, or cobalt) are easily magnetized. These randomly arranged magnetic domains can be lined up in an orderly pattern by the presence of a strong magnetic field.

Making magnets If the atomic dipoles all line up in the object, it becomes magnetized. The object becomes demagnetized if the atomic dipoles become unaligned.

Permanent magnets Atomic dipoles in very hard materials like steel are hard to move. They are "sticky"; to line them up, a strong magnetic field is needed. However, they will continue to stay aligned even when the magnetic field is not present.

Temporary magnets Atomic dipoles in softer materials are easier to move. They are "slippery" and can be aligned temporarily by a weak magnetic field.

Activities and Procedures

I. Natural and Man-Made Magnets

1. Mystery Rock

Materials *Magnetite/loadstone; a strong magnet; cardboard.

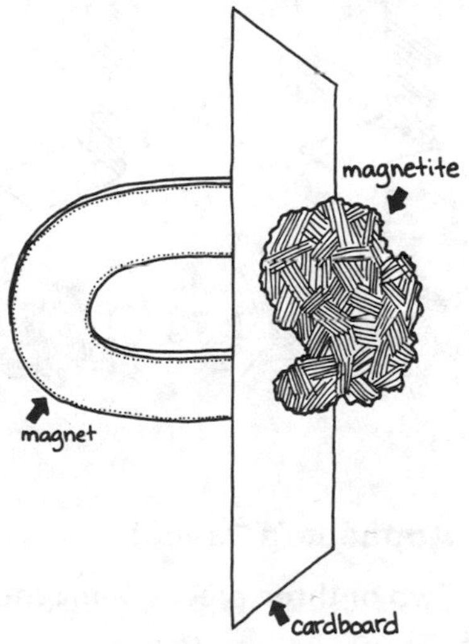

*Magnetite/loadstone can be purchased at a rock store, or from a science supply store or natural history museum.

Procedure

- Place a magnet on one side of the cardboard and the loadstone rock on the other side so that the magnet can be seen but the rock cannot be seen.
- Ask the children, *"What is holding up the magnet?"*
- Have them guess. They will probably say another magnet. Then show them what is on the other side. (They will be surprised to see that it is a magnetic rock.)
- *Explain:* This rock is special. It is called a loadstone. It is made out of a mineral called magnetite. Magnetite has iron ore in it. Iron ore has magnetic properties and can attract things that have iron in them.

2. Detecting Magnetite

Materials Magnetite; assorted small rocks that are black, white, and brown; a strong magnet.

Procedure

- Display a loadstone and assorted small rocks that are black, white, and brown.
- Have a child approach the rocks with a strong magnet and try to guess which rock is the loadstone before the magnet approaches it.
- Have the children observe how the loadstone "rocks" back and forth when the magnet approaches it.

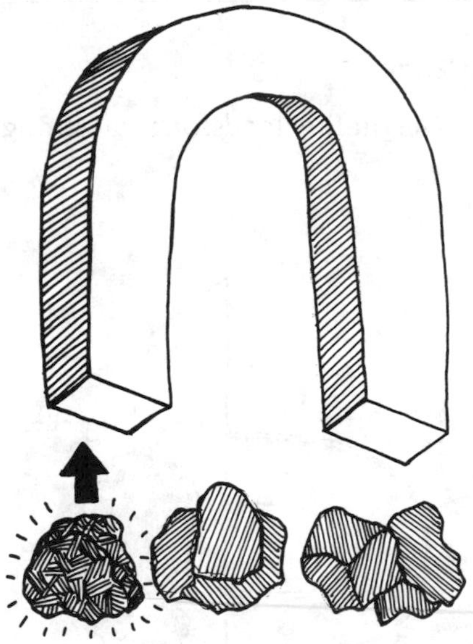

3. Testing Magnetite's Strength

Materials Two or three pieces of magnetite; a box of paper clips.

Procedure

- Place the paper clips in a bowl or on the floor. Approach with the magnetite. Test to see if each piece of magnetite picks up the same number of paper clips, or if one piece of magnetite is stronger than the other.
- Have children experiment to find out which picks up the most paper clips.

Fine points to discuss with children

How can we tell when a magnet is strong?
(By seeing how much it can pick up.)

Do size and shape affect the strength of a piece of magnetite?
(No.)

Can magnetic force go through things?
(Yes.)

How do we know?
(Because we can observe that it does. Remind the children of the magnet and the magnetite going through the cardboard from the first activity.)

4. Comparing the Strength of a Man-Made and a Natural Magnet

Materials Magnetite; bar magnet; paper clips.

Procedure

- Hold up a man-made bar magnet. Tell the children it is a man-made magnet. Hold up a piece of magnetite and tell the children it is a natural magnet found in nature.
- Have children experiment to see if the magnetite can lift up the bar magnet. (Find out which kind of magnet picks up more paper clips.)

Fine points to discuss with children

How can we tell a natural magnet from a man-made magnet?
(Natural magnets look like black rocks. Man-made magnets have a definite shape.)

Is there a difference in their strengths?
(Yes.)

II. Magnetic Force

1. Fishing for Magnetically Sensitive Materials

Materials Plastic basin; "fishing bowl" filled with assorted things* in the center along with a "yes" tray and a "no" tray; a magnetic "fishing pole" (a wood dowel attached to a piece of yarn tied to a magnet).

*"Assorted things": sponge, nail, key, paper clips, butter container, toy cars, aluminum foil, pill container, pen, pencil, paper, shoelaces, bottle cap, etc.

Procedure

• Let's find out which things a magnet attracts or pulls. We will use this magnetic "fishing pole" to test the objects. Have the children sort the things that have been tested into the "yes" or the "no" tray.

• Discuss which things will go into the "yes" tray, and which things will go into the "no" tray. Have the children guess before you bring the magnet to it. See if they guessed right.

Fine points to discuss with children

Does a magnet pick up all things that are made of metal?
(No, only metals that contain iron.)

What other things in the room might attract a magnet?
(Discuss and then have the children find out by going on a magnet hunt around the classroom with a magnet on a stick to find out what the magnet is attracted to.)

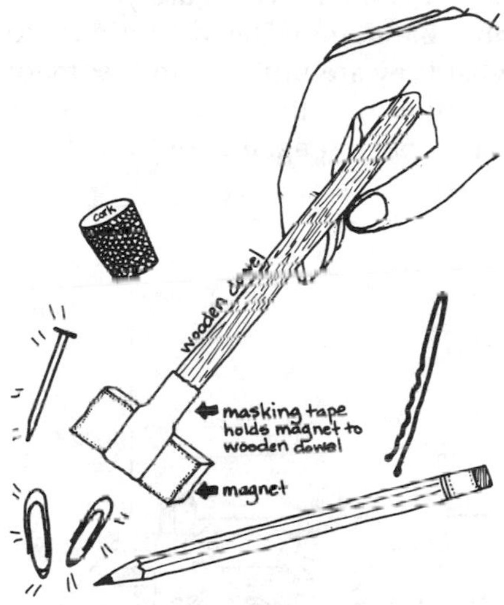

MAGNETIC POLE

2. Jumping Paper Clip

Materials Paper clips; bar magnet.

Procedure

• Place a paper clip on a table. Have a child slide a magnet toward it to find out what happens to the paper clip. (It jumps toward the magnet.)

• Have a child hold a paper clip in his or her palm. Approach the paper clip with a magnet to find out what happens to the paper clip. (It goes up.)

Fine points to discuss with children

Can we feel magnetism?
(No.)

Can we feel its force?
(Yes.)

Can we see magnetism?
(We can see its effects.)

What is a magnetic force?
(A push or a pull.)

3. Moving Paper Clip

Materials Paper clips; magnet; paper.

Procedure Demonstrate magnetic force by pulling and pushing a paper clip across a paper with a magnet held underneath the paper and the clip on top of the paper.

4. Feeling a Magnet

Materials Magnet.

Procedure

• Place a magnet on a child's face, or other body part.

• Ask the child if he/she can feel the magnetism when the magnet touches his/her skin.

• Discuss how they can feel the magnet, but not the magnetism.

5. Feeling Magnetic Force

Materials Two bar magnets.

Procedure

• Have a child hold his/her hand open, palm up. Place one bar magnet on the child's fingers and another bar magnet on the back of his/her fingers (immediately below the first magnet). Now, have the child turn his/her hand vertically. See if the magnets will stay in place. (They will.)

• Discuss how a magnetic force is going through the child's hand. (They cannot feel it penetrate, but they can feel its force.)

MAGNETIC FORCE

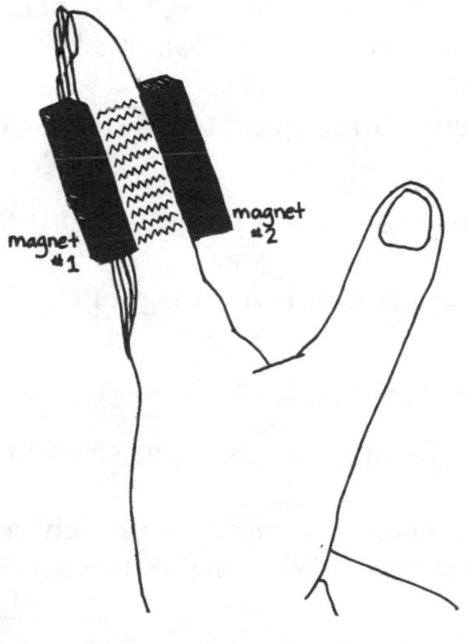

6. Make a Nail Feel Wavy

Materials Two bar magnets; a large nail.

Procedure Have a child hold part of a strong magnet in one hand and a nail or another strong magnet in the other hand. Then bring one magnet close to the other magnet or the large nail. When the magnet is close enough to the other magnet or to the nail, the child will be able to feel a push or a pull of the force in his or her hands. It will fell "wavy," as the two approach each other.

7. Lifting a Piece of Paper with a Magnet

Materials Paper clip; paper; magnet.

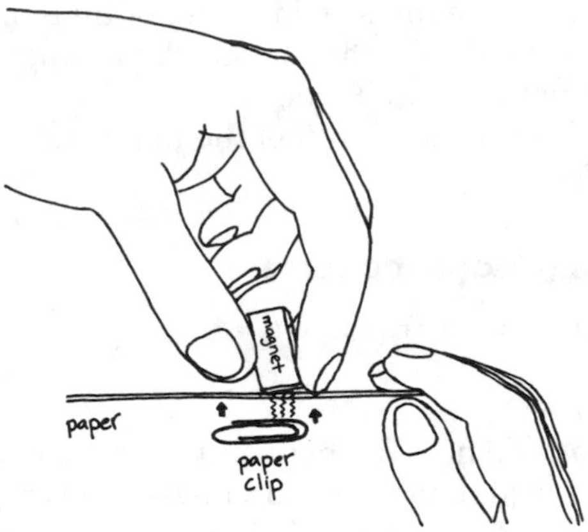

Procedure

- Cover a paper clip with a piece of paper. Have a child slide a magnet on top of the paper, above the paper clip, and lift the magnet up. (The paper will lift up.)
- Discuss why the paper can be lifted by the magnet.

What happens when the magnet is placed above the paper clip when a piece of paper is between it and the paper clip?
(A magnetic force penetrates [goes through] the paper.)

Can the magnet lift the paper without the paper clip under it?
(No, the paper itself is not magnetic.)

8. Make a Tin Can Roll

Materials Empty tuna fish can; strong magnet.

Procedure Have a child approach a can with a magnet. Ask the child to make the can roll forward or backward by holding and keeping the magnet too far away from the can to allow the magnet to attach itself to the can, but close enough to make the can roll.

9. Play a Circle Game Called "Let's Pretend"

Materials Long piece of yarn and assorted materials: bottle caps, keys, pencils, crayon, paper clip, rubber bands, etc. Place the assorted materials in the center of the yarn circle.

Procedure

- Play "Let's Pretend"* (circle game). Adult and children sit crosslegged in a circle.
- To play: One child chooses one object from the assortment. Adult says, "Let's pretend that I am a strong magnet. What are you, David?" David replies, "I am a nail." Adult says, "Then we'll stick together." Adult will hold David's hand. David says to next child, "I am a magnetized nail. What are you?" If Jenny says she's a rubber band, then David continues to ask other children what they are until he finds someone to stick to. Game continues until the adult ends the game by saying, "I am a person again, you're children."

LET'S PRETEND

III. Magnetic Strength

1. Testing Magnets

Materials Paper clips; nails; bolts; different sized magnets.

*Game adapted from Jean Harlan, *Science Experiences for the Early Childhood Years*, 2nd Edition. Charles E. Merrill, 1980.

Procedure

• Display the materials and a variety of magnets in different shapes and sizes. Proceed by letting children find out which magnet has the most pulling power.

Fine points to discuss with children

• Some magnets are stronger than others. Magnets stay stronger with a keeper. A "keeper" is a bar that goes across the ends of a horseshoe magnet. Magnets need to be put away in pairs to stay strong. One magnet helps keep the other magnet strong.

• We can find out how strong a magnet is by testing it, and finding out which magnet can lift up the most things at the same time.

2. Observing Magnetic Force and Strength

Materials Strong magnet; paper clips; plastic tub-shaped container with lid.

Procedure

• Fill a plastic tub-shaped container with paper clips and cover with fitted plastic lid. Have a child experiment to see if the magnet can lift the plastic container.

• Discuss why the plastic container can be lifted. (It can be lifted because magnetic force goes through the plastic.)

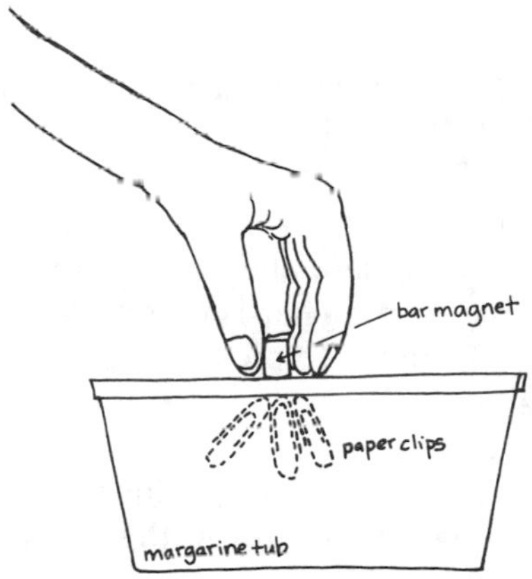

3. Taking Away a Magnet

Materials See Procedure 2 above.

Procedure

• Ask the child to remove the lid to the plastic container and to remove the magnet.

• What will happen to the paper clips and why?

• Discuss why the paper clips fell. (They fell because the magnetic force was taken away.)

4. Magnetic Sweeper

Materials Strong magnet; lots of paper clips.

Procedure

• Have the children spill all the paper clips on the floor.

• Ask the children what is the easiest way to pick up the paper clips.

• Demonstrate how you can use the magnet to pick up all the paper clips. The magnet will act like a "sweeper."

5. Experimenting with Magnetic Strength

Materials Different-sized magnets; paper clips; nails and bolts.

Procedure Let the children experiment with different-sized magnets to find out which one picks up the most, or how long a paper clip chain can be made by attaching them by magnetic force. Have the children test the magnets to find out which magnet picks up the most nails and bolts.

IV. Lines of Force

Seeing Lines of Force

Materials Plastic see-through envelope; iron filings; assorted magnets.

Procedure

• Explain to children that the plastic see-through envelope contains iron filings. Iron filings come from iron when it has been sawed. It is iron dust (as sawdust is to wood). Iron filings are very small pieces of iron. They are inside the sealed envelope. You can see them and not breathe the dust into your lungs. The iron dust is not good for your body. The iron filings must stay inside the sealed envelope. The envelope has been taped closed for safety.

• Place a magnet on a flat surface (floor or table) underneath the see-through envelope. Tap your finger gently on the envelope. Magnetic force lines should appear. Iron filings show you a picture of the area around a magnet where its force can be felt. This area around a magnet is called its magnetic field. The lines formed around the magnet are called lines of force.

• Ask children what shape the force lines will be that surround a circle magnet. (A circle.)

• Ask children what shape the force lines will be that surround a rectangle magnet. (A rectangular shape that looks like an ellipse or "squared" circle.)

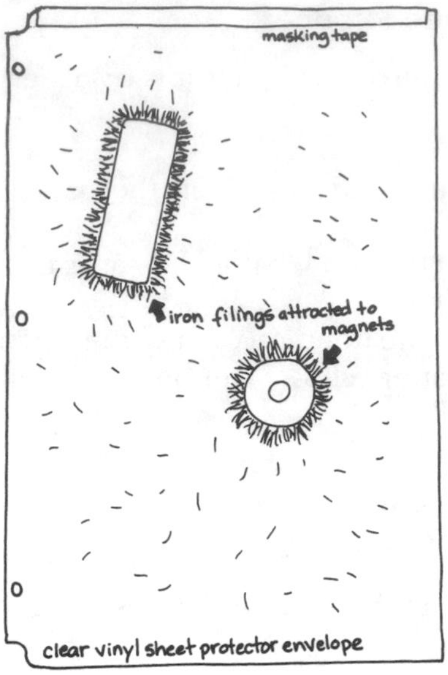

SEEING LINES OF FORCE

V. Magnetic Field

Demonstrating a Magnet's Magnetic Field

Materials Paper clip strung to a berry basket; book; paper; magnet; rocks to weigh down the berry basket.

Procedure

- Explain to children that lines of magnetic force from a magnetic field can go through the air.
- Demonstrate with a paper clip whose wire has been strung with a string tied to a weighted object like an empty berry basket.

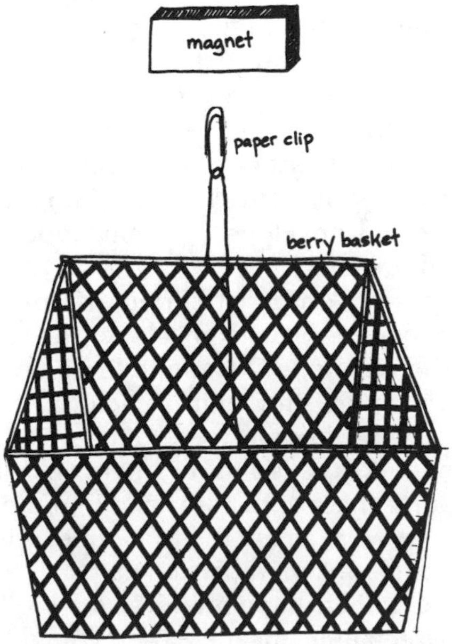

- Approach the paper clip with the magnet. Try not to touch the paper clip with the magnet. Instead, wait for the clip to point vertically on the thread because of its attraction caused by lines of force in the magnetic field.
- While the paper clip is in a vertical position held up by magnetic force, have children test to see if the magnetic field goes through their hands, a thin book, a piece of paper, etc. Have children place the item being tested between the magnet and suspended paper clip.

Fine points to discuss with children

What makes the paper clip fall?
(If the magnet moves too far away from the paper clip, the lines of force from the magnet cannot reach the paper clip. Strong magnets have longer lines of force than weak magnets do.)

Why does the paper clip stay in the air?
(Magnetic force from the magnet holds the paper clip up.)

How far away can the magnet move and still hold up the paper clip?
(It can move a little, but not a lot. If the magnet moves too far away, the lines of force become too weak to act on the paper clip.)

VI. Temporary Magnets

Making a Temporary Magnet

Materials Strong magnet; nail; paper clip; hammer.

Procedure

- Demonstrate how to make a temporary magnet. Use a strong magnet, a nail, and paper clip.
- Allow the nail to hit a hard cement floor so it will not be a magnet. Then try to pick up a paper clip with the nail. The nail cannot pick up a paper clip because it is not a magnet.
- Then ask the children if they think they can make the nail into a magnet. Wait for their response. Then attach the nail head or point to the magnet. Pick up the paper clip.
- Discuss why the paper clip can be lifted. (It is in the magnetic field of the nail, which has become a temporary magnet.)
- Remove the magnet from the nail. Observe what happens.
- Discuss why the paper clips are still attracted and attached to the nail. Hit the nail with a hammer or let it fall onto a hard floor. Will it still be a magnet? (It might be, but it will lose some of its magnetic force. It will not be as strong as it was.)

Fine point to discuss with children
Magnets lose much of their magnetism if they are treated roughly.
(Their molecules get all shook up and out of line.)

• Demonstrate with paper clips how molecules are lined up. (Arrange several paper clips in a line. Hit the paper clips with a hammer and observe how they bounce around and jump out of the straight-line arrangement. The same thing happens to the insides of magnets when they are dropped.)

VII. Making a Magnet

1. Making a Permanent Magnet

Materials Bar magnet; stainless steel needle.

Procedure Have children stroke a stainless steel needle in one direction about 200 times with a strong bar magnet. It will become a magnet. Have the children bring the needle next to a paper clip to test it. If the paper clip reacts then you will know that the needle has become a magnet.

2. Making a Floating Magnet

Materials Magnetized stainless steel needle; sliced wine-bottle cork; bowl filled with water.

Procedure Have a child place the magnetized stainless steel needle on a sliced piece of wine-bottle cork. Then float the cork with the needle on it in water. Have children observe what happens to the needle. It will tend to stabilize in one direction. If you spin it, it will continue to point in the same position over and over again when it stops.

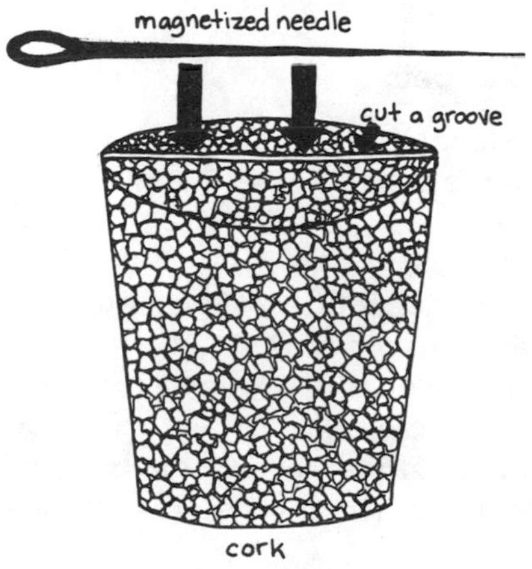

VIII. Laws of Magnetism

1. Experimenting with a Pair of Marked Magnets

Materials Two marked magnets (each magnet has a red spot on one side and a blue spot on the other side).

Procedure
• Have a child bring the two marked magnets near each other and observe what happens. (If the two red spots touch, they push away. If the two blue spots touch, they push away.)
• Discuss what can be done to make the magnets attract each other. Wait for the children to respond. Then try to put a red side together with a blue side.

2. Repelling a Magnet

Materials Two marked magnets (same as Activity VIII, Procedure 1).

Procedure Can one magnet push another magnet away? How can this be done? Have children put two red sides or two blue sides together. (One will repel the other and produce a push reaction.)

3. Making a Magnet do Somersaults

Materials Two marked magnets (same as Activity VIII, Procedure 1).

Procedure After your demonstration, let the children experiment with making the magnets do somersaults. Place one magnet in your open palm and the other on the back of your hand. Hold your open palm parallel to the floor. Now turn the bottom magnet over. The top magnet will flip over too.

4. Magnetic Somersaults on a Tray

Materials A Styrofoam tray; two marked magnets (same as Activity VIII, Procedure 1).

Procedure Place one magnet on a Styrofoam tray. Place another magnet on the bottom of the Styrofoam tray. Have the children make it do somersaults, or pull it across the tray. (The repel force causes somersaults to happen; attract force causes the pull to take place.) See diagram.

Fine points to discuss with children *Explain:* The Laws of Magnetism (likes repel; unlikes attract).

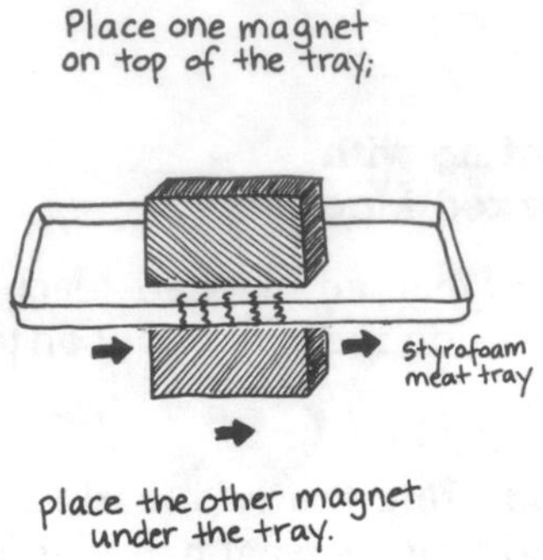
Place one magnet
on top of the tray;
styrofoam
meat tray
place the other magnet
under the tray.

What does repel mean?
(Push away.)

What does attract mean?
(Pull together.)

When one magnet pushes another magnet, is that an attraction force or a repulsion force?
(A repulsion force.)

What "colors" have to come together to create an attraction force?
(Red and blue.)

What "colors" have to come together to create a repulsion force?
(Red, red or blue, blue.)

5. Repelling and Attracting Magnets on a Wooden Dowel

Materials Four marked magnets with holes in their centers; a thin wooden dowel that fits through the holes in the magnets.

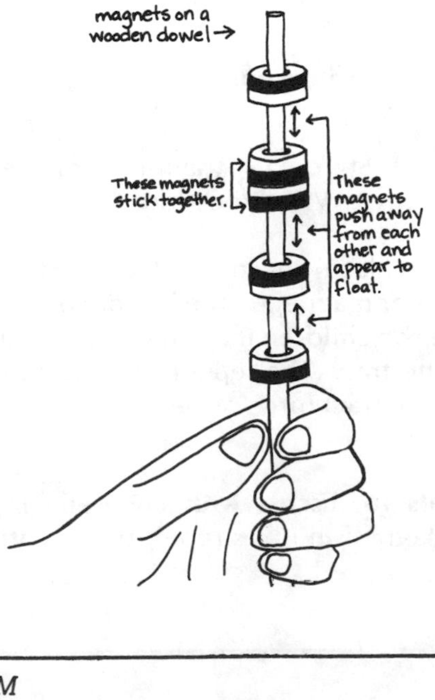
magnets on a
wooden dowel
These magnets
stick together.
These
magnets
push away
from each
other and
appear to
float.

Procedure
- Demonstrate floating magnets (magnets with holes in their centers). Using a thin wooden dowel, show how they appear to float up and down the stick. Place the magnets together so "unlike" colors touch. They will all connect. Now place the magnets so "like" colors touch. They will repel each other and appear to be floating up and down the dowel.
- After the demonstration, let the children experiment making magnets float on a dowel.

Fine points to discuss with children
- The magnets appear to be floating as you move the bottom magnet up and down the dowel because they are repelling each other. The magnetic force is causing a push. (Likes repel and opposites attract.)

6. Magnetic Toys

Materials Magnetic toy frogs or turtles, or other novelty magnetic toy set.

Procedure Demonstrate frog magnets. (One frog can make the other frog spin.) Then let children experiment with them.

Fine points to discuss with children
- Attract means to stick together; repel means to push away.
- Discuss why the frogs can make each other spin.

7. Demonstrating Attract and Repel Through Body Language

Materials None.

Procedure
- Clasp hands together to show attraction.
- Separate hands to show repulsion.
- Have children think of other body language to demonstrate attract and repel with each other.

8. Magnet Puppets

Materials Magnetic puppets (with paper clip feet), shoe-box puppet stage;* two magnets; thumbtacks.

Procedure
- Demonstrate magnetic puppets and shoe-box puppet stage with two magnets.
- *How do the puppets move?* (The puppets have thumbtacks or paper clips on their feet. A magnet is moving underneath them in the box. The magnet makes them move. The thumbtacks or paper clips are

*Adapted from Rose Wyler.

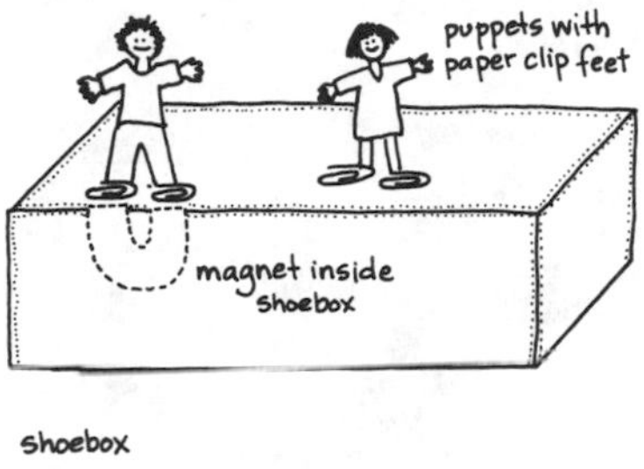

attracted to the magnet. The two magnets repel and attract each other, which also causes the puppets to come together and/or to separate.)

- Let children experiment with the magnetic puppets and/or design their own magnetic puppets.

IX. Magnetic Poles

1. Compass

Materials Compass; marked loadstone on a string.

Procedure

- Show children a compass. Explain that the needle in the middle is a little magnet. When it stops spinning it always points in a north/south direction. In the olden days, sailors used the sun and stars to navigate, using a loadstone for a compass. They hung the loadstone by a string and used the stone to help lead them toward their destination. If they knew where north was, it was easy to determine east and west.
- Let children experiment with the compass. Tell them to spin it and to observe where it points when it stops.
- Hang a marked loadstone on a string. Spin it. See where it points when it stops spinning.

2. A Floating Compass

Materials See Activity VII, Procedure 2.

Procedure Let the needle float. Place a compass near it. When the needle stops, have the children compare the direction the compass needle points with the direction the floating needle points.

Fine points to discuss with children
How can you tell if the needle has been magnetized? (If it has been, then it should be able to make the needle on the compass spin.)

3. Finding a Magnet's Poles

Materials Strong magnet; paper clips.

Procedure The ends of a magnet are called its poles. Like poles repel and unlike poles attract just like the colors which marked the magnets. Magnets are strongest at their poles. How can we prove this with paper clips? Where will most of the paper clips stick? Have children experiment to find out. (Most of the paper clips will stick on the ends of the magnet.)

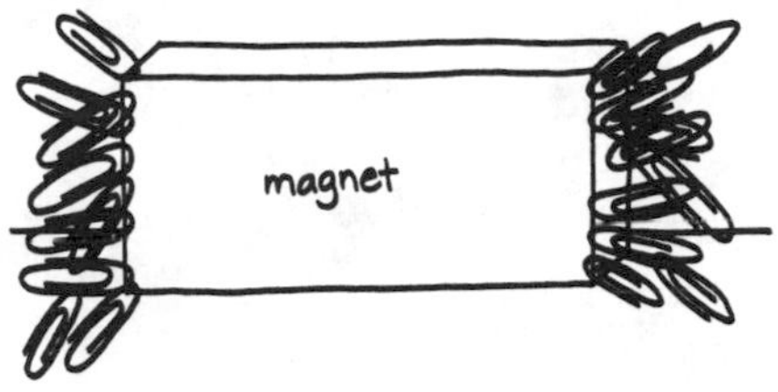

Further Resources

Suggested Books for Children

Dewey Decimal Classification Number for magnetism is: J538.

Freeman, Mae, *The Real Book of Magnets.* New York: Scholastic, 1967.

Kirkpatrick, Rena K., *Look at Magnets.* Milwaukee, Wisconsin: Raintree, 1978.

Pine, Tillie, and Joseph Levine, *Magnets and How to Use Them.* New York: McGraw-Hill, 1958. (Good sketches on what magnets can do.)

Schneider, Herman and Nina, *Secret Magnets.* New York: Scholastic, 1979. (Describes how to make a "magnetic detector" to help look for hidden magnets in your house.)

Wyler, Rose, *First Book of Science Experiments.* New York: Franklin Watts, 1971.

Wyler, Rose, and Gerald Ames, *Prove It.* New York; Scholastic Book Services, 1967.

Resource Books for More Ideas

Amery, Heather, and Angela Littles, *The Fun Craft Book of Magnets and Batteries.* New York: Scholastic Book Service, 1976.

Catherall, Ed, *Magnets.* Morristown, NJ: Silver Burdette Co., 1982. (Good color sketches on what magnets can do.)

Fernando, Rocco V., *Junior Science Book of Magnets.* Champagne, Illinois: Gerrand, 1960.

Holden, Raymond, *Magnetism.* New York: Golden Press, 1962.

Keen, Martin, *The Know-How Book of Experiments with Batteries and Magnets.* New York: Grosset and Dunlap, 1976.

Lieberg, Owen S., *Wonders of Magnets and Magnetism.* New York: Dodd, Mead & Co., 1967.

Podendorf, Illa, *True Book of Magnets and Electricity.* Chicago: Children's Press, 1972.

Sootin, Harry, *Experiments in Magnetism and Electricity.* New York: Watts, 1962.

Sootin, Harry, *Experiments with Magnetism.* New York: W. W. Norton, 1968.

Valens, Evans G., *Magnet.* Cleveland: World, 1964.

5
STATIC ELECTRICITY

Objectives

• For children to develop an awareness of static electricity's presence.

• For children to become aware that static electricity can be produced on a dry day by the action of friction.

• For children to develop an awareness that static electricity can be collected, but that it is hard to hold on to.

• For children to develop an awareness of the meaning of force.

• For children to develop an awareness of how small "small" can be.

• For children to become aware that water reduces or eliminates static electricity.

• To give children an understanding of static electricity.

General Background Information for Parents and Teachers

Static electricity Creates a cracking noise or a shock from electric charges. It can be obtained by vigorously rubbing two different dry materials together. Friction from rubbing and close contact causes electrons to transfer from one dry material to another. Static electricity cannot harm anyone. It is not powerful like current electricity. It is okay and safe to play with static electricity, but it is not safe to play with current* electricity (unless the voltage is low, as with 6-volt batteries).

Static Comes from a Greek word that means standing. Static electricity is usually at rest. It can be found on the surfaces of most materials. When the weather is dry, it can be temporarily collected.

Electricity A term referring to the movement of electrons.

****Atoms** Everything alive, dead, and never living is made up of atoms. Atoms are microscopically miniscule units of matter. (No one has ever seen an atom; they exist in theory.)

It is theorized that:

a. The nuclei of atoms are made up of protons and neutrons. Protons are positively charged. Neutrons are neutral.

b. Electrons are negatively charged and orbit around the positively charged nucleus.

c. When static electricity is not able to be easily collected due to a lack of transfer by free electrons,

*Current electricity refers to electricity that flows, like the current in a stream or river. When the current is turned on, it is constantly in motion.

**All items with double asterisks indicate that the information is too abstract and too complicated for young children to understand or comprehend. It is included to enhance parent or teacher background only.

then atoms are electrically neutral. The positive protons in the nucleus cancel out the orbiting negative electrons. Nuclear forces hold atoms together.

d. The protons and neutrons in the nucleus are "heavy" and stay together as a tight-knit group in the center of the atom.

e. The electrons of the atom are much "lighter" in weight than the nucleus. Electrons travel alone and far away from each other in separate orbits (as the planets do around the sun). The paths of the individual electrons do not meet because their like negative charges repel one another.

Nuclear force Energy derived from the nuclei of atoms.

Electrons Electrons are very tiny particles that orbit around the nucleus of atoms. Electrons carry negative electric charges.

Electric charges Can be positive, negative, or neutral.

Electrically positive A positive charge is caused when atoms lose electrons. It has a force. A force is a push or a pull. The force makes it possible for paper to stick to a wall or for items that are electrically charged to "stick together."

Electrically negative A negative charge is caused when atoms gain electrons. Like a positive electrical charge, it too has a force which causes it to push or pull, thus causing materials to "stick together."

Electrically neutral A neutral charge has an equal number of positive and negative electric charges which have cancelled each other out. It does not have a force.

"Free" or separated electrons Cause static electric charges. Electrons become free and transfer to other materials when they are attracted to a material that has a stronger attraction. This transfer occurs when two different dry materials are rubbed together vigorously.

a. The atoms of the two dry materials are jostled through the friction action of vigorous rubbing. The heat from friction and the collisions of electrons caused from jostling cause the outer orbiting electrons to separate from their atoms.

b. One of the two materials will have temporarily lost electrons and will carry a positive charge. The other material will have temporarily gained electrons and carry a negative charge.

c. Rubbing two different dry "electrically neutral" materials together does not produce electricity. It merely creates a temporary imbalance in the number of electrons possessed by the atoms of each material.

Use of static electricity Static electricity has no real practical use except to help young children understand simple concepts about electricity. It is easy to collect on a dry day, but hard to hold on to. Moisture shortens the time span of a charge's force. Moisture helps a charge neutralize itself. Only separated or "free" electric charges (+ or −) carry force. When an electron is no longer separated or "free" from its atom, it is neutral and carries no force. (No force equals no charge.)

A law of electricity As in magnetism, like electrical charges repel and unlike electrical charges attract. Positive attracts negative. Positive repels positive. Negative repels negative.

Conductors Materials that allow electric charges to pass and spread through them easily (like metal and water or moisture). Static electricity cannot accumulate and collect on things when electrons flow easily. If there is no conduction path to remove a charge, then static electricity stays at rest and separated and static force results. (Force equals charge.)

Insulators Materials that do not allow electric charges to pass or spread through them easily (like rubber, glass and plastic). Electrons cannot move easily through an insulator. Insulators help keep a charge in place. (Wires are covered with insulation to keep the electric charge concentrated in the wires and to protect materials that the live electricity could hurt or damage.)

Activities and Procedures

I. Creating Static Electricity

1. Creating Static Electricity with Balloons

Materials Balloon.

Procedure

- Blow up a balloon. Rub the balloon against a wool sweater. It will start to sound "crackly." Bits of dust and fiber in the air will stick to the charged balloon.
- Place the balloon against the wall. It will stick to the wall.

Fine points to discuss with children

Why does the balloon stick to the wall?
(It has an electric charge.)

What is a charge?
(In science, it is not the way we pay for things. A charge is a scientific word that means something has been energized or given energy. The electric charge is caused by static electricity. The charge makes it "cling" to materials like the wall, which are not charged.)

How does rubbing help us get a charge?
(Rubbing creates heat, and a "closeness" between two materials that are rubbed. Rubbing causes static charges to transfer from one material to the other. When the transfer happens, charges collect on the surface of the balloon, and the charges give the balloon energy or power to stay on the wall.)

2. Feeling Heat from Friction

Materials None.

Procedure Have children rub their hands together hard and fast. Ask children what they feel in their hands. They should feel heat. Heat is energy. The heat is created from the friction caused by rubbing.

Fine points to discuss with children
Where is electricity?
(Electricity is everywhere. But most materials are usually "electrically balanced" so we do not feel or see the effects of the energy. When materials are not neutral, we can feel the effects of the temporary energy. It is called static electricity.)

3. Attracting a Charged Balloon

Materials Blown-up balloon; string.

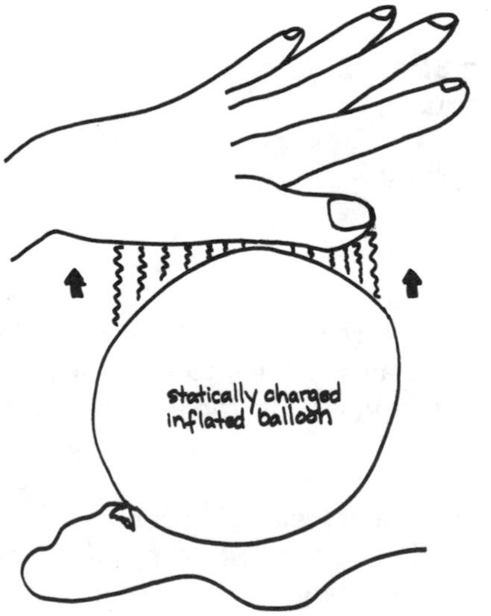

Procedure
- Tie a string to the end of a charged balloon. Tie the balloon so it will hang freely. Have a child approach the charged balloon with the palm of his or her hand opened. The balloon will be attracted to the child's hand because his or her hand is not charged (it is electrically neutral).
- Have a child hold his or her hand flat against the side of the balloon. The child's hand will lift the balloon up because the charge stays attracted to the child's hand and causes lift to occur when his or her hand goes up. See diagram.

4. Attracting and Repelling Charged Balloons

Materials Two balloons; string.

Procedure
- Blow up two balloons. Cut a piece of string about two or three feet long and tie one end of the string to each balloon.
- Hang the two balloons suspended on a hanger. (If there is no place to hang the hanger, then if necessary, hang the hanger from a broom handle supported by two chairs, or two tables.)
- Allow the two balloons to hang freely. Have the children observe what happens to the balloons. (If left to hang free, they will touch each other.)
- Now charge each of the balloons by rubbing them on wool or animal fur. Have the children observe what happens to the balloons. (The balloons repel each other because they have like charges.)

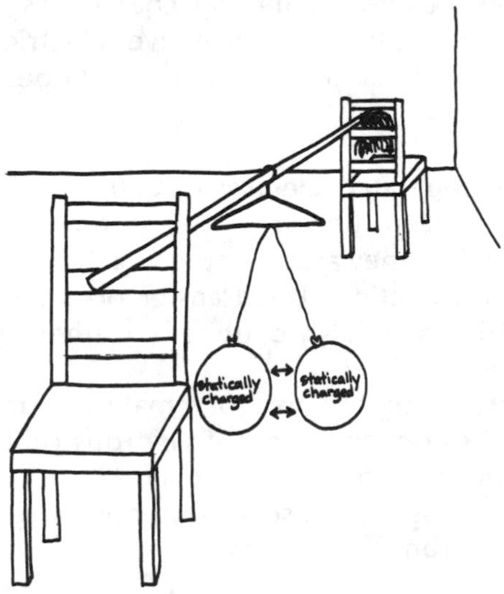

- Place a child's hand between the two balloons that are repelling each other. Have children observe what happens to the balloons. (The charged balloons touch the child's hand because they are electrically neutral and unlike charges attract each other.)

Fine points to discuss with children
How are electrical charges like magnets?
(Electrical charges behave as magnets do; likes repel and unlikes attract.)

What do we know about charges, particles, and electrons?
(Charges are caused by very tiny particles that we cannot see called electrons. No one has ever seen an electron. Scientists have theories which help explain things. Sometimes scientists talk about electrons, atoms, and molecules to explain why things happen.)

5. Creating Static Electricity with Newspaper

Materials Newspaper; pencil.

Procedure
- Place a half sheet of newspaper or newsprint on a flat, smooth wall. Have the children rub the sheet of newspaper or newsprint with a pencil held flat (horizontally) against the wall. Have the children observe what happens. (The paper is able to stay put on the wall. Static electricity is holding the paper on the wall.)
- After a while, the paper will stop clinging and fall to the floor. (The paper will become electrically neutral or balanced again.)

Paper sticks to the wall when rubbed with a pencil.

Fine points to discuss with children
Why was the paper able to "stick" to the wall?
(Extra electrons were collected on the paper from the pencil. A static charge was caused by extra electrons. The static charge caused the paper to "stick" to the wall. When the air is dry, extra electrons can be collected on the surface of some materials that are rubbed.)

Why did the paper fall?
(The extra electrons found another place where they could stay. It is difficult to hold on to extra electrons. They do not stay put.)

6. Creating Static Electricity with an Empty Plastic Container

Materials Empty plastic margarine container with a lid; puffed rice; salt; pepper; a piece of wool.

Procedure
- Fill the container with about ten pieces of puffed rice, cereal, a dash of salt, and a dash of pepper.
- Remove the lid and empty the contents (puffed rice, salt, and pepper) onto the lid. Have a child lift the empty margarine tub up and hold it about half an inch above the lid. Observe whether the empty plastic container will lift any of the particles on the lid. (It might.)
- Place a child's hand inside a plastic container so that the child's hand is touching the bottom of the inside of the container. Have the child use his or her other hand to rub the outside bottom of the container vigorously with a piece of wool to create static electricity.

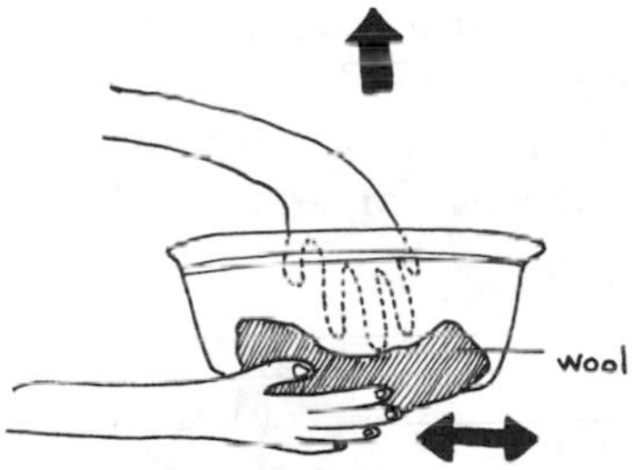

RUB TO CREATE STATIC ELECTRICITY

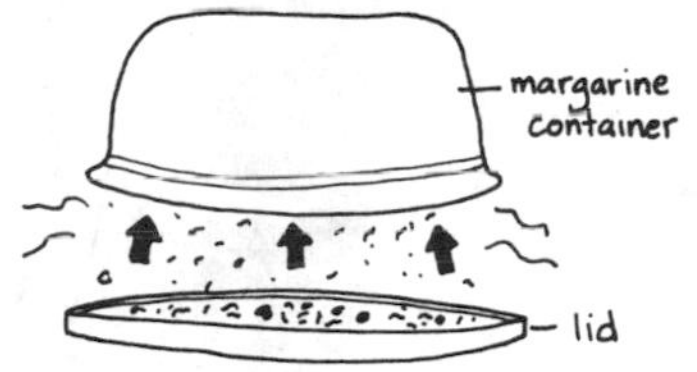

- Again lift the empty but charged plastic container up and hold it about half an inch above the lid with the puffed rice, salt, and pepper. Again have the child observe what happens. (The puffed rice will be lifted up, along with some of the salt and pepper particles.)

Fine points to discuss with children
Why was wool rather than something else used to rub the bottom of the margarine tub in order to create a static charge?
(Wool comes from lamb's fur and it contains protein. Hair and fur contain protein. Protein can create static charges, especially on dry days when the materials are

rubbed against plastics. Electrons are scraped off of the wool and are collected on the bottom of the plastic tub.)

Why are the particles of cereal, salt, and pepper lifted? (The particles of cereal, salt, and pepper are very light in weight and are uncharged. Unlike charges are attracted to the charged piece of plastic.)

II. Understanding Force

1. Make a Tin Can Move

Materials Empty tin can, a magnet.

Procedure
• Place a tin can on its side. Ask the children how the tin can can be made to move.
• Use your hand to push or pull the can.
• Ask the children if the can can be moved without touching it. (By blowing on it.)
• If they do not respond by saying "blowing on it," then show them how it can be moved by blowing on it.
• Ask if a magnet can make the tin can move.
• Demonstrate how the magnet can make it move without touching the can.
• *Explain:* Our hands, the air, the magnet, and static electricity are all forces. Forces can pull or push things.

Fine point to discuss with children
What does a force do?
(It pushes or pulls things.)

2. Bouncing a Ball

Materials A ball.

Procedure
• Drop a bouncing ball. Observe how high it bounces.
• Ask the children if we can make the ball bounce up higher. How? (By moving our hand down fast before we let go of the ball.)

Fine points to discuss with children
How can we control the force of the ball's bounce?
(The fast movement of our hand before we let go of the ball gives energy to the ball. The extra energy adds more force to the bounce of the ball. The ball will push off the floor with more force, and the ball will bounce higher than when it is just dropped.)
(Charges can have a weak force or a strong force. A strong charge has a lot of energy. The energy comes from the loose electrons. If the electrons stay loose, the charge stays "strong." If the electrons do not stay loose or separated from their atoms, then the static electric charge is weak and becomes neutral.)

III. The Very Small

1. Breaking Cereal into Particles

Materials Puffed rice; toothpicks.

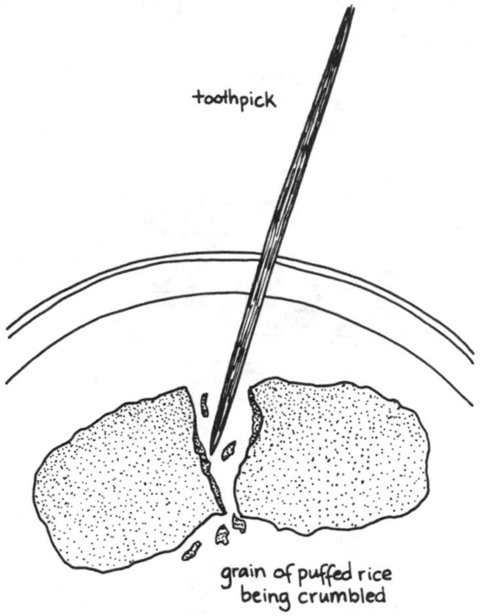

Procedure Have the children take a piece of puffed rice cereal and pick it apart. Have them find out how small a piece of puffed rice can be picked apart and still be a piece or particle of puffed rice. (The piece can be extremely small.)

Fine point to discuss with children
How small is small?
(Too small to see. Salt and pepper are very small particles. A piece of puffed rice is made up of many particles.)

2. Crushing Salt and Pepper

Materials Salt and pepper; magnifying lens.

Procedure

• Have children crush or grind the salt and the pepper down. Have them find out if it can be made into salt dust and pepper dust (obviously it can). Keep the two kinds of dust separate.
• Have the children test to find out if these small particles are still salt and pepper by tasting the dust.
• Allow each child the chance to make his/her own salt or pepper dust and to taste it.
• Have the children look at the tiny particles through a magnifying lens and have them observe whether or not the particles are all the same size. (They are not. They are different shapes.)

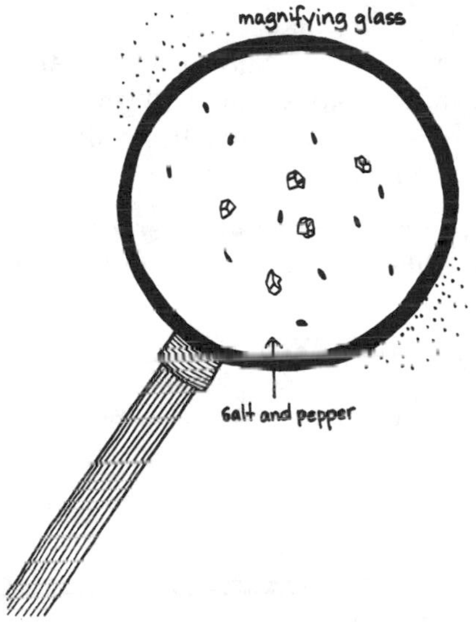

3. Jumping Salt and Pepper

Materials Empty plastic container; salt dust; pepper dust; a piece of wool.

Procedure Have a child rub an empty plastic margarine container with a piece of wool to get it charged. Have child bring it near the particles of salt dust and pepper dust and then observe what happens. (The particles jump on to the bottom of the tub and stay charged longer.)

Fine points to discuss with children
Why do the particles stay charged longer?
(The particles weigh less and are more sensitive to static electric charges. They are more sensitive than the larger pieces of puffed rice were.)
(The dust of salt, pepper, and puffed rice is made up of very small particles. When we compare the size of these dust particles to the size of an electron particle, the particles of salt, pepper, and puffed rice dust are gigantic—as gigantic as an elephant would look if it were standing next to an ant.)

4. Model of an Atom Made from Basketballs and Tennis Balls

Materials Two basketballs; two tennis balls.

Procedure Demonstrate how electrons collide when they are jostled and brought close together through rubbing and friction. Use two large basketballs and two tennis balls as a model of an atom. The tennis balls are models of electrons orbiting around the basketballs, which are models of the nucleus. When the tennis balls collide, they bounce off away from their orbit. They are shaken loose from the atom by the collision.

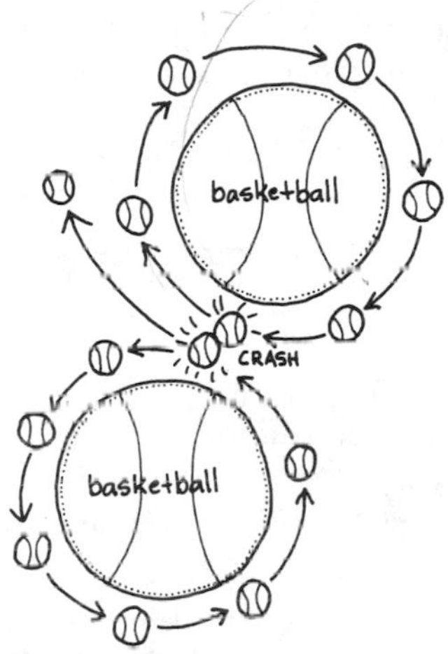

COLLISION OF ORBITING ELECTRONS

Fine point to discuss with children
What happens to the two balls when they collide?
(They bounce off in a new direction. They get shaken off their path or orbit. The same thing happens when two materials are rubbed vigorously. Electrons get shaken loose. Electrons that are separated or shaken loose cause static electricity to occur.)

IV. Lightning

1. Creating Sparks with Leather Shoes on a Rug

Materials Children with leather-soled shoes.

Procedure

• Explain to the children that when static electricity charges are exchanged, sparks fly.
• Have the children rub their leather-soled shoes against a carpet and then touch a metal doorknob. A

shock can be felt. If the room is darkened, it is sometimes possible to see a spark.

Fine points to discuss with children
What causes lightning?
(When clouds exchange charges, lightning is created and energy can be seen. The energy from the charge has been let loose and is in the air. Lightning is caused by huge charges of static electricity.)

Why does lightning occur during a wet storm?
(Lightning occurs when a lot of moisture is present. Moisture helps carry or conduct electrons either toward each other or away from each other.)

Why is it difficult to create static electricity on a wet day?
(On a wet day, electrons flow easily. Static occurs when electrons are at rest and shake loose easily. On wet days, electrons do not separate easily. They flow through the moisture. The moisture acts as a conductor.)

V. Playing with Static Electricity

1. Static Hair

Materials Clean hair recently washed, a plastic comb.

Procedure Comb a child's hair briskly. If it is a dry day and the hair has just been washed and is not greasy and wet, static will be created. It may be necessary to comb hair awhile to generate the static.

Fine points to discuss with children
How can we tell that static has been created?
(Hair starts to sound crackly, and is attracted to the comb. The hair appears to stand on end.)

Why is static created?
(The friction of the comb rubbing against the hair causes the electrons to separate. The separated electrons are collected on the comb from the hair. **The comb has a negative charge and the hair has a positive charge. **The hair has lost electrons and is positive. **The comb has gained electrons and is negative.)

2. Hair Raising

Materials Hair with static electricity.

Procedure Observe that the hair appears to stand on end when the comb is no longer near the hair.

Fine points to discuss with children
Why does the hair appear to stand on end when the comb is no longer near the hair?
(The individual hairs, like the balloons from Activity #1, Procedure 4, are repelling each other with a like charge. The hair is attracted to the comb when the comb comes near. The comb has a different charge and attracts the hair.)

• Review the point that static electricity is similar to magnetism—"likes" repel and "unlikes" attract.

3. Making Paper "Walk"

Materials Tissue paper or newspaper; sewing thread; plastic drinking straw.

paper dolls

Procedure
• Cut out two "people shapes" from tissue paper or newsprint.

• Tie a piece of sewing thread to each of the paper people's heads.
• Hang the two threads from a plastic drinking straw.
• Keep the two paper dolls about two inches apart.
• Rub another plastic straw through a child's hair. (For best results, be sure hair is squeaky clean.) Keep rubbing or stroking the child's hair with the straw until the straw is charged.
• Have a child gently rub the "paper people dolls" with the charged straw.
• Have a child approach the paper doll with the charged straw and observe what happens to the paper dolls. (They will move in circles.)
• Let children experiment with making paper "walk."

Fine points to discuss with children
Why do the paper dolls move and turn in circles?
(The charged straw carries extra electrons that carry an invisible electronic force.)

4. Getting Rid of Static

Materials Atomizer filled with water; static charges on hair or on newspaper.

Procedure Have a child spray the static electric charge with an atomizer. The spray of water will create a moist situation. Have children observe what happens to the static. (It will disappear.)

Fine point to discuss with children
Why does the static disappear?
(The moisture helped the electrons flow back to an atom. The water acted as a conductor that led the way for the separated electron to find an atom that needed an electron.)

Further Resources

Suggested Books for Children

Dewey Decimal Classification Number for electricity is: J557.

Branley, Franklyn, *Flash, Crash, Rumble and Roll.* New York: Thomas Y. Crowell, 1964.

Zim, Herbert, *Lightning and Thunder.* New York: Morrow, 1952.

Resource Books for More Ideas

Bonsall, George, *The How and Why Wonder Book of Weather.* New York: Grosset and Dunlap, 1960.

Pine, Tillie, and Joseph Levine, *Friction All Around.* New York: Whittlesey House, McGraw-Hill, 1960.

Schwartz, Julius, *Now I Know.* New York: Whittlesey House, McGraw-Hill, 1955.

6

SOUND

Objectives

- For children to develop an awareness that sounds are caused by vibrations.
- For children to become aware that many kinds of vibrations can be seen, felt, and heard.
- For children to become aware that an action of force or energy is needed to start a vibration.
- For children to develop an awareness that a lot of force creates a loud noise, but a little bit of force creates a soft noise.
- For children to become aware that vibrations can make things nearby vibrate.
- For children to develop an awareness that vibrations can travel through objects.
- For children to become familiar with the meaning of the terms vibrate, energy, echo, reflection, bounce, absorb, wave, pitch, frequency.
- For children to develop an understanding of the relative differences between volume terms (loud and soft), and pitch terms (low and high).
- For children to develop an awareness that different sizes of vibrating objects can create different frequencies and pitches when they vibrate.

General Background Information for Parents and Teachers

Sound The source of all sound is movements or vibrations. When there is no movement, there is no sound to be heard.

****The speed of sound** 1,100 feet per second. Light travels faster than sound. During a lightning storm, we see the lightning before we hear the sound of the thunder.

Vibration A back and forth motion. When vibrations stop, sound stops. Vibrations can cause other things nearby to vibrate.

Sound waves Sound travels in waves. Sound waves can move through things. Waves move best through solid objects like the earth, metals, and wood. Sound waves do not travel as well through a gas such as air or through spongy materials like pillows which contain air pockets. All vibrations cause sound waves.

Measuring a wave The length of a sound wave is measured from one crest to the next, or from one trough to the next.

Crest The high part of a wave.

Trough The low part of a wave.

Sound absorption Materials that absorb sound waves often have air pockets. Air pockets trap sound waves. Some building materials are designed to catch and absorb sounds. (Have the children examine a piece of acoustical ceiling tile and observe the holes.)

**All items marked by double asterisks indicate that the information is too abstract and too complicated for young children to understand or comprehend. It is included to enhance parent or teacher background only.

Echoes An echo is caused by a sound wave that bounces back from an object, like a ball bouncing off a wall.

Reverberation A prolonged echo effect.

****Refraction** When sound waves are bent, and parts of the sound wave travel at different speeds. This happens on a windy day because the different air currents refract or bend sound waves.

Feeling sound vibrations Many sound vibrations can be seen as well as felt. Deaf people take advantage of their other senses to "hear" what their ears cannot hear.

Energy In physics, the term energy refers to the capacity to do work.

Energy transfer When energy is released and causes other things nearby to vibrate. Once the energy is used to start a vibration, the vibration stays in motion until that energy given to start the "reaction" of vibration is dissipated.

Chain reaction A self-sustaining "reaction" of energy being transferred that does not dissipate.

****Conservation of energy** A law of physics which states that the input of energy is equal to the output of energy. Energy can neither be destroyed nor created. It can be changed from one form into another, but the total amount of energy in our universe is always constant. It never changes.

Kinetic energy The energy of motion.

Potential energy Stored energy, or energy of position.

Audible sound Sound vibrations that can be heard.

Inaudible sound Sound vibrations that cannot be heard because the frequency is too high or too low for our ears to be sensitive to. Dogs, dolphins, and bats can hear sounds at higher frequencies than are audible to human ears.

Ultrasonic waves Bats and dolphins can hear ultrasonic waves which are inaudible to human ears. These animals make use of echoes in conjunction with their hearing.

Frequency The rate or speed of a vibration. Frequency measures the distance and time between crests.

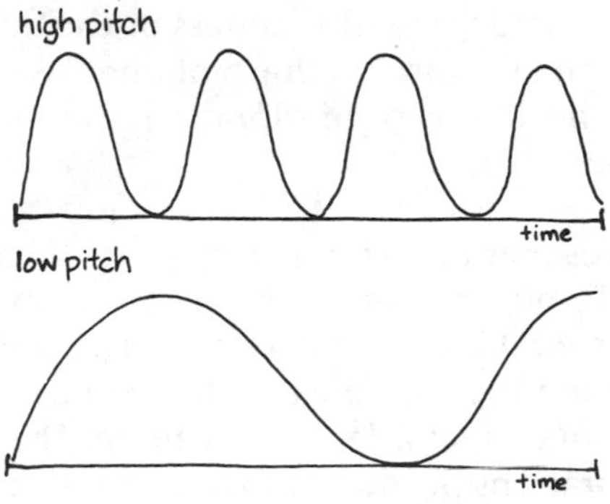

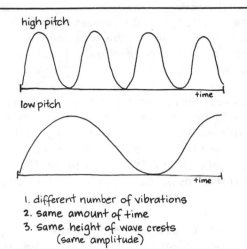

1. different number of vibrations
2. same amount of time
3. same height of wave crests (same amplitude)

Pitch The "highness" or "lowness" of a note on a musical scale. Pitch corresponds to frequency. On a musical scale, the low notes have a lower frequency. When vibration of low notes occurs, they sound lower, slower, and heavier, whereas the high notes on a musical scale have a higher frequency. When they vibrate, they sound faster, higher, and lighter.

Musical scale Composed of musical notes with increasing pitch at regular intervals.

Noise A combination of sound tones or notes or unrelated frequencies.

Decibel Refers to the amount of pressure received at the eardrum from sound vibrations.

Amplify To intensify or to make something louder.

Amplitude The intensity and loudness of a sound. It is measured in decibels. Amplitude measures the height of a wave's crest.

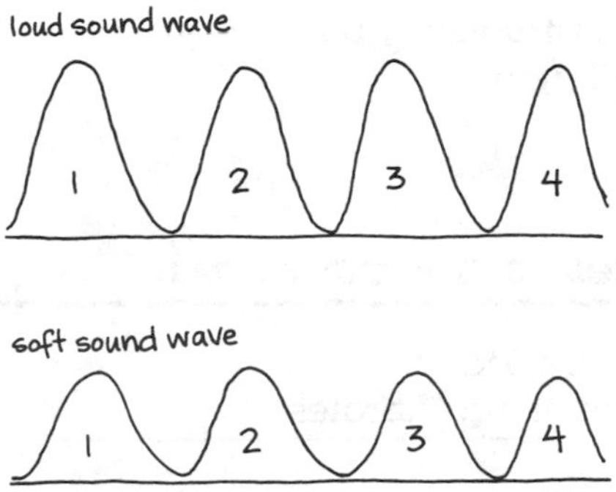

1. same number of vibrations
2. same length of time
3. different heights of wave crests (different amplitude)

Volume The degree of loudness or the intensity of a sound. When we turn up the "volume," we amplify or increase the intensity of vibrations. Volume can be loud or soft.

Musical resonance The quality which increases and lengthens musical tones resulting in an increased amplitude or loudness of sound. This resonance is caused when the sound waves from one object cause another object that is larger to vibrate. The additional sound vibrations produce a louder sound by putting a larger amount of air into motion.

The design of musical instruments that produce musical tones Musical tones are created by instruments. The tones can be modified through an understanding of the force or energy needed to make loud or soft sounds, and through an understanding of how to mechanically change or vary the frequency or speed of a vibration to control pitch. Pitch can be high or low.

Creating string instruments When creating string instruments with pitches, it is helpful when designing them to know that:

1. Loose strings vibrate at a low frequency and tight strings vibrate at a high frequency.

2. Long strings vibrate at a lower frequency than short strings.

3. Heavy strings vibrate at a lower frequency than light strings.

4. On a piano, the weight, rather than the thickness, affects lower pitches.

5. On a rubber band, the pitch goes up as the tension is increased.

****Quality or timbre** The characteristic of an individual musical instrument. The quality that makes a clarinet sound like a clarinet and a French horn sound like a French horn. The same pitch can be played on different instruments, but the quality of the sounds will be different.

Activities and Procedures

I. Sounds Are Made
When Something Vibrates

1. Noisy Paper

Materials A piece of notebook paper.

Procedure
• Ask the children if the paper can make a noise. (They will probably respond "no." Or they might suggest that it needs to be "rattled" in some way.)
• Hold the piece of paper with two hands and shake it. *Is there a noise?* (Yes.) *When does the paper make a noise?* (When it is moved.)

2. Vibrating Ruler

Materials An 18-inch wooden ruler.

Procedure
• Extend the wooden ruler over the edge of a table. Hold one end of the ruler with your hand and pluck the extended edge with your thumb. The ruler will make a sound.
• Ask the children, *"What happens to the ruler when it makes a sound?"* (It moves.)
• *Explain:* The ruler moves back and forth very fast. This kind of very fast movement back and forth is called a vibration.

3. Humming

Materials None.

Procedure
• Have the children place their fingers on their throats and say "mmmmmm" in a low tone.
• Ask them how their fingers feel. (Their fingers should feel "tickly.")
• Have the children find a partner. Each child should feel the other child's throat while they each say "mmmmm" or talk to each other. (*Note:* The children should be cautioned to hold their fingers straight and not to press hard on the other child's throat.)
• Ask the children if it is easier to feel the vibration on their own throat or on someone else's throat. (It is easier to feel on someone else.)

Fine points to discuss with children
Can our fingers "hear"?
(Some people who cannot hear very well, or who cannot see or hear, can "hear" what someone is saying by feeling the person's throat when the person is talking. Every sound has a different feel. Our fingers can be trained to "hear" what our ears cannot hear. Helen Keller was blind and deaf, but she was able to train her fingers to "hear.")

Note: You might want to encourage children to stay with their partner and to feel and "hear" different throat sounds with their fingers so that they can understand better how sensitive their fingers are to vibrations.

4. Wiggling

Materials None.

Procedure
• Have the children wiggle around, slap their knees and clap their hands. Then ask them to sit very still.
• Ask the children when they heard more noise, when they moved or when they stayed still. (When they move there is more noise.)

II. We Can See Things Vibrate

1. Vibrating Rubber Bands

Materials A rubber band.

Procedure
• Pluck a stretched rubber band.
• Ask children what they see and hear. (They can see a vibration and hear a sound.)
• Ask if the rubber band can make sound when it is not vibrating. (No, it cannot.)

2. Vibrating Rice

Materials An empty coffee can with a plastic lid; some uncooked rice grains; and a spoon.

Rice vibrates or bounces on a coffee can drum when the drum is struck.

Procedure
• Place a few grains of rice on top of the coffee can drum. Strike the top of the can with a spoon.
• Observe what happens to the rice grains. (They will bounce on top of the plastic lid.)
• Ask the children what causes the rice to bounce, and why we can see the rice bouncing. (We can see the rice bouncing because sometimes we can see the effects of a vibration.)

2. Noisy Bell

Materials A small metal bell with a clacker.

Procedure
• Hold the bell by the clacker and shake it.
• Ask the children why there is no sound from the bell. (The clacker is not hitting the bell and causing a vibration.)
• Allow the clacker to hit the bell. Ask the children what they see when they hear the bell ring. (They see the clacker strike against the metal on the bell. They hear the metal on the bell vibrate when it is struck.)

3. Tuning Fork Splash

Materials A tuning fork; a pie pan filled to the top with water; newspaper.

Procedure
• Hit the tuning fork against your palm. Place it near each child's ear so that they can hear that a sound is coming from it.
• When the fork is not making a sound, and is therefore not vibrating, place the tuning fork in the pan of water. Observe what happens to the water. (Nothing much.)
• Hit the tuning fork against the palm of your hand so that it will vibrate. While it is vibrating, submerge a tip of the fork into the water. Observe what happens. (A splash effect should occur.)

Hearing a tuning fork vibrate.

Creating a splash with a vibration.

Fine points to discuss with children

What causes the water to splash when the vibrating tuning fork hits the water?
(The vibrations.)

How do we know the tuning fork is vibrating when it makes a sound?
(We can see the vibration effect in the water. We can also see the blurry look of the prongs when they are vibrating.)

What has to happen to the tuning fork for it to make a sound?
(It has to be moving.)

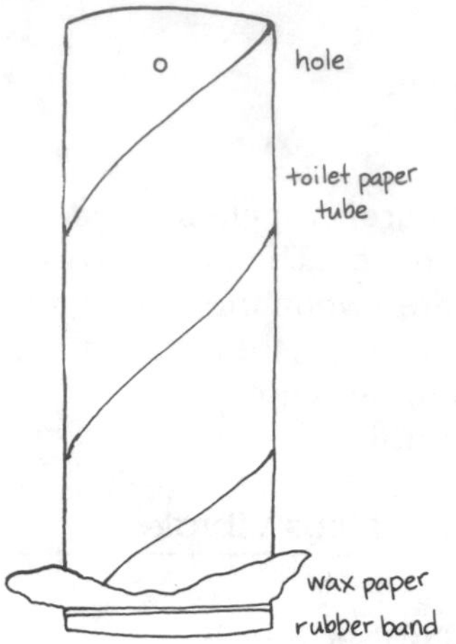

KAZOO

III. We Can Feel Things Vibrate

1. Humming Straws

Materials Drinking straws.

Procedure

- Pass out a straw to each child. Let the children blow through them. Ask them to hum a note through the straw and to feel the other end of the straw with their palm.
- Ask the children how their humming felt through the straw on their palm. (It should feel tickly.)
- Have the children place a finger over the end of the straw while they are humming. Observe what happens to the sound. (The sound becomes muffled. It is not free to move outside of the tube.)
- Have the children tap the end of the straw while humming and listen to the different rhythmic effects that can be created.

2. Kazoo

Materials Cardboard tube from paper towels or toilet paper; waxed paper; rubber band; sharpened pencil for poking a hole through tube.

Procedure

- Have each child make his/her own kazoo. To make a kazoo, place a small, square piece of waxed paper on the end of the cardboard tube and secure it tightly with a rubber band. Poke a hole through the tubing with a sharp pencil.
- Have the children hum through the kazoo and feel the end of the kazoo with their fingertips while humming. (Children will feel vibrations from their own sounds in the tube.)
- Ask the children what happens to the kazoo sound when they cover the end of the tube with their hand or when they cover the little hole in the tube. Have them experiment to find out. (When the air hole is left open, the sound is louder; when the hand covers the end, the sound is very muffled.)

3. Feeling a Radio Vibrate

Materials A radio.

Procedure

- Turn the radio on. Turn the volume up. Have the children feel the sound vibrations from the radio's speaker.
- Have the children feel the difference between loud and soft volume on the radio's speaker.

IV. Vibrations Can Cause Other Things Nearby to Vibrate

1. Megaphone Model

Materials Tuning fork; paper cup or Styrofoam cup.

Procedure

- Hit the tuning fork against your palm. While it is vibrating, allow the tip of one prong of the fork to lightly touch the bottom of a paper cup.
- Ask the children why the sound of the tuning fork can be heard when it touches the cup. (It can be heard because the vibrations from the tuning fork cause the paper to vibrate. This creates a louder sound. More air is made to vibrate [at a larger amplitude]. The sound is intensified or amplified.)
- Have the children experiment touching other parts of the cup. Ask if the sound is as loud when the vibrating tuning fork touches the sides or the rim of the cup as when it touched the bottom of the cup. (It is loudest when it touches the bottom of the cup. The sound coming from the cup at the bottom is amplified more because the cup is shaped somewhat like a

megaphone. The sounds are able to resonate on the cup, creating an amplification and a prolongation of the sound.)

2. Tuning Fork Amplification

Materials Blown-up balloon; tuning fork or comb.

Procedure
• Lightly place the side of one prong of a vibrating tuning fork on an inflated balloon. Observe what happens.
• Ask the children why the sound of the tuning fork became louder when it touched the balloon. (The vibrations from the tuning fork made the surface of the balloon vibrate. Vibrations cause other things nearby to vibrate.)
• Repeat the same procedure with a comb vibrating on a balloon. Ask the children to use their fingers to make the teeth of the comb vibrate on the balloon's surface.

3. Waxed Paper Vibrations

Materials Toilet paper or paper towel tube; a homemade kazoo made from toilet paper or paper towel tube.

Procedure
• Hum through the cardboard tube. Then hum through the homemade kazoo.
• Ask the children why the humming sounds different in the kazoo. (It sounds different in the kazoo because the humming at the top of the tube causes the waxed paper at the end of the tube to vibrate. The added vibrations cause a different sound to occur.)

4. Paper Clip Vibrations

Materials Empty coffee can with plastic lid; long, thin rubber band or string; a paper clip.

Procedure
• Thread the paper clip with a long, thin rubber band or string.
• Allow the threaded paper clip to dangle in front of the empty coffee can with a plastic lid lying on its side. The paper clip should be touching the surface of the plastic lid at about the center of the lid.
• Have a child gently tap the metal end of the coffee can lying on its side. Have children observe what happens to the paper clip when the can is tapped gently and when the can is tapped harder.
• Ask the children why the paper clip is jumping, and why the paper clip jumps more when the can is tapped harder. (The paper clip jumps or moves because the

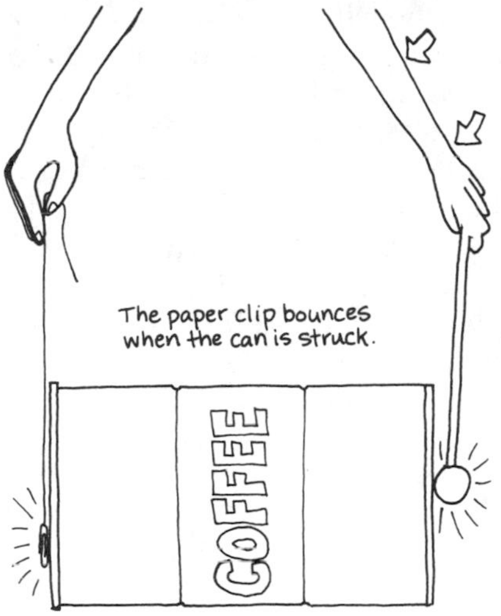
The paper clip bounces
when the can is struck.
COFFEE

vibrations caused by the tapping cause other things to vibrate. The vibrations bounce around on the inside of the can and continue to vibrate, causing the paper clip to bounce or vibrate.)

V. Vibrations Can Be Absorbed and Stopped or Left Free to Bounce

1. Holding Sound

Materials Toy xylophone; a mallet.

Procedure
• Have a child strike the metal plates with the mallet. It should make a short, light sound.
• Have a child strike the plates again but this time have the child hold the mallet on the plate after striking it to create a pounding sound, rather than a light, bouncing sound.
• Ask the children which kind of sound is prettier or more pleasant to listen to—the bouncing mallet sound or the pounding-and-holding mallet sound.
• Explain to the children that sound vibrations can be left free to vibrate or can be held and stopped. When the mallet stays on the metal plate after it strikes, it is holding and absorbing the vibrations, and the sound vibrations are not free to bounce.

2. Muffling Sound

Materials A jingle bell.

Procedure
• Shake the jingle bell in your cupped hand.
• Close your hand around the jingle bell and shake your hand while holding the jingle bell in your closed fist.

• Ask the children which way the bell sounded louder and prettier to hear. (It sounds prettier to hear and louder when your hand is left open because the sound vibrations are left free to travel and bounce. When the sound is muffled inside your closed fist, it is harder to hear and does not sound as light and as long. When sounds are able to echo or bounce around after they are started and then fade away or blend with a new vibration, they are called resonant sounds.)

3. Knocking

Materials Something soft like a pillow or a sweater.

Procedure

• Have the children knock on the floor or a desk with their fists.

• Then have children knock on the same surface, but this time have them place "something soft" between their fist and the surface.

• Ask the children if both knocks sounded the same and if not, why not. What does the "something" that is soft do to the sound? (The "something" that is soft absorbs or isolates the sound vibrations. The hard surface allows sounds to bounce and echo.)

Fine points to discuss with children

Is it quieter to walk across a floor that has a rug than on one that does not have a rug?

(It is quieter to walk across the floor that has a rug because the rug absorbs or isolates some of the sound.)

What are some other things in the room that help absorb sounds?

(Draperies, ceiling tiles, soft furniture, almost anything that is soft or has a lot of holes like the ceiling tile.)

What are some of the things in the room that bounce sound off?

(Most of the hard surfaces, like the walls, the uncovered floor, the desks or hard chairs.)

VI. Resonance and Echoes Cause Amplification of Sound Vibrations

1. Amplifying a Music Box

Materials A music box outside of its casing with absolutely no amplification or resonance. (A commercial product that fills the bill for this activity is the *Hurdy Gurdy,* found in many gift shops, especially airports, as a novelty item. It is distributed by Alfred E. Knobler and Co., Moonachie, N.J.)

Procedure

• Hold the music box up in the air and turn the crank. It will be difficult to hear the music. The sound vibrations will be absorbed in the air and will scatter.

• Place the music box on a hard surface like a desk, the wall, or a window. Turn the crank and the children will hear a drastic difference in volume coming from the music box.

• Ask the children why we can hear the music box better when the music box is placed on the desk, door, wall, or window, but not so easily when it is held in the air. (The hard surface allows the sound vibrations to resonate and amplify themselves. The hard surface allows the music to sound more resonant or full.)

Note: The volume and the quality of the sound are directly related to the size of the surface and the kind of material from which the surface is made. Have the children experiment with the music box by placing it on different kinds of surfaces like windows, a clock face, the sink, a wooden door, cinderblock walls, metal pots, plumbing pipes, an unopened tissue box, an empty tissue box.

VII. Sound Vibrations Travel in Waves

1. Making Waves with Water

Materials Metal broiling pan half-filled with water; a hammer; newspaper (to absorb possible spills).

Procedure

• Have a child gently tap the top edge of the broiling pan with a hammer. Have the children discuss their observations. (The water will vibrate from the sound vibrations. Little waves will be visible on the surface of the water. They will look like ripples.)

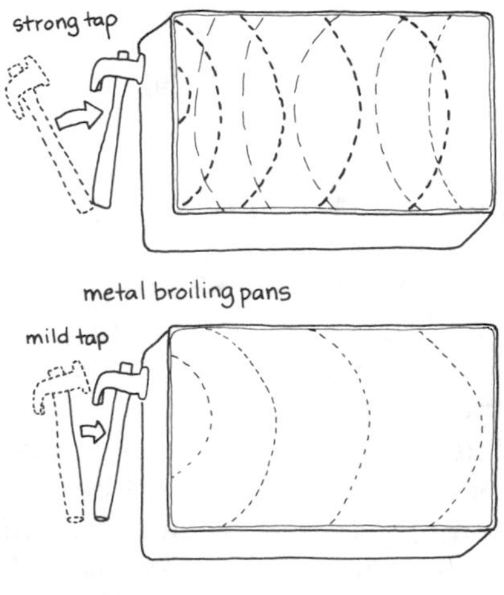

TOP VIEW OF
HAMMER STRIKING A PAN OF WATER

• Ask the children if the hammer actually hit the water, and if not, why the water appears to be moving. (The water itself was not hit. The water is moving because the vibrations from the pan, and the sound waves were started by the tapping on the pan.)
• Ask the children what will happen to the ripples on the water if the pan is hit very hard and fast with the hammer. Will the waves get bigger? The children will probably respond that the waves will get bigger and will splash. Have a child hit the pan hard several times quickly. Have the children observe what happens.

2. Making Waves with Rope

Materials A piece of rope about 12 feet long or less tied to an object about 3 feet off the ground.

Procedure
• Hold the rope in your hand and dangle it. Have the children observe what happens to the rope. (Children will see a wave effect.)
• Ask the children whether the wave will look different if the rope is moving fast or slow. Experiment and discuss what happens. (When the rope moves faster it begins to look blurry. The rope will begin to make a whirring or "windy" sound.)
• Ask the children which wave has more energy, the low, slow wave or the fast, high wave. (The fast and high wave has more energy.) The children can feel how tired their arms will become making a fast, high wave, and how much less energy they will need to make a low, slow wave with the rope.

Fine points to discuss with children
Do these rope waves look like other waves you have seen before? Where do you usually see waves?
(At the beach.)

What kinds of waves at the beach can knock you over?
(Large waves with crests.) Explain to children that a crest is the highest part of the wave.

Do all waves at the beach carry enough energy or force to knock you over?
(No. Waves vary in their intensity of strength and force. Waves that are small and have a low crest are not very powerful.)

Do all waves carry energy?
(Yes.)

Can large sound waves knock you over?
(No, but if they are too loud for a long period of time they can damage your eardrums. If our eardrums are damaged, we can lose some of the sensitivity that allows us to hear well. Our ears are very delicate and sensitive sense organs.)

3. Air Molecules Carry Odors and Sound

Materials Perfume and atomizer to spray perfume.

Procedure
• Ask the children if they have ever been able to notice that supper was ready when they were not in the kitchen.
• Did their nose help them know?
• *Explain:* Molecules are very small things in the air. They are invisible. We cannot see them, but sometimes we can smell them. When we smell someone's cooking in another room, we are smelling molecules of the cooking odors in the air. The odors travel to our noses through molecules in the air. We cannot see molecules, but we can sometimes smell them. Molecules of air also carry vibrating sound waves.
• Spray the perfume in the air from a far corner in the room. Ask the children to raise their hands when they smell the molecules of perfume in the air.

Smell the aroma of perfume molecules in the air.

4. Seeing Wave Energy Transfer

Materials A "Slinky"* (a commercial toy that looks like a giant spring made of plastic or metal).

Procedure
• Have a child hold one end of the Slinky. Stretch the Slinky out. Hold a clump of the spring and let go of one coil. Have the children observe the bounce and the vibration that takes place up the spring and back to you. The vibration or wave will continue until it

*Manufactured by James Industries, Inc.

runs out of or transfers the energy that was set into motion when the coil was let loose.

• Continue to let coils loose while a child holds one end of the stretched-out Slinky. Compare the difference in the kind of vibration or energy release that takes place when one or several coils are let loose at the same time.

• Explain that when we let go of a coil on the Slinky, we are observing a chain reaction of energy being transferred. The Slinky is an observable model to look at to better understand how a sound vibration behaves. A sound vibration is really an invisible wave that carries energy. The sound from a sound vibration continues until all of its energy has been absorbed and then it stops.

5. Molecule Model of Energy Transfer in an Oscillating or Vibrating Wave

Materials Two 12- or 18-inch plastic rulers with a groove down the center; about 10 or 12 glass marbles all the same size; one marble much larger than the others; two wooden blocks; masking tape.

Procedure

• Tape the two plastic rulers together with masking tape so they will stay together. Emphasize the groove with the tape so that the integrity of the groove will still be apparent. Rest each end of the taped rulers on a wooden block to create a double ramp. See diagram.

• Line all of the marbles up on the ruler except for the largest one. Have a child take one marble and lift it up the "ruler ramp" to the top end of the ruler, then let go of the marble. Have the children observe what happens and discuss it with them. (If you let go of one marble, only one marble will bounce off on the chain of marbles. The energy from the moving marble will transfer to the other marbles that are in line and the last marble will receive the energy. The last marble will then give its energy back to the chain of marbles and the first marble will bounce off. This energy transfer will continue as it did in the Slinky until all of the energy from the original marble has been absorbed.)

• Ask the children what they think will happen if two marbles are lifted up on the ramp and then the marbles are let loose. Then have a child lift two marbles and let them go. (This time two marbles will bounce off the end of the chain of marbles.)

• Continue to observe what happens with two, three, four, five, and six marbles being lifted up the ramp and then being let go. Have the children make a prediction and then test it out. Discuss the results after each trial.

• Set up all the marbles in a row on the groove of the ruler. Show the children the large marble. Ask them what will happen if you send the large marble down the ramp. Let them make predictions. Then have the children test it out and see what happens. (The large marble will make only one marble bounce off the end. The one large marble will carry more energy in it than the one smaller marble did, so the bounce at the end of the chain of marbles will be more dramatic.)

• Explain to the children that each of the marbles is a giant model of a molecule. The marbles show what happens to a molecule of air that is carrying energy from a sound vibration. The model shows what happens when energy is transferred or moved from the first object to the next object in a line until it reaches the end of the line of objects. *Note:* This same effect can be demonstrated with dominoes standing in a line or with a deck of playing cards standing on their edges.

Fine points to discuss with children

How is energy transferred in a sound vibration?
(One molecule of air makes another molecule of air move.)

How do vibrations of molecules affect sound?
(When more molecules of air vibrate, the sound is louder.)

MARBLES ON A RULER

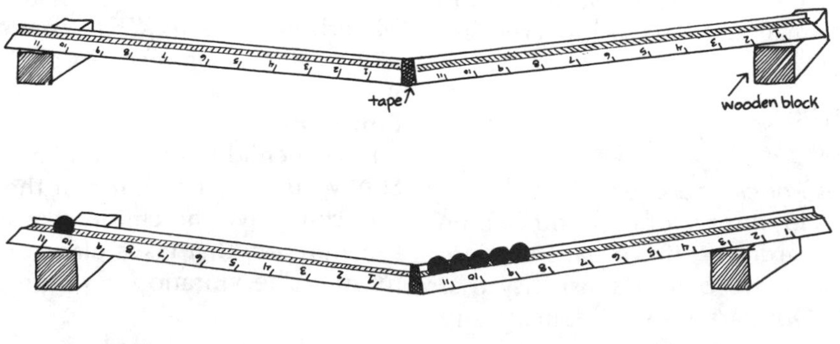

Two grooved rulers taped together with masking tape, resting on two wooden blocks.

Where does energy come from in a sound wave?
(Energy comes from movement or action. When there is no action, there is no sound.)

What is energy?
(Energy is power or strength that can create an action. Energy is needed to create sound. Energy comes in many forms: heat from the sun, food we eat, gasoline for the car. It can be stored for future use or put into use. Energy usually involves movement or action.)

VIII. Sounds Are Able to Travel Through Things

1. Floor Sounds

Materials None.

Procedure
- Have the children place one ear directly on the floor and listen to footsteps. Do this on the playground, in the classroom, or in the house.
- Ask the children whether the sounds seem louder on the ground or in the air. (On the ground.)

2. Sounds Through Wood

Materials A board or wooden mop handle.

Procedure
- Demonstrate to children how to listen through a board. Place one end of the board on the ground outside and the other end of the board at your ear. (The sound travels from the ground through the wood.)
- Have children listen to sound through wood.

3. Sounds Through Tubes

Materials A wind-up toy or ticking alarm clock or a timer; a cardboard tube.

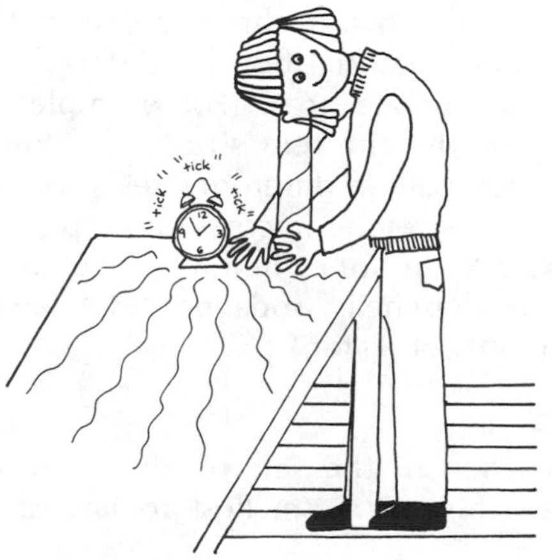

Procedure
- Have the children listen to the ticking object on a table and then put the cardboard tube next to the ticking sound.
- Ask the children if the ticking sounds louder through the tube, and if so, why. (The vibrations sound louder through the tube because they are confined to the tube.)

4. Stethoscope

Materials A toy stethoscope (commercial product).

Procedure
- Have the children listen to a sound with a stethoscope in their ear and without it in their ear. Rub on the end of the stethoscope lightly with your finger. It will not sound very loud, but it will be very loud when the stethoscope is in the child's ears.
- Discuss with children where the sound in the stethoscope goes, and why it sounds so much louder when the stethoscope picks up a sound. (The sound is confined to the tube. The sound goes directly to the listener's ear.)

5. Whispering Hose

Materials Two funnels and a length of old hose or clear plastic tubing about 6 to 8 feet long; some masking tape to secure funnels to the ends of the hose. See diagram.

Procedure Make a Whispering Hose Phone. Demonstrate the hose to the children. Explain that it is only used for whispering because the sounds will be too loud for their ears if they talk in the funnels instead of whispering in them. Have two children use the phone.

One child listens while the other child whispers. Discuss how the sound travels with the children.

6. Tin Can "Telephone"

Materials Two tin cans; awl to punch holes in bottom center of cans; two plastic buttons; length of string about 12 feet long.

Procedure

• Make a tin-can telephone. Place the button inside the can. Tie the button to the string. The button helps amplify the sound inside of the can.

• Let the children talk through the cans. Discuss how the sound travels through the string.

7. "Chime" from Metal

Materials A metal grill from the inside of a broiler pan or a metal spoon; a piece of string about 3 feet long.

Listen to the chime-like sound when the metal is struck.

Procedure

• Place the spoon or the grill in the middle of the piece of string and tie the string around the metal so that each end of the string can reach the child's ears.

• Have a child strike the metal with an object. (The sound will travel up the string to the child's ears.) Discuss with children how the metal sounds when it is tapped and how the sound traveled to their ears. (The metal should sound like a pretty chime or bell.)

8. String Sound

Materials A piece of string about one foot long.

Procedure

• Hold onto the string with both hands. Ask the children if the string can make a sound. Snap the string by pulling your hands apart quickly. Have the children observe what happens to the string. Ask the children why the string made a sound. (The string moved or vibrated and we could hear the movement which produced a sound.)

• Have children experiment shaping a string.

9. Sound Through Pipes

Materials A piece of metal pipe.

Procedure Demonstrate to children how sound travels through a pipe. Bang on the pipe with a pebble. Place the pipe near a child's ear and bang on the pipe softly. Discuss how the sound travels and why it sounds so much louder when your ear is on the pipe.

IX. Different Sounds Can Be Made with the Same Objects if They Are Different Sizes

1. Sound Vibrations

Materials Sets of two or three objects that are made from the same material but are different in length, thickness, or surface area. (For example: matching metal pot lids in different sizes, clay flowerpots in different sizes, nails in different sizes, rubber bands in different sizes stretched across an empty and lidless cigar box, a xylophone, hollow pieces of bamboo, different-sized pencils, soda bottles filled with different amounts of water.)

Procedure

• Arrange each of the sets of objects in order according to their size, smallest to largest. The size differences should be extreme and very obvious. *Note:* No need for subtle size differences here; contrasts are important. Each set of objects should contain two or three items so that the pitch differences of each set will be distinct.

• Tap, strike, or pluck an object in a set. Then do the same to the other objects in that set. Have children observe the different sounds that are made from each of the objects in the set. Ask the children which object makes a sound that is very deep, heavy, and low. Which object makes a much lighter, higher, and "thinner" sound?

• Proceed to have children experiment with each set of objects. Observe the kinds of sounds that the biggest and the smallest items in each set make. (The larger, longer, or thicker objects will make slower lower sounds when they vibrate, whereas the smaller, shorter, or thinner objects will make faster and higher sounds.)

2. Piano Strings

Materials A piano.

Procedure

• Have children look inside the piano and at the keyboard. Push some low piano keys and some high piano keys. Have the children observe the inside strings and hammers moving while the piano keys are being pushed in. Discuss the appearance of the strings. Ask the children how the strings on the inside of the piano look different from one another, and how they can tell by just looking at some of the strings whether they will make a higher sound or a lower sound.

• Explain and demonstrate to the children that the long, large, thick, and heavy strings make a slower, lower, and heavier sound, while the short, thin strings make a faster, lighter, and higher sound.

3. Rubber-band Guitar

Materials An empty and lidless cigar box; assorted rubber bands in different thicknesses and lengths arranged in sequence from thinnest to thickest; a wooden dowel; ruler or a long slender piece of Styrofoam to be used as a bridge underneath the rubber bands.

Procedure

• Show children the cigar box with rubber bands. Tell them it is called a sound box. Have a child pluck the rubber bands. Listen to the sounds. If they are played in sequence, they will create sounds like those on a musical scale. The sounds will sound like they are moving up or down.

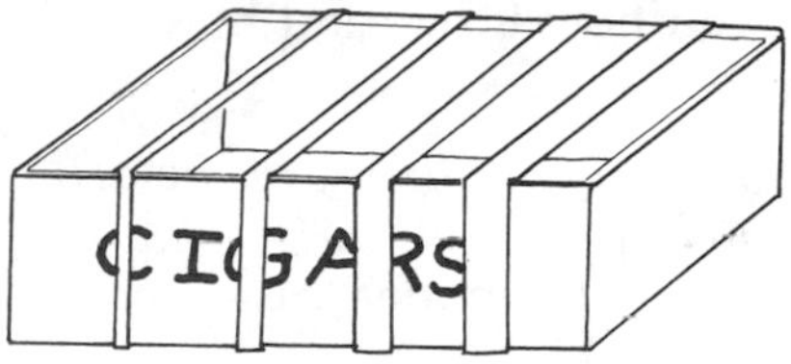

A cigar-box guitar

SOUND BOX

• Place the bridge made of wood or Styrofoam underneath the rubber bands. Have a child pluck the bands again. Ask the children if the sound is the same. (It will sound different because the bridge makes the rubber band shorter by absorbing some of the vibrations and making the length of the rubber band that is able to vibrate shorter.)

• Move the "bridge" off center or to a diagonal position so that one side of the rubber band is short and the other side is long. Have a child pluck the rubber bands and hear the different sound pitches the rubber bands make. Discuss why this happens with the children. (The longer length of rubber band makes a low, long, heavy sound and vibrates at a slower rate or frequency. The shorter length of rubber band makes a high and short sound and vibrates at a faster rate or frequency.)

4. Quality of Sound

Materials Toy cymbals; coffee-can drum or toy drum; a drumstick.

Procedure

• Hit one of the cymbals at the edge with a drumstick, then in the center of the cymbal. Ask the children if the sounds are the same. (They are not. The sound from the center has a thinner, less resonant sound. The circle is small. At the edge there is a more resonant tone quality. The circle or area that is vibrating is larger.)

• Have a child use a drumstick to hit one of the cymbals with a fair amount of force. Then hit the same cymbal very softly. Ask the children if they notice a difference in the sound. (The strong hit creates a louder volume of sound.)

• Repeat the same procedure with the drum. Have the children test the sound quality at different spots on the drum and the effect the force of the hit has on the volume or relative loudness of the sound.

Fine points to discuss with children

Does a drumstick hit with a lot of force or a little bit of force?

(It depends on how it hits and how much force it is given.)

How does the force in the hit of the drumstick affect the sound quality?
(The more force, the louder the sound.)

Does it matter where a drumstick hits a surface?
(Yes; if the hit is in the center of a drum, it will sound more resonant. On a flat piece of metal such as the cymbal, however, it will vibrate more if it is hit on the edge because the entire surface is free to vibrate. It will sound like a gong. When a drum is hit near the edge, the framing material of the drum prevents the drumhead from vibrating.)

Do materials made from the same stuff sound the same when they vibrate?
(The size of the material and the force of the hit affect the sound.)

X. Up and Down the Scale

1. Monochord

Materials A monochord—a thin 1-inch by 2-inch board that is 36 inches long with an eye-screw at each end securing a nylon fishing line tightly; a small plastic tub or box to use as a resonator; and a bridge which can be slid freely up and down the spine of the monochord underneath the "string" of fishing line. See diagram.

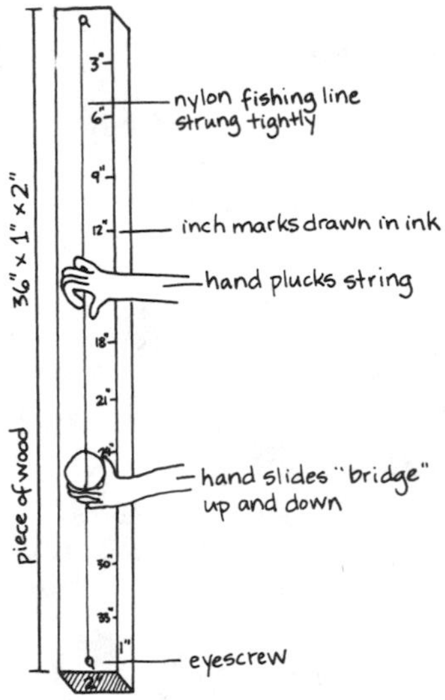

Procedure
- Have a child pluck the "string" of the monochord and listen.
- Ask the children if they can think of a way to make the pitch or tone that the string makes sound different. (They will probably suggest that you move the box up or down the spine of the monochord.)
- Move the resonator bridge box to the very top of the spine on the monochord. Have a child pluck the string on each side of the bridge box. Ask the children if it sounds different than it did before. (The sound will be very high on the top side with the short string and very low on the bottom side with the long string.)
- Have the children move the "box" up and down the spine and listen to all of the different sounds or pitches of sound that can be created on one string.

Fine points to discuss with children
As the box moves up and the string becomes shorter, what happens to the sound?
(It becomes a higher pitch.)

As the box moves down and the string becomes longer, what happens to the sound?
(It becomes a lower pitch. It sounds like you are going down a flight of stairs.)

What is a sequence of musical tones called?
(A musical scale.) Demonstrate what a scale sounds like on a piano or other musical instrument.

2. Bottle Sounds

Materials A small empty soda bottle or thin jar; newspaper; water inside a pitcher; a funnel; a wooden spoon.

Procedure
- Pour a small amount of water into the soda bottle. Have a child tap it with the wooden spoon and listen to the sound. Pour some more water into the bottle. Have another child tap it and listen again. Continue to do this several more times until the bottle is almost full.
- Ask the children why the sound is able to change. (A different amount of water and air are vibrating each time the amount of water changes.)

Fine points to discuss with children
How is the bottle being filled with water like the monochord?
(The pitch or tone can be changed. A scale can be created by changing the amount of water and the amount of air above the water. Different vibrations create different sounds and can be arranged in an order or sequence.)

How could the bottle be made into a musical instrument?

(By using several bottles filled with different amounts of water.)

Note: Bottle organ—You might want the children to create a soda-bottle organ consisting of 6 to 8 bottles filled with different heights of water. The "organ" can be "tuned" by filling the bottles while playing piano keys or xylophone keys to find sequential pitches. If the organ is tuned properly, a musical scale and possibly some simple tunes like "Mary Had A Little Lamb" and "Jingle Bells" can be played. Place a piece of masking tape with a number on it on each bottle to indicate where the water level should remain if it accidentally spills or evaporates. The numbered bottles can be played as "notes" if a melody is written for them.

3. Wind Instrument

Materials A fluteophone (wind instrument) or recorder.

Procedure

• Show the children the wind instrument. Cover all the holes with your fingers and blow through the fluteophone or recorder. While you are blowing, cover one hole at a time from the bottom of the instrument. Listen to the sound. It will sound as though you are going up a flight of steps. **When the vibrating air column grows shorter as the holes are uncovered, the pitch of the note goes up.

• While blowing, cover the holes one at a time from the top. It will sound as though you are going down a flight of stairs. **The column of air that is vibrating as you blow is getting longer; therefore the pitch becomes lower.

4. Paper Straw Whistle

Materials Several paper straws; a pair of scissors.

Procedure

• Flatten out one end of a paper straw. Cut off two small triangles from the flattened end. See diagram.

• Blow through the "forked end" that has been cut. It will sound like a whistle.

• Cut off small snips from the end of the paper straw while blowing through it. The note or tone will become higher and higher.

• Ask the children if they can think of another way to make the note get higher in pitch without cutting the end off. (They might suggest adding some holes to the straw so that it looks like a flute.)

• Have children experiment making different sounds with different lengths of forked paper straws.

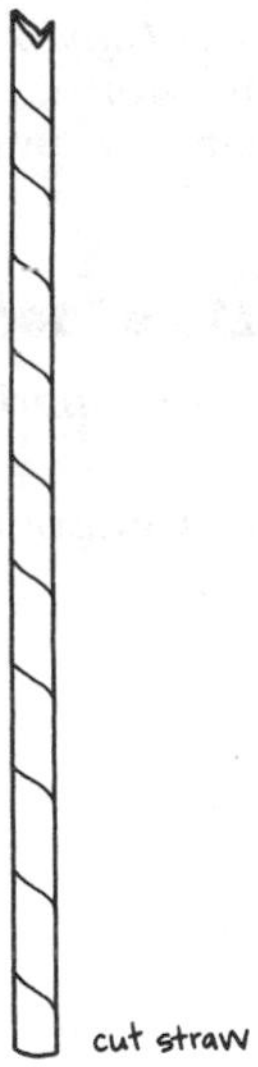

5. Paper Straw Flute

Materials Same as above.

Procedure

• Make another "paper straw whistle" as described above in Procedure 4.

• Cut or punch holes in the straw with the scissors.

• Blow through it and find out if the one straw can produce many pitches if the holes are covered and uncovered one at a time. (It can be done, but it requires patience.)

• Have children make their own paper straw flutes.

• *Note:* Paper straws stop vibrating if they get too wet. If they do get too wet, cut off the wet end and recut it to shape the end.

Further Resources

Suggested Books for Children

Dewey Decimal Classification Number for sound is: 534.

Alexenberg, Melvin, *Sound Science.* Englewood Cliffs, New Jersey: Prentice-Hall, 1968. (Illustrates many concepts and experiments young children can do by themselves.)

Branley, Franklyn, *High Sounds, Low Sounds.* New York: Thomas Y. Crowell, 1967.

Branley, Franklyn, *Timmy and the Tin Can Telephone.* New York: Thomas Y. Crowell, 1959.

Holl, Adelaide, *Listening for Sounds.* Indianapolis: Bobbs-Merrill, 1970.

Pine, Tillie, and Joseph Levine, *Sounds All Around.* New York: McGraw-Hill, 1959.

Podendorf, Illa, *Sounds All About.* Chicago: Children's Press, 1970.

Sanday, Allan P., *Sounds, A Ladybird Book.* Loughborough, England: Wills and Hepworth, 1975. (Illustrates many concepts and experiments young children can do by themselves.)

Resource Books for More Ideas

Baer, Miriam E., *Sound, an Experiment Book.* New York: Holiday, 1952.

Freeman, Ira, *Sound and Ultrasonics.* New York: Random House, 1968.

Ganat, Charles, *Sound and Hearing.* New York: Abelard, 1965.

Hawkinson, John, and M. Faulhaber, *Music and Instruments for Children to Make.* Chicago: Whitman, 1969.

Keen, Martin, *The How and Why Wonder Book of Sound.* New York: Grosset and Dunlap, 1962.

Kettlekamp, Larry, *Magic of Sound.* New York: Morrow, 1982.

Scott, John M., *What Is Sound?* New York: Parents Magazine, 1973.

7
LIGHT

Objectives

- For children to become aware that beams of light come from the sun and other sources.
- For children to develop an awareness that light is a form of energy.
- For children to develop an awareness that some materials allow light to pass through them, and some materials do not.
- For children to understand that shadows are formed when light beams are blocked.
- For children to become aware that light can be reflected.
- For children to develop an understanding that mirror reflections can create multiple images.
- For children to develop an awareness that lenses have a curved surface and that curved surfaces can bend light beams to make objects look bigger, smaller, or upside-down.
- For children to develop an awareness that we need light to see.
- For children to develop an awareness that light is made up of many colors.
- For children to understand that when colors are mixed or blended together, new colors are created.

General Background Information for Parents and Teachers

Light Any source of illumination is called light. Light can be found in nature or made by humans. We need light to see. If there is no light there is no sight.

Natural light Sources that are natural, like the sun, lightning, and fire, are natural sources of light. They are very hot and give off their own light.

Artificial light Man-made lights are artificial sources of light. They do not appear in nature. Man has created the light source from resources. Electric lights are man-made. Electric light bulbs have filaments which give off enough heat to create light.

****Incandescent light** Lights which produce enough heat to give off light.

****Fluorescent light** Light produced or created from a source that is cool. Electric sparks flow through a fluorescent tube which contains special gases. Lit fluorescent tubes do not feel as hot to the touch as lit light bulbs with filaments.

**All items marked by double asterisks indicate that the information is too abstract and too complicated for young children to understand or comprehend. It is included to enhance parent or teacher background only.

****Energy** Light gives off heat or thermal energy, which can be transformed into energy of motion, and/or stored as potential energy.

Transparent Light can pass through materials that are transparent. A clear window pane and a piece of cellophane or clear plastic are examples of transparent material.

Opaque Light cannot pass through an opaque material. Opaque materials are usually solid. Opaque materials can absorb and reflect light. Some examples of opaque materials are tinfoil, cardboard, furniture, and books.

Translucent Some light can pass through materials that are translucent. The light is scattered and images cannot be seen clearly. Examples of translucent materials are waxed paper, frosted glass, tissue paper, a silk scarf, shedded snakeskin.

****Diffused light** Light that is scattered. Translucent materials give off diffused light.

Reflect Light that bounces off of one surface onto another is reflected. Materials that reflect stay cooler than materials that absorb light.

Absorb Light that does not bounce from one surface to another is absorbed. Materials that absorb light become warmer than materials that reflect (for example, a blacktop surface becomes very hot on a sunny day).

Shadows A shadow occurs when a light source is blocked. Opaque materials create shadows. So do translucent materials. Opaque materials make solid shadows because part of a beam of light is entirely blocked. Translucent materials make lighter, less solid-looking shadows because only some light is blocked.

Night Earth's own shadow creates night. The sun can only shine on one-half of the earth's surface at a time. The other half is in the dark.

Light beams Beams of light can cause a direct or indirect lighting effect.

Direct light Direct lighting occurs when a beam of light shines directly from a light beam to a surface.

Indirect light Indirect lighting occurs when a direct beam of light reflects or bounces off another surface. For example, a direct light becomes an indirect light if it bounces off a wall or ceiling and throws indirect light into a room.

Reflection A mirror image is called a reflection.

Image An image is an illusion. It looks like the original, but it is a duplicate or copy of the original.

****Law of reflection** A law that helps explain reflections. The law states that the angle of incidence is equal to the angle of reflection. This means that when light enters or hits a surface it will bounce or reflect off that surface, continuing forward in a straight line at the same angle as when it hit the surface (before it was reflected). See diagram.

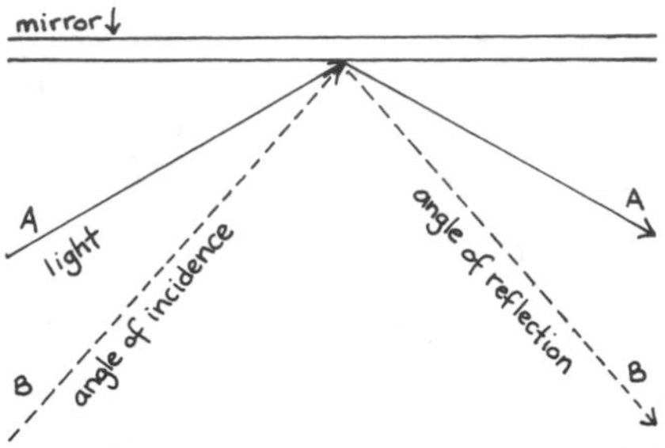

REFLECTION

Angle An angle is formed when two lines meet at a point.

Kaleidoscope A device that allows us to see multiple mirror images, by using more than one mirror to cause reflections of reflections.

Periscope A device that uses two mirrors to reflect images. A periscope helps us see things around corners or above our heads. A periscope helps us see an image of a reflected image.

Refraction The bending of a light beam is called refraction. Refraction occurs when light enters one medium like oil, glass, air, or water on a diagonal. Each time the light enters or leaves one clear substance and travels through diagonally to another substance the parts of the slanted light beam travel or penetrate the next clear substance at a slightly different angle. This difference in angles creates an illusion that an object like a straw or a spoon is broken or bent. See diagram. Light slows down as it enters the surface of a medium that is thick or dense. It increases its speed when it leaves the (thick or dense) medium. This difference of speed at surfaces causes the light beam to bend. Refraction sometimes makes objects in liquids appear closer and bigger than their real-life size.

Mirage Mirages are caused by refraction of light in the air. When the layer of air next to the ground is at an extremely high temperature (this often occurs in a desert) and the layer of air directly above that layer of air is at a different temperature, a mirage will occur.

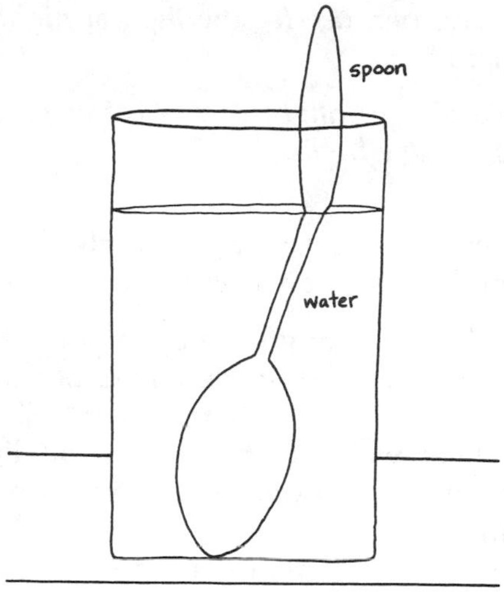

REFRACTION

Lens A transparent curved surface that causes light to bend. A lens can enlarge an object, make an object look smaller, or make an object look upside-down.

Microscope Two lenses that work together to make objects look much larger. Microscopes magnify.

Telescope Two lenses working together that make things that are far away look closer.

Concave The shape of a lens when it caves in in the center and looks like a valley or the inside of a bowl. The lens causes things to diverge or separate and spread out from a focal point.

Convex The shape of a lens when it curves out in the center and looks like a hill. The lens causes things to converge or come together at a focal point.

Lenses Can be:

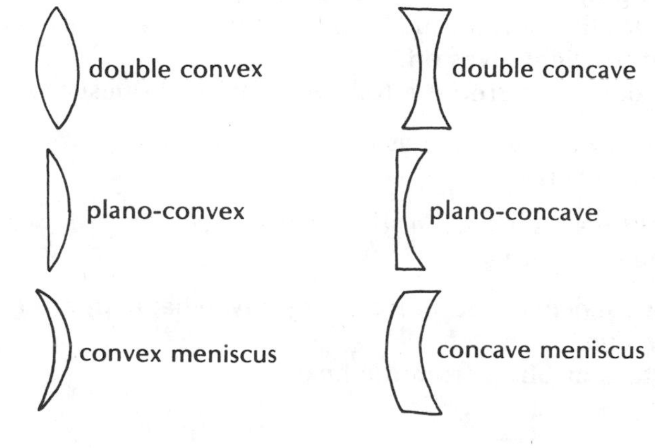

Color The amount of light reflected off an object gives the object its color. Every color has its own wavelength. The higher the light wave in amplitude, the more energy it has and the brighter the color is.

****Chromatography** The separation of complex mixtures (liquid, powders, or other small particles) by the passage through a selectively absorbing filter, resulting in distinct layers or colors.

Prism A diagonal piece of crystal-clear material like glass, plastic, or water in a glass that is able to bend (refract) a light wave two times causes a separation of the light beam to occur. The separation of the light beam causes a rainbow effect.

Rainbow The rainbow is a spectrum of all of the colors of visible light. The violet colors bend the most and appear on the inside of a rainbow's arc. The reds bend the least and appear on the outside edge of the rainbow's arc.

Primary colors Red, yellow, and blue are the primary colors. When they are mixed together they create the secondary colors of orange, green, and purple.

Tint Colors that have white added to them to lighten them are called tints. Red can become a very light pink if enough white is added to it. Colors that have black added to them to darken them are called shades. Red can become very dark and almost black if enough black is added.

Color wheel All of the colors arranged in a circle according to their sequence on a rainbow's spectrum.

Complementary Colors that are opposite each other on the color wheel are called complementary colors. When two complementary colors are blended together they form a very dark-brownish neutral color. Examples of complementary colors are: red and green; orange and blue; yellow and purple.

A Comparison of Light and Sound

To develop a better understanding of light, it is helpful to compare light to sound:

Sound waves Both sound and light travel in waves. However, light travels much faster than sound. Sound travels like a snail, in comparison to light, which travels like a bullet.

Travel Sound needs to travel through something to be heard. Something needs to vibrate. Whereas, light does not need to travel through anything to be seen.

Eyes and ears When our eyes are closed we cannot see, but our ears never close. If our ears are healthy and normal, they cannot be turned off.

Frequency The frequency of light waves affects the hue of color, whereas the frequency of sound waves affects the pitch of sounds.

Hues All of the colors seen in the rainbow. Each color has its own frequency.

Pitch Pitch refers to musical notes. Every musical note has its own frequency.

Mixtures Waves of light can be mixed together to form new hues of color. Two or more different hues of color mixed together will blend to form a new color.

Timbre If one instrument, several instruments, or a complete orchestra plays a tune, the timbre or quality of the sound may change, but the tune will still be the same. If several colors are mixed together, they will blend together, becoming a totally new color. The number of colors added will change the quality of the original color (hue) beyond recognition.

Amplitude The height (amplitude) of a light wave affects the brightness of color. Whereas, the height (amplitude) of a sound wave affects the loudness of sound.

Activities and Procedures

I. Sources of Light

1. Seeing in a Dark Closet

Materials A well-lighted room and a closet.

Procedure Promote a discussion about light by asking the children the following questions:

What gives us light in this room?
(The sun and/or an electric light.)

What gives us light during the day?
(The sun.)

What gives us light during the night?
(The moon, stars, candles, electric lights, fire, fireworks, sparks.)

If there were no electricity, how would we have light at night?
(Only natural sources like fire, candles, moonlight, and starlight.)

What did cavemen use for the light at night?
(Natural light.)

If there were no sunlight or any other kind of light, what would a day be like?
(Dark.)

**The poles of the earth are in nearly total darkness for six months out of every year.

• Darken the room, or go to a closet and turn out the lights. Ask the children if the colors of things are as bright as they were when there was more light. If not, why? What can we do to make the room light again? (Turn the lights on, or open the closet door to let the sunlight in.)
• Ask the children if there is a difference between how much light there is indoors and outdoors. Where is there more light? (During the day when it is sunny, there is usually far more light outside than inside. When we take photographs inside a room, we usually need to use a flashbulb because there is not enough light indoors for the picture to turn out well.)

Fine points to discuss with children
What kinds of things give off natural light?
(The sun, fire, fireflies, sparks, and lightning.)

How can we create or make artificial light when it is dark and there is no natural light from the sun?
(By using man-made lights which use electricity, or lamps that use oil or gas; by making a campfire, or lighting candles.)

II. Light Reflects and/or Absorbs Heat

1. Light Feels Warm

Materials A small light or Tensor lamp.

Procedure
• Ask the children if they can feel, touch, see, or taste light. (They will respond that they can see light, but that they cannot feel or taste light.)
• Turn the light on and have the children feel the heat that the light gives off.
• Ask the children the following kinds of questions:

Is it as warm at night as it is during the day?
(Not usually).

What makes it warmer during the day?
(The sunlight.)

If we stay in the sun on a sunny day, what happens to our skin?
(It tans or burns from the heat.)

• Have the children stick their tongues out under the light. Ask them if they can taste the light. (Light does not have a taste, but it does feel warm on our tongue.)

2. Light Can Burn a Hole

Materials A small magnifying glass with a handle; a small pail filled with water; sunglasses or pieces of colored cellophane; pieces of black and white construction paper; white tissue paper.

Procedure

• Ask the children if the rays of sunlight can burn a hole through a piece of paper. Listen to their responses.

• Take the children outside or near a window on a bright sunny day. Have them wear sunglasses or place a piece of colored cellophane in front of their eyes to protect them from the bright light they are about to see.

• Catch a light beam from the sun with a magnifying glass. Concentrate a small sunlight beam on a piece of black construction paper (the smaller the beam, the higher the concentration of light). Hold the magnifying glass very still. After about 15 to 30 seconds, you will see and smell smoke. If the magnifying glass stays focused longer it will actually burn a hole in the paper. ***It is very important not to stare at the bright spot of light because it can harm our eyes.*

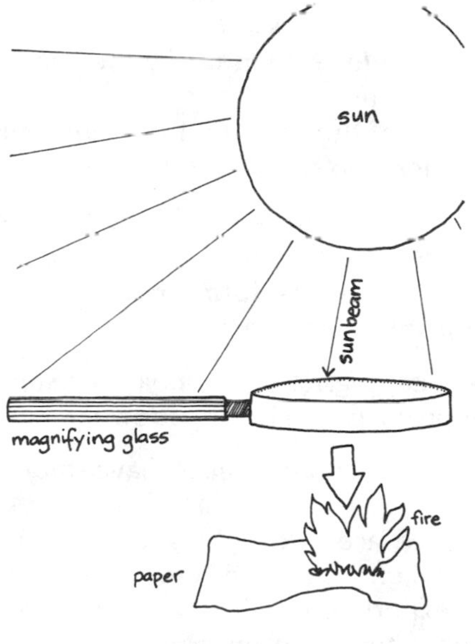

• Do the same thing again with the piece of white tissue paper and the piece of white construction paper. (They will burn eventually, but it will take a great deal of patience.) Ask the children if they know why the white pieces of paper do not burn as quickly as the black one did. (Black absorbs heat; white reflects heat.)

• Let each piece of paper sit in the sun for a few minutes. Have the children feel each piece of paper. Ask them which feels the warmest and which feels the coolest. (Black will feel the warmest.)

Fine points to discuss with children

What can our body tell us about light?
(Light feels warm.)

What is the magnifying glass able to do to light?
(It is able to concentrate the power or energy of light to show us what light is. It is a form of energy. The energy is a form of heat that we can feel on our bodies and that can affect other materials like paper.)

What does the paper tell us about light?
(Different colors absorb light differently. Some colors become very hot, some remain cool.)

What would be good colors to wear on a hot day if you wanted to feel cool?
(White or other light colors.)

On a very hot, sunny day, which would feel cooler to walk on: a blacktop surface or a concrete sidewalk?
(A sidewalk.)

III. Light Can Go Through Some Materials and Not Others

1. Does Light Go Through?

Materials An assortment of paper products: waxed paper, paper towels, tinfoil, black and white construction paper, cellophane in different colors, cardboard, cardboard tube, tissue paper, clear plastic wrap, clear vinyl, a pin, flashlight.

Procedure

• Turn the lights out and darken the room.

• Show the children the various materials by holding them in front of the lighted flashlight one at a time. Ask the children if they think the light can shine through the various materials. Then have the children experiment to find out if they were right.

• Pierce the tinfoil with a pin. Ask the children to predict what the light will look like and whether it will shine through the tinfoil. (It will shine through the tiny hole and look like starlight. More pinholes will produce more lights.)

• Have children shine the flashlight through the cardboard tube and see what happens. (It will appear as a concentrated beam of light with a slight shadow, like a stage light.)

2. Seeing Through a Balloon

Materials A large balloon that blows up to approximately 9 inches.

Procedure

- Hold the uninflated balloon up to a light. Have the children see if they can look through it. Ask them what needs to happen to the balloon for it to become thinner so they can see through it. (It needs to be blown up or inflated with air.)
- Blow the balloon up with air. Have the children look through it. (They will be able to see things that are close up, but things that are farther away will look hazy and blurry.)

Fine points to discuss with children

Can light pass through all materials?
(No, but it can pass through some. Explain to the children that when materials are clear like a window, they allow light to pass through and are transparent. Materials that are opaque do not allow light to pass through. They simply block light. When materials allow some light to pass through in a scattered kind of way they are called translucent. Waxed paper, tissue paper, and frosted glass are examples of translucent material. Translucent materials make objects look blurry.)

Are translucent materials always translucent?
(No, if they become too thick or dense they lose their translucency and become more solid or opaque. We can see through one thin piece of tissue paper, but we cannot see through several layers of tissue paper. We can see through a blown-up balloon, but not through a balloon that has lost its air. Thinness allows a material to become translucent.

IV. Shadows

1. Making Shadows

Materials A tensor light, or a film or slide projector; a clear plastic cup.

Procedure

- Ask the children if they know what a shadow is. Have them look for their own shadows.
- Darken the room, and turn the lights off. Ask the children if when the room was well lit it was easier to see and to make shadows of themselves.
- Shine a bright light on a wall. Have the children observe the light and notice if there are any shadows. (There will be a shadow if something is blocking the light.)

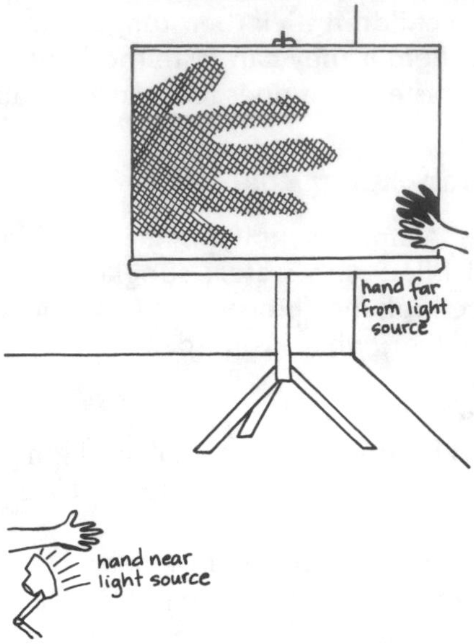

SHADOWS

- Choose a child to stand in front of the light holding a clear plastic cup. Have the children observe the child's shadow as the child walks away from the light. Discuss what happens to the shadow. The child's shadow grows smaller as it moves away from the light, but it becomes gigantic when it is near the light.

Fine points to discuss with children

When the light shines on the child holding a clear plastic cup and creates a shadow of the child and the cup, is the whole child lit up by the light, or just one side of the child?
(Just the side of the child that the light shines on is lit up. The other side of the child remains in the dark.)

Why doesn't the light shine through the child?
(The child is a solid object. Light is blocked by solid objects. Solid objects form shadows of themselves when light shines on them.)

Does the clear plastic cup appear as a solid shadow?
(No, it appears as a lighter shadow.)

Can a person or an object have more than one shadow?
(Yes, if there are two light sources shining on the object each light source will create a shadow. Have the children experiment with two lights or flashlights shining on a toy from different angles to check this out.)

Does the brightness of the light affect the shadow?
(Yes, when the light is brighter, the lines of the shadows appear sharper and clearer.)

Can you tell how solid an image is by looking at its shadow?

(Yes, solid objects do not allow light to pass through. Solid objects appear darker than translucent objects.)

2. Shapes of Shadows

Materials A Tensor light; various-shaped objects such as a small tin can, a pair of scissors, a rectangular block, a pencil, a fat round crayon, a paper cup, a cone shape, a jar lid, a large thin book.

Procedure

- Darken the room and turn the lights out. Shine the light on a wall. Display the various-shaped objects. Place one of the objects on a table in front of the Tensor light so that the object on the table creates a shadow.
- Have the children experiment moving each of the shapes around one at a time to different positions so that the shapes are standing up or lying down, or at a different angle to the light. Ask the children to experiment to find out how many different kinds of shadows each of the different-shaped objects can make. Ask them to make a prediction before they look at the shadow about what the shape of the shadow might look like.

Fine points to discuss with children

What happens to round and curved objects when they make shadows?
(They look flat and lose their roundness. The shadows of some things look very different from what we expect them to look like. A pair of scissors lying flat can look like a straight line, a pencil held straight up can look like a small circle.)

What happens to shapes or objects when they are very close to the light?
(The shadows of the objects get much larger.)

What happens to shapes or objects when they are further away from the light?
(The shadows of the objects more accurately represent their true size.)

Which part of the shape or object is always in the light?
(The part facing the light source.)

What part of the shape or object is always in the dark?
(The part of the object that is not facing the light.)

V. Night Is Earth's Shadow

1. Earth Model

Materials A small model of a globe; a flashlight or Tensor light; a small piece of clay; a toothpick.

Procedure

- Turn the lights out and darken the room. Shine the light on the globe.
- Explain to the children that the globe is a model of the Earth. The Earth is the name of the planet we live on. All of the blue represents oceans of water. Show the children where North America and the United States are on the globe and where their state and city are located. Place a small dab of clay with a toothpick in it on the state that the children live in, to represent a person.

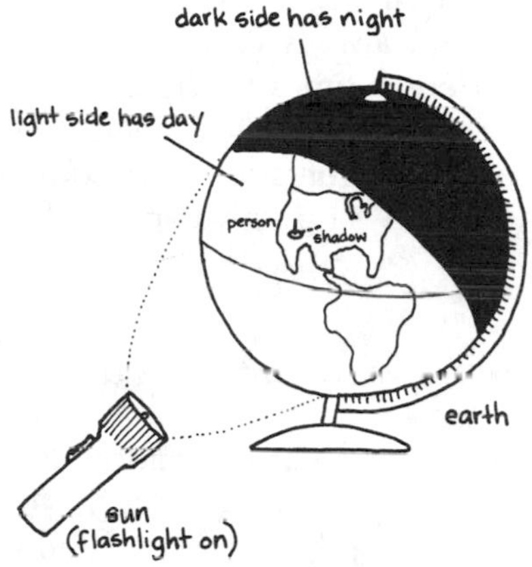

- Rotate the Earth around slowly until the light is shining on the dab of clay with a toothpick in it. Ask the children if they know what the bright light that shines on the Earth is called. They will probably respond that it is the sun. If they don't, tell them that the light is a model that represents the sun shining on the Earth.
- Have the children observe that one side of the Earth is in the dark and one side is in the light. Ask them if they can tell which side of the Earth is having night and which side of the Earth is having day. (The answer is rather obvious. The lit-up side is having day; the dark side is having night.)
- Continue to turn or rotate the Earth so that the dab of clay with a toothpick in it is in the dark. Explain to the children that the Earth is continuously moving, but that we cannot feel it moving because everything is moving with us. The sun stays still.
- Have individual children continue to shine the light on the globe and to rotate the globe to experience where the light shines and to experience how night is caused by Earth's shadow.

2. Shadows Change

Materials A globe with dab of clay and a toothpick; a Tensor light.

Procedure

- Turn the lights off and darken the room. Shine the light on the Earth.

• As you rotate the Earth, have the children observe where the sun is located. Ask the children if the sun is always located in the same spot on the Earth or if the sunlight would appear to be moving. (The sunlight would appear to be moving. It would appear to be rising and setting.)
• Ask the children how the rising and setting sun would affect shadows. Have them observe the toothpick's shadow.

Fine points to discuss with children
Will our shadows always look alike or will they be different at different times of the day?
(Although the sun stays still, it appears to be making an arc in the sky. When the sun is low, our shadows are long. When the sun is directly overhead, our shadows are short.)

How can you tell where the sun is by looking at your shadow?
(The sun will always create a shadow in an opposite direction from where it is shining. If you turn your back to the sun when the sun is low you will see your shadow in front of you. You can always tell where the sun is by looking at where the shadows are.)

3. The Sun's "Arc"

Materials A flashlight or Tensor light.

Procedure
• Turn the lights out and darken the room.
• Choose a child to shine a light on, and another child to hold the flashlight.
• Explain to the children that the light from the flashlight is going to represent the sun. Although the sun does not move, it appears to move by rising and setting every day. Have a child hold the flashlight. The child is to pretend that the light coming from the flashlight is the sun rising and setting. Have the child move the light in an arc. You may need to assist the child in moving the flashlight to form an arc.
• Have the children begin the arc on the floor by holding the flashlight parallel to the floor. Slowly have the child create an arc shape by moving the flashlight into an upward position. Be sure the light is shining down onto the other child. Have the child end the arc on the floor on the opposite side from where he or she started. Have the rest of the children discuss how the size and shape of the child's shadow changed as the sun "rose and set."

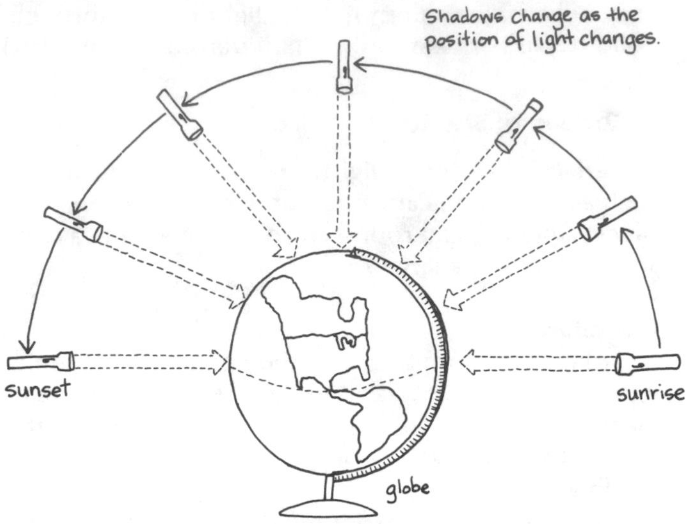

The sun's arc in the sky as seen from the Earth. The flashlight represents the sun.

SHADOWS CHANGE

VI. Light Can Bounce (Reflect)

1. Catch a Sunbeam

Materials A small mirror.

Procedure
• Have a child stand near a window on a bright sunny day and catch a sunbeam with a mirror.
• Ask the child to shine or reflect the beam onto a wall or the ceiling so everyone can see the beam of light. Ask the children if the light is going through the mirror, and if it is not, how can they tell. (The mirror makes a shadow and the light hitting the mirror bounces off the mirror and is thrown to another place.)

REFLECTED SUNLIGHT

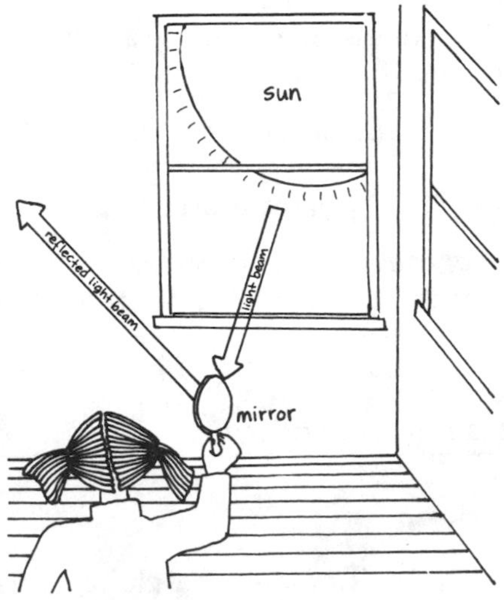

• Explain to the children that when light is thrown this way by an object like a mirror, it is called a reflection. Ask them if they can think of other things that cause reflections. (Examples: red bike reflector lights, colors that glow in the dark, chrome on cars, shiny surfaces, water.)

2. Making a Ball Bounce Against a Wall as a Model of a Reflection

Materials A ball; a long hallway wall with no obstructions.

Procedure

• Have the children roll a ball against a wall. Ask them to predict what will happen to the ball. Where will it bounce off to when it hits the wall?

• Have the child roll a ball directly in front of him- or herself so that it will hit the wall head-on. (The ball will roll back to him or her.) Then have the child roll the ball at an angle. (The ball will hit the wall at an angle and roll off at an angle away from him or her.)

• Have the children line up and sit down parallel to the wall a few feet from the wall. Place a marker on the wall for the children to aim at. Ask them to predict which child will receive the ball that they roll at an angle. (The children should be able to notice how the ball bounces differently according to the angle it is thrown from.)

• One child can do this activity by his/herself, by extending and holding his/her arms apart. If the child rolls the ball from his/her extended right arm, the ball will bounce against the wall and roll back to the child's extended left arm.

Fine points to discuss with children

How is the rolling ball bouncing against a wall and reflecting off it like a light beam hitting a mirror?

ANGLE OF INCIDENCE EQUALS ANGLE OF REFLECTION

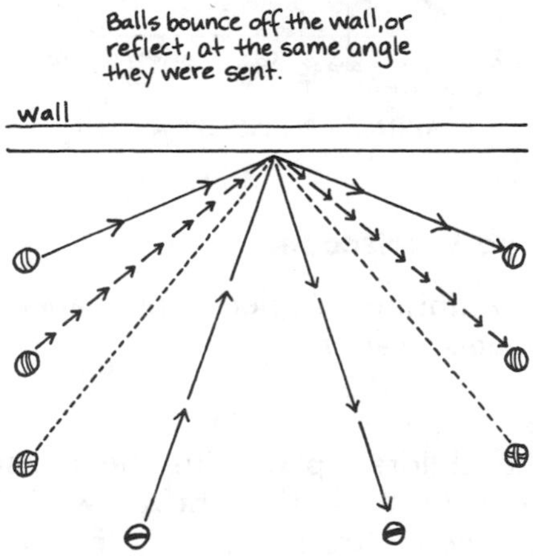

Balls bounce off the wall, or reflect, at the same angle they were sent.
wall

(Light behaves like a bouncing ball. It reflects or bounces off a surface to another place. Light travels in a straight line just as the ball does.)

**See *Law of Reflection* at beginning of this chapter under General Information for Parents and Teachers.

3. Black and White, Bounce or Absorb?

Materials Black and white construction paper; a shiny piece of vinyl material; a shiny piece of glossy paper or tinfoil; a flashlight.

Procedure Have children shine a flashlight on the different pieces of paper and plastic. Ask them if light bounces off or reflects off each kind of material in the same way. Discuss the differences. Ask which kind of surface bounces off more light, and what color reflects more light. (The shiny surfaces reflect more light. White reflects more light than black. Black absorbs light; that is why the magnifying glass was able to burn the black paper. White feels cool because it reflects light and heat.)

4. Water Reflection

Materials A black, flat pan filled with water; photographs from travel magazines that depict pictures of lakes with mirror images of scenery.

Procedure

• Have children observe their reflection in the pan of water. They will be able to see themselves if they are directly over the pan, but if they look into the water from an angle they will be able to see other children or other things that are in front of them.

• Show children the travel pictures of lakes with mirror image reflections. Turn the picture upside-down and ask the children how they can tell the picture is upside-down. (The reflection will probably have waves in it from the water, or the colors of the reflection may not be as bright.)

5. Mirror Writing

Materials A mirror; a piece of paper for each child; a black marking pen.

Procedure

• Write the child's name on the paper and underline it.

• Place the mirror perpendicular to the paper on top of the child's written name. (The letters will appear to be upside-down.)

• Place the mirror perpendicular to the paper on the bottom of the child's written name so that the word is upside-down, and the word will appear to be written backwards in the mirror. See diagram.

• Lift the paper up and turn it over to the other side. The word can be seen through the paper. Place the mirror next to the word and it will appear in the usual form in the mirror.

• Explain to the children that a mirror reflects an image. The image is a picture. The real you and the real word are not in the mirror. The mirror creates a reflection of real things. Mirrors can trick you into thinking you see things that are "there," that are not really "there."

• Have the children continue to experiment with the mirror held perpendicular to letters, words, or pictures.

6. Multiple Images

Materials One small mirror and a large wall mirror.

Procedure Have a child hold a small mirror under his or her chin, while standing in front of a large mirror so that the child can focus on his or her image holding a mirror under his or her chin. If the mirror is tilted at an appropriate angle to catch the child's reflection, the child will be surprised to see a multiple image of him- or herself that goes on for what appears to be forever inside of the mirror. It will appear to be an endless tunnel. Each image inside the image will appear to be smaller, less clear, and darker. Each time something is reflected it loses some light.

7. Periscope Model

Materials Two small mirrors; two pieces of cardboard; some tape; two empty half-gallon milk cartons; a pair of scissors.

Procedure Make a toy periscope by wedging a piece of cardboard to the bottom of each of the opened empty half-gallon milk containers at about a 45° angle. Mount a mirror to the cardboard. Cut a two-inch square hole directly in front of where the mirrors are mounted. Secure the cardboard in place with some tape. Secure the mirror in place on the cardboard with some tape. Slip the two cartons together. Be sure that the two holes are "katty-korner" to each other. See diagram.

Periscopes are used in submarines. They are also used for seeing around corners. The mirrors inside them reflect light.

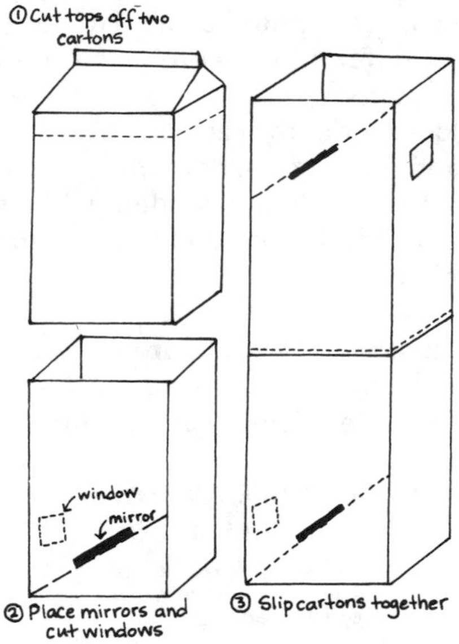

MAKING A PERISCOPE MODEL

8. Take Apart Periscope

Materials A finished toy periscope; paper; two small round magnets; marking pens.

Procedure

• Have the children play with the periscope and experiment with it. Ask them how it works. (It works because the two mirrors work together to reflect an image. It creates an image of an image.)

• Ask the children to disconnect their periscope and connect it so that both holes are on the same side. Then ask them to look through the hole and to explain what they see. (Everything will appear to be upside-down, because the light reflects off the mirrors in straight lines. Light reflects the way it enters the periscope.)

• Ask them to visualize soldiers walking along a reflected light beam in one direction. See diagram.

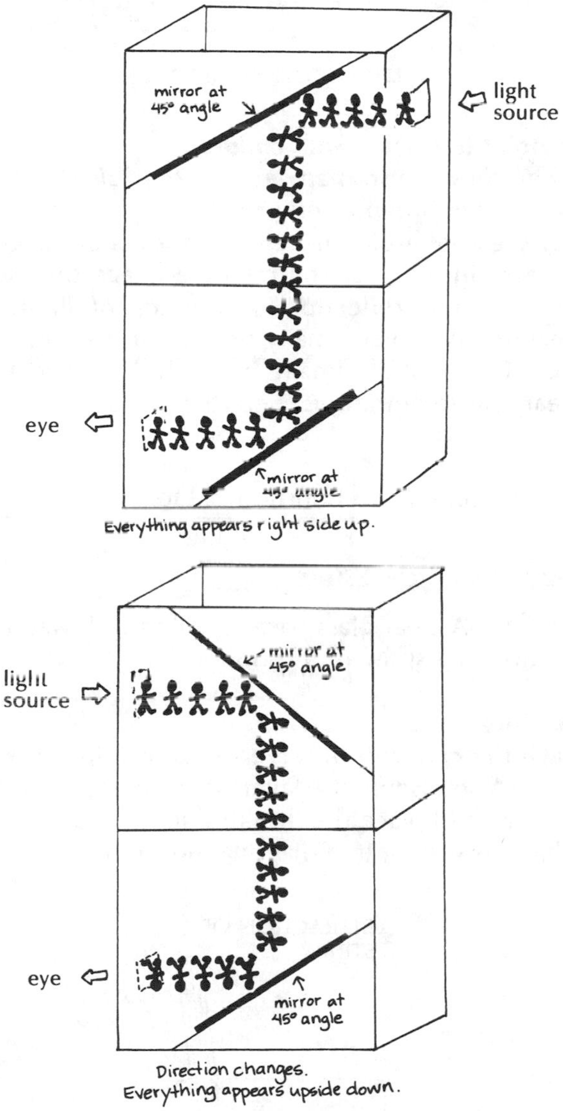

PERISCOPE ANGLES

• Draw the two sketches that appear in above diagram on a piece of typing paper. Use a set of small round magnets as markers to move on the two sketches. Ask the children to look at the first sketch and to try to imagine little toy soldiers marching on a reflected light beam or boats floating down a reflected light beam inside the periscope. When they hit the first mirror they follow the light beam to the next mirror and continue to march or float out of the periscope on the reflected light beam. The reflected light beam has continued to move in the same direction and moves in a straight line.

Then have them look at the second sketch and try to imagine those same soldiers marching or the boats floating on the reflected light beam again, but this time when they hit the first mirror, the reflected light beam bounces down to the second mirror and that mirror reverses the direction of the light beam. Because the soldiers or boats follow the light beam as it reverses direction, they are forced to march or float upside-down along the reflected light beam as they leave or exit from the periscope.

9. Curved Reflections

Materials Several shiny metal spoons in different sizes; a curved mirror or shiny pot lid.

Procedure

• Have the children look at their reflections in the various curved shapes. Ask them if their reflections look the way they would in a mirror or if they look different. (Their reflections will be distorted.)

• Have them now look at themselves inside of the curve of the spoon (the concave side that caves in). They will notice that they look upside-down.

• Have the children look at themselves on the convex side of the spoon—the side of the spoon that curves out (the part that children might call the bottom of the spoon).

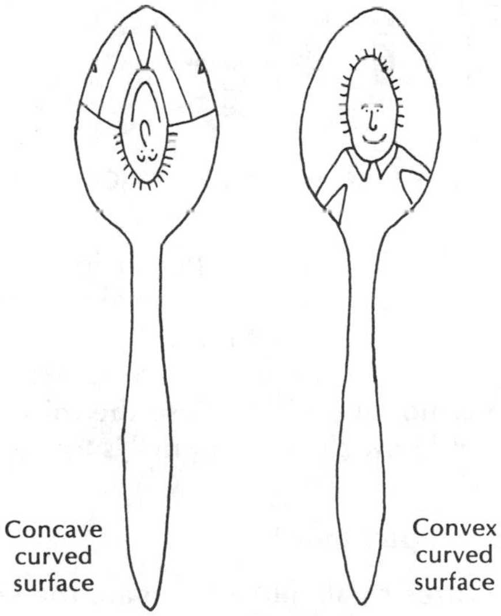

REFLECTIONS ON A SPOON

Fine point to discuss with children

Why do reflections look so different on the curved or rounded surfaces?

(Light that hits a curve reflects or bounces on a tangent of the curve so it appears to reflect light differently from light that hits a flat surface. This causes a twisting and a bending of the images that are reflected and is called a distortion.)

10. Hinged Mirrors

Materials Two small mirrors of the same size taped together on one side to form a hinged effect; a pencil.

Procedure

• Stand the hinged mirror perpendicular to the surface of a table. Have the children look inside the mirrors and count how many mirrors they see. (There will be a range of four to twelve mirrors. The number will depend on the angle that the mirrors are opened to.)

• Have the children experiment with the angle of the two mirrors (to be acute and obtuse). Ask the children if they see more images when the mirrors are standing close together or when they are opened far apart. (When they are held close together they will see more images.)

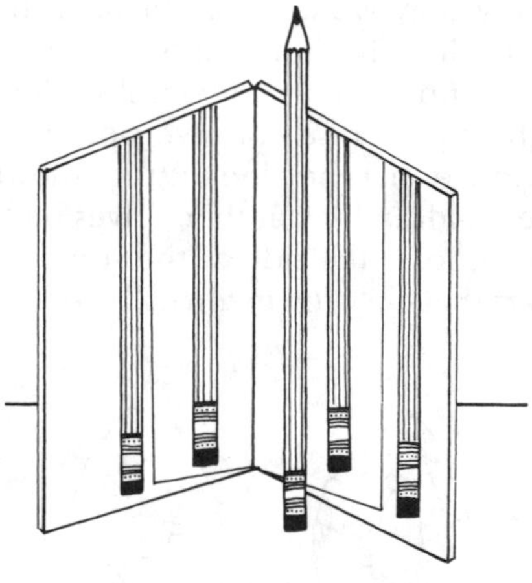

MULTIPLE IMAGES OF A PENCIL

• Have the children place a pencil in front of the hinged mirror, but ask them to make a prediction about how many pencils they will see before they place the pencil in front of the mirrors. (The number will vary depending on how close the mirrors are to each other and how close the pencil is to the mirrors.)

11. Kaleidoscope Model

Materials Three small mirrors that are the same size, taped together on their sides to form a triangular-shaped tunnel; one other small mirror.

Procedure Have the children look through the homemade kaleidoscope. Have them place the one extra mirror in front of the "triangle tunnel." Then ask them to discuss what they see.

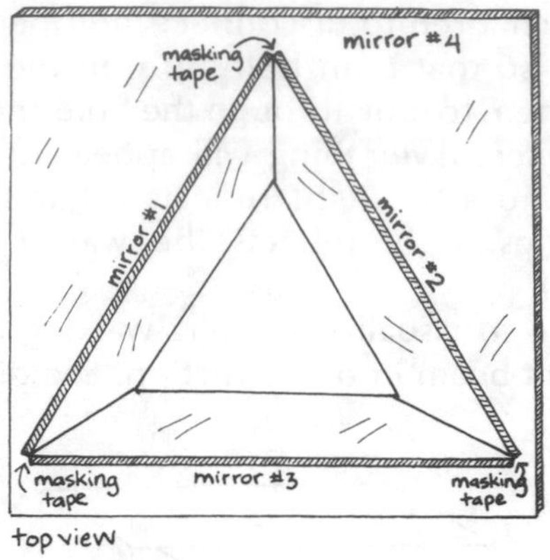

KALEIDOSCOPE OF MIRRORS

Fine point to discuss with children

Why do they see so many eyes in the kaleidoscope if only one eye is being reflected?

(They see a multiple image of their eyes or images of their eyes in mirrors. The multiple image they see is caused by the reflection or bounce of light. The reflection takes place many times, causing a multiple image. The multiple image is an illusion. It makes it appear that something is there that is not.)

VII. Refraction (The Bending of Light)

1. "Broken" Straw Effect

Materials A clear glass partially filled with water and oil; a drinking straw or a spoon.

Procedure

• Have the children observe the separation of water and oil. Also discuss the layer of air on top of the oil.

• Have a child place the drinking straw into the water so that it is resting in a diagonal position.

REFRACTION OF A STRAW

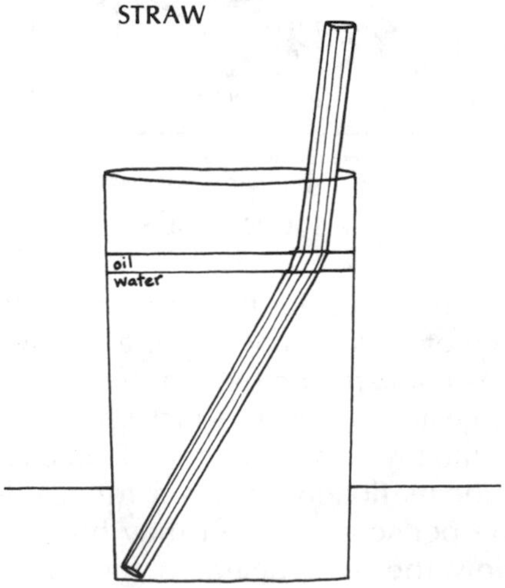

• Have the children discuss what they see. (The straw will look strange, as though it has been cut.) **This phenomenon is called *refraction.* Refraction is the bending of light. For more information, see General Information for Parents and Teachers at the beginning of this chapter.

Fine points to discuss with children
Does the size of the water drop affect what you see? (Yes. When the drop of water is smaller, the curved surface of the drop is higher and the magnification effect is greater. A large water-drop lens has a flatter surface.)

VIII. Lenses

1. Water-Drop Lenses

Materials A Styrofoam meat tray; a clear plastic bag; used postage stamps; Scotch tape; eye dropper; water; clear plastic vinyl or waxed paper.

Procedure
• Mount the used postage stamps on the meat tray with Scotch tape. Slip the meat tray into the clear plastic bag.
• Have a child use an eye dropper to drop a few drops of water onto the clear vinyl or waxed paper. Have the child place the waxed paper or clear vinyl with water drops on it over the Styrofoam meat tray that has the postage stamps mounted on it under a clear plastic bag. See diagram.

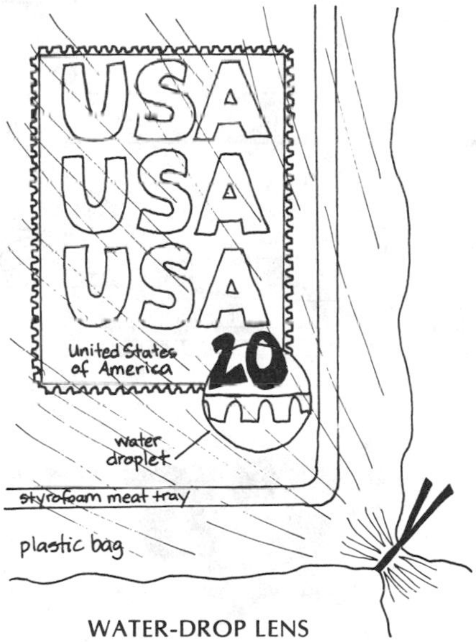

WATER-DROP LENS

• Have the child slide the vinyl or waxed paper around with the water drops on it, and then observe the postage stamps under the water lens. Discuss what is seen. (The parts of the stamps that are underneath the water-drop lenses will be magnified.) Ask the child why they are magnified. (They are magnified because they are seen through a curved surface.)

2. Water Magnification

Materials A clear plastic glass filled with water; a page of print from a newspaper or magazine.

Procedure
• Have a child place a page of print behind a glass filled with water. Ask the children what happens to the print when it is seen through the glass. (The print becomes bigger or magnified.)
• Place the glass on top of the page of print and have a child look through the bottom of the glass. Ask the child if the words look as big as they did when they were seen through the sides of the glass. (No, the print will not be magnified. The curve on the side of the clear drinking glass creates a lens effect. A lens needs to have a curve and be transparent to be a lens.)

3. Magnifying Glass

Materials Magnifying glasses; page of print; other items of interest to magnify.

Procedure
• Have the children look through a magnifying glass at their skin, and at other items of interest. Have them discuss what they see, and what the magnifying glass is able to do. Ask them if it is easier to use a magnifying glass to make things look bigger or to use a drop of water.
• Ask the children to look for and to feel the curve on the magnifying glass. Discuss the shape of the lens. Is it similar to the shape of the water-drop lens? (Yes, they both curve up like a round hill and are called convex lenses.)

4. Convex and Concave Lenses

Materials Old prescription lenses from eyeglasses and/or various cheap, defective, or surplus lenses purchased from a science supply house; or lenses from old cameras or binoculars, old watch-face crystals, or clear marbles.

Procedure
• Have the children examine the various lenses and see the effect they create. Ask them to observe

whether thickness or thinness affects the lens, and how the curve of the lens affects what they see.

• Have the children observe how things appear through different lenses. Have the children observe whether all of the lenses are convex or if some of them are concave. (Concave is shaped like a valley: it caves in, in the center.)

**You might want to show children the spoon again so they can see the difference between a convex and a concave curve

5. Microscope Lens Model

Materials A water-drop lens (see Procedure #1 from this activity section); a postage stamp or other interesting item to magnify; and a plastic magnifying lens.

Procedure Set up the water-drop lens over a postage stamp. Have the children look through a plastic magnifying lens through the water-drop lens at the postage stamp. Have them discuss what they see. (It will be like looking through a microscope. The tiny dots and lines on the stamp will become very large.)

6. Seeing Through Two Lenses

Materials Two plastic magnifying glasses; interesting things to look at with the magnifying glass like feathers, snakeskin, a grain of salt, a drop of water, a leaf.

Procedure

• Place the items out on display. Have the children observe the items by looking through two magnifying glasses. Have them discuss what they see. (If the two magnifying glasses are held together on the surface of the object, the two magnifying glasses will act like one strong magnifying glass. However, if the two magnifying glasses are lifted up off the surface, everything will look upside-down and small. If one magnifying glass is removed while it is away from the object being looked at, everything will look blurry and out of focus.)

• Explain to the children that they can create a telescope effect with the two magnifying lenses. A telescope makes things that are far away look closer. Show the children how to focus the two magnifying glasses onto something far away in the room. Have the children close one of their eyes and hold one magnifying glass in front of their other eye. Move the other glass approximately 3 to 4 inches in front of the first magnifying glass until it feels focused. (It will be focused when things can be seen clearly through both of the lenses. Everything will look upside-down and small, but things will look closer than they really are.)

• Explain to the children that they can also create a microscope effect with the two magnifying glasses. A microscope makes things that are small look bigger. Show the children how to focus the two magnifying glasses onto something close to their nose. Have them close one of their eyes and hold one magnifying glass in front of their other eye. Have them move the other magnifying glass approximately one inch in front of the first magnifying glass. The second magnifying glass should be about one-half inch away from the material being focused on. When it is focused, things will look very large.

7. Projector Magnification

Materials A Tensor light or flashlight; a magnifying glass; a clear transparent ruler or shedded snakeskin or piece of transparent film.

Procedure Darken the room. Have a child hold a transparent ruler a few inches in front of a lit Tensor light or flashlight. Have another child hold a magnifying glass a few inches in front of the ruler until the light is focused through the ruler and part of the ruler is projected onto the wall or ceiling. The ruler will look magnified when it is projected.

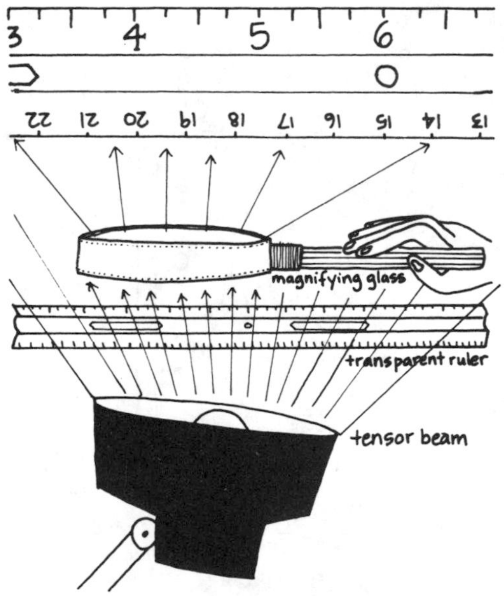

Fine points to discuss with children

What do lenses do for us?

(Lenses help us focus so we can see things better. They also make things look larger or smaller than they really are.)

What is a lens?

(A lens is a curved surface that refracts or bends light to help us see better.)

1. No Light, No Sight

Materials An empty shoebox with a lid; a small colorful picture; Scotch tape.

Procedure

- Use Scotch tape to mount the colorful picture on the inside of the box. Make a small peephole in front of the picture at the opposite end of the box.
- Show children the empty shoebox with a small picture mounted on the inside. Discuss what the picture shows. Cover the shoebox with the shoebox lid. Have the children look through the peephole at the picture. Ask them if they can see the colors in the picture. (They might be able to, but it will be hard to see.)
- Open the lid of the shoebox while the children are looking through the peephole. Ask them if they can see the colors in the picture better when there is light. (The objects will be easier to see, and the intensity and brightness of the colors will be greatly improved.)

Fine point to discuss with children

Why do we need light to see?

(Colors are reflected. If there is no light, there is no reflection of the color to our eyes.)

2. Make a Rainbow

Materials A sunbeam; a piece of white paper; a prism or clear glass partially filled with water (the glass can be made of clear plastic).

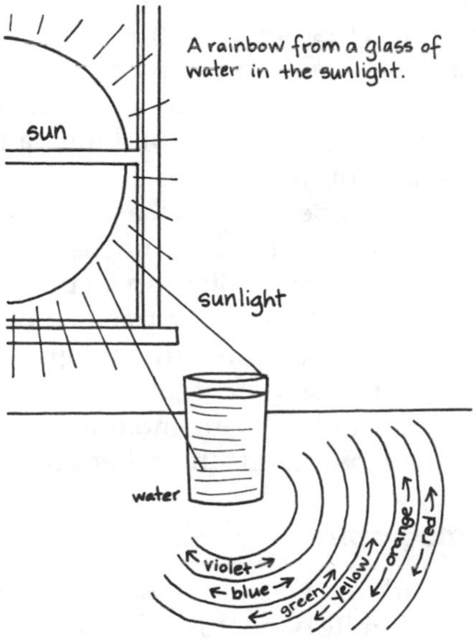

Procedure

- Place the prism in a window that has a light beam shining through it. Discuss the rainbow effect that can be seen. Have the children place the white paper underneath the rainbow to see if the colors become brighter and more distinct.
- Explain to the children that the light is being bent by the water. It is being bent twice: once when it enters the glass, and once when it leaves the glass. This bending of light twice causes the light to separate. When the light beam separates, we can see a rainbow.
- Ask the children to name the colors in the rainbow from the top band down to the bottom band. (There are seven colors in the rainbow: red, orange, yellow, green, blue, indigo, and violet.)

3. Spinning Colors

Materials A toy top or hand drill; a round cardboard disk; crayons in the following colors: red, orange, yellow, green, blue, purple; a ruler; a pencil.

Procedure

- Divide the disk into six sections with a ruler and a pencil. Have a child color in each of the six sections with one of the crayon colors in the order that the color would appear in a rainbow spectrum.

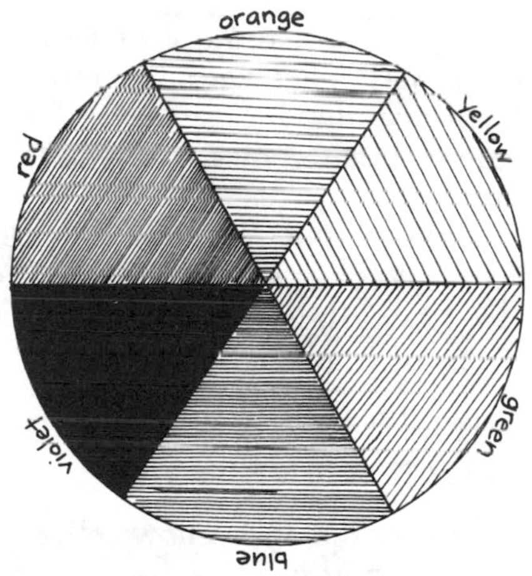

COLORED PAPER DISK

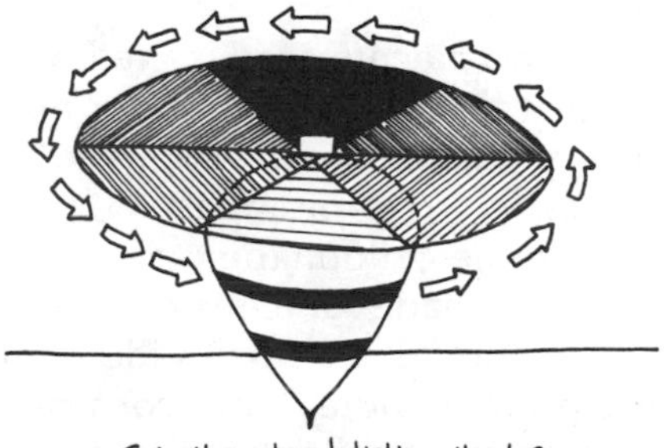

Spin the colored disk on the top.

• Have the child place the center of the colored cardboard disk on top of the toy top or on top of the hand drill. Then have the child spin the disk. Ask the children to observe what happens to the colors on the disk. (The colors will blend together and begin to look white or have a white cast.)

4. Combining and Mixing Colors

Materials Pieces of colored cellophane; pieces of colored transparent plastic; three small jars filled with water; red, yellow, and blue food color; red, yellow, and blue poster paint; toothpicks; white paper.

Procedure

• Have the children arrange the pieces of colored cellophane on top of each other in a random pattern on a piece of white paper, then discuss with the children the new colors that are created by the overlapping pieces of cellophane.

• Have the children place food color in each of the three small jars of water so that one jar has red in it, one jar has yellow in it, and one jar has blue in it. Tell them to use a lot of food color in the jars so that the colors are fairly intense. After the colors are fairly intense, tell the children to observe the colors and then observe them through another color. Discuss the new colors that can be seen through the overlapping colors.

• Have the children use toothpicks to lift drops of water from the jars filled with colored water onto white paper. Have them observe and discuss the colors that can be created by combining two or three colors of water.

• Show the children the poster paint colors. Have them predict what colors will be made by combining two colors together. Then have the children mix two toothpick-drops of color together to see the result.

5. Seeing Color Through Filters

Materials Pieces of red and yellow cellophane; construction paper; staples or masking tape; red, yellow, and blue crayons; white paper.

Procedure

• Place one or two pieces of red (or yellow) cellophane together so that they are able to filter out that color. (When you look through red cellophane at something red, it will look white or disappear.)

• Staple or tape the cellophane together, and place a frame around it made of construction paper. The cellophane can look like a small slide or can be large like a ping-pong paddle. The construction paper frame will make the "cellophane window" easier to hold and more sturdy.

• Have the children draw simple designs on white paper with red, yellow, and blue crayons. Then have the children look at their drawings through the red or yellow cellophane windows. The color yellow in the drawings will seem to disappear when it is viewed through the yellow cellophane. The color red in the drawings will seem to disappear when it is viewed through the red cellophane.

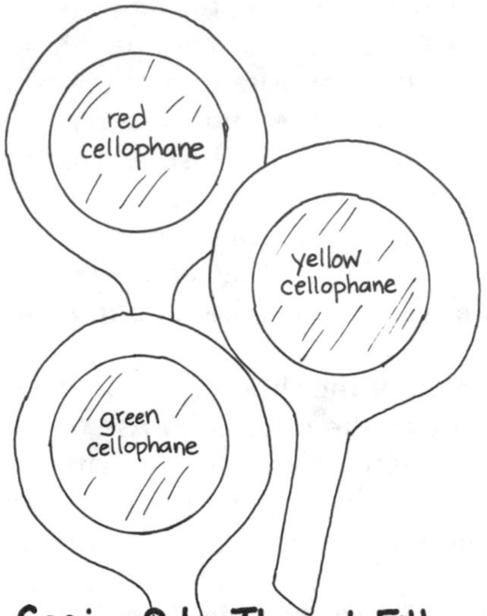

Seeing Color Through Filters

Fine points to discuss with children

Why do colors appear to change or to disappear when they are seen through other colors?

(All of the colors we see are reflected colors. Colored transparent materials act as a filter. They filter out all of the other colors from the light beam except the color of the filter. The crayon colors cannot be reflected back to our eyes when a colored filter absorbs the other wavelengths of color from the light beam.)

**A colored crayon on white paper does not absorb or add to color. It takes out certain wavelengths of light and reflects them back to us. When an object looks blue to our eyes, it is because every other color is absorbed by the object except blue, and blue is reflected back to our eyes.

**Grass appears to be green because the only wavelength of light that grass does not absorb is green. Grass cannot absorb green light so it appears green to our eyes. The grass absorbs or traps all of the other colors in light. A plant in green light would die because all colors would be filtered out except green. The green filter would absorb and trap all of the other colors, but the plant needs the other colors to live.

6. Chromatography

Materials Marking pens in assorted water-soluble colors; a pile of white paper towels cut in 4-inch circles; several clear plastic glasses; water; scissors.

Procedure

• Partially fill the glasses with water. Have the children make two cuts into each paper-towel "filter." The two cuts should be parallel to each other and form a strip or tongue that hangs down from the center of each circle. See diagram.

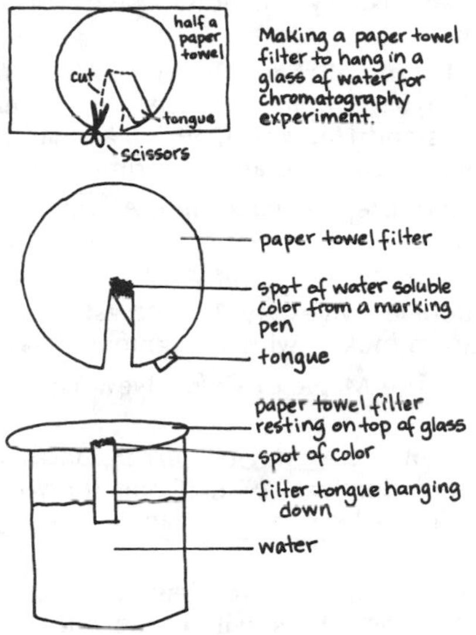

• Have the children color the top near the center of the circles of each "filter" tongue with a color from a marking pen. See diagram.

• Have the children place the "tongue" or strip in the water and the rest of the paper circle on the rim of the glass. (The water will rise* up the strip onto the colored pen mark. The colors in the pen mark will separate into all of the component colors or dyes that were needed to create the color made by the marking pen.) **There should be one filter and one glass with water for each marking pen color used. A comparison can be made afterwards of the results. It will be hard to remember what the original color was before the chromatography process occurred, so you might want to mark the outer perimeter with the original color. The chromatography process takes about 15 minutes per color.

7. Camouflage

Materials Magazine pictures of animals that depict camouflage*; colored paper in various colors; crayons in assorted colors.

Procedure

• Show the children the pictures of animals and discuss what camouflage means and how the coloration of these animals helps protect them in their habitats. (Examples are: tigers' stripes protect them in tall grass; lions' color protects them on the plains; polar bears' white coat protects them in the snow; bright colors on some insects protect them on flowers, etc.)

• Have the children create a camouflage texture on the colored paper with colored crayons, and another that is not as camouflaged but uses contrasts that are easier to see. (Example: red spots on red paper, and one that shows red spots on white or yellow paper.)

*The water rises up the strip due to capillarity. Capillarity also helps leaves of plants receive water from their roots.

**Ranger Rick*, or other wildlife magazines, are a good source for such pictures.

X. The Energy from Light Can Affect Plants and Animals

1. Plant and Light

Materials Two plants that are healthy and identical in size and species; one empty half-gallon milk container.

Procedure

• Cut a "window" hole about one inch square on the side of the milk carton. Open the top of the milk carton.

• Place the two plants in a sunny window. Invert the open milk carton and place it on top of one of the plants. Be sure the "window" on the box is facing the sun.

• Remember to have the children water the plants daily, and check their growth in a few days. (After a few days there will be a noticeable difference in the way the two plants look. The plant that is covered will be twisted. It will be growing in the direction of the "window" on the milk carton.)

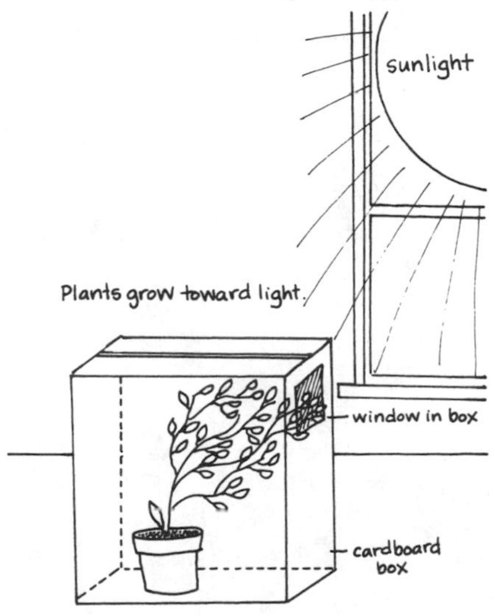

Fine points to discuss with children
Why is the plant growing toward the "window" of the milk carton?
(The light enters through the window and the plant seeks light. The plant needs the energy from the light to grow and produce its own food supply.)

2. Invertebrate Animal and Light

Materials Earthworm or mealworms (beetle larvae); black paper; white paper; Tensor light.

Procedure
- Place the black and the white papers side by side so that one sheet of paper is tucked slightly under the other. Have a child shine the light on the papers. Place the animal on the paper so that it is touching both sheets of paper.
- Have the children observe where the animal moves. Does it move toward the black or the white paper? Have the children repeat the experiment a few times to see if there is a consistency to the animal's response or behavior.

Fine points to discuss with children
Why do these animals prefer one piece of paper to the other?
(The black paper will feel warmer to these animals because the black paper will absorb heat from the light, whereas the white paper will reflect heat off and will feel cooler to them.)

Do these animals prefer black or white?
(These animals usually prefer black. They are accustomed to living in or on the ground where it is warm, damp, and dark.)

Further Resources

Suggested Books for Children

Dewey Decimal Classification Numbers for light are: 535 and 612.

Alexenberg, Melvin L., *Light and Sight.* Englewood Cliffs, New Jersey: Prentice-Hall, 1969. (A cartoon-style picture book illustrating experiments, with helpful explanations.)

Branley, F. M., *Light and Darkness.* New York: Thomas Y. Crowell, 1975.

Bulla, Clyde, *What Makes a Shadow?* New York: Scholastic Book Services, 1962.

Goor, Ron and Nancy, *Shadows.* New York: Thomas Y. Crowell, 1981.

Newing, F. E., and Richard Bowood, *Light, Mirrors, and Lenses, A Ladybird Junior Science Book.* Loughborough, England: Wills and Hepworth, 1962. (A small picture book with excellent illustrations and experiments.)

Pine, Tillie, and Joseph Levine, *Light All Around.* New York: McGraw-Hill, 1961.

Schwartz, Julius, *Magnify and Find Out Why.* New York: Scholastic Book Services, 1972. (Interesting illustrations of simple things to look at with a magnifying glass.)

Simon, Hilda, *The Magic of Color.* New York: Lothrop and Lee, 1981.

Walter, Marion, *The Magic Mirror Book.* New York: Scholastic Book Services, 1971. (Good for young children. Comes with a small mirror that can be used on the pages while the book is being used.)

Watson, Philip, *Light Fantastic.* New York: Lothrop, Lee and Shepard, 1982. (Pages filled with numerous colorful illustrations of experiments.)

Resource Books for More Ideas

Beeler, Nelson Fredrick, and Franklyn Branley, *Experiments with Light.* New York: Thomas Y. Crowell, 1964.

Freeman, Mae and Ira, *Fun and Experiments with Light.* New York: Random House, 1963. (Interesting experiments illustrated with large black and white photographs.)

Gramet, Charles, *Light and Sight.* New York: Abelard, 1963.

Healey, Frederick, *Light and Color.* New York: Golden Press, 1966.

Highland, Harold, *The How and Why Wonder Book of Light and Color.* New York: Wonder Books, 1963.

Ruchlis, Human, *Wonders of Light, A Picture Story of How and Why We See.* New York: Harper, 1960.

Scott, John, *What Is Sound?* New York: Parents Press, 1973.

8
AIR AND WATER

Objectives

- For children to become aware that air is practically everywhere.
- For children to develop an awareness that air takes up space.
- For children to understand that air has force that can push or pull objects.
- For children to develop an awareness that air pressure can create a suction that can lift or hold things in place.
- For children to develop an awareness that moving air can cause movement and/or lift.
- For children to become aware that water has and exerts pressure.
- For children to develop an awareness that the surface of still water is "sticky" and can stretch.
- For children to become familiar with some of the common properties of water such as: water is transparent, flows easily, has weight, can dissolve things, can act as a filter, can be absorbed.
- For children to become familiar with the kinds of materials that can float in water.
- For children to develop an awareness of buoyancy, boat design, and load.

**All items with double asterisks indicate that the information is too abstract and too complicated for young children to understand or comprehend. It is included to enhance parent or teacher background only.

General Background Information for Parents and Teachers

Air It is an invisible gas that does not weigh much. It is all around us. We live in an ocean of air. It is essential to plant and animal life. Air is the fuel of life. We can live for a few days without food, but no more than five minutes without air.

Oxygen A part of the air we breathe in. People use oxygen and give off carbon dioxide.

Carbon dioxide A part of the air we breathe out. Plants use carbon dioxide and give off oxygen. Plants help purify our air.

Bubble A small globule of gas that is trapped in a liquid or a solid, as in carbonated soda or in hardened glass.

Displacement of air Air takes up space. When another substance moves in to occupy the space the air is in, the air is displaced.

Displacement of water by air This occurs when air forces or pushes water out of a space it is occupying. For example: Liquids flow more easily from closed cans when two holes are punched into the lid. Two holes allow the air to displace the liquid; air goes in one hole, and liquid comes out the other hole. Otherwise, the air pressure outside the can would slow down the liquid flow. Air entering the can equalizes the air pressure on the outside of the can, allowing the liquid to flow.

Compressed air Air that has been squeezed and compressed into a smaller area than it originally occupied. Compressed air has energy. Examples of machines that use the force of compressed air are: spray cans, air hammers, and pneumatic drills.

Air pressure Air pressure is the force of air per square inch. Differential air pressure occurs when the force of air is not the same in all directions. We usually say "air pressure" rather than "differential air pressure." Differential air pressure is like Indian arm wrestling. If both forces are equal no movement takes place. If one force is stronger than the other, the stronger force or pressure overpowers the weaker force or pressure and movement takes place. Examples of machines that use differential air pressure to do work are: vacuum cleaners, plungers, eye droppers, drinking straws.

Pressure The amount of force per unit of area. The larger the area over which a force is distributed, the less pressure on a given point. The smaller the area over which a force is spread, the more pressure will be felt on a given point. For example: The corner of a brick feels heavier resting on the palm of your hand than a brick lying flat on your palm.

Cohesion The ability of a substance such as water to stick to itself.

Surface tension It is caused by the force per unit of area on the surface of the liquid due to the cohesion of the liquid.

Water pressure The force per unit area due to the weight of a volume of water. The pressure or force of water increases with depth. When an object is submerged beneath the surface of water, the water pressure at any given depth is the same in all directions.

Matter Matter refers to anything that has weight and takes up space. Everything that "is" is matter.

Mass Refers to the amount of material or matter in an object or substance. For example: A marshmallow is a marshmallow whether it is thick and compressed, or light and fluffy. The matter in the marshmallow remains that of a marshmallow.

Weight Refers to gravitational pull. It is the force of gravity on an object. Weight is equal to the mass of an object times the pull of gravity.

Volume The amount of space "matter" occupies. It is found by measuring an object or substance by its length, width, and height (or depth). ($V = l$ times w times h.) Objects that have the same weight do not necessarily have the same volume.

Density The formula for finding density is: $D = \frac{W}{V}$. This means that density is equal to weight divided by volume. Denser liquids such as salt water have a greater buoyant force than less-dense liquids. This is why oil and water separate and level off in a bottle. Denser liquids buoy up less-dense liquids. Water is denser than oil.

Buoyancy The tendency or ability to stay afloat is caused by the balancing of forces, such as water pressure pushing up and gravity pulling down on a floating or immersed object. An object that is placed in water floats when the buoyant or upward force is greater than its own weight. It sinks when the force of its own weight is greater than the buoyant force.

Why large steel ships float Large steel ships are able to float because they are filled with passenger and cargo areas. They are not solid steel because passenger and cargo areas are filled with things lighter than water such as air, or oil. Also, the density has nothing to do with the size. Large ships have a relatively low density. A ship displaces a weight of water equal to its own weight. The lighter the ship, the higher in the water it will ride. As cargo is added, the ship will ride lower and displace more water. When a ship does not displace an amount of water equal to its own weight, it sinks. A steel ship compacted into a ball would be the same weight but would have less volume and would sink. When ships fill with water their density or weight increases and the buoyant force from the water cannot support their weight. So ships that fill with too much water sink.

Why submarines can dive and surface in water When a submarine surfaces, it takes in air, and compressors compress air into bottles. The bottles of compressed air are stored. When the sub dives beneath the surface, special chambers called ballast tanks fill with water. As the water enters the sub ballast tanks, the sub sinks to lower depths. When the crew decides to surface, the crew changes the density of the sub by opening up the valves on the bottles of compressed air. The compressed air pushes or blows the water out of the ballast tanks. As the water is pushed or blown out by air, the ballast tanks fill up with air and the density changes. This makes the sub weigh less. When the sub weighs less, the net force from the water exceeds the weight of the submarine and the sub is pushed upward due to the buoyancy of water.

Volume of water displaced Water cannot be compressed easily. For everyday purposes, we assume it is incompressible. When objects are submerged in water, they displace an amount of water equal to their own volume, and the water level rises. An object with more volume displaces more water. Two objects cannot occupy the same space at the same time. A completely submerged balloon filled with air will displace the same amount of water as a heavy rock with the same volume.

Archimedes A Greek philosopher, mathematician, and scientist who lived in 200 B.C. He made discoveries about mechanics, and water at rest.

Archimedes' Principle The weight of water* displaced by a floating object is exactly equal to the weight of the object. For example, because standard measuring cups are calibrated to the density of water, water can be weighed by measuring its volume in a measuring cup. You can find out how many ounces a given amount of water weighs by reading the measuring cup. If you place water in a large-capacity measuring cup and place a piece of fruit like a pear or an orange in the measuring cup, partially filled with water, you can then measure the weight of the piece of fruit by observing how much the water level rises in the measuring cup. The actual increase in ounces of water is the weight of the fruit. The fruit will displace an amount of water equal to its own weight.

WEIGHING FRUIT IN WATER

Activities and Procedures

I. Air Is Practically Everywhere

1. Catching Air

Materials Plastic bags.

*Archimedes' Principle applies to all liquids.

Procedure

- Catch some air in a plastic bag by pulling the opened bag through the air. Twist the end of the bag so that the air stays inside.
- Ask the children what is inside the bag. They will probably respond "air." If they don't, explain to them that air is inside the bag and that we are surrounded by an ocean of air. Tell them to move their arms around in a swimming style. They will be able to feel their arms pushing air around.
- Give each child a plastic bag and tell them to catch some air. (**Do not be surprised if very young children try to catch air where you caught your air. They may not understand that air is everywhere and that they can catch it in front of themselves.)

Fine points to discuss with children

Where is air?
(Air is practically all around us.)

Can we see air?
(Not usually.)

Can we feel air?
(Yes, if we move around quickly.)

Can we smell air?
(Yes, if there are molecules of odors mixed in the air. We can smell odors in the air from such things as food, flowers and plants, animals, decaying materials, and moisture, and/or odors caused from some pollutants in the air.)

2. An Empty Bottle

Materials An empty plastic detergent squeeze bottle; a feather; a bucket of water; newspaper to absorb possible mess from water.

Procedure

- Show the children that the bottle is empty. Ask them if there is anything in it. Some children may respond "air."
- Tell them you are going to squeeze the bottle. Place a feather in front of the squeeze hole. Ask them if they think anything will come out of the empty bottle and how they will be able to know.

If air comes out of the bottle, what will happen to the feather?
(It will move.)

- Have a child squeeze the bottle into the water. Ask the children to observe if anything comes out of the bottle into the water. (They will observe little bubbles coming out of the bottle into the water.) Ask the children if they know what has caused the bubbles to appear. (Air inside the bottle has made the bubbles appear. Air is inside the bubbles.)

3. Finding Air in Seeds

Materials Seeds like lima beans or peas; a clear plastic glass of water.

Procedure

• Show the children the seeds. Ask them if air is inside the seeds.

How can they find out?
(By placing the seeds in water. If air bubbles can be seen, that means the seeds contain some air.)

• Place the seeds in water and observe whether air bubbles appear.

4. Lungs

Materials None.

Procedure

• Take a deep breath. Have the children do the same. Ask them what they are breathing in and out. (Air.)
• Have the children take another deep breath, but this time tell them to hold their breath for as long as they can.
What happens?
(We cannot stop breathing. Our body forces us to take another breath.)

• Ask the children to feel their rib cage as they take a deep breath and let their breath out.

Where does the air go when it enters our body?
(It enters our lungs.) *Explain:* Our rib cage protects our lungs. When new air comes into our lungs, our lungs and rib cage expand. When used air leaves our lungs, our rib cage contracts or gets smaller. All living things need air to live.

• **Explain to children that plastic bags are dangerous to play with. If a plastic bag is near our mouth it can prevent us from breathing.

II. Air Takes Up Space

1. Containment of Air

Materials Balloon.

Procedure

• Blow up the balloon.

• *What is inside the balloon?*
(Air.)

• *If the air was not inside the balloon, what would happen to the balloon?*
(The balloon would be flat. Air takes up space.)

• *What happens to a tire that loses its air?*
(It becomes flat. If air does not fill a space, an object loses its shape.)

2. Displacement of Air by Water

Materials A large empty juice can with a small hole in the bottom end; a bucket of water.

Procedure

• Turn the juice can upside-down so that the end with a hole is on top. Have the children place their hands near the hole as the can is pushed down into the water. They will feel a surge of air come out of the can as the can enters the water.

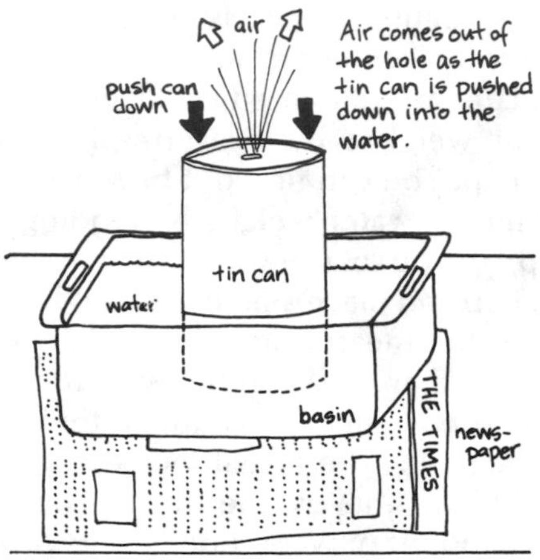

• Ask the children what they feel coming out of the can. They will probably respond "air." Ask them where the air came from. (It was inside of the can.)
• Ask the children what is pushing the air out of the can. (The water is pushing the air out. Two things cannot take up the same space at the same time. As water comes in, it pushes the air out.)

3. Air Pocket

Materials A bucket of water; a clear plastic glass; a tissue; newspaper to absorb possible mess from water.

Procedure

• Push the tissue into the glass so that it stays in place when the glass is turned upside-down.
• Tell the children that you are going to choose a child to place the glass with the tissue into the water. Ask if they think the tissue will get wet.
• Have a child hold the glass upside-down vertically and push it down into the water. Have the children observe that the tissue is still dry.

Fine points to discuss with children
Why can't water enter the glass?

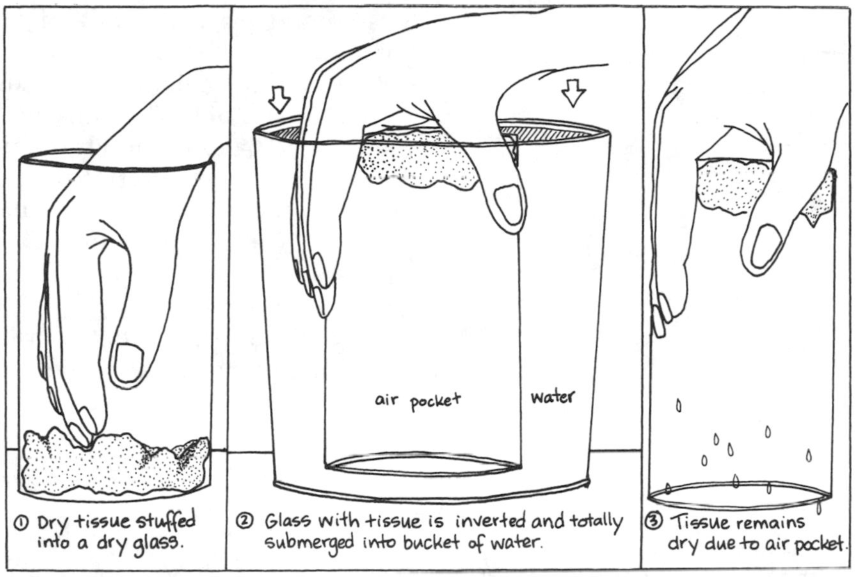

air pocket
water
① Dry tissue stuffed into a dry glass.
② Glass with tissue is inverted and totally submerged into bucket of water.
③ Tissue remains dry due to air pocket.

AIR POCKET

(Air has already taken up the space inside the glass. Air and water cannot take up the same space at the same time.)

Why is the tissue still dry?
(Air takes up space. The water cannot move into the area that is occupied by the air. The tissue is in the space where the air is, so the tissue stays dry. The air has formed a pocket around the tissue inside the glass. There is no water inside the glass, only air.)

4. Air Takes Up Space

Materials A cork from a wine bottle; a clear plastic glass; a large bowl of water; newspaper to absorb possible mess from water.

Procedure
- Float the cork in the bowl of water. Ask the children if they can think of a way to make the cork sink. Listen to their responses and try their ideas.

Air Takes Up Space

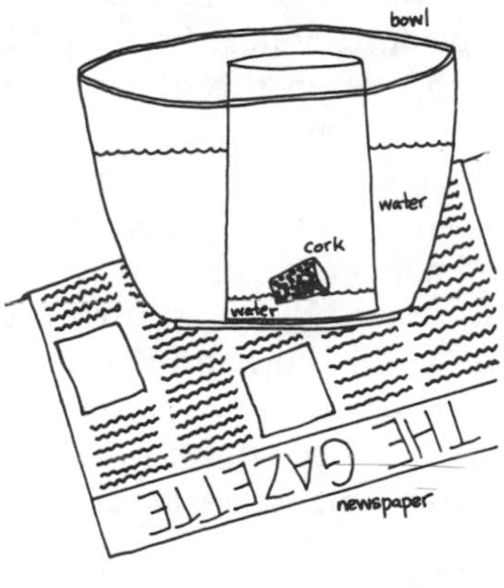

- Turn the empty plastic glass upside-down and place it on top of the floating cork. Have a child push the glass down into the water vertically. (The cork will sink.)

Fine points to discuss with children
Why does the cork sink?
(The air inside of the glass pushed the water out of the space it was occupying. The cork sank because the water was no longer lifting it up. Corks do not float in air. Corks float in water because they weigh less than the water. Corks are heavier than air so they do not float in air.)

5. Displacement of Water by Air

Materials A basin filled with water; a glass jar; a piece of plastic tubing or an old garden hose about 3 feet long; newspaper to absorb possible mess from water.

Procedure
- Place the jar inside the basin filled with water. Lay the jar on its side so that it can fill with water. Turn the jar upside-down in the water so that the bottom of the jar is protruding above the water line in the basin. Place one end of the tubing into the upside-down jar filled with water. See diagram on next page.
- Tell the children you are going to blow on one end of the tubing. Ask them what they think will happen. Ask the following kinds of questions:

What will be inside of the tube when you blow through it?
(Air.)

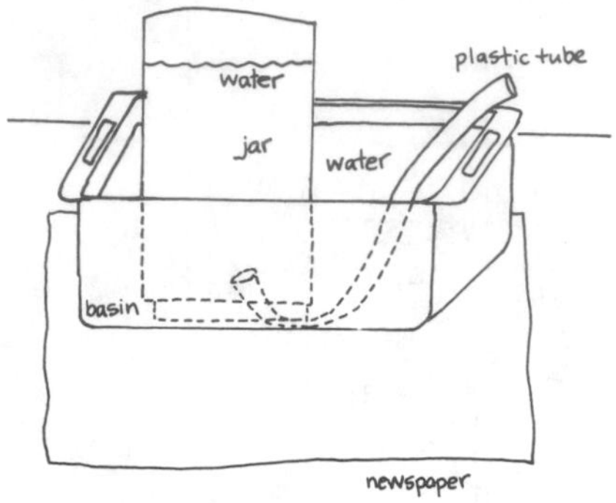

AIR DISPLACES WATER

Where will the air go?
(Into the glass jar.)

What will happen to the water inside of the jar?
(It will be forced out of the jar because the air takes up space.)

How will you know that air is going into the jar?
(Bubbles will be seen in the water. Then there will be no more water in the jar and the jar will fall over on its side in the water.)

When you drink milk with a straw and blow into your drink, what happens?
(Bubbles of air appear.)

III. Air Has Force

1. "Breath" Power

Materials Pencil.

Procedure
- Ask the children what will happen to the pencil if it is blown on. They will most likely respond that it will move.
- Have a child blow on the pencil. Have the children observe the movement that takes place.

Why does the pencil move?
(The air which takes up space is being pushed. The movement of the air from one place to another causes the pencil to move. A push or pull that causes movement to take place is called a force. One of the properties of air is force or pressure.)

2. Air's Accelerated Force Lifts

Materials Several large books; a long balloon.

Procedure
- Ask the children if they think that a balloon can lift a pile of books. Then place the balloon near the edge of a table and place the pile of books on top of the balloon.
- Blow up the balloon while the pile of books is resting on top of it. The children may be surprised to see that the balloon can lift the pile of books.
- Explain to the children that the force from your air added to the air inside of the balloon has lifted the books. **The air pressure inside the balloon per square inch is more than the pressure per square inch from the pile of books.
- If the children can inflate a balloon, give them one to inflate so they can repeat the experiment by themselves.

AIR'S FORCE CAN LIFT

3. Air Supports Water and Weight

Materials A clear plastic glass; a bucket of water; newspaper to help absorb possible mess from water; a top from a cottage cheese container or a piece of cardboard.

Procedure
- Fill the glass with water. Cover the top of the glass with a cover from a cottage cheese container or a piece of cardboard. Tell the children you are going to turn the glass upside-down. Ask the children what will happen to the top when the glass is turned upside-down. Listen to their responses.
- Carefully turn the glass of water upside down while holding the lid on top of the open end of the glass.
- Remove your hand from the lid when the glass of water is upside-down. You can turn the glass on its side and shake the glass up and down. The water will not come out. The force of air is pressing the lid to the rim of the glass. The force of air pressure seals the lid in position on the rim. If the air seal is broken, the

water will fall out. If you press hard on the sides of the plastic glass, it will break the air seal.
• Have children do the experiment on their own.

4. Air Lifts Liquids

Materials Drinking straws; a drink or water in glasses.

Procedure
• Have children place their drinking straws inside their drinks.
• Ask them if they can think of a way to lift their drinks without putting their mouths on their straws.
• Show the children how to place their fingers on the top end of the drinking straw while it is in their drinks. Have them lift their straws out of the drink; part of the drink will still be in the straw.
• Ask the children what is inside the straw that has helped lift the drink up and has kept it inside of the straw. (The force of air pressure supplies a push or a pull to keep the drink inside of the straw.)

5. Jet Power

Materials A balloon.

Procedure
• Inflate the balloon, but do not tie it shut. Hold the inflated balloon.
• Tell the children you are going to let the balloon lose its air. Ask them what they think will happen if you let go of the balloon. Listen to their responses.
• Let the balloon go. Have the children observe what happens. (The balloon will "fly" around wildly until all of the air is out.)
• Explain to the children that air is a gas. When the air in the balloon was squeezed into a tiny space, the air became compressed gas. Compressed gas has stored energy. When air is compressed into a balloon, it has stored energy. The air in the balloon was like a fuel. It made the balloon move forward. When all of the air was out of the balloon, it was out of gas and the balloon stopped moving.

Fine points to discuss with children
Why did the balloon fly?
(The air coming out of the balloon forced the balloon to move. The air coming out pushed or propelled the balloon.)

Does the amount of air inside the balloon affect how long it can fly around?
(Yes. The more air or fuel there is the longer the flight will last.)

Is there a way to make the balloon fly in a straight path?
(Yes, but the design of the balloon has to change. The balloon's force of air has to be controlled for it to fly straight.)

6. Guided Jet Power (Equal and Opposite Reaction)

Materials A long balloon; a paper bag; two paper clips; two chairs; 15 feet of nylon fishing line.

Procedure
• Tie the fishing line on to two chairs. Pull the two chairs apart so that the fishing line is fairly taut.
• Open up two paper clips so that one end of each paper clip can be hooked on to the top side of the paper bag.
• Place the balloon inside of the paper bag and inflate the balloon while it is inside of the bag.
• Mount the "balloon bag" on to the stretched fishing line with the paper clips that have been opened. See diagram.

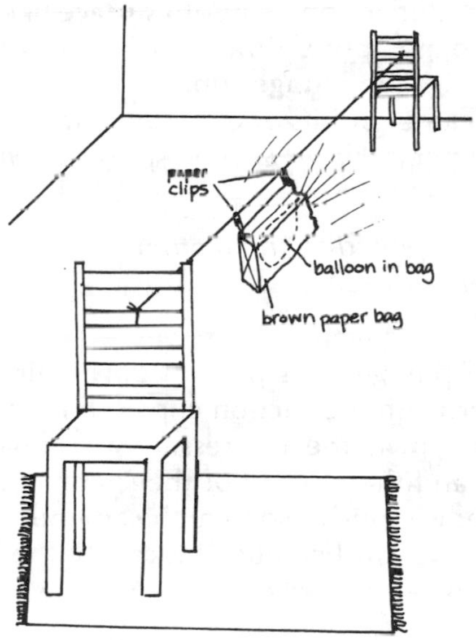

• Let the "balloon bag" loose. Have the children observe how the balloon travels in a straight line on the fishing line, which acts as a "guidance system" to control the flight direction of the balloon.
• Give each child a paper bag, a balloon, and two paper clips to do the experiment on their own.
• *Note:* With older children, measurements can be taken to see which jet-powered balloon bag travels the farthest, and the variables that affect distance can be analyzed.

Fine points to discuss with children
Why does the balloon push forward in a straight line?
(It moves in a straight line because it is guided by the

fishing line. It moves forward because air is being released. Jet engines operate in the same way.)
**Newton's classic Third Law of Motion states that for every action there is an equal and opposite reaction. The movement is in the direction opposite to that from which the force is applied. In the example of the balloon, the air that is being released is under pressure and the compressed air comes out of the balloon nozzle. This causes a movement to occur in the opposite direction, which causes the balloon to propel itself forward.

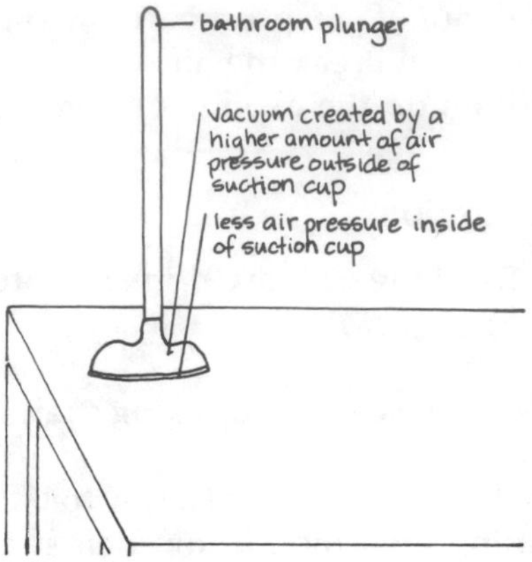

AIR PRESSURE HOLDS THINGS IN PLACE

IV. Air Pressure

1. "Plunger" Power

Materials Bathroom plunger; a feather or bits of paper; spoon or screwdriver.

Procedure

• Place the plunger on a smooth surface like a desk or a floor. Do not press down on it. Ask one of the children to lift the plunger up.

• Place a feather or bits of paper near the suction cup of the plunger. Have a child press down on the plunger.

What has happened to the feather?
(It has been moved.)

What caused the feather to move?
(When the plunger was pushed down, air came out from underneath the suction cup. Before the plunger was pushed down, the air pressure was equal on both the inside and the outside of the suction cup. When the plunger was pushed down, the air underneath the suction cup was pushed out. This caused the feather or the bits of paper to move.)

• Now that the plunger has been pushed down, ask a child to lift the plunger up. It is very difficult to do unless the suction seal of air is broken. (To do this, slide a spoon or screwdriver under the plunger's suction cup to break the air seal or suction.)

Fine points to discuss with children
Why is it so difficult to lift the plunger?
(The air pressure on the outside of the suction cup is greater than the air pressure on the inside of the plunger's suction cup. There is no air to push up from underneath the suction cup. So, the downward push of air is stronger and the pressure or force from the outside air is extremely strong. This makes it difficult to lift the plunger up.)

How does air pressure hold things in place?
(By pressing in on them.)

2 The Ruler Breaks (Pressure from Volume)

Materials A slat of wood from an orange crate or a thin yardstick; large sheets of newspaper; a hammer.

Procedure

• Place the slat of wood or the yardstick on a desk. Cover the wood with a few pieces of newspaper. Allow the edge of the wood slat to stick out beyond the desk. Be sure that the newspaper is flat and centered on the wood slat.

• Tell the children you are going to hit the wood with your fist or with a hammer. Ask them what they think will happen.

Will the newspaper pop up?
(No.)

Will the wood break?
(Yes.)

• Hit the wood hard and *fast* with a tight fist or a hammer. (The wood will break.)

A protruding ruler will break when held in place by a newspaper, then struck hard and fast.

Fine point to discuss with children
Why did the wood break?
(The wood broke because the newspaper had a great deal of air pressure pushing down on it. This large amount of air pressure prevented the wood from popping up.)

3. The Water Stops

Materials A nail; a hammer; an empty plastic liter soda bottle with screw-on cap; water.

Procedure
- Use the hammer to puncture the plastic bottle with the nail. Make the hole on the side of the bottle about 3 inches up from the bottom.
- Hold the bottle over the basin. Fill the bottle with water. The children will be able to observe the water leaving the side of the bottle through the hole.
- Ask the children if they can think of a way to keep the water from flowing out of the hole in the bottle.
- Tell the children that you are going to screw the cap on to the opening of the bottle. Ask them if they think this action will keep the water from flowing out. (It will.)
- Have the children repeat the step above on their own.

Fine points to discuss with children
Why does the water stop flowing out of the hole on the side of the bottle when the cap is screwed on tightly to the bottle?
(In order for the water to flow out of the hole, air is needed to displace the water. When the cap is screwed on very tight it prevents air from entering the bottle. When there is no air to equalize the pressure, the water stops flowing because a vacuum is created within the bottle. A second hole allows air to displace water and equalizes the air pressure.

Many children have the misconception that air pushes the water out of the container. Air does not "push out" the water. It merely equalizes the air pressure, takes away the vacuum, and allows the force of gravity to pull the water out due to its own weight.)

4. Two Holes Are Needed

Materials A full can of juice; a can opener; glasses to pour drink into.

Procedure
- Open the can of juice by puncturing one hole in the top of the can. Try to pour the juice. It will not flow evenly. Ask the children if they can suggest what to do to make the juice flow from the can easier.
- Puncture a second hole in the top of the can. (The juice will flow out faster and easier.)

Fine points to discuss with children
Why does the juice can make sounds when there is only one hole in the can?
(As the juice leaves the can, air enters the can and takes up space in the can.)

Why does the juice flow out more easily when two holes are in the top of the can rather than one hole?
(In order for the juice to flow out, air has to enter the can. The first hole allows air to enter the can, but the air flow restriction prevents the air from entering and prevents the juice from flowing out easily. When there are two holes the flow of air and hence liquid is more even and quiet.)

5. Coins "Stick" (Holding Power from Pressure)

Materials A quarter, dime, or penny.

Procedure
- Show the children the coin or coins. Tell them that you can make the coin or coins stick to their forehead. Ask them if they can guess how this can be done.
- Press the coin on a child's forehead hard and count to ten, or place some moisture on the coin and place it on the child's head. Either way it will stay stuck until the air seal is broken. Air pressure will hold the coin in place.
- Have children repeat this procedure alone or with another child.

6. Fountain from Compressed Air

Materials Newspaper to absorb possible mess from water; an empty liter soda bottle; a wad of clay; a drinking straw; a large basin of water.

Procedure

• Fill the bottle with about two cups of water. Pack clay around the drinking straw and insert the straw with clay on it inside of the bottle opening. The clay should be packed between the straw and the neck of the bottle opening so that the top has an air-tight seal. The water level in the bottle should be high enough so that part of the straw is underneath the water level.

• Tell the children that you are going to blow air into the straw. Ask them what they think will happen.

• Blow into the straw with your mouth. Put as much air into the straw as you can. Then when you cannot blow any more, step aside quickly so you will not be sprayed with the water coming out of the straw.

• Give each child a plastic drinking straw, a plastic soda bottle, and some clay so that children can repeat this procedure on their own.

Fine point to discuss with children

What happened to the air inside of the bottle when more air was blown into the bottle?

(The addition of more air increased the air pressure inside of the bottle. This increase in air pressure was able to push the water up the straw to create a fountain effect. The additional air caused the air inside of the bottle to be squeezed. Compressed air has stored energy.)

7. Pull the Bag out of the Can

Materials A large empty juice can; a plastic bag large enough to fit inside of the juice can and hang over the rim of the can; a rubber band large enough to fit over the can.

Procedure

• Place the opened plastic bag inside the large juice can. Press all of the air out of the can so that the plastic bag liner is touching the inner sides of the can. Pull the plastic liner over the rim and secure it with a rubber band.

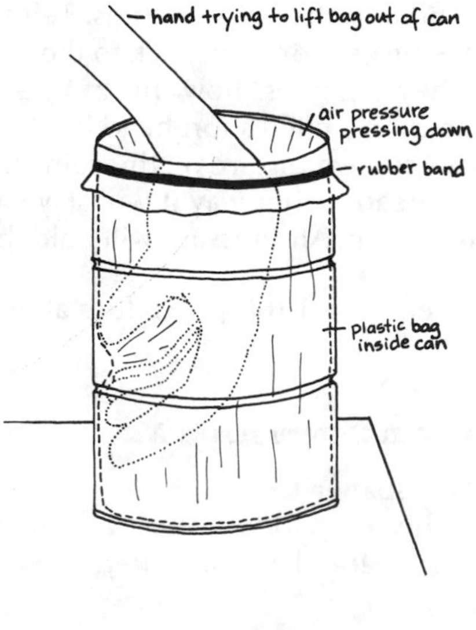

• Ask a child to reach inside of the can and try to remove the bag from the can without making a hole in the plastic bag. The force of air pressure pressing in on the plastic bags makes it practically impossible to pull the bag out. The air pressure is too strong. Unless the bag breaks or the rubber band pops, the plastic bag cannot be pulled out.

8. Suction Power

Materials Two clear plastic cups; a round balloon.

Procedure

• Tell the children that you intend to lift the two plastic cups up and have them stick to the balloon when it is blown up. Ask them if they can suggest how this feat can be accomplished. Try out their suggestions.

• Place the balloon in your mouth so it will be ready to inflate. Hold the two plastic cups in each hand so that the openings of the two cups are facing the balloon. The cups should almost be touching and the deflated balloon should be hanging in-between the two glasses. See diagram.

When the balloon is inflated, remove your hands from the two cups so the cups will stick to the balloon due to suction.
balloon

• As you blow the balloon up, the two cups will stick to the balloon.

• Give each child a balloon and two plastic glasses so children can repeat this procedure alone.

Fine point to discuss with children

Why do the cups stay put on the balloon?

(As the air inflates the balloon it creates an air seal over the openings of the cups. The force of air pressure holds the cups to the surface of the balloon. If the air escapes from the balloon the air pressure inside of the cups will become equal to the air pressure outside of the cups and the cups will fall off the balloon.)

9. Siphon

Materials Two basins, one filled with water; a clear plastic hose or tubing about 3 feet long; newspaper to absorb possible mess from water.

Procedure

- Place the basin filled with water on a table or chair. Place the empty basin on the floor near the basin filled with water. **It is important that the basin filled with water be situated so that the water level is at a higher level than the empty basin. **Water seeks its own level.
- Fill the rubber hose with water. Be sure there is no air left in the hose. You can tell when there is no more air left in the hose because air bubbles will stop coming out of the hose. Cover each end of the hose with a thumb.
- Tell the children you are going to make the water move from the basin filled with water to the basin that is empty. Ask them if they know how that can happen. Listen to their responses.
- Place one end of the hose into the basin filled with water. Be sure that the end of the hose is in the water and that no air is inside of the hose. Keep your thumb on the end of the hose.
- Place the other end of the hose in the empty basin. Remove your thumbs from the ends of the hoses.
- Have the children observe what happens to the water. It will move from one basin to the other. The hose or tube is acting as a siphon.
- Let children experiment with the siphon on their own.

Fine point to discuss with children

Why does the water flow through the tube or hose from one basin to another basin?

(The water in the hose flows downward. One basin is lower than the other. Water is pulled down because of the force of gravity. A partial air vacuum is created in the hose. The water is forced up the hose before it flows down the lower basin. It flows up because air pressure is pressing down on the surface of the basin filled with water. The flow of water will continue as long as the water level of one container is at a higher level than the water level of the other container and as long as there is no air in the hose to break the partial vacuum.

V. Air Streams and Air Currents Can Cause Movement and/or Lift

1. Moving Air Causes Lift

Materials Two clear plastic glasses that are identical in size.

Procedure

- Gently put one glass inside of the other.
- Hold the two glasses near your mouth. Blow on the side of the glasses near the top rim. The glass inside of the other glass will pop up.
- Explain to the children that the force of air pressure from the air being blown on the rim of the glass creates a current or wind that causes a lift action to take place.
- Have children repeat second step above on their own.

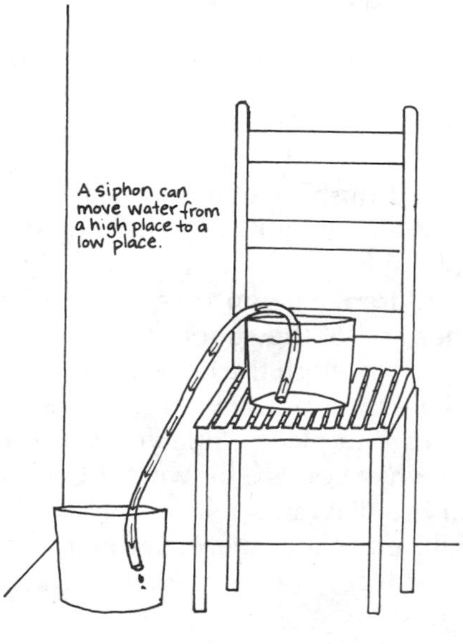

A siphon can move water from a high place to a low place.

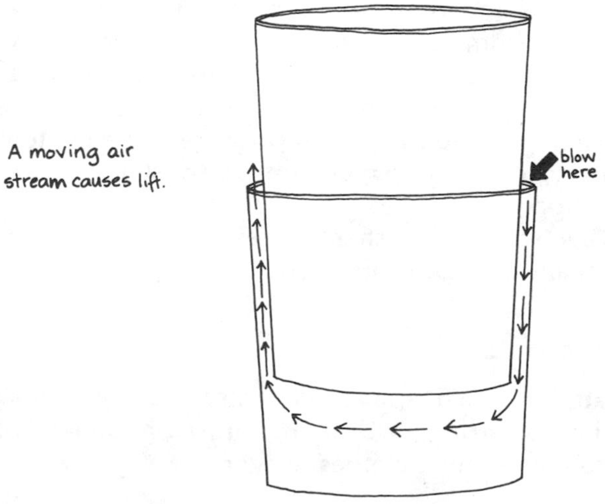

A moving air stream causes lift.
blow here

2. Moving Air Keeps Things Put

Materials A newspaper; an index card.

Procedure

• Place a flat sheet of the newspaper on your chest. Move quickly and the newspaper will stay put. (Moving air helps hold things in place. Gravity pulls the paper down, while frictional force against the chest helps keep the paper up. The frictional force occurs due to the pressure of the paper against the chest, which in turn is due to pressure from the moving air.)

• Fold the index card so that two of the long sides are folded down to form a tunnel. See diagram.

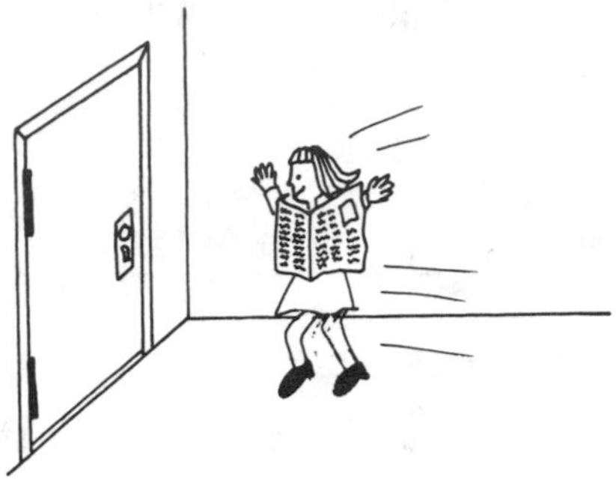

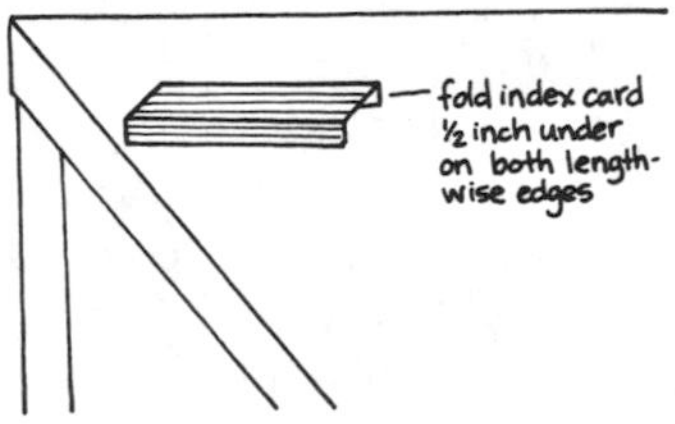
fold index card ½ inch under on both length-wise edges

• Blow on the tunnel. Try to make the card tunnel turn over. Blow very hard, blow soft. Ask the children if they can blow hard enough to make the paper tunnel blow up and/or over. (It cannot be done. The air coming from your breath is blowing a strong wind. The wind is pushing the air forward and lowering the air pressure. The top or roof of the paper tunnel is caving in due to a loss of air pressure inside the tunnel. This causes the paper tunnel to stay in a fixed position.)

• Give each child a sheet of newspaper to experiment with and to repeat first step above.

3. Bernoulli Effect

Materials Two apples with stems or two inflated balloons; string; a drinking straw or tube to blow through; a metal clothes hanger.

Procedure

• Cut two pieces of string about two feet long. Tie a piece of string to each apple stem or to each of the inflated balloons. Tie the other end of each string to a metal clothes hanger. Hook the clothes hanger onto the wood molding of a doorway or other suitable object. Separate the two strings on the hanger so that the two hanging apples or balloons are about one inch apart. See diagram.

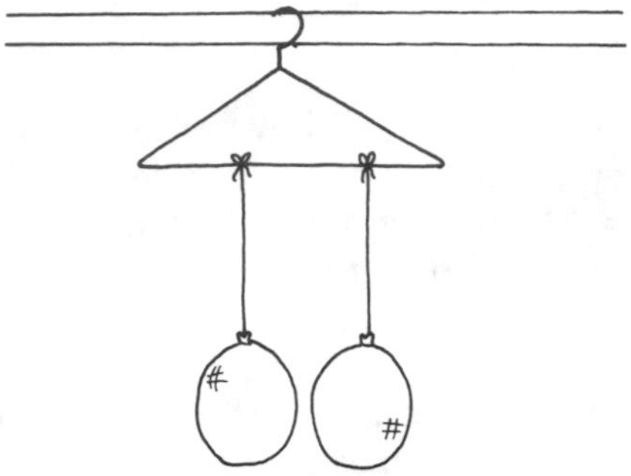

• Wait for the two apples or balloons to be hanging motionless. Tell the children you are going to choose a child to blow air through the straw between the two apples or balloons. Ask them what they think will happen to the two apples or balloons.

Will the balloons move away from each other or will they move closer together?

(They will move closer together. When the air between the two apples or balloons is pushed away by the air coming out of the drinking straw, the air pressure in the middle will be lower. The lower air pressure in the middle will cause the two apples or balloons to bounce together.)

4. The "Card" Stays up

Materials A spool of thread; a 3 × 5 index card; a straight pin.

Procedure

• Have a child push a straight pin through an index card. Place the card with the pin going through it on the hole of a spool.

• Tell the children that you are going to place your lips on the other end of the spool's hole and that you will be blowing air through the hole of the spool on to the index card with the pin going through it.

• Hold the card in place while you blow. Then let go of the card while you are blowing. (It will stay next to the spool.) See diagram.

• Have children repeat the experiment on their own with a different spool of thread.

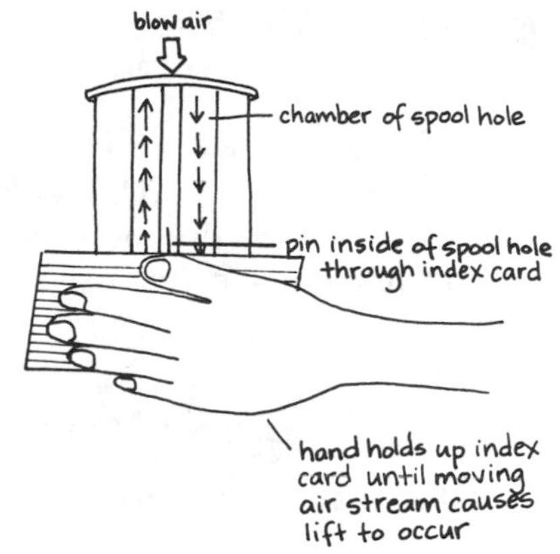

Fine points to discuss with children
What happens to the index card?
(The card stays close to the spool. The air pressure becomes lower because there is a stream of moving air coming through the spool's hole.)

When does the the card fall?
(The index card falls when the air stream stops flowing because you stop blowing.)

5. Atomizer Model

Materials Newspaper to absorb possible mess from water; a clear plastic glass; one drinking straw; a pair of scissors.

Procedure
• Cut a straw in half. Place one straw into a glass of water. Hold the straw vertically in the water with your fingers. The straw should not be touching the bottom of the glass. Place the other straw in your mouth and blow through it hard, directly over the top end of the straw that is in the glass of water. See diagram.

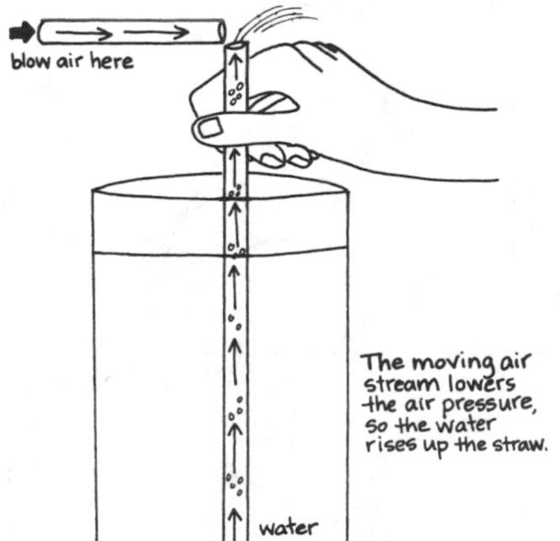

• Have the children observe what happens to the water. It will rise up the straw and be sprayed or atomized.
• Give each child a straw to cut in half so the children can repeat the first step on their own.

Fine points to discuss with children
Why does the water rise through the straw?
(The water rises through the vertical straw because the moving air stream from the horizontal straw lowers the air pressure in the vertical straw.)

Why does the water become a spray?
(When the water reaches the top of the vertical straw it is met with fast-moving air. This fast air current causes the column of water to break into little water drops which form a mist or spray. The faster the air moves, the finer the mist is from the water droplets.) **Spray bottles and some perfume bottles use the same principle. You might like to examine a few. Find out how they work and where the air comes from that helps create the mist.

VI. Water Pressure

1. The Difference Between Pressure and Weight

Materials About two cups of clay or Play-Doh (see below); a plastic liter bottle of soda capped tightly and filled with water or soda; a small unopened can of tomato sauce or soup.

Homemade Play-Doh Recipe:
Ingredients

1 cup salt	2 cups water
food color	2 cups flour
4 teaspoons cream of tartar	2 tablespoons veg. oil

Mix salt and water. Add a few drops of food color. Add flour. Stir until mixed. Add remaining ingredients. Cook over a low flame, stirring until thick. Put mixture on a floured surface, and knead. (This play-doh will last several months if it is stored in an air-tight container.)

Procedure
• Have a child shape the clay or Play-Doh into a round ball and then flatten it out to make a circle about 4 inches in diameter.
• Have a child place a bottle filled with liquid on top of the clay circle. Then lift the bottle up. Have the children notice the indentation the bottle has made on the surface of the clay (shallow imprint).

• Have a child turn the bottle filled with liquid upside-down and place it on top of the clay. You will have to help balance the bottle with your finger. (See diagram.) Lift the bottle up. Have the children notice the indentation in the clay made by the filled bottle when it was upside-down (deeper dent).

THE DIFFERENCE BETWEEN PRESSURE AND WEIGHT

Was the bottle heavier when it was upside-down?
(No, but more of the weight was concentrated on a smaller surface so the bottle made a deeper imprint into the clay. There was more pressure from the small area of the filled bottle on the clay than there was from the larger surface of the bottle on the clay.)

• Have a child place an unopened can on the clay. Lift the can up. Have the children observe the imprint from the can on the surface of the clay. Ask the children how the imprint could change. Have them suggest other ways to place the can in the clay so the dent will be deeper.
• Have a child place the can in the clay at an angle so that only part of the can's rim touches the clay. (The can will not stay in this position unless you help balance it with your finger.)

Fine points to discuss with children
Why was the imprint deeper in the clay?
(The imprint was deeper when there was more pressure. The imprint had nothing to do with weight, but rather with the amount of force coming down on one area. The more force that comes down the more the pressure is on a given point.)

If you are holding a book, is there less pressure if you hold it flat and horizontal, upright and vertical, or on a corner at an angle?
(The least pressure would be in a flat, horizontal position. The most pressure would be felt if the book were held on its corner because more of the book's weight would be felt on one small section of your finger.)

2. Water Pressure Increases with Depth

Materials A nail; a hammer; a large open juice can with one lid removed, or an empty plastic liter soda bottle; water; a basin; newspaper to absorb possible mess from water; a marking pen.

Procedure
• Use the hammer and nail to puncture the can and/or the plastic bottle with holes. Place three or four holes in a vertical line about two inches apart from the bottom of the container up the side to the top of the container. Number the holes with a marking pen. The hole next to the bottom should be numbered one.
• Have a child hold the container over the basin. Fill it with water. Have the children observe the water streams coming out of the can. Ask them to tell you which "numbered" hole has water shooting out farther than the other streams. (Number one on the bottom.) See diagram.
• Ask the children which stream of water is shooting out the least. (The one near the top of the can.)

Fine point to discuss with children
Which stream has the most water pressure pushing on it?

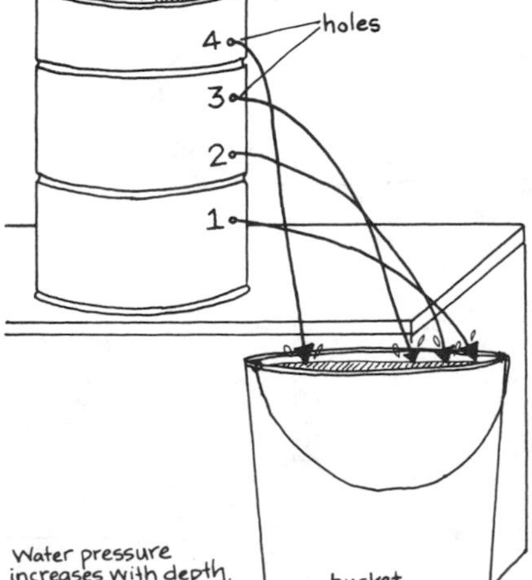

(The stream at the bottom of the bottle has the most water pressure. The weight of the water [and air] sitting above the hole opening is pressing down and making the water shoot out farther. Whereas, the top hole is a mere dribble. It does not shoot far from the container.)

3. Water Pressure Is the Same in All Directions

Materials Same as materials for preceding procedure.

Procedure

• Use the hammer and nail to puncture the can and/or plastic bottle with holes. Place three or four holes in a horizontal line about one or two inches apart near the bottom of the container.

• Have a child hold the container over the basin. Fill it with water. Have the children observe the water streams. (They will all be shooting streams of water out in different directions. Each stream of water will be shooting out the same length from the can.)

Fine point to discuss with children

Why are the streams of water all the same length?
(Each stream of water starts its flow from the same water depth. The pressure of water [and air] pushing down is the same in all directions.)

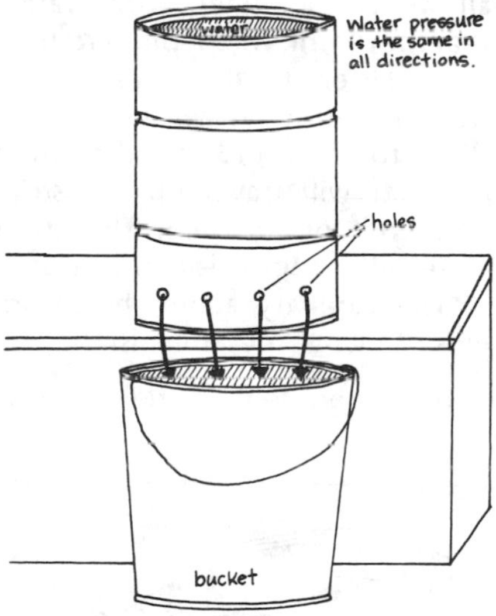
Water pressure is the same in all directions.
holes
bucket

4. Water Seeks Its Own Level

Materials A clear plastic tube or hose; a basin filled with water; newspaper to absorb possible mess from water; food color to color the water; a funnel.

Procedure

• Choose a child to add food color to the water so it can be seen more easily inside of the hose. Attach the funnel to the hose. Fill the hose with water. Lift the hose out of the water. Hold the hose so that it forms a "U" shape. Have the children observe the water level in each side of the tube. Have them notice how the water level remains the same in each side of the tube even when the tube is raised or lowered.

• Tie a loose knot in the center of the tubing. Have a child fill the knotted tube with water. (The water will still be at the same level in each side of the hose.)

• Tie the knot tighter while the water is in the hose. Have a child raise and lower the tubing. Tell the children to observe what happens to the water level. (The water level will even out on both sides of the tube, but the water will move more slowly because of the tight knot.)

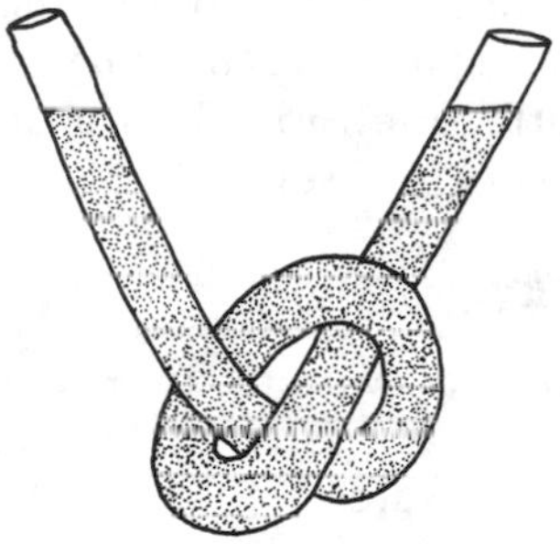
The water in the tube stays at the same level on each side of the tube.

Fine points to discuss with children

Why does the level of water on both sides of the tube stay the same?
(The air pressure on both sides of the tube is the same. This "sameness" of air pressure keeps the water level the same on both sides. When the water level is not the same, but the pressure from air is the same, as in the example of the tightly knotted tube, the water will "seek" to be at an equal level with itself.)

In which direction does water flow?
(Water tends to flow down. The force of gravity pulls it down. When water is not in a container it flows down toward sea level. When water is enclosed in a container like a hose it can move or flow up if there is water pressure to push it up.)

VII. Surface Tension

1. How Full Is Full?

Materials Two clear plastic cups; water; a basin; newspaper to absorb possible mess from water; an eye dropper or a straw; a paper towel.

Procedure

• Slowly pour water into a cup until it is full. Be sure the rim of the cup is dry.

• Fill an eye dropper or use a straw to lift water one drop at a time. Drop drops of water into the full glass of water. Ask the children how many more drops they think you will be able to drop into the full glass of water without making the water overflow from the glass. Continue to drop additional drops of water into the glass. (Many drops can be added to the full glass.)

• Have children repeat this procedure on their own.

Fine points to discuss with children

What happens to the surface of the water as more drops are added to the cup?
(The surface begins to look curved, like a lens.)

Why is the full glass able to hold so many additional drops of water after it is already full?
(Water has a surface tension. This property of water allows water to stick to itself.)

2. Water Is Sticky

Materials A cup of water; an eye dropper or a drinking straw; waxed paper; newspaper to absorb possible mess from water.

Procedure

• Place a drop of water between your thumb and index finger. The shape of the water drop can be changed by moving your thumb and index finger. It will appear as though the drop of water is being stretched or squeezed. (Water itself cannot be stretched or squeezed. It is basically incompressible. However, the shape that water assumes can be changed or deformed.) See diagram.

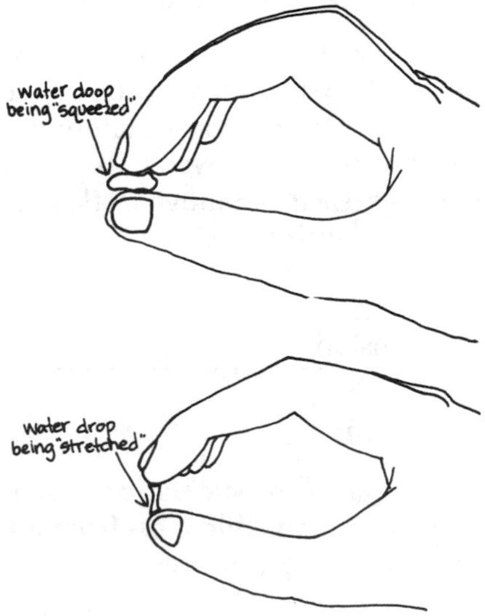

• Drop some drops of water on the children's hands. Ask the children if the water is sticking to their hands. Have them shake their hands. Ask the children if the water is still there. (Some of the water will be there. For the water to come off it has to be wiped off or evaporate.)

• Drop a drop of water onto waxed paper. Have the children observe what happens to the drop. (The drop forms a round curved shape like a ball and can roll on the paper.) Have a child add some more drops of water to the waxed paper. Have the children observe what happens to the drops as they are rolled on the paper. (Some of the drops will combine or stick together to form a larger drop.)

Fine point to discuss with children

Why do the water drops combine to form larger drops of water?
(Water is sticky. It sticks to itself. When water drops meet, they combine.)

3. Capillarity

Materials A cotton washcloth; a shallow pie pan filled with water; newspaper to absorb possible mess from water.

Procedure Place the corner of a dry cotton washcloth into a shallow pie pan filled with water. Ask the children what they think will happen to the water and the washcloth. Listen to their responses and wait awhile to see the results. It will take *time!* (If water naturally sticks to itself and to other materials like cotton, the water will travel up the strings in the washcloth and out of the pan. The strings in the washcloth are like tubes for the water to flow through.) **The capillary action helps liquids flow through veins of plants and animals.

• Have children experiment on their own with a cloth and water.

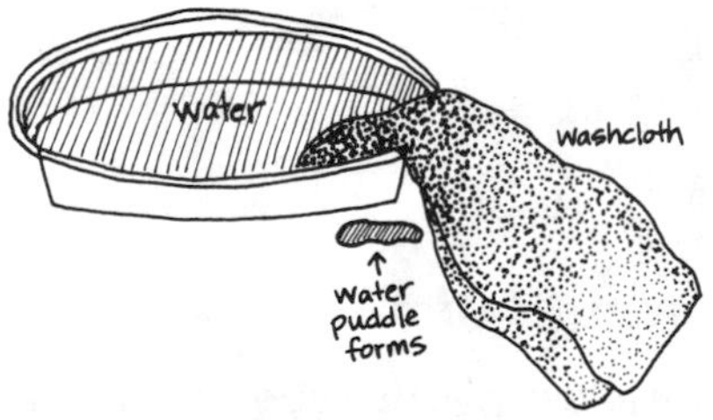

CAPILLARY ACTION

4. A Water Rope

Materials An empty can with the top removed; a basin; water; newspaper to absorb possible mess from water; a nail; a hammer.

Procedure

- Use the hammer and nail to punch out four holes in a horizontal line around the side of the can very close to the bottom rim. The holes should be very close together, about ¼-inch apart or less. As you pour water into the can to fill it, hold it over the basin. Have the children observe how the water comes out of the can in four separate streams of water.
- Ask the children if they think it is possible to make all of the streams of water combine into one stream. Listen to their responses.
- Either pinch the stream of water together with your thumb and index finger or twist them together and the four streams will appear as a rope of streams flowing together. To separate the streams, rub your finger horizontally across the holes on the can. The surface tension of the water causes the streams of water to stick to each other and form a water rope.
- Let children experiment with the can and the water stream on their own.

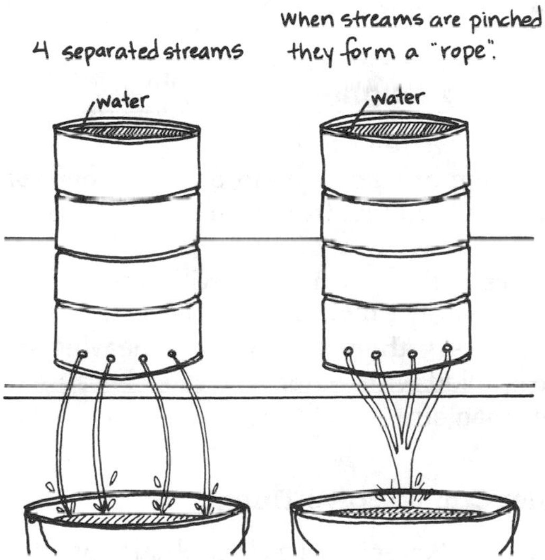

5. The Hairs Form a Point

Materials A round-tipped easel paintbrush; a clear plastic cup of water; newspaper to absorb possible mess from water.

Procedure

- Have a child dip a paintbrush into a clear plastic cup of water. Have the children observe how the hairs on the paintbrush separate and fluff out in the water. Ask the child to pull the paintbrush out of the water. Have the children observe that the brush hairs are now held together and form a point.
- Ask the children if they know why the hairs are sticking together. (The surface tension from the water is causing the hairs to stick together.)

6. A Waterproof Handkerchief

Materials A handkerchief; a rubber band; an empty tin can without a lid; a basin of water; newspaper to absorb possible mess from water.

Procedure

- Fill water to the top of the can. Wet the handkerchief. Place the wet handkerchief on top of the tin can and secure it on the can with a rubber band.

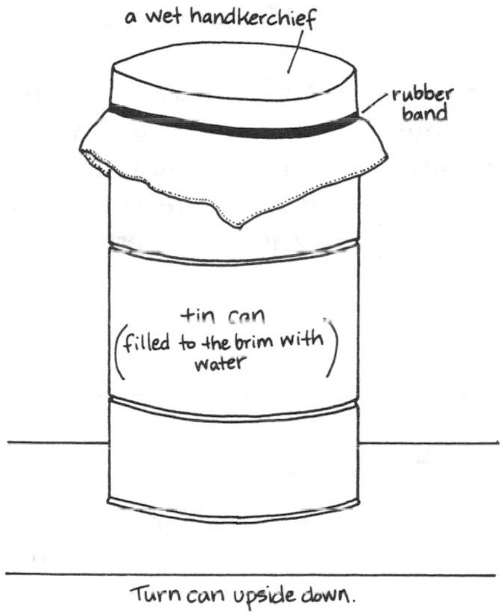

- Tell the children you are going to turn the can of water with the handkerchief on it upside-down. Ask them if they think the water will stay in the can or if the water will pour out. (It will stay in the can. The wet handkerchief has swollen threads. When the can is held upside-down, the surface tension of the water and the outside air pressure keep the water from pouring out of the can through the handkerchief. When the can is held on its side, the water dribbles out because the surface tension of the water is broken.)
- Let children continue to experiment on their own with the two steps above.

7. Soap Reduces Surface Tension

Materials Ground black pepper; a bar of soap; a basin of water; a bowl; newspaper to absorb possible mess from water.

Procedure

- Fill the bowl with water. Sprinkle pepper on top of the water. Some of it will sink, but most of the pepper will float on the surface of the water.
- Dip the corner of a bar of soap into the water. Have the children observe what happens to the particles of

ground pepper. (The particles will scatter and move away from the bar of soap.)

• Let children continue to experiment with pepper, soap, and water.

Fine points to discuss with children

Why does the pepper float?
(The pepper is lighter in weight than the water.)

Why does some of the pepper sink?
(As the particles of ground pepper absorb water they become heavier and sink.)

Why does the soap make the pepper scatter and move away?
(Soap has oil in it. Oil and water do not mix. Oil feels slippery to touch and it breaks down the sticky cohesive quality of water. Oil disconnects the surface tension or "skin" of water. The rupture of surface cohesion by the soap causes the pepper to scatter.)

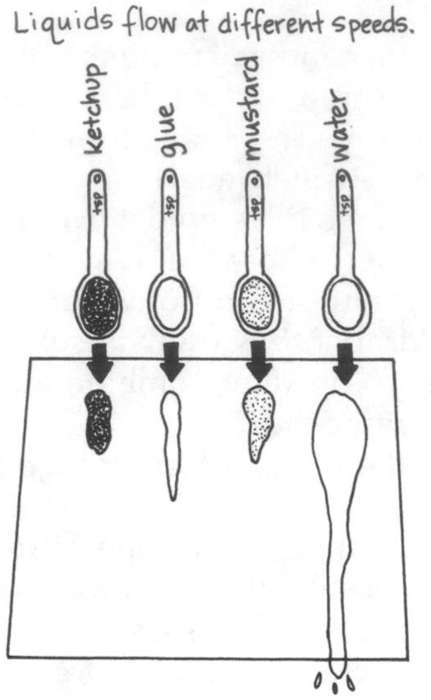

VIII. Description of Water

1. Water Is Transparent

Materials A hand mirror; a clear plastic fish-bowl or cup filled with water; newspaper to absorb possible mess from water.

Procedure Have children look through a clear plastic container filled with water. (It is clear.) Have a child place his or her hand behind the container of water and look at it through the container. Then have the child place the mirror behind the clear water container. Ask the child to look through the container into the mirror. (The child will see his or her reflection through the curved lens of the container. It will appear as though the child's face is inside the container like the image in a crystal ball.)

2. Water Flows Easily

Materials Water and other heavy liquids such as thick ketchup, glue, mustard; a piece of cardboard; teaspoons.

Procedure

• Explain to children that water is a liquid. Liquids are able to flow. Some liquids flow faster than other liquids.

• Have the heavy liquids on display and let the children experiment with each of the liquids to see if they flow and how fast they flow. Have the children drop a teaspoon of each liquid onto the piece of cardboard. Then have them tilt the cardboard at a slight angle. Have the children observe which liquid moves the fastest or appears to flow the easiest. (Water will be an obvious answer.)

3. Water Has Weight

Materials Two empty cans that are the same size, each missing one lid; a basin of water; newspaper to absorb possible mess from water.

Procedure Fill up one can with water. Leave the other can empty (filled with air). Have the children lift both cans. Ask them which can is heavier and why. (The can filled with water is heavier because water is heavier than air.)

4. Water Can Dissolve Things

Materials Alka-Seltzer; a clear plastic cup of water; a basin filled with water; newspaper to absorb possible mess from water; several clear plastic cups; salt; flour; sugar cube; granulated sugar; teaspoons for stirring and tasting water.

Procedure

• Drop the Alka-Seltzer into the glass of water. Have the children observe as the large white pill disintegrates in the water and lets out bubbles of air. (The bubbles of air are carbon dioxide.) Ask them what happens to other things that are placed in water—for example, powder that makes punch drinks, frozen lemonade, powder for Jello.

• Place several cups of water out on a table. Put a different "powder" into each cup. Have children stir the various containers filled with water and powder until the powder is dissolved. Ask the children to observe how the various powders of sugar, flour, salt, and the cube of sugar mix with the water. Discuss the results.

Does the cube dissolve as quickly as the granulated sugar?
(No.)

What happens to the water? Is it still clear?
(Flour and salt make the water appear less clear.)

How can we tell if the water has the powder in it?
(Taste it.*)

What happens if a lot of powder is added to the water?
(The powder will float and eventually sink to the bottom. The solution will become saturated.)

What happens if the "powder" does not dissolve?
(If the solution is left undisturbed, the water will eventually become clearer. The sediment of the undissolved powder will settle to the bottom of the container.)

5. Water Can Be Purified

Materials Small pebbles; sand; soil; paper towels; coffee filter; cotton; a basin of water; newspaper to absorb possible mess from water; a large funnel; a large pickle jar.

Procedure
• Create some dirty water in the basin by mixing soil into the water. Ask the children if they think the water can be made clean again.

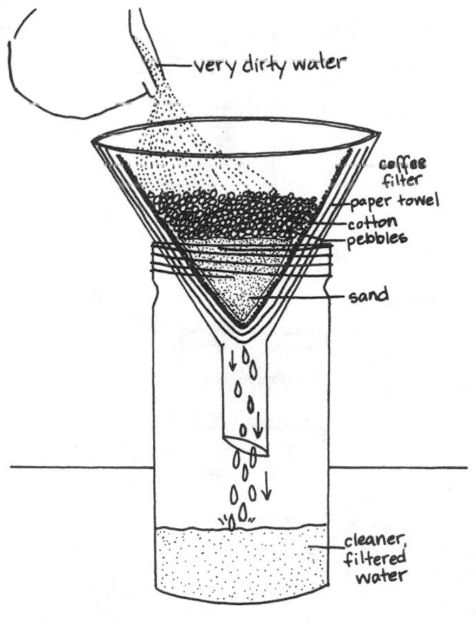

*Explain to the children that some powders are dangerous and that they should *never* taste substances known to be dangerous or unknown that they experiment with.

• Create a filter by arranging layers of materials inside of the large funnel. Place the coffee filter in first, then a paper towel and some cotton, a layer of sand, and the top layer should be a layer of pebbles. Have a child pour a cupful of the dirty water slowly from the basin into the funnel. (The funnel with filters should be resting on top of the large empty pickle jar. The dirty water will enter the pickle jar through the filter system in the funnel. When it enters the jar it will be much cleaner. To get the water still cleaner, continue to refilter the water through the filter system from the pickle jar. It may be necessary to reassemble the filtration system with a clean coffee filter, paper towel, and cotton.)

6. Water Can Act as a Filter

Materials A clear plastic cup; salt; sand; pebbles; a large pickle jar with a lid; a measuring cup; a basin of water; newspaper to absorb possible mess from water.

Procedure
• Mix sand and salt together. Ask the children if they can think of a way to separate the two "powders." Then add water to the mix and stir. (The salt will dissolve in the water and the sand will sink to the bottom of the container.)
• Mix equal portions of pebbles, sand, and soil together in a pickle jar so that it is not more than half full. Fill the remainder of the jar with water. Screw the lid on the pickle jar. Shake the filled jar vigorously. Let the jar sit for several hours. (The heavier materials will sink to the bottom.)

7. Water Can Be Absorbed

Materials Assorted objects that absorb water like: paper towels, sponges, cotton, a washcloth, yarn, a handkerchief; assorted objects that do not absorb water like: a plastic lid, a paper clip, tinfoil, a painted pencil, a bottle cap, a feather; a basin of water; newspaper to absorb possible mess from water; an eye dropper or an atomizer to spray water.

Procedure 1 Show the children the assorted materials that can and cannot absorb water. Have the children predict which materials will absorb water and which will not. Then have the children experiment to find out if their predictions were right by using an atomizer to spray water or an eye dropper to drop drops of water onto the various materials.

What happens to water that is absorbed?
(It spreads out flat.)

What happens to water when it is not absorbed?
(It forms little beads and it rolls.)

Why do we wear a material that will not absorb water in the rain?
(So we will not get wet.)

What kinds of materials are good to wear in the rain?
(Plastic and rubber materials, or materials that have been treated not to absorb water.)

Do bird feathers get wet in the rain?
(No, the outer feathers on birds do not absorb water because birds have natural oils in their feathers. These oils repel water.)

Materials A marking pen; dried lima beans; pebbles; two empty juice cans, one without a lid.

Procedure 2 Fill one large can half-full of beans and the other can half-full of pebbles. Place a line on the containers with a marking pen to show where the top of the beans is and where the top of the rocks is. Fill the remaining half of the cans with water. Ask the children what they think might happen to the beans and pebbles if they are in the water for awhile. (The beans will absorb water and will become practically twice their original size. Nothing much will happen to the pebbles, but their color will become more intense when they are wet.)

IX. Boats and Buoyancy

1. Floaters and Sinkers

Materials Basin of water; newspaper to absorb possible mess from water; assorted materials that will float or sink when placed in water, for example: seeds, feather, plastic materials, bar of soap, sponge, comb, crayons, pen, golf ball, popsicle sticks, marble, grapes, buttons, penny, drinking straw.

Procedure Place the objects that are to be tested on the floor or table near the basin of water. Tell the children that each object will either sink or float in the water. Have them make a prediction about each object and then test their prediction by placing each object one at a time into the basin of water.

2. Floating and Sinking Cans, Bottle Caps, and Closed Containers

Materials A basin of water; newspaper to absorb possible mess from water; bottle caps; empty tin cans that come with plastic lids, in assorted sizes: tuna fish can, coffee can, soup or vegetable can (or other containers with removable lids).

Procedure

- Place the objects on the table or floor near the basin of water. Tell the children that each item can be made to sink or to float. Have them experiment to find out how each item can be made to sink or float.
- Discuss their findings. The following are some of the things they will be able to observe from their experimenting:

a. When most containers are filled with air and shut tight with a cap, they will float.

b. When metal containers fill with water they usually sink, whereas plastic containers will continue to float.

c. A metal cap can be made to float if the top (flat side) touches the water.

d. An upside-down cap (flat side up, rim in water) will float if a layer of air is between the flat side and the water.

e. A can with short sides (tuna can) will float if the bottom (the flat side) touches the water.

f. A can with tall sides will float at an angle.

g. A can with tall sides floats upright if water is added to the inside of the can.

h. A can with tall sides filled with some water rests or floats deeper in the basin.

3. Will a Sieve or Colander Float?

Materials A colander or sieve without a handle; a basin of water; newspaper to absorb possible mess from water; plastic wrap like Saran Wrap; Crisco or other solid shortening.

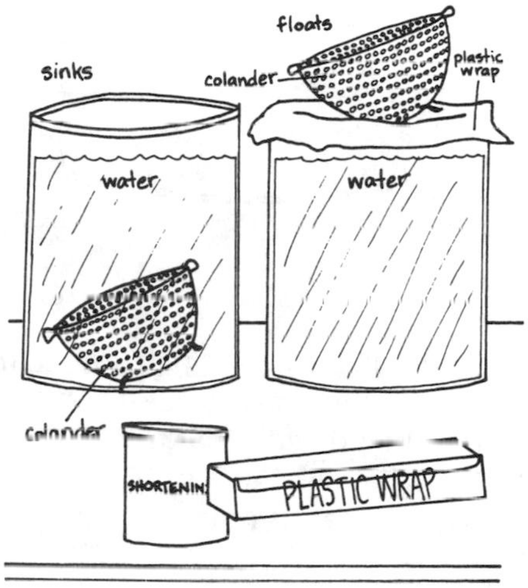

Procedure

- Place the colander in the water. (It will sink.) Ask the children if they can think of a way to make the colander float. Listen to their ideas.
- Rub the holes with shortening to fill in the holes. Place the colander in the water. (It will sink. The water will still seep through the holes.)
- Cover the colander's holes with two long strips of plastic wrap. The plastic wrap will stay in place with the shortening that is on the colander.
- Place the colander in the water. (It will float. The plastic wrap will keep the water from seeping through the holes.)
- Let children experiment on their own to see if they can make the colander float.

4. What Makes a Boat Sink?

Materials Small toy boats or homemade barge boats made from pie tins, tin cans, Styrofoam, cardboard or plastic meat trays from the grocery store, empty half-gallon plastic ice cream containers; a basin filled with water; newspaper to absorb possible mess from water; a large can of pebbles, rocks, or marbles to be used as weights. (If rocks or pebbles are used, their weights will vary. If marbles are used, their weights will be more consistent and constant. Children may discover that if they use only marbles to load their tin boats it may be easier for them to make predictions of how many marbles a tin boat can hold.)

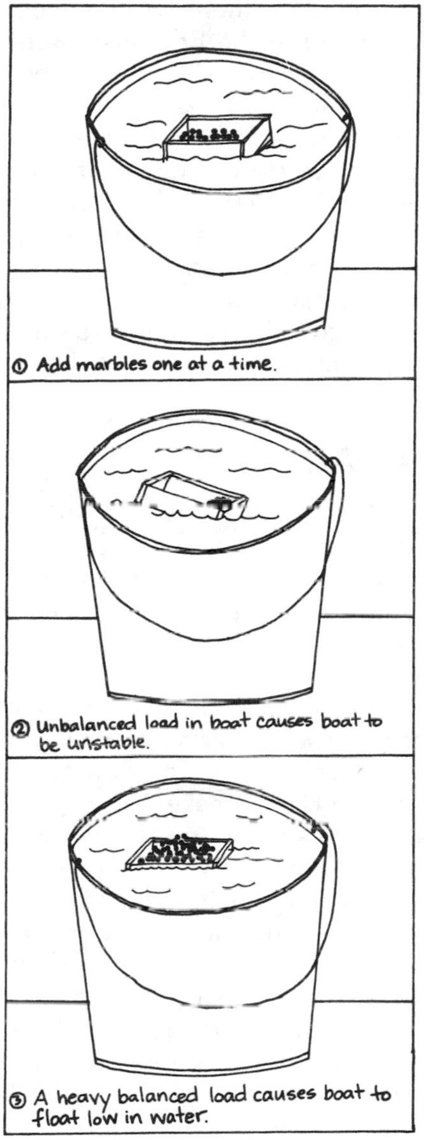
① Add marbles one at a time.
② Unbalanced load in boat causes boat to be unstable.
③ A heavy balanced load causes boat to float low in water.

Procedure

- Have children load the barge boat with pebbles, one pebble at a time. Ask the children to predict how many pebbles the barge boat might be able to hold. Have the children continue to add pebbles until the boat sinks. Ask the children what made the boat sink. (It will sink because of too much weight.) Ask the children if there are other reasons a boat would sink.
- Tell the children to add pebbles to the boat again, but this time you will add them to only one side of the

barge boat. Ask them how many pebbles the boat might be able to carry when the load is not balanced and what they think will happen to the boat from the uneven load. (It will eventually tilt, fill with water, then sink. If it is a styrofoam boat barge, it will spill its load and then right itself in the water or turn upside-down [capsize].)

- Have children punch holes in the bottom of the barge boat. Then have them add the pebbles. (When pebbles are added to the tin "boat," sediments will probably fall from the pebbles. It would be helpful for the children if an adult made them aware of the sediment and where the sediments came from.) Tell the children to observe the reaction of the barge boat as the pebbles are added. (This is especially interesting to watch if the barge boat is a tinfoil pie tin. When the tinfoil pie tin "boat" starts to sink, stop adding pebbles. The sinking will continue very slowly, but once it starts to sink it will continue to sink until it hits the bottom of the basin.)

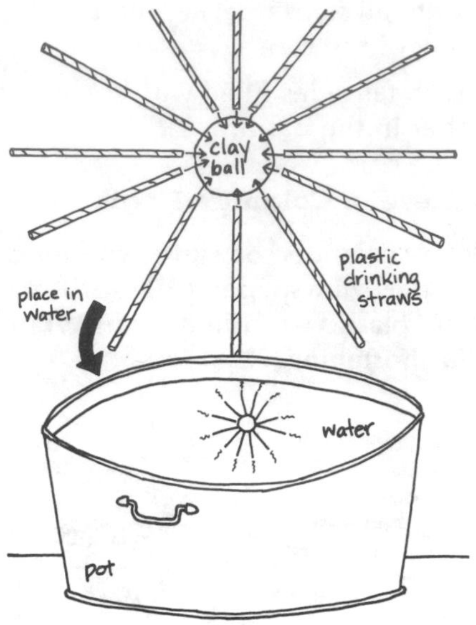

5. Shaping Clay to Float

Materials Clay, plasticine or Play-Doh; a small, round-bottomed bowl; a rolling pin; a basin filled with water; newspaper to absorb possible mess from water; waxed paper; paper towel; paper clips.

Procedure

- Shape the clay or Play-Doh into a round ball. Drop it into the basin of water. Have the children watch the ball sink. Ask them if there is a way they could change the shape of the clay to make it float.
- Blot the clay on a paper towel. Then use the rolling pin to flatten it out. Roll out the clay on a piece of waxed paper. When it is fairly flat and thin, turn a small bowl upside-down and use the bottom of the bowl as a mold to shape the clay into a bowl-shaped boat. Place the bowl-shaped boat into the basin of water. Be sure there are no holes in the clay and that the edges of the clay are pinched together to be solid. (The clay bowl will float. It will be able to carry a small, light load like a paper clip or two.)
- Let children experiment with the clay to see if they can make the clay float.

6. Making a Clay Ball Float

Materials Clay, Play-Doh or plasticine; drinking straws; scissors; paper towels; basin filled with water; newspaper to absorb possible mess from water.

Procedure

- Roll clay into a ball. Blot it on a paper towel to absorb any extra water that it might be holding. Cut about 5 or 6 drinking draws in half. Pierce the clay ball with the 10 or 12 pieces of drinking straw. Place the straws around the perimeter of the clay. See diagram.
- Place the clay ball with straws protruding from it in the water. (It will float. If not, add more straws or use less clay.)
- Let children experiment with the clay and drinking straws to see if they can make a clay ball float.

Fine points to discuss with children

Why is the clay ball unable to float without straws supporting it, but able to float when it is thin and shaped like a bowl?

(The clay ball is very thick and dense. The clay bowl is much thinner than the ball shape. The water is able to support the clay when it is shaped like a bowl because the bowl holds a lot of air. The water is unable to support the clay when it is shaped like a ball because the clay ball contains less air.* An object can float when the object has less density than the water has.)

How do straws help the clay ball stay afloat?

(The drinking straws contain air; the straws are less dense than the clay.)

7. When Does Something Float?

Materials A bucket filled with water; a newspaper to absorb possible mess from water; an empty half-gallon plastic container; a large flat basin; a measuring cup; two blocks of wood that are the same shape, size and weight.

*The density of the clay remains the same, but the shape and enclosed volume of air changes density as the shape of the clay "boat" is changed.

Procedure

- Place a wooden block inside the basin and a wooden block inside the half-gallon plastic container. Tell the children you are going to add water to each of the containers, one cup at a time. Ask them how much water they think needs to be added to the container before the wood block will float. Ask them if they think the blocks in each container will float with the same number of cups of water or whether the smaller container will make the wood float with less cups of water. Test out their ideas. (The smaller and deeper container will need less water to create a depth of water deep enough to lift the wood block.)
- Let children continue to experiment with the wooden blocks, the basins, and the water.

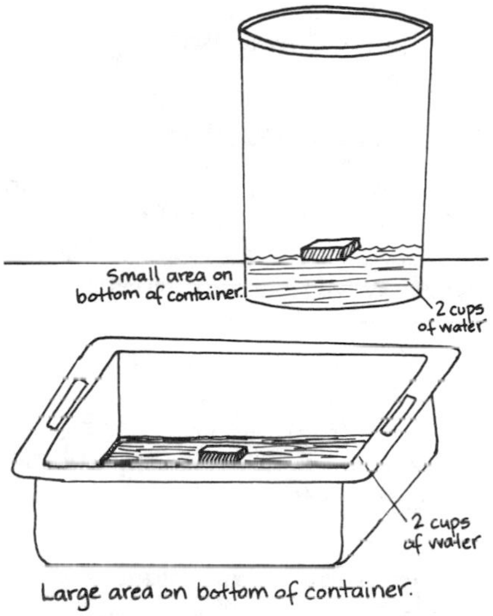

Fine point to discuss with children

Why does the wooden boat float in the small container with less water?

(The wooden block could not float in the water until the water was deeper than the wooden block.)

8. A Balloon in Water

Materials A bucket half-filled with water; an inflated balloon; newspaper to absorb possible mess from water.

Procedure Tell the children that you are going to choose one of them to place an inflated balloon into the bucket. Ask them what they think will happen. (The balloon will float on the water.) Ask them what will happen if the balloon is pushed into the water. (The water will rise. The volume of space taken up by the air in the balloon will displace or push away the water that is occupying that space. As the balloon is pushed down the water pushes up.)

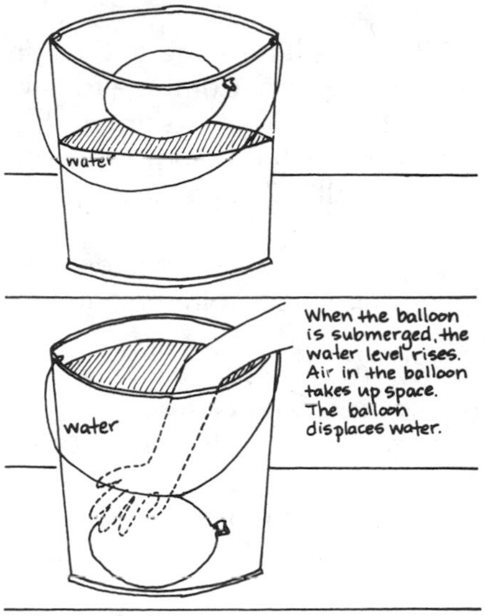

water
water
When the balloon is submerged, the water level rises. Air in the balloon takes up space. The balloon displaces water.

Fine point to discuss with children

Why does the balloon push back up from the water? Isn't the water heavier than the balloon?

(The water is heavier than the balloon, but the air inside the balloon is less dense than the density of the water. The water pushes up the balloon with great force because the density of water is much greater than the density of air inside the balloon.)

9. Water Makes a Brick Feel Lighter

Materials A bucket half-filled with water; a brick or heavy rock; a piece of rope or twine about 18 inches long; newspaper to absorb possible mess from water.

Procedure Tie the rope to the brick. Give the free end of the rope to a child. Ask the child to lift the brick up. Have the child observe and feel how heavy the brick feels on the end of the rope. Then have the same child lift the brick and gently lower it into the bucket of water. Tell the child not to let the brick touch the sides of the bucket or the bottom. (As the brick enters the water, the child should notice an immediate difference in the weight of the brick.) Ask the child why the brick feels less heavy. (The brick feels lighter because the weight of the water is pushing up against the brick and is supporting some of the brick's weight.)

10. Eggs Float in Salt Water

Materials Two clear plastic cups filled with water; an egg; salt; a teaspoon.

Procedure

- Have a child pour salt into one of the cups of water and stir it with a teaspoon. Continue to have the child add salt until the solution is saturated. (It will be saturated when the water cannot hold all of the salt and some of the salt will sink to the bottom of the cup.)
- Place an egg into the clear water. (It will sink.) Remove the egg and place it in the salty water. (It will float.)

Fine points to discuss with children

Why can an egg float in salt water but not in clear water?
(Salty water is heavier or more dense than clear water. The increased density of the salt water makes it possible for the egg to float.)

Do ships float higher in salt water than in clear water?
(Yes, the ship displaces less water if the water is denser.)

Further Resources

Suggested Books for Children

Dewey Decimal Classification Number for air and water is: 551.

Branley, Franklyn, *Air Is All Around You.* New York: Thomas Y. Crowell, 1962.

Brewer, Mary, *The Wind Is Air.* New York: Children's Press, 1975.

Milgrom, Harry, *ABC Science Experiments.* New York: Children's Press, 1975.

Newing, F. E., and Richard Bowood, *Air, Wind and Flight, A Ladybird Junior Science Book.* Loughborough, England: Wills and Hepworth, 1963.

Pine, Tillie, and Joseph Levine, *Water All Around.* New York: Whittlesey House, 1959.

Podendorf, Illa, *The True Book of Science Experiments.* Chicago: Children's Press, 1972.

Simon, Seymour, *Wet and Dry.* New York: McGraw-Hill, 1969.

Smith, Henry, *Amazing Air, Science Club.* New York: Lothrop, Lee and Shepard Books, 1982.

Watson, Philip, *Liquid Magic, Science Club.* New York: Lothrop, Lee and Shepard Books, 1982.

Wyler, Rose, *First Book of Science Experiments.* New York: Watts, 1971.

Wyler, Rose, and Gerald Ames, *Prove It.* New York: Scholastic Book Services, 1963.

Zubrowski, Bernie, *Messing Around with Water Pumps and Siphons.* Boston: Little, Brown, 1981.

Resource Books for More Ideas

Arnov, Boris, *Water.* New York: Lothrop, Lee and Shepard, 1980. (Introduces concepts about water's relevance to life.)

Benish, Jean, *Water, Water Everywhere, Science Through Water Waterplay.* Winston-Salem, North Carolina: Kaplan Press, 1977.

Berger, Melvin, *The New Air Book.* New York: Thomas Y. Crowell, 1974.

Bird, John, *Science from Water Play, Teaching Primary Science.* Milwaukee, Wisconsin: MacDonald-Raintree, 1979.

Freeman, Mae, *When Air Moves.* New York: McGraw-Hill, 1968.

Keen, Martin, *The How and Why Wonder Book of Science Experiments.* New York: Grosset and Dunlap, 1971.

Zim, Herbert, *Waves.* New York: Morrow, 1967.

9

WEATHER

Objectives

- For children to develop an awareness that weather is the result of interactions between air, water, and heat from the sun.
- For children to develop an awareness that air can be cooled by water and heated by the sun.
- For children to become aware that wind is fast-moving air.
- For children to develop an awareness that when two different air masses with different temperatures meet, a wind occurs.
- For children to develop an awareness that when temperatures change, so does air pressure.
- For children to develop an awareness of how water is recycled by nature.
- For children to become aware of the meaning of the terms associated with the water cycle: water vapor, evaporation, condensation, precipitation.
- For children to become aware of the various kinds of clouds and how they form.
- For children to develop an awareness of how air masses form, and why their temperatures are different.
- For children to become aware of some of the instruments used to measure and predict weather.
- For children to become aware of what weather data means, and why weather data records are kept.

General Background Information for Parents and Teachers

Weather It is created or caused by a combination of air, water, and the sun's heat. It involves changes in air pressure and temperature, wind speed and direction, and the amount of moisture in the air. When these factors change, they affect the movement of air masses, which creates short-term changes in the atmosphere called weather.

Temperature Temperature is a measure or degree of warmth or coldness.

Thermometer An instrument that measures temperature.

Air pressure The amount of weight or force that air exerts on a surface per square inch.

Warm air It has a low air pressure. Warm air tends to rise and expand because it is lighter in weight per square inch than cool air. Warm air has energetic molecules which bang against each other and disperse or bang apart. This results in reducing the air density. See diagram.

**All items with double asterisks indicate that the information is too abstract and too complicated for young children to understand or comprehend. It is included to enhance parent or teacher background only.

When warm air and cold air meet, turbulence occurs.

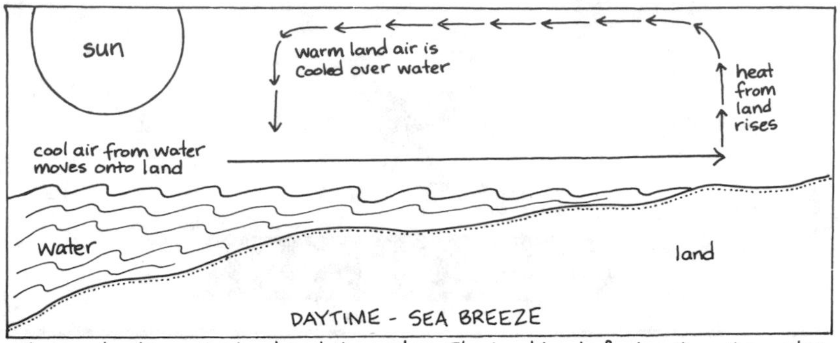

The sun heats up the land and the water. The land heats faster than the water. The warm land air rises. Cooler air from the water moves on to the land.

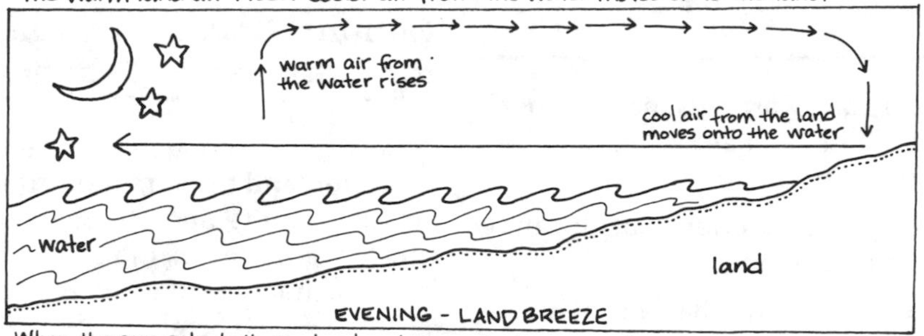

When the sun sets, both the land and the water become cooler. The land becomes cool quicker than the water. The warm air from the water rises. Cooler air from the land moves onto the water.

Cool air It has a high air pressure. Cool air tends to sink and contract because it is heavy in weight per square inch. It has a higher density than warm air. See diagram.

Density Weight per square inch.

****Moist warm air** Has less pressure than warm air. It takes up a lot of space. Moist air contains water (molecules) and is therefore denser than dry air. In turn, the atmospheric pressure of moist air is higher than that of dry air at the same temperature. See preceding diagram.

****Dry cool air** Has more pressure than cool air. It contracts more than cool air. See preceding diagram.

Ice Ice is water in the "solid" state. When water freezes, it turns into ice. Ice is able to float because it is lighter than water. The process of expansion makes water lighter in weight than an equal amount of water before it freezes. When ice forms, it crystallizes on exposed surfaces first and in the center last.

Land Refers to continents and islands of the Earth. During the day, the air above continents and islands warms up. At night, the air above them cools off. See diagram above.

Water Refers to the large and small bodies of water on the Earth: oceans, lakes, rivers and streams. During the day, water tends to absorb the heat from the sun slowly. At night, water tends to slowly lose the heat it absorbed. At night, the air above water bodies tends to feel warmer than the temperature of the air above land areas. See diagram above.

Land breeze An evening breeze that blows from the land to the water. See diagram above.

Sea breeze A daytime breeze that blows from the water to the land. See diagram on page 96.

Low air pressure Warm air has low air pressure.

High air pressure Cool air has high air pressure.

Wind and currents Changes in air temperature bring about changes in air pressure. Air tends to move from an area of high pressure to an area of low pressure. When air moves it is called a wind or an air current.

Wind Air that moves parallel to the ground.

Current Air that moves up or down.

Direct sun rays Sunlight that shines directly down on the earth.

Indirect sun rays Sunlight that shines down at a slant so that a given quantity of sunlight is spread over a larger area than if it shines directly down.

Water cycle The process by which water is recycled into the atmosphere over and over again. Water evaporates from the earth and becomes water vapor. Then it condenses and forms a cloud. When the air in the cloud becomes saturated, precipitation occurs, which starts the whole cycle over again.

Water vapor Is the form water takes when it is diffused as a gas. It is invisible.

Evaporation The process of liquid water appearing to disappear as it diffuses and changes into water vapor.

Condensation The process whereby water changes from a gas back into a liquid.

Precipitation Condensed water that falls from clouds as rain, hail, sleet, or snow.

Acid rain Neutral and pure raindrops that become polluted (mixed with acid) as they fall through the atmosphere.

Saturated Air that is filled with water. When air is 100 percent saturated, it rains.

Humidity The amount of moisture in the air.

Moisture The amount of water vapor in the air.

****Dew point** The temperature at which condensation occurs.

Droplets Miniscule drops of water. Droplets are extremely light in weight.

Cloud A large mass of moist air containing tiny suspended water droplets or ice particles. Clouds can be categorized by their appearance. They can also form at different altitudes in the sky.

Fog A very low cloud that touches the ground.

Dew A condensation that can be seen on surfaces as little water droplets. It occurs when temperatures change dramatically between daytime and nighttime.

Frost A condensation that can be seen on surfaces as small ice crystals. It occurs for the same reason dew does, but the water vapor freezes when the temperature is at freezing point or below.

Stratus clouds Clouds that look long, flat and thin. When they are dark looking they are called nimbostratus. Nimbostratus are rain clouds.

Cumulus clouds Can be seen on sunny days. They look like puffs of cotton. Cumulonimbus clouds form when the temperature cools off dramatically. They are big vertical rain clouds, and hold a lot of water.

Cirrus clouds They appear at a high altitude in the sky and look like thin, wispy curls. They indicate that the weather may change.

Air mass A large body of air that forms over the land or the water and that has a fairly consistent temperature and moisture level.

Tropical air mass A tropical air mass will have warm moist air if the air mass formed over water, and warm dry air if the air mass formed over land.

Polar air mass A polar air mass will have cool dry air if the air mass formed over land, and cool moist air if the air mass formed over water.

Turbulence Occurs when two air masses with different temperatures collide. A "battle" over air space ensues, and the weather changes.

Front The boundary line between two air masses with different temperatures.

Warm front A warm front is a warm air mass that overtakes a cold air mass. A warm front brings about a slow and gradual change in the weather which lasts several days.

Cold front A cold front is a cold air mass that overpowers or invades the air space occupied by a warm air mass. A cold front brings about a sudden change in weather, and lasts for a few hours. Thunderstorms occur when a cold front moves in. The air becomes very turbulent and violent during a thunderstorm. The cold air is denser than the warm air. It rushes in and pushes a warm mass of air up quickly. The warm air cools off fast as the cool air pushes against it and the warm air condenses, causing precipitation to occur. Then the sky clears and it is sunny.

Stationary front The boundary between two non-moving masses of air.

Meteorologist A weather scientist. Meteorologists study and record weather data and make predictions about the weather.

Weather data Information about the weather: temperature, air pressure, wind speed, wind direction, relative humidity, etc.

Weather instruments Instruments that help measure weather data: thermometer, wind vane, anemometer, barometer, rain gauge.

Wind vane Tells you from which direction the wind is blowing.

Anemometer Tells you how fast the wind is blowing.

Barometer Tells you the air pressure.

Rain gauge Tells you how much rain fell.

Hurricane A tropical low-pressure storm that forms at sea near the equator. The low pressure creates a vortex or whirlwind of strong, powerful winds that often move a hurricane toward a continent or island. If a hurricane does not blow out to sea, it arrives on the land and can be quite destructive.

Tornado A funnel-shaped low-pressure storm with very powerful winds resulting from the low pressure induced by a vortex or whirlwind. It forms over land. It brings much destruction as it passes over a small area of land for a short time.

Vortex A strong flow involving rotation about an axis, resulting in a whirlwind or whirlpool.

Activities and Procedures

I. Air Plus Sun Plus Water Make Weather

1. What Is Weather?

Materials The word "weather" written on a card or blackboard; teacher- or parent-made pictures of each of the following: sun; raindrops; snowflakes; clouds; lightning. See diagram.

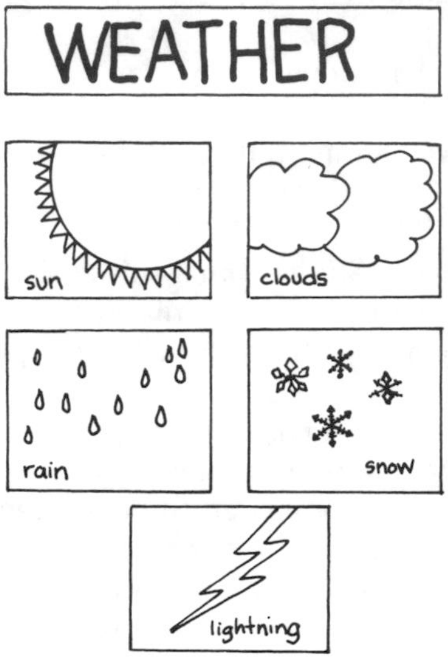

Procedure

• Show children the word "weather." Ask them if they can tell you what weather is. Ask them if they can name different kinds of weather.

• Hold up the teacher- or parent-made pictures one at a time. Explain to the children that the pictures are models or symbols of different kinds of weather. Ask them to describe the kinds of weather each picture represents. Then ask the following kinds of questions:

Why isn't every day sunny or rainy?
(Weather changes.)

Why does weather change?
(Wind blows in new kinds of weather and/or the temperature changes after it rains.)

Where is the sun on a cloudy or rainy day?
(The clouds are between the sun and the earth.)

Where do rain and snow fall from?
(The clouds.)

When do we see lightning?
(Sometimes during or before a storm.)

• *Explain:* We are surrounded by an ocean of air. Ask the children to make a swimming motion with their arms or to flap their arms like a flying bird. (They will feel the air being pushed away.)

2. Wind Is Fast-Moving Air

Materials A paper fan folded accordion style; a deflated balloon.

Procedure

• Wave the paper fan in front of each child's face. Ask the children what they feel as the fan moves quickly in front of them. (Wind.)

What is wind?
(Fast-moving air.)

• Inflate the balloon. Hold the neck between your fingers. Tell the children you are going to let go of the balloon. Ask the children what will happen to the balloon. (It will fly around.)
• Let go of the balloon. Observe what happens. Ask the children the following kinds of questions:

What came out of the balloon?
(Fast-moving air or wind.)

What caused the balloon to move or "fly"?
(The reaction to the fast-moving air or wind coming out of the balloon.)

• *Explain:* Wind can make things move. Wind can cause air to move. When large masses of air move, weather changes.

3. Water Cools Air

Materials A sunny day; a bucket filled with water at room temperature.

Procedure

• Take the children outside. Have the children dip their hands into the water. When their hands hit the outside air, their hands will feel cool, especially if there is a gentle breeze. The water and breeze from moving air will cool the air before it touches their skin. (If there is no breeze, the children can move their hands around to create a breeze.)
• Spill some water onto a cemented or blacktopped area. Have the children feel the blacktop and/or cement after some water has been poured on it. Have the children compare the difference in heat or temperature their hands feel from the wet area and the area that is still dry.
• **Be sure the wet and the dry area are either both in the sun or both in the shade.

4. The Sun Heats Air and Water

Materials A sunny day; a shade tree; two dark-colored basins; water.

Procedure

• Take the children outside. Stand with them in the sun and then in the shade of a tree or a building. Discuss the difference in temperature.

Where does the air feel warmer?
(In the sun.)

Where does the air feel cooler?
(In the shade.)

• Fill each basin with one inch of water. (**If you begin with the water at a shallow level in a dark-colored basin, it will absorb more heat. The final results will be more dramatic.) Place one basin in the shade and the other basin in the sun. Wait about an hour. Then observe the temperature in both basins by feeling the water in each basin. Discuss the differences. (Results will differ according to the season. On a warm day, the water left in the sun may evaporate. On a freezing day, the water left in the sun may turn into ice. But in any event, the temperature of the water in the basins should feel different.)

II. Temperature, Currents, and Air Pressure

1. Thermometer

Materials Two identical weather thermometers; two cups of warm water; ice cubes; paper towel; newspaper to absorb possible mess.

Procedure

• Show children a thermometer. Ask them the following kinds of questions:

What is this tool or instrument called?
(A thermometer.)

What is it used for?
(Measuring temperature.)

What is temperature?
(How hot or cold something is.)

How does it work?
(The temperature makes the liquid inside of the tube go up or down.)

• Have the children try to see the liquid column.
• Fill both cups with warm water. Place the thermometer into one of the cups. Have the children

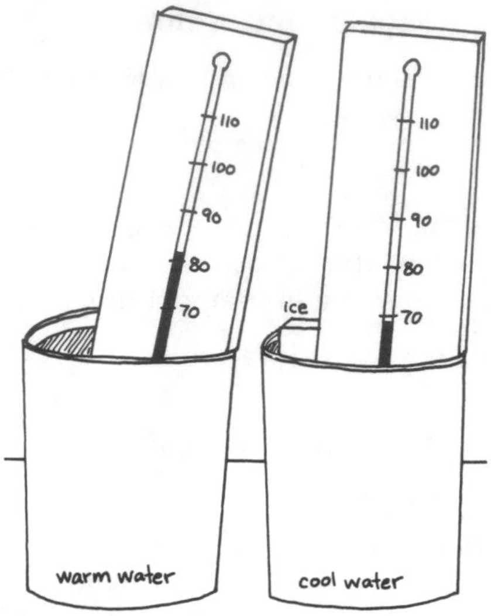

Thermometers measure the air temperature.

compare that temperature reading to the temperature on the other thermometer, which should be at room temperature.

Which thermometer has a longer line?
(The one in the warm water.)

• Place an ice cube in the other cup of warm water.

What will happen to the ice cube?
(It will melt.)

• Place one ice cube on the paper towel.

Which ice cube will melt faster, the one on the paper towel or the one in the water?
(The one in the water.)

Why?
(The water is warmer so the ice will melt faster.)

When the ice melts in the warm water, how will the water feel, warmer or colder?
(Colder.)

How can you find out if that is so?
(By feeling the water, and by measuring the temperature of the water with the thermometer.)

Will the column of liquid in the thermometer be higher and longer, or lower and shorter after it measures the warm water with melted ice?
(Shorter than the other thermometer.)

Does the liquid in the thermometer go up or down when the air is cold?
(Down.)

Where does the liquid move when the air is warm?
(Up.)

2. Balloon on a Coke bottle

Materials Small empty glass soda bottle; a small deflated balloon; bucket of hot water; bucket of ice water.

Procedure

• Pass an empty soda bottle around for the children to feel. Then place the bottle in the bucket of ice water. Leave it in the bucket for a few minutes. Ask the children how they think the bottle will feel when you take it out of the ice water. (The bottle will feel cool. The air inside of the bottle will be cool.)

• Stretch the neck of a deflated balloon around the neck of the cooled bottle. See diagram below.

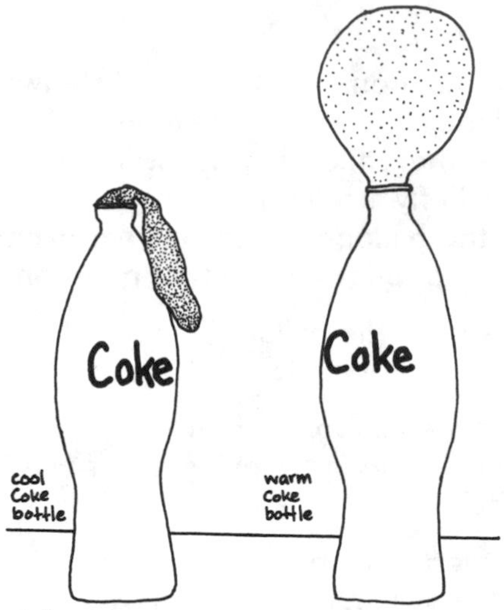

Cool air takes up less space. Warm air takes up more space.

• Pass the cooled bottle with the balloon on its neck around for the children to feel again. Have them hold the bottle with both hands for a few seconds. Ask them to tell you how the bottle feels. At first, it will feel cool. After it passes through a few sets of hands, the air in the bottle will become warmer. As the air in the bottle becomes warmer the balloon will start to inflate as the warm air moves up or rises.

• Place the warmed bottle back into the bucket of ice water. Have the children observe what happens to the balloon. (It will deflate. If the water is very cold, the balloon may become inverted inside of the bottle.) After it deflates, place the cooled bottle into the hot bucket of water. Have the children predict what will happen to the balloon when the bottle is placed in the bucket of hot water. (The balloon will expand or fill with air again.)

• *Explain:* A special kind of wind has been created in the bottle. It is called a current. Currents are winds that move up or down.

What happens when the air in the bottle warms up?
(The balloon inflates.)

What happens when the air in the bottle cools down?
(The balloon deflates.)

Fine points to discuss with children
How is the balloon on a bottle like a thermometer?
(Warm air goes up. Cold air sinks.)

Why does the balloon fill with air?
(Warm air takes up more space and rises.)

Why does the balloon lose its air?
(Cold air takes up less space and is heavier than warm air, so it drops or falls.)

How does the temperature of the water affect the air?
(The temperature of the water changes the temperature of the air.)

How do changes in temperature affect air?
(Changes in temperature cause currents to occur. Currents are up or down movements of air.)

What current direction is caused when air cools off?
(Downward movement.)

What current direction is caused when air warms up?
(Upward movement.)

What is wind?
(Wind is moving air.)

Was wind created in the bottle?
(Yes, wind was created when hot and cold air met. This caused the balloon to inflate and to deflate. Wind is created whenever two different temperatures of air meet.)

3. Collapsing a Plastic Bottle

Materials An empty plastic liter bottle with a cap; access to a freezer or outside temperature below freezing; a bucket of hot water.

Procedure
• Place an empty bottle into a bucket of hot water. Allow the air inside the bottle to become warm. Cap the bottle and allow the children to feel its warmth with their hands. Tell the children you are going to place the bottle filled with warm air into a place where the temperature is below freezing. Ask them what they think will happen to the bottle. (It will cave in or collapse.)
• Place the bottle with warm air capped tightly in the freezing air. Tell the children to observe what happens to it. *Explain:* Warm air takes up a lot of space. When the warm air inside of the bottle cooled off, it took up less space. This caused the bottle to cave in.

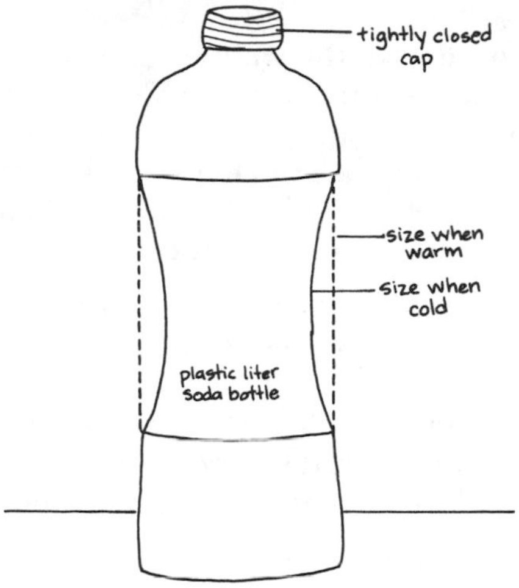

Fine points to discuss with children
When the air in the bottle cooled off, where was the force of air pressure greater, on the inside or the outside of the bottle?
(On the outside of the bottle, so the bottle caved in.)

What happened to the air inside of the bottle?
(The warm air cooled off and took up less space.)

Which air takes up more space, warm air or cool air?
(Warm air.)

Which air has more air pressure, warm air or cool air?
(Cool air.)

4. Hot and Cold Water

Materials Two colors of food coloring; large two-quart clear glass or plastic bottle; two eye droppers; water; two small containers; hot water; ice cubes; water at room temperature; newspaper to absorb possible mess from water.

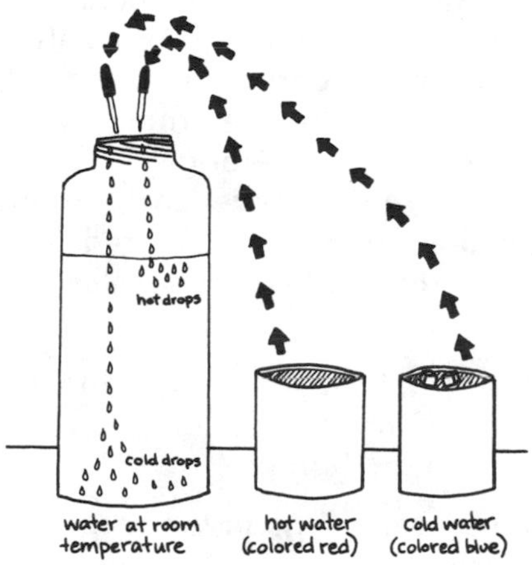

Procedure

• Fill a two-quart bottle with water at room temperature. Pour some water into a container and add ice cubes. Pour some hot water into another container. Ask the children if they can tell by looking at the water whether it is hot or cold. (They will probably say that the water with the ice cubes is colder.)

When the ice cubes melt, will they be able to tell by just looking, which water is hot and which water is cold?
(Yes, condensation will occur on the outside of the colder container, but it will be harder to tell which is which by just looking at the surface of the water.)

• Show children two food colors. Tell them you are going to add one color to the cold water and the other color to the warm water.

Will the food color make the cold water colder or the warm water warmer?
(No.)

Will color added to the water make it easier to tell, by just looking, which water is warm and which water is cool?
(Yes.)

• Add several drops of food color to each container of water so that the color is fairly dark. Have the children observe the drops as they enter the water and spread or diffuse into the water.

Does the food color spread (diffuse) faster in the hot water or the cold water?
(The hot water.)

Does the color spread out faster in still water or moving water?
(Moving water.)

• Use two eye droppers, one for each container of colored water. Draw some warm colored water up with the eye dropper. Drop the warm colored water from the eye dropper into the large two-quart bottle filled with water at room temperature. Have the children observe where the drops go after they enter the bottle. They will observe that the colored warm drops of water from the eye dropper will float to the surface of the water in the bottle.

• Tell the children you are going to use the eye dropper to draw some cool colored water and that you will drop the cool colored water into the large bottle.

Will the cool drops of water float to the surface or will they go to the bottom?
(They will go to the bottom.)

Which kind of water stays in the shape of a ring?
(The cold water.)

If the hot colored water is sent far down in the water, will it still come up to the surface?
(Yes.)

• Let the children continue to do this experiment on their own using eye droppers to drop colored water at different temperatures into a bottle filled with water.

Fine points to discuss with children

How does the hot and cold water behave?
(Hot water moves up and cold water moves down.)

Does hot and cold water behave like the liquid inside of a thermometer?
(Yes, warm temperature forces the liquid mercury to go up or expand and cool temperature forces the liquid mercury to go down or contract [inside the thermometer tube].)

5. Ice Floats

Materials A bucket of water; ice cubes; a milk carton; a can filled to the brim with water and then frozen; newspaper to absorb possible mess from water.

Procedure

• We have found out that cold air and cold water sink and that hot air and hot water float.

What does ice do when it is in the water?
(It floats.)

• Place some ice cubes in the bucket of water and tell the children to observe what the ice cubes do.

Does the entire ice cube float above the water?
(Only part of the ice cube floats above the water.)

• Have children observe a can of frozen water and a milk carton filled with water and frozen. (They will notice the ice has a bump, and/or that it is taking up more space than the container. The frozen water has expanded.)

Fine points to discuss with children

If ice is cold, why does it float?
(Ice floats because it weighs less than water. When water freezes, it expands and it takes up more space. It also becomes less dense than water, so it is able to float in water. See Chapter 8, Air and Water, Activity IX, Boats and Buoyancy, Procedure 6, Making a Clay Ball Float, Fine Points to Discuss With Children.)

How much of a floating iceberg can we see?
(About one-ninth is above the water, and eight-ninths is hidden beneath the water.)

6. The Center Freezes Last

Materials A bucket of water; a semi-frozen block of ice (use an empty half-gallon milk container as a mold for the block of ice); newspaper to absorb possible mess from water.

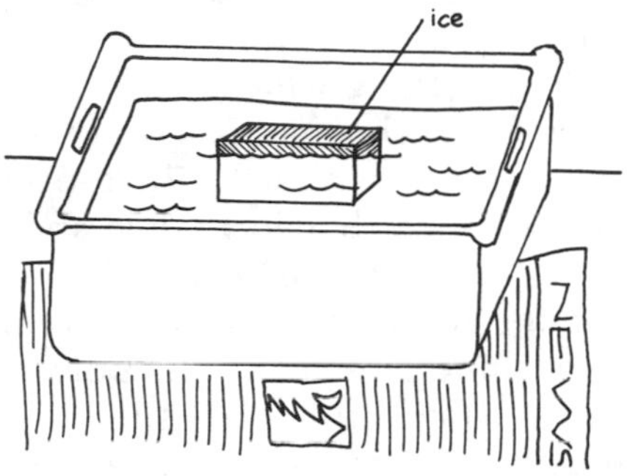

Procedure Unmold the block of ice. Allow it to float in the bucket of water. Have the children observe the center of the block. (It will still be filled with water. The water can be emptied out of the center, and the center will be hollow.)

What shape was the frozen block?
(The same shape as the container it was frozen in.)

What appears to be the last part of the block that froze?
(The center.)

What appears to be the first part of the block that froze?
(The sides.)

Why is it important to know how something freezes?
(It helps us understand how living things can live in water in the winter.)

Where do fish swim in the winter when the lake they live in freezes over?
(They live underneath the ice. The lake freezes on the top before it freezes in the center. This allows plant and animal life to continue during the winter in a pond or lake.)

Does the water move underneath the ice?
(Yes, there is a current that continually turns water over in a circular pattern. The water near the ice becomes cold and sinks to the bottom. Warmer air moves up near the ice and is cooled and sinks. This movement of water creates a current because the water temperature differs at different depths underneath the ice. The uneven temperature creates a current.)

7. Land and Water

Materials Dark brown paper; light blue paper; two basins, one filled with topsoil, the other filled with water; two thermometers.

Procedure
- *Explain:* In order to understand weather better, we are going to conduct an experiment to observe how land and water absorb heat or become warmer from the sun. Show the children the two basins. The basin with topsoil will represent a "piece of land." The basin with water will represent a water area like an ocean or lake. Show the children the colors of construction paper and ask them which color might represent land and which color could represent water. (Land, dark brown; water, light blue.)
- Place the two basins in the sun, either outside or inside on a window-sill. Allow the basins to absorb sunlight for about one hour or more. Ask the children if they think the temperature will be the same in each basin. Check the temperature at the beginning of the experiment and after several hours to find out if there has been a change. (The soil should become warmer than the water. The dark color of the soil should absorb more heat from the sunlight.) **Record the temperatures after they are taken and explain that it is important to record this kind of data because it is easy to forget the exact numbers.
- After recording temperature data from the sunlight, place the two basins in the shade or away from sunlight. Have the children check the temperature of each basin, then let each basin sit in the shady area for about 15 minutes or more. Have the children check the temperature again. (The water should stay at a fairly constant or even temperature, whereas the soil will lose a lot of its heat.)
- Place the pieces of colored paper in the sunlight. After about 30 minutes have the children check the way the papers feel.

Does one color feel warmer than the other color?
(The dark brown paper will most likely feel warmer than the light blue paper.)

- Discuss observations and results of the experiments with the children. You might want to ask the following kinds of questions:

What happens to the soil and to the water when the sun shines on them?
(They become warmer.)

Which becomes hotter in the sun, the "piece of land" or the water?
(The soil or "piece of land.")

During the night when the sun is not shining on the land or the water, which cools off faster?

(The "piece of land" or soil cools off faster because it does not retain heat. Soil heats up and cools off faster than water.)

Fine points to discuss with children
How does the temperature of the land and the water affect the air and the weather?
(The different temperatures of the air from land and water create a breeze or gentle wind near water.)

Explain: In the daytime when the sun shines, the air above the land warms up faster than the air above the water. The warmer air is very light and tends to rise. As the warm air rises, a low pressure area is created and the cooler air from above the water rushes in to take the place of the warm air above the land that has floated upward. Cool air is heavy and has a higher pressure than warm air. When the cool, high-pressure air rushes into the low pressure area vacated by the warm air, a sea breeze or wind is felt from the water. The reverse happens at night.

Why does a sea breeze become a land breeze at night?
(When the sun goes down, the land cools off quickly and loses its heat. The water stays warm. It cools off much more slowly than the land. At night the air above the water is warmer than the air above the land, so a cool breeze comes from the land toward the water to replace the warm air that has floated upward.)

**You might want to review the results of this experiment again. Water takes a longer time to heat up but once it is warm it stays warm a longer time. Land warms up quickly and cools off quickly. You might also want to discuss and review with the children the results of the soda bottle and balloon experiment or the hot and cold water experiment described earlier in this section, so that they will better understand how and why air currents occur.

**With older children you might want to look at a globe with the children and discuss the land and water formations on the globe. Land breezes and sea breezes occur on and from the continents and on and from the oceans. These "breezes" affect our weather. Sometimes major storms begin as little winds.

8. Direct and Indirect Rays from the Sun

Materials A globe on an axis; a flashlight or projection light.

Procedure
- Show children the globe and rotate the globe on its axis. Shine the light from a flashlight or projector on to the equator of the globe as it spins.
- *Explain:* The globe is a model of the Earth. It rotates or spins on its axis. The flashlight or projector is a model of the sun's light. The sun stays still. Half of the Earth faces the sun and has daylight while the other half of the Earth is in darkness and has night. Every twenty-four hours, the Earth rotates on its axis and a day is completed. The sun shines directly over the equator. Point to the equator area on the globe. This area of the Earth is always very warm. The rays from the sun shine directly on the equator in a straight line. The sunlight is very strong at the equator and warms the water and the land. The sunlight is not as strong at the top and bottom of the Earth. The top and bottom of the Earth are called the North Pole and the South Pole. It is very cold at both the North Pole and the South Pole because the Earth is round and curved. The sunlight does not shine directly on the poles. The poles receive indirect rays from the sun. The equator receives direct rays from the sun. The sun's heat and light are not as strong at the poles as they are at the equator. This difference in heating at different places on the Earth causes winds to occur when the air masses from the equator and the poles meet.

III. Water Cycle

1. Seeing Water Vapor

Materials A mirror or eyeglasses.

Procedure Have the children breathe through their mouths onto a mirror or eyeglasses. The moist air that has come from their lungs will cloud the surface of the mirror or eyeglasses. The cloud will then evaporate or disappear.

Explain: The cloud on the mirror or eyeglasses from their own warm moist breath is called water vapor. The water vapor disappears before their eyes because it evaporates or goes into the air. Warm moist air floats up or rises because it is lighter than cool, dry, heavy air.

2. Feeling Water Vapor

Materials None.

Procedure Tell the children to put their hand up to their mouth and to breathe on it. Ask them how their breath feels on their palm. It will feel warm and moist.

Where does the moisture they feel on their hand go?
(Into the air.)

What is the moisture they feel on their hand called?
(Water vapor.)

3. Evaporation

Materials A blackboard; two sponges; water.

Procedure

• Wipe a blackboard with a wet sponge. Ask the children how long they think the blackboard will stay wet. Ask the following kinds of questions:

Will the blackboard dry by itself, or does it have to be wiped dry?
(It can dry by itself.)

Where will the water go that was on the blackboard?
(Into the air.)

Will the wet sponge dry by itself?
(Yes.)

Where will the water go that was in the sponge?
(Into the air.)

• Wet two sponges. Place one sponge in the sunlight or over a heating vent and the other sponge in a shaded and cool area. Ask the children which sponge they think will become dry faster.

Where will the water go?
(Into the air.)

Can they see the water as it leaves the sponge?
(No.)

• *Explain:* When the water goes into the air, it is called water vapor. Water vapor is invisible. The process of water going into the air is called evaporation.
• Ask them if they can think of things that are affected by evaporation. Suggested things to discuss might be: where the water from puddles goes after a rain; how wet clothes become dry; how wet paint becomes dry; how dishes dry on a drainboard; how Play-Doh dries in the air; how a wet body becomes dry after swimming; etc.

**You might want to do experiments to find out which kind of container shape and container opening will make water evaporate faster. If you color the water with food color, it will leave a residue when the water evaporates and the children will be able to see the water mark left by the water that evaporated. For example: Does the same amount of water evaporate faster from a shallow pan or a deep pan? (A shallow pan or area.) Does the size of a jar opening or the length and size of a jar's neck affect how much water evaporates? (The larger-size jar opening has faster evaporation; the shorter-necked jar also has faster evaporation.)

4. Condensation on a Glass of Water

Materials A glass or an empty tin can; ice cubes; water; newspaper to absorb possible mess from water.

Procedure

• Place several ice cubes into a glass or an empty tin can. Add some water so that the glass or can is about three-quarters full. Let it stand for about ten minutes. Have the children observe what happens to the outside of the glass or tin can. At first, the outside is dry, but after about ten minutes, tiny water droplets begin to form like beads of sweat and cling to the outside of the glass or can. Ask the children where the water came from.
• *Explain:* The beads of water on the outside of the glass or can came from the air. Air contains a lot of water or moisture that we cannot see. It is called water vapor. Water vapor is like air. Usually we cannot see it, but sometimes when it is dense or thick, we can.

The air surrounding the outside of the cold glass or tin can filled with ice water became cooler. Cool air cannot hold as much water vapor as warm air. The extra water vapor came out of the surrounding air that cooled off. The extra water vapor condensed or turned into water and clung to the outside of the glass or tin can. When a gas changes into a liquid it is called condensation.

**You might want to introduce the three states of water to the children: ice/solid; water/liquid; water vapor/gas.

5. Making It "Rain" Inside a Jar

Materials A large empty Pyrex jar; very hot water; a tin lid for the jar; an empty tin can filled with ice cubes; a flashlight.

Procedure

• Tell the children that you are going to create a cloud in a jar from water vapor and that the cloud will become very heavy with moisture and will condense. The condensation will fall as large water drops. (That is, you're going to make rain!)

Explain: When a cloud's moisture condenses and it begins to lose its moisture, this is called precipitation. Precipitation can be in the form of rain, snow, hail, dew, drizzle, or sleet.
• Pour some very hot water into a large empty Pyrex jar. (About half a cup of water will do—just enough to form a lot of steam inside of the Pyrex jar.) Cover the jar with a lid. Place an empty tin can filled with ice cubes on top of the jar lid. See diagram (next page).

• Notice what happens inside the jar.
1. The heat inside the jar from the hot water warms the air.
2. The warm, moist air in the jar begins to look steamy.
3. The steamy, moist warm air evaporates and turns into water vapor.
4. The water vapor forms a cloud in the jar. It will appear white, especially if you shine a flashlight through the jar. (The flashlight is like sunlight.)
5. As the small, light droplets of water in the steam become larger and heavier droplets, the white steam will appear grayer in color.

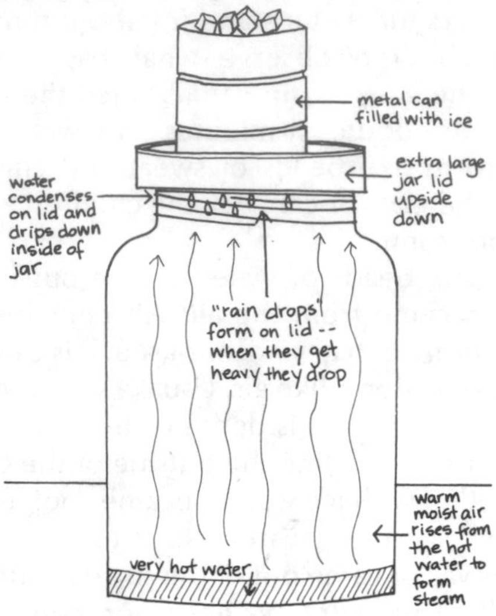

MAKE "RAIN" INSIDE A JAR

6. The warm, moist air mass inside of the jar becomes cooler when it hits the cool lid of the jar, which has been cooled by the ice cubes (that are filling the tin can on top of the lid of the jar.)
7. When the warm, moist air becomes cooler, the cloud inside the jar becomes darker because the large water droplets form shadows and block the light of the sun or flashlight from shining through.
8. Large water drops begin to form on the lid of the jar. The water vapor has changed back to water. This is called *condensation.* If you lift the lid off the jar, you will be able to see the large water droplets forming.
9. When the condensed water droplets fall, many will roll down the side of the jar or just drop. When they fall it is called *precipitation.*

Precipitation means that water or moisture is falling out of the clouds onto the land or water below.

6. Water Cycle Chart

Materials A teacher- or parent-made chart of the water cycle. See diagram for what the chart should look like.

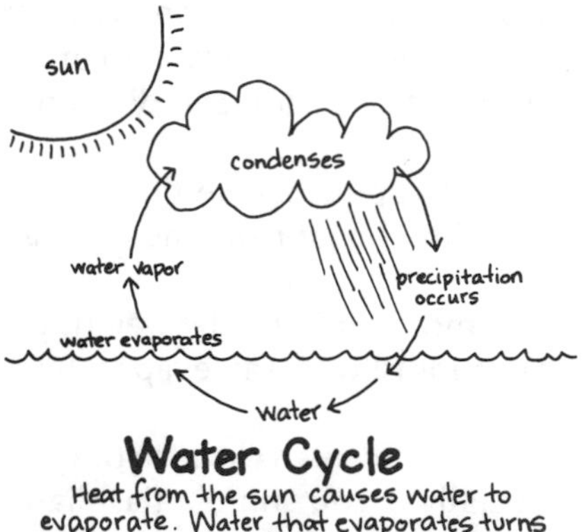

sun
condenses
water vapor
precipitation occurs
water evaporates
water
Water Cycle
Heat from the sun causes water to evaporate. Water that evaporates turns into a gas called water vapor. Water vapor rises and forms a cloud. When the water vapor becomes heavy, the vapor condenses and forms large water droplets. When water droplets fall it is called rain or precipitation.

Procedure Show the children the Water Cycle Chart. Ask them to explain what the chart is showing a picture of or trying to represent. You might ask the following kinds of questions:

Where do the arrows begin?
(They do not begin. They continue in a circle over and over again. There is no beginning.)

What is a cycle?
(Something that continues to happen over and over again with no beginning or end.)

**You might want to use a bicycle chain as an example of a cycle. The links on the bicycle chain turn or move around continuously as the bike is pedaled. As long as the wheels are in motion, the chain continues in motion until it is stopped, but there is no real beginning or end to the circular motion. Each section or link of the continuous chain is necessary for the system to be complete and whole. If a link of the chain were missing, the pedals would not be able to move the wheels, and the system would not work.

What happens to the water in the ocean?
(The heat from the sun and air evaporates some of the water. When it evaporates, the water turns or changes into water vapor.)

Where does the water in the ocean come from?
(Some of the water from rain flows into streams, which flow into rivers, which flow into the ocean.)

What happens after the water from the oceans and lakes and our yards evaporates?
(The warm water vapor floats up and forms clouds.)

What happens when the clouds become large and cool off?
(They become heavy and the water vapor in them changes back into water again. This is called condensation. When condensation occurs, precipitation usually follows. Precipitation means water or moisture falls into the ocean, lakes, or rivers and onto the land.)

Does new water fall from the sky or is it the same water that fell before?
(It is the same water that fell before. Since the time of the dinosaurs or earlier, the water on our Earth has been continuously recycled—that is, used over and over again. The water cycle has no beginning or end.)

**You might want to discuss what "recycled" means—how aluminum cans can be melted down and reused, how paper products can be turned into pulp again and reprocessed, etc.

How does dirty and polluted water become clean?
(When water evaporates, only the water turns into vapor. The other things that were in the water remain behind. When water falls from clouds, it is pure water

unless it falls through polluted air; then it becomes acid rain.)

What is acid rain?
(When rain falls from the clouds, sometimes it comes in contact with pollution in the air. The rain clings to the pollutants and brings the pollution in the air down with it to the ground and water below when it falls. Acid rain is harmful to living things. Our government has a special agency called the Environmental Protection Agency [EPA] which tries to protect our country's environment from pollutants.)

7. Pure Water Evaporates

Materials A Styrofoam meat tray or a jar lid; food color; water; a cup; a tablespoon.

Procedure
• Have the children mix several drops of food color into 3 tablespoons of water. Then pour the colored water mixture into the styrofoam meat tray or into the jar lid.
• Ask the children what will happen to the water mixture if you let it sit on a sunny surface in the room. (It will evaporate.) Ask them if they think the color will evaporate too. (It will not.)
• Have the children check back in a few days to see if the water evaporated. Discuss the results with the children. (The color remained behind. Only the water evaporated.) Ask the children how this experiment shows us that when water evaporates, it is pure and not dirty. (The dirt or color stays behind; only the water disappears.)
• Ask the children what will happen to the color if you add water to it. (It will mix with the water.) Add the color and let the children see the mixture form again and the water evaporate again. **The color is like a pollutant. It does not disappear. It remains and spreads when the water mixes with it.

IV. Clouds

1. Water Vapor

Materials Deflated balloon marked with a thick water-soluble marking pen.

Procedure
• Show the children the balloon with the black mark on it. Tell them you will be inflating or blowing the balloon up with warm air from your lungs. Ask them what they think will happen to the black spot on the balloon when the balloon is filled with warm air. (They may suggest that the black spot will become much larger. Actually, the black spot will become so much larger that the spot will appear to have disappeared. It will be stretched out so much that it will become very light in color.) Proceed to inflate the balloon and discuss the results.

Is the black spot still there?
(It seems to have disappeared.)

• Allow the air to escape from the balloon. The black spot will reappear. Ask the following kinds of questions:

Did the black spot really disappear?
(No, it was there all the time. It seemed to disappear because the molecules of ink from the marking pen were spread apart so far on the surface of the balloon that the mark appeared not to be there any more.)

How is the black spot on the balloon like hot air?
(Hot air takes up a lot of space and spreads out. It becomes very thin and light like the black spot on the balloon.)

How is the black spot on the blown-up balloon like water vapor?
(Water vapor is in the air. Most of the time it is invisible and difficult to see. When the balloon is inflated, the black spot is like water vapor. It is difficult to see. Although the black spot seems to disappear, it is really still there. Water vapor seems to disappear when it evaporates, but it does not disappear. It floats up or rises and forms a cloud with other particles or molecules of water that have also floated up.)

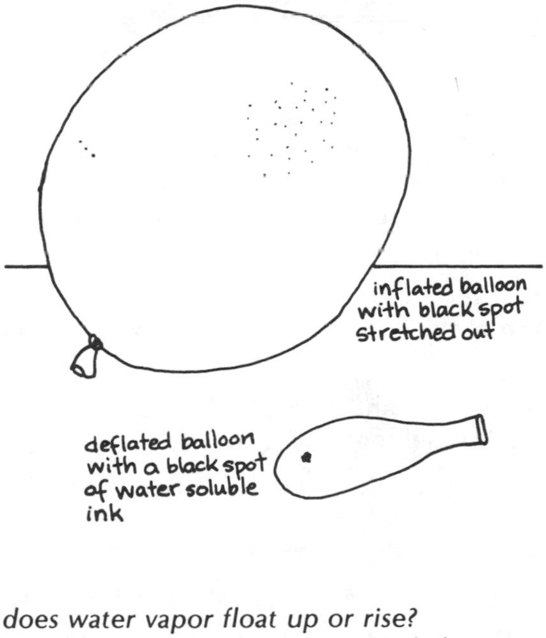

Why does water vapor float up or rise?
(Like air, water vapor is a gas. It is very light in weight. It is warm, thin, and moist. It weighs less than thick, heavy, cool, dry air. Since it weighs less, it floats up above cooler air.)

2. Clouds Float

Materials Two clear plastic glasses the same size; masking tape; very hot water; newspaper to absorb possible mess.

Procedure

- Pour a small amount of very hot water into a plastic glass. Quickly place another plastic glass upside-down on top of the first glass so that the lips of the two glasses are touching. Secure the two glasses (with the small amount of hot water inside) with masking tape so that the container is sealed and the water will not be able to run out. See diagram.

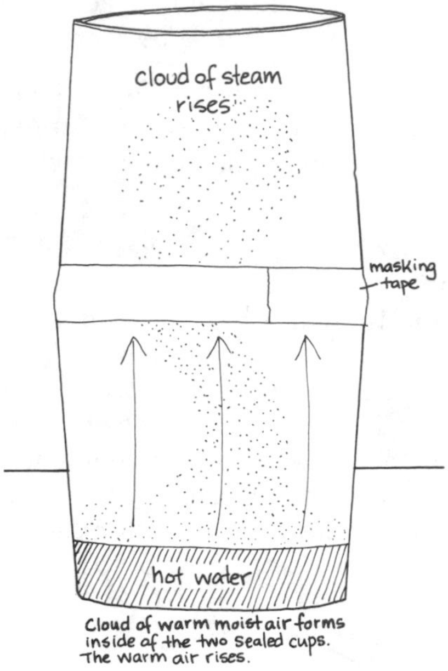
cloud of steam rises
masking tape
hot water
Cloud of warm moist air forms inside of the two sealed cups. The warm air rises.

- Have the children observe the steam or water vapor forming above the water. Discuss the children's observations. You might want to ask the following kinds of questions:

Where is the cloud forming?
(On top of the container, above the warm water.)

Why is the cloud forming?
(The air is warm and moist. Moist, warm air moves up or rises. It is lighter than cool, dry air.)

If the container is turned upside-down, what will happen to the cloud?
(It will form on top of the container again.)

- Turn the container upside-down and observe what happens to the cloud of steam.

Why does the steam rise to the top again?
(The steam is filled with warm, moist air. Warm, moist air is lighter than cooler air, so it rises or floats up.)

Fine points to discuss with children

What are clouds made of?
(Clouds are made up of tiny water droplets and ice crystals. When warm, moist air evaporates and turns into water vapor it expands and cools as it rises. Cool air cannot hold as much water vapor as warm air. When the warm, rising air cools off it begins to condense and changes into very tiny water droplets. Sometimes the temperature in the air above is so cold it is freezing. If the temperature above is freezing, the water droplets change into crystals of ice.)

Why do clouds float?
(Clouds float because they are made up of very tiny water droplets or ice crystals. These tiny droplets of water and crystals of ice are so small and light that the force of warm rising air keeps the tiny water droplets and ice crystals that form clouds from falling to the earth. When the tiny water droplets and ice crystals become heavier and larger they fall out of the cloud. The cloud then loses its moisture and becomes smaller or blows away.)

3. Colliding Water Drops

Materials An eye dropper; water; food color; a piece of waxed paper; a paper cup to mix water and food color together.

Procedure

- With an eye dropper, drop some water drops colored with food color onto a piece of waxed paper. Have the children notice how the water forms little beads on the waxed paper. The beads stay separate unless they touch. When the drops or beads of water touch, they collide and the small drops become bigger.
- Lift the waxed paper up at one of the corners or edges. Have the children observe the speed at which a larger drop of water rolls in comparison to a smaller drop of water. The larger drop rolls much faster. When water drops roll and collide or touch they become much larger. All of the little drops can be rolled to touch each other and can be made to form one large drop on the paper. **One of water's properties is its ability to stick to itself.
- Ask the children how this experiment can help us understand how small water droplets in a cloud can become large water droplets. (Water droplets in a cloud collide. The more activity or turbulence there is in a cloud from wind or air currents caused by differing air temperatures mixed together, the more collisions take place between water droplets. As water droplets become larger, they become heavier and move faster. If they become too heavy they drop from the cloud.)

• Let the children continue to experiment with the eye dropper, waxed paper, and colored water to study water drops and how they roll to form larger drops, and how large drops roll faster on the waxed paper.

4. Saturation

Materials A basin; a sponge; water; newspaper to absorb possible mess.

Procedure

• Pour some water into a pan. Place the sponge into the pan. The sponge will absorb some of the water from the pan. The amount of water absorbed will vary with the size of the sponge in relation to the amount of water. If a lot of water is in the pan, the sponge will only be able to absorb a certain amount of the water. When the sponge reaches its capacity for absorbing the water it will not be able to hold any more water. Ask the children the following kinds of questions:

How will they know when the sponge has reached its limit?
(If they lift the sponge out of the basin, it will drop water.)

How will they know the sponge has not reached its limit?
(If they lift the sponge out of the water, it will hold all of the water it has absorbed without dripping water.)

When does the sponge stop soaking up or absorbing water?
(When it is full.)

• *Explain:* When the sponge reaches its holding peak, it is saturated. When it is saturated, it cannot hold another drop. A sponge that is filled beyond its capacity drips water.
• Ask the children how an overly saturated sponge is like the air in an overly saturated cloud. (They will both drip water, but when water drops fall from a cloud or clouds, it is called precipitation. Precipitation can be in the form of drizzle, rain, snow, hail, or freezing rain, which is called sleet.)
• Discuss air's ability to hold water. Ask the following kinds of questions:

What kind of air holds more water, warm air or cool air?
(Warm air.)

What happens when warm air cools off?
(It cannot hold as much water as it did and condensation occurs.)

What does a professional weather person on TV mean when he/she refers to the "relative humidity"?
(Humidity refers to the amount of water in the air. When it is raining there is 100 percent relative humidity. On a hot, muggy day, the humidity is very high. On a dry, non-muggy day, the humidity is low.)
**Water vapor is always present in the air of our atmosphere.

5. Types of Clouds

Materials An encyclopedia (under "Clouds"), or pictures of clouds cut from magazines that illustrate various kinds of clouds: stratus, nimbostratus, cumulus, cumulonimbus, cirrus, fog, dew, and frost.

Procedure

• Ask the children what clouds look like. Listen to their responses. Ask the following kinds of questions:

Do clouds always look alike?
(No.)

What color are clouds?
(Many colors at sunrise and sunset, but usually white, or shades of gray.)

Are some clouds higher in the sky than other clouds?
(Yes.)

Can clouds ever be touched?
(Yes, fog can be touched.)

On a cloudy day, where is the sun?
(Behind the clouds.)

When you fly in an airplane, can an airplane go above the clouds?
(Yes.)

When you stare at a cloud, does it stay still or does it move?
(It moves, and sometimes appears to form interesting and imaginative shapes.)

What are clouds made up of?
(Water vapor and ice particles.)

• Show the children the various pictures of clouds from magazines. Discuss the pictures, and discuss the kinds of weather that usually result with the appearance of the different kinds of clouds. You might want to give the following kind of explanation to the children as you show them the various cloud pictures:

There are three basic kinds of clouds: Stratus, Cumulus, Cirrus. *Stratus clouds* are layered, flat, blanket-like and spread out. They usually mean rain will come soon. Sometimes they make the sky look overcast or "white." When stratus clouds become heavy with moisture and turn "grayish" they are then called nimbostratus clouds. "Nimbo" refers to rain. Rain, snow, and/or sleet fall from nimbostratus clouds. *Fog and Haze* are very low stratus-type clouds that can be touched. Fog feels cool and moist. It has a high relative humidity. *Dew and Frost* are special kinds of condensation. Dew and frost occur when water vapor condenses before it rises high in the air to become a cloud. Dew appears frequently the morning or evening after a warm, sunny day. The air is heated during the day after the sun goes down and the air cools off quickly. The fast change in temperature from warm to cool causes much of the water vapor in the air to condense. When the water vapor condenses, it is called dew. In the morning when the sun comes up the air is heated and the dew evaporates and becomes water vapor again. When the temperature outside drops to freezing or below, frost occurs. Frost forms like dew, but when the water vapor condenses it freezes directly into ice crystals.

Cumulus clouds are usually rounded, puffy, and white. They look like heaps of cotton, and usually mean sunny weather. When a lot of cumulus clouds blow or connect together they can form a large, tall cloud mass. If the large, tall cloud mass is surrounded by cooler air, condensation occurs in the cloud. The cloud grows darker and the cumulus cloud becomes a cumulonimbus cloud. Nimbus refers to rain. Cumulonimbus clouds carry a lot of water. The water falls out of them as heavy rain or hail. Thunder and lightning are often heard and seen during a heavy rain from cumulonimbus clouds.

Cirrus clouds look like feathery curls very high up in the atmosphere. They appear in dry weather and usually are a warning that the weather will be changing soon. They often indicate that a storm is coming.

6. Making Models of Clouds

Materials Blue construction paper; white chalk; cotton balls; black chalk; glue.

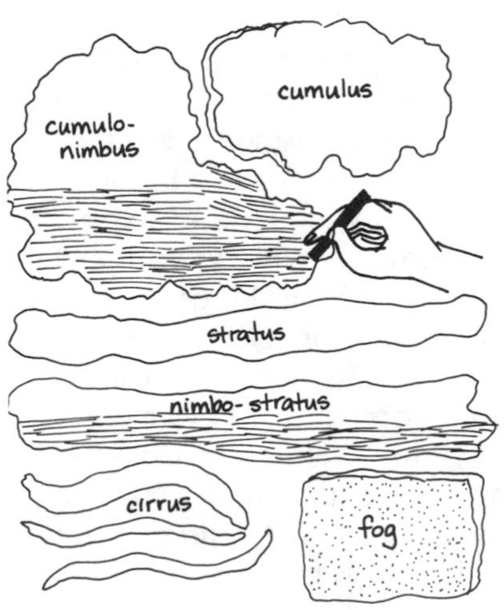

Procedure Show the children the materials. Ask them how they could make a model of what a cumulus cloud looks like. Listen to their responses. Demonstrate how to make a cumulus cloud and other cloud types from the materials. See diagram for ideas on how to construct cloud models from cotton balls and chalk.

V. Weather Formation and Measurement

1. Air Masses

Materials A physical relief globe; a teacher-made diagram or commercial store-bought diagram illustrating the various climate zones on the Earth. See diagram.

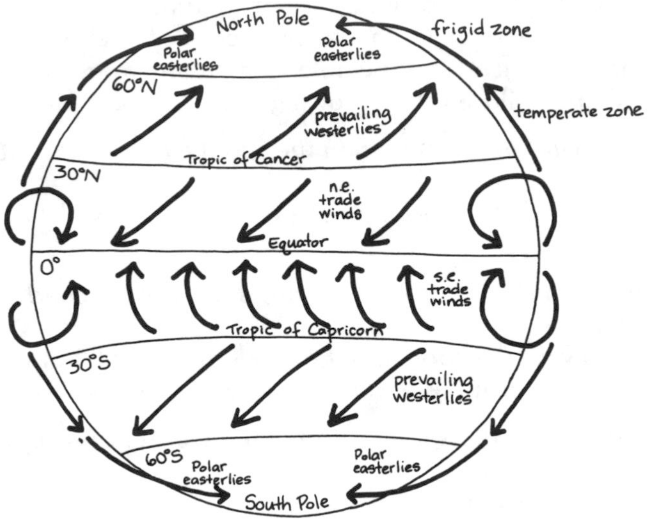

CLIMATE ZONES: CIRCULATION OF PREVAILING AIR MASSES

Procedure

• Show the children the globe, a model of the Earth. Explain that it is a model of the Earth. Discuss how the colors on the globe represent where land and water areas are located and what these land and water forms look like. Discuss how usually the blue colors represent water areas. Different shades of blue usually mean different depths of water. Browns, greens, and yellows usually represent land areas. Greens usually represent tropical and warm areas. Yellows usually represent dry desert areas and white usually represents cold and icy areas.

• Study the globe with the children and help them make observations about what the climate or weather might be like at different locations on the globe. Then show them the climate zone chart and discuss how the earth's land and water areas shown on the globe can affect climate.

**You might also review with the children the experience with direct and indirect rays from the sun (or from the flashlight on the globe) which was described in Activity II, Procedure 8 of this chapter.

Ask the children the following kinds of questions:

When a large body of air is over the ocean and another large body of air is over the land, which would be cooler during the day?
(The air over the ocean.)

Which air would be warmer during the day?
(The air over the land.)

Which air would feel more moist, the air over the land or the air over the water?
(The air over the water would feel more moist.)

Which air would feel drier?
(The air over the land or the continents would feel drier.)

Which air is warmer, the air above the poles or the air above the equator?
(The air above the equator is warmer.)

Where does cooler air form?
(Above the poles or ice caps.)

• *Explain:* Air masses form over the land or the water. An air mass formed over the land or water can be very cold if it is near the poles, and very warm if it is formed near the equator. Air masses formed at the poles are called polar air masses; those that are formed near the equator are called tropical air masses. If the air mass is formed over land, it is called continental. If it is formed over water, it is called maritime. In general, air masses that form over land are dry, those that form over water are moist, those that form near the poles are cold, and those that form near the equator are warm. Winds are created when air masses with different temperatures meet. These winds blow the different air masses around the globe. Weather changes come about because of shifting or moving air masses. Air masses can be warm or cool, moist or dry.

**The different combinations of air, its temperature, and humidity bring about changes in weather, especially when two different air masses meet.

2. Air Masses Meet

Materials Two small glass jars with wide mouths; food color; a piece of cardboard; hot water; cold water; an ice cube; a large basin; newspaper to absorb possible mess from water.

Procedure
• Tell the children you are going to demonstrate for them what happens when two air masses with different temperatures meet. Explain to them that because air is difficult to see you are going to do your experiment with colored water. Fill one of the small jars to capacity with hot water. Fill the other small jar to capacity with cold water. Add an ice cube to the jar filled with cold water. Add food color to the jar filled with hot water.
• Ask the children how you can tell if the air surrounding the water is hot or cold. (By feeling it.) Ask them what they think will happen to the hot water if you place the jar of cold water on top of it upside-down. Listen to their responses. Then place the jar filled with hot water in a basin. Take a piece of cardboard and place it on top of the lip of the jar filled with cold water. As you turn the jar upside-down, push down on the cardboard so that the water does not spill out of the jar. Gently place the two jar lips together with the piece of cardboard placed between them. Slowly remove the cardboard by sliding it out from between the lips of the two jars. See diagram.

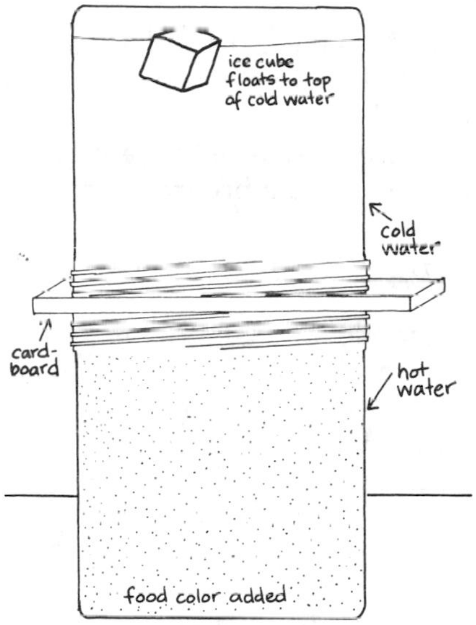

OBSERVE AIR MASSES MEETING

• Discuss the results with the children. The hot water will move up into the cold water in a swirling pattern. They will be able to see the hot water moving up because it will have had food color added to it. If they look closely at the water near the ice cube they will notice that a current is floating down from the ice cube as the cube melts. Eventually, the cold water is the same color as the colored hot water. It all happens in less than a minute.
• Explain to the children that all of this motion that happens so quickly is called wind or turbulence. It is a fast, violent action. Wind or turbulence happens to large air masses when they meet, if they have different air temperatures. Storms grow out of turbulence. Storms are winds that move extremely fast. The stronger the wind blows, the more force it has.

3. Beaufort Wind Scale

Materials A chart illustrating the symbols that represent the Beaufort Wind Scale (can be homemade). (See NOAA Hurricane Warning by Branley and Kessler, stock # 003-018-00075-0, 35¢ each, U.S. Government Printing Office.)

Procedure

• In 1805, Sir Frances Beaufort invented a way to record wind speed or force of the wind. He described the wind as happening at a force between 0 and 12. A force of 1 means a calm, gentle breeze. A force of 12 is a strong, powerful, and destructive wind called a hurricane. He suggested that you could tell how fast the wind was blowing by looking at what the wind did to other things.

What does the force of wind tell us?
(How fast a weather change might occur and the kind of weather it might bring.)

• Show the children the chart and discuss the different kinds of wind they have experienced. Ask them what kind of wind is blowing outside the window now. A wind can be described as light, gentle, moderate, or strong. It can be called a breeze, a gale, or a storm.

4. Anemometer

Materials A model of an anemometer made from: a paper plate, three paper fasteners, three paper cups, a headless nail, half of a drinking straw, a small block of wood, and a marking pen.

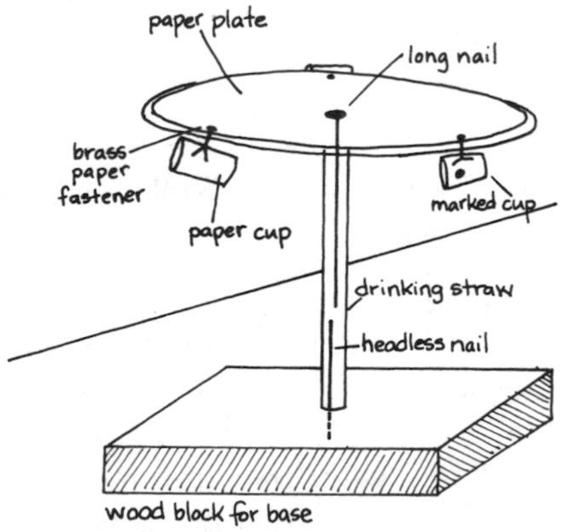

MODEL ANEMOMETER

Procedure

• Another way that we can find out how fast the wind is blowing is by using an anemometer. An anemometer is a special instrument that weather people use to measure how fast the wind is blowing. Demonstrate how the model of an anemometer works. Explain that the little black mark has to be counted each time the anemometer turns so that you know how many times it turned during a certain amount of time like a minute. The wind speed can be figured out by counting the number of times it spins per unit of time.

• Have children make their own model of an anemometer.

5. Weather Vane

Materials A model of a weather vane made from: an arrow that can spin, tagboard, glue, a headless nail, half of a drinking straw, a small block of wood, a marking pen. See diagram.

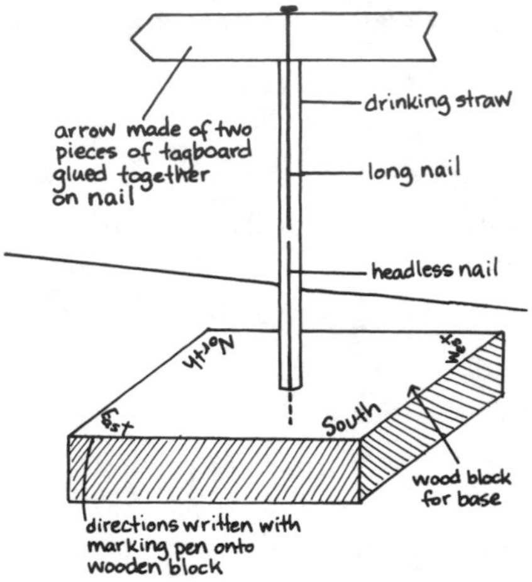

MODEL WEATHER VANE

Procedure

• Explain to the children that another weather instrument that weather people use to help them record weather is a weather vane. Show them the model of a weather vane. Have the children blow on it. It will spin. The weather vane shows us which direction wind is blowing from. When the arrow points, it points away from the direction in which the wind is blowing. If the arrow points south, that means the wind is coming from the north.

• Have the children make their own model of a weather vane.

6. Thermometer

Materials Two basins; hot water; cold water; two weather thermometers; newspaper to absorb possible mess; front page of morning newspaper for weather report.

Procedure

• Show the children the thermometer. Ask them if they know what it is, and what it is used for. (It measures the amount of heat in the air.) Ask the following kinds of questions:

How can you tell what the weather and temperature are like outside without going outside to find out?
(By reading an outside thermometer through an indoor window, by listening to the radio or television weather report, or by looking at the front page of the morning newspaper. Have children look at the front page of the paper to see the weather summary located in the top left- or right-hand corner of the front page. A full weather report is also listed in the index at the bottom of the page.)

What is inside a thermometer?
(A liquid which is very sensitive to changes in air temperature. The liquid is usually a metal called mercury. It expands and contracts with changing temperature.)

Will the liquid inside a thermometer go up or down when it is cold?
(Down.)

What sinks down when it is cold?
(Air is heavy when it is cold and sinks.)

• Show the children the two thermometers. Pour hot water into one of the basins and cold water into the other basin. Place a thermometer into each basin. Look for the results on the thermometer. (Hot will register high, cold will register low.)

7. A Bottle Thermometer

Materials A small empty soda bottle; water; a drinking straw; plasticine or clay; a bucket of ice water; a bucket of hot water; an index card; Scotch tape; food color; newspaper to absorb possible mess.

Procedure

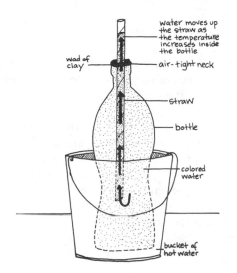

• Fill the empty soda bottle with colored water. Place a wad of clay around the perimeter of a drinking straw. Put the drinking straw with clay wrapped around it on top of the soda bottle so that half of the straw is in the bottle and half of the straw is sticking out of the bottle. Be sure the clay is squeezed in between the straw and the neck of the soda bottle so that it is airtight. See diagram.

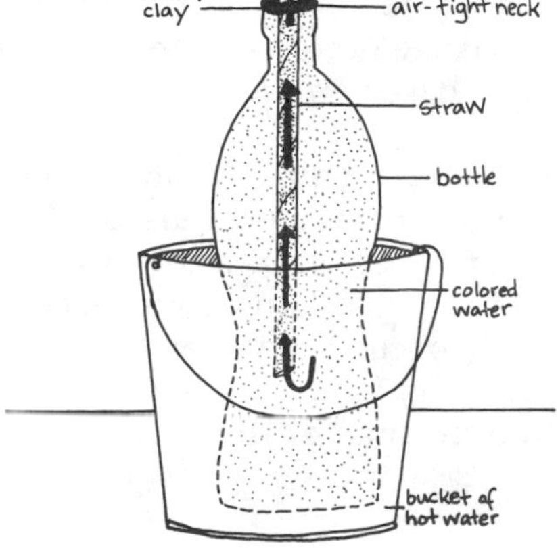

• Put the bottle in the bucket of hot water. Observe what happens to the colored liquid in the bottle. It will start to rise. It may even go out the top of the straw.
• Put the bottle thermometer in the bucket of ice water. Observe what happens to the liquid in the straw. It will go down, just like a real thermometer.
• Ask the children to explain why the liquid goes up and down inside the straw. (The liquid moves up and down in the straw because it is affected by temperature. Warm things expand and take up more space; cool things contract and take up less space.)

**You can use the index card as a marker. Scotch-tape it to the straw. Take a reading on the bottle thermometer when it is hot and mark it on the card with a line. Take another reading when it is cool and mark it on the card. Take another reading that is at room temperature. Compare the readings to that of the mercury thermometer. You can put degree numbers on the line marks on the index card by taking another measurement with a mercury thermometer at the same time.

8. Weather Fronts

Materials Teacher- or parent-made models of sun, rain and clouds to represent a warm front and a cold front made from: tagboard, crayons, and marking pen.

Procedure

• Explain to the children that air masses can be warm or cold. When the air masses meet they form a front. A front is the line that forms between two air masses before the "battle" occurs. When the "battle" occurs, weather changes.
• Show the children the models of the rain, the sun, and the clouds that represent a warm front and a cold front. Code the clouds with different colors like red for warm and blue for cold, or with symbols: + for warm, and − for cool. Let the children decide.
• Tell the children that you will be using these models of the rain, the sun, and the warm and cold air masses to demonstrate how weather fronts move and how they "battle" each other. Use the cloud models as you explain about fronts. You might want to explain fronts in the following way:

A *warm front* contains a mass of warm air. Warm air has low pressure. It is light in weight. It spreads out and rises.

A *cold front* contains a mass of cool air. Cool air has high pressure. It is heavy and sinks.

A *stationary front* is a stalemate on the "battle" line between two masses of air that do not move. A

When air masses meet they form a front. The weather changes. Warm air rises up and cool air settles down. The air masses "battle" and wind and turbulence are seen and felt. Circular movements occur both up and down and sideways.

WEATHER FRONT DEMONSTRATED BY CHILDREN

stationary front can change quickly or can stay around awhile. If the stationary front moves on quickly so that the two air masses slide past each other, the weather does not change much. If the stationary front stays for a few days, the weather will gradually change. First, it will rain for a few days and then the sky will clear.

9. Barometer

Materials A real aneroid barometer (with a dial) or a mercury barometer (with a long glass tube); a model of a barometer made from: tagboard, paper fastener, marking pen, crayons. See diagram.

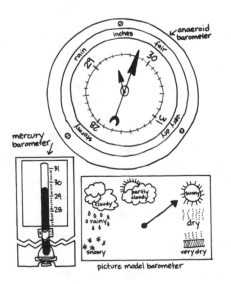

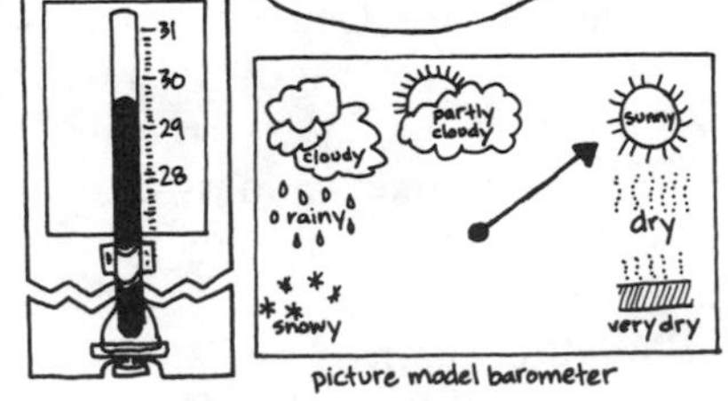

picture model barometer

Procedure

- Show the children the barometer and the model of a barometer. Explain that a barometer is a special weather instrument that measures the amount of pressure in the air. Barometers help us to predict the weather. Move the pointer on the model barometer. Tell the children that when the pointer moves it tells us about the weather and when the barometer does not change it also tells us about the weather.
- Move the pointer on the dial as you give the following kind of explanation:

If the pointer on the dial moves down to a low number, it means that the pressure is low. When the pressure is low it means that a warm front is approaching and that rainy days may be arriving soon. If the pointer on the dial stays still or steady it means that the weather is not changing or is stationary. A stationary front means that two air masses have met, but they are not moving. If a stationary front moves on or only stays for a short time, the weather does not change much. If the stationary front stays put for awhile and does not move, then the weather does change. The change is gradual and slow. It will rain or snow for a few days and then the sky will look clear again.

If the pointer on the dial moves up to a high number, it means that the pressure is high. When the pressure is high, it means that a cold front is approaching. A quick rainstorm or snowstorm that will last only a few hours will occur, and then the sky will clear and sunny days will follow.

- Have children make their own model of a barometer.

10. Rain Gauge

Materials Make a model rain gauge from: an empty tin can, a funnel, a ruler, a sprinkling can filled with water, newspaper to absorb possible mess from water.

Procedure

• Tell the children that when it rains, weather people like to record how much rain fell. They keep records of rainfall. They measure the rainfall by collecting the rain when it falls. Demonstrate how to use the model rain gauge. Explain that because it cannot rain indoors you are using a sprinkling can filled with water to represent a cloud that is dropping rain. Let the "rain" fall into the funnel on top of the can. See diagram.

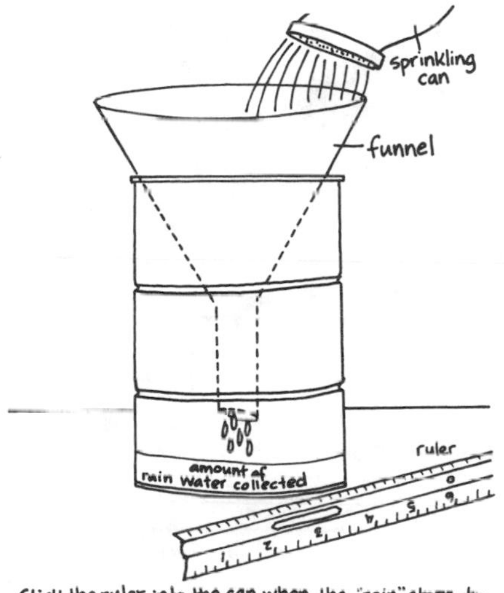

Stick the ruler into the can when the "rain" stops, to measure how much rain fell.

• Let it "rain" for a minute or less. Then measure with the ruler how much "rain" fell. Stick the ruler in the water and take a reading. Explain that a real rain gauge is much larger than the model, but that a real rain gauge measures rain water in the same way.

• Have children make their own model of a rain gauge.

11. Record Keeping

Materials Tagboard calendar for a weather-keeping chart; ruler; crayons and marking pens; cut paper symbols of the sun, clouds, rain and snow.

Procedure

• Tell the children that the chart represents a month. It is like a calendar. Weather people record their day-to-day measurements. The measurements are called data. Ask the children the following kinds of questions:

What kinds of data do weather people collect?
(Temperature, air pressure, rainfall, humidity, wind speed and wind direction, cloud formation, sunrise and sunset, high tide and low tide.)

What are the names of some of the weather instruments that weather people use?
(Thermometer, wind vane, anemometer, barometer, rain gauge, satellite pictures of clouds.)

What kinds of things could you collect data on during a month?
(Temperature, rainfall, the kind of day it was, *i.e.*, sunny, cloudy, rainy, snowy. The other data would depend on the weather instruments available to you.)

• Suggest that children make and keep their own record of weather for a month. Supply them with materials to make their own charts.

Further Resources

Suggested Books for Children

The Dewey Decimal Classification number for weather is: 551.5

Blackwood, Paul E., *The How and Why Wonder Book of Weather*. New York: Grosset and Dunlap, 1978. (Appropriate for older children.)

Branley, Franklyn M., and Leonard Kessler, *Hurricane Warning*. Washington, D.C.: U.S. Dept. of Commerce, National Oceanic and Atmospheric Administration, and National Weather Service, Stock No. 003-018-00075-0, U.S. Government Printing Office. 35¢ each.

Branley, Franklyn M., *Flash, Crash, Rumble and Roll. Let's Read and Find Out*. New York: Thomas Y. Crowell, 1964. (Describes and illustrates how and why electrical storms occur.)

Branley, Franklyn M., *Rain and Hail, Let's Read and Find Out*. New York: Thomas Y. Crowell, 1963. (Picture book for young children and older children with large illustrations explaining the process of precipitation and the water cycle.)

Chisholm, Jane, *Finding Out About Our Earth*. Tulsa, Oklahoma: Hayes Books, 1982. (Colorful illustrations, a summary of Earth Science.)

dePaola, Tomie, *The Cloud Book*. New York: Holiday House, 1975. (Colorful picture book about clouds for young children.)

Gans, Roma, *Water for Dinosaurs and You, Let's Read and Find Out*. New York: Thomas Y. Crowell, 1972. (Picture book appropriate for young children. It describes the water cycle.)

Updegraff, Imelda and Robert, *Weather*. New York: Penguin Books, 1982. (Picture book with illustrations that can be lifted up to illustrate before-and-after scenes.)

Webster, David, *Snow Stumpers*. Garden City, New York: The National History Press, 1968. (Numerous thought-provoking black and white pictures depicting snow scenes captioned with a question. Answers to questions provided at end of each section. Excellent for children in the middle elementary grades and up.)

Resource Books for More Ideas

Bendick, Jeanne, *The Wind.* New York: Rand McNally and Company, 1964. (Old but well thought out, very inclusive. The text and illustrations are both humorous and interesting.)

Burnett, Will R., Paul E. Lehr and Herbert Zim, *Weather, A Golden Guide.* New York: Golden Press, 1975. (An illustrated summary of many ideas and concepts related to weather.)

Courtney, William, *What Does a Barometer Do?* Boston: Little, Brown and Company, 1963. (Helpful illustrations and text.)

Hitte, Kathryn, *Hurricanes, Tornadoes and Blizzards.* New York: Random House, 1960. (Large print book, helpful illustrations, good explanation about how storms form and behave.)

Kaufman, John, *Winds and Weather.* New York: William Karoom and Company, Inc., 1971. (Black and white illustrations, text describes the formation and circulation of winds on the planet.)

Minnesota Environmental Sciences Foundation, Inc., *Snow and Ice, An Environmental Investigation.* Washington, D.C.: National Wildlife Federation, 1971. (Interesting investigative experiments.)

Schneider, Herman, and Jeanne Bendick, *Everyday Weather and How It Works.* New York: McGraw-Hill, 1961.

Schneider, Nina and Herman, *Let's Find Out, A Picture Science Book.* New York: William R. Scott, Inc., 1966. (Interesting presentation and facts about air, heat and water.)

Stone, A. Harris, and Herbert Spiegel, *The Winds of Weather.* Englewood Cliffs, New Jersey: Prentice Hall, 1969. (Interesting air experiments to conduct related to wind; helpful illustrations.)

10

VOLCANOES, ROCKS, AND EROSION

Objectives

• For children to become aware of what volcanoes are.

• For children to develop an understanding of why an eruption occurs.

• For children to develop an awareness of what a cross-section model represents.

• For children to develop an awareness of what seismic waves are.

• For children to develop an awareness of the differences between the inside interior layers of the Earth and the outside layer of crust on the Earth.

• For children to develop an understanding that islands do not float in the ocean, but are really tall mountainous mesas that stick up above the water line.

• For children to be able to distinguish rocks from one another.

• For children to become aware of the various properties of rocks and the terms used to describe those properties.

• For children to become aware that rocks can be classified or grouped by the way they were formed.

• For children to become aware of erosion and how it can occur by mechanical action or through chemical action.

• For children to become aware of how sediments can be loosened, moved, and built up.

• For children to develop an awareness of how mountains can form from pressure.

General Background Information for Parents and Teachers

Volcano An opening in the Earth's crust. Magma, gases, rock fragments, lava, and ash are expelled from the opening or vent. It is often shaped like a mountain.

Shield Volcanoes are basically flat-looking in their appearance. Magma can erupt from several vents at the same time. Lava flows very fast and is very liquid.

Cinder Volcanoes are shaped like flat-topped mountains. The lava from this kind of volcano flows slower and is sticky. It tends to have more rock fragments, ash, and dust than does the more fluid liquid lava which erupts from a shield volcano.

Composite Volcanoes are shaped like high-peaked mountains. They are formed from both sticky and highly liquid lava in alternate layers.

Volcanic eruption A volcanic activity that allows magma, gases, ash, and rocks to move up and emerge from the interior of a volcano. Eruptions are often sudden and violent.

**Items marked by two asterisks indicate that the information is too abstract and too complicated for young children to understand or comprehend. It is included to enhance parent or teacher background only.

Volcanic activity Volcanoes can be active, inactive, or extinct.

Active Volcanoes still have eruptions.
Inactive Volcanoes have infrequent eruptions.
Extinct Volcanoes no longer have eruptions.

Volcanologist A scientist who studies volcanoes.

Magma Hot liquid rock. Igneous rocks are formed from magma.

Lava Magma that emerges from a volcano's interior.

Crater Opening or vent on top of a volcano.

Cone Shape of some volcanoes.

Magma pipe Located in the interior of the volcano. It is a vertical space or tunnel shape that is formed from the pressure of magma pushing up.

Magma chamber Located deep within the Earth, under the volcanic area. It contains a large mass of magma.

Caldera A very large vent or crater opening caused by the collapse of a volcano's top.

Seismologist A scientist who studies the vibrations caused by earthquakes. The discoveries and findings of seismologists have helped us create theories and gain knowledge about the earth's interior and about the movements of the earth. Seismologists make predictions about sites and approximate times for future earthquakes and volcanic eruptions based on their knowledge gained from previous movements they have observed.

Seismic waves Waves or earth tremors that can be measured by a seismograph machine. There are three kinds of seismic waves:

Primary Waves are often called P Waves. They are the first set of waves that are sent out from an earthquake. They travel the fastest and penetrate deeply. They create a ricocheting pattern of pushes and pulls.

Secondary Waves are often called S Waves. They travel slower than the primary waves. S waves arrive after the P waves. They travel in an up-and-down or side-to-side pattern like an S.

Surface Waves or L Waves arrive last but do the most damage. They travel the slowest of the seismic waves. They travel along the crust or surface of the Earth and cause much destruction.

Seismograph A machine that measures and records vibrations on the Earth's surface or crust.

Seismogram A picture of wave lengths made by a seismograph machine. The actual recording on paper by the machine.

Richter Scale A scale ranging in numerical value from 1 to 10. It indicates how violent or calm an earthquake's seismogram reading was. A numerical value of 1 indicates that the quake had the least amount of energy. A numerical value of 10 would indicate an enormous amount of energy was expended.

Gas A state of matter. Gases have the ability to expand and contract greatly depending on the relative changes in the amount of temperature and pressure. Gases also have the ability to spread out easily and uniformly.

Cross-section A diagram that depicts an internal slice of something that has dimensions.

Globe A model of the Earth.

Earth's crust The relatively thin outer layer of the Earth that we live on. It consists of the land and the water we see. It is the outside layer of the Earth, and is believed to be about 25 miles thick. Under the ocean it is about 3 miles thick.

Bedrock Layer of solid rock that lies underneath the soil. Also, loose gravel, sand, and clay on the Earth's crust.

Earth's mantle The interior layer of the Earth beneath the crust. It is believed to be about 1,800 miles thick, and is thought to be made up of solid rock.

Core The innermost part of the Earth. The core consists of an inner and an outer core. The inner core is thought to be a solid area made up of iron and nickel. The outer core is thought to be a nonsolid area that is molten (hot liquid).

Fault A broken section of the Earth's crust along which movement occurs.

Fault line A weak section of the Earth's crust where earthquakes and volcanoes might occur.

Volcano or earthquake zones There are three principal areas where volcanic and earthquake activity frequently occur. They are:

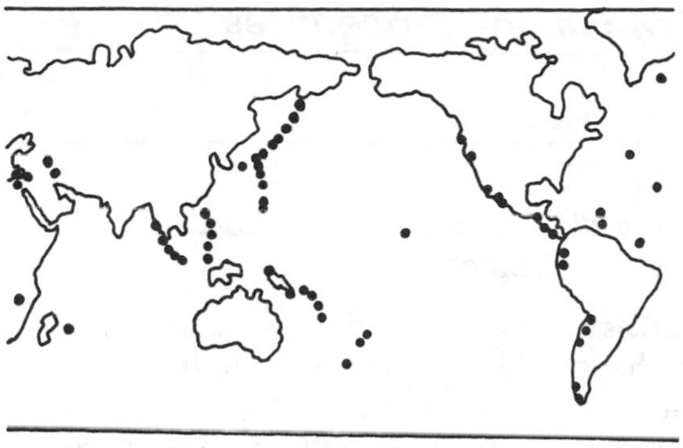

Dots represent volcanic activity and eruptions.

The Ring of Fire—A circular line that runs along and near the edges or coastlines of the continents that border the Pacific Ocean.

The Mid-Atlantic Ridge—A line that runs from Iceland to the South Pole under the midline of the Atlantic Ocean.

The Mediterranean Region is actually a perpendicular extension line branching off the Mid-Atlantic Ridge. It runs under the Mediterranean Sea past Asia and India and connects to the Ring of Fire between Australia and New Zealand.

Earthquake When the earth's crust breaks apart suddenly and slides in two different directions, creating a disturbance of existing natural and man-made structures on the crust.

Atom Rocks and minerals are made up of atoms.

Rock A combination of two or more minerals.

Mineral A mineral is something that is found in nature that was never alive. No matter where it is found it always has a nearly uniform chemical composition. Also the atoms of a mineral are arranged in a regular pattern which forms a unique crystal structure. Minerals have fairly constant physical properties. Their physical properties are described in terms of: hardness, crystal formation, color, streak, luster, weight, and cleavage. Many minerals end with the suffix "ite." There are about 2,000 kinds of minerals. Only about one hundred of them are common.

Element A substance made up of molecules which consist of only one kind of atom.

Crystal formation A crystal is a pure mineral. The atoms of a crystal are arranged in a unique pattern. Every mineral has its own special crystal structure and formation or pattern.

Chemical bond A bond that holds the atoms together in a crystal.

Cleavage Refers to the way a rock breaks. Weak chemical bonds along an atomic structure or crystal formation form cleavage or breaking points where crystals or rocks break apart.

Luster Refers to the shine and sparkle of some rocks. Luster can be metallic, nonmetallic, pearly, dull, brilliant, glossy, etc.

Hardness Rocks vary in their degree of hardness and softness. Hard rocks can scratch softer rocks.

Moh's Hardness Scale A scale that is numbered 1 through 10, placing a numerical value on the relative hardness or softness of rocks in relation to other rocks. #1 is the softest, #10 is the hardest. The complete scale is: #1 talc; #2 gypsum; #3 calcite; #4 fluorite; #5 apatite; #6 feldspar; #7 quartz, #8 topaz; #9 corundum; #10 diamond. #1 and #2 can be scratched by a fingernail. #3 can be scratched by a copper coin. #4 and #5 can be scratched by a knife, scissor blade, or window glass. #6, #7, and #8 can scratch a knife, scissor blade, or window glass. #10 scratches most other materials.

Color Rocks with different kinds of minerals have different colors.

Streak A line of luster that runs through some rocks. Also the line of color that is left on an unglazed ceramic tile when certain rocks are rubbed on to the tile.

Weight or density Refers to the solidness of a rock. The more solid the density, the heavier the rock. A difference in density gives two rocks that are the same size a different weight.

Igneous rocks Rocks made from fire, formed by the cooling of hot liquid magma. The magma solidifies and forms igneous rocks. The original magma for igneous rocks comes from the inner depths of the Earth. Lava, granite, and quartz are examples or forms of igneous rocks.

Metamorphic Refers to change. It means a change takes place.

Metamorphic rocks Rocks that began as another kind of rock and that have undergone a change. Rocks undergo metamorphosis or change when they are subjected to extreme amounts of pressure and/or heat. Metamorphic rocks were originally igneous or sedimentary rocks. For example, marble is formed from limestone, slate is formed from shale.

Gemstone A precious or semiprecious stone that can be used as a jewel after it has been cut and polished. Most gemstones are forms of metamorphic rocks.

Lapidary A person who specializes in cutting, polishing, and engraving gemstones.

Sedimentary rocks Rocks that were formed over a period of time in layers. Often formed in low areas or under water from sediments of mud and silt that have been deposited by rivers and streams. The sediments become cemented together over time to form layers of sedimentary rock. Clay and limestone are examples of sedimentary rock.

Sediment Small pieces of dust and soil that have been broken away from larger pieces of land and rock.

Erosion A natural process that wears away rock and earth. Erosion can take place from weathering, from wind, from glacial action, from corrosion, from grinding action, and from movement of earth and rocks from one place to another.

Fold An area on the Earth's crust that has been bent due to enormous internal pressure from gas or magma deep inside the earth. It can be an upward, downward, or lateral movement of the crust. Some mountains are formed due to folding. Some folds take 1,000 years or more to form. Some folds form quickly. Some folds are small, others are enormous.

Activities and Procedures

I. Volcanoes

1. Three-dimensional Cardboard Model of a Volcano

Materials Pieces of cardboard; paper rolled into a tube shape; pieces of yellow, red, black, and orange construction paper cut into strips ¼-inch wide by 8 inches long; corner of a cardboard box; masking tape; marking pens in assorted colors.

Preparation

- Roll masking tape around the wad of colored construction paper strips. Crinkle the strips up. It should look like a mini-pompom. See diagram.
- Mount the corner of a cardboard box onto the piece of cardboard. Cut a hole at the top of the corner and through the piece of cardboard. Stuff the piece of paper rolled into a tube shape through the two holes. Use colored marking pens to create an imaginary landscape on the piece of cardboard and on the cone-shaped cardboard corner.

Procedure

- Show the children the three-dimensional cardboard model after it is constructed. Explain that it is a model of a volcano. Identify the parts of the model volcano for the children. Use the following terms to describe its parts:

Crater for the hole on the top of the cone.
Cone for the cardboard corner.
Magma pipe for the paper tube.

VOLCANO MODEL

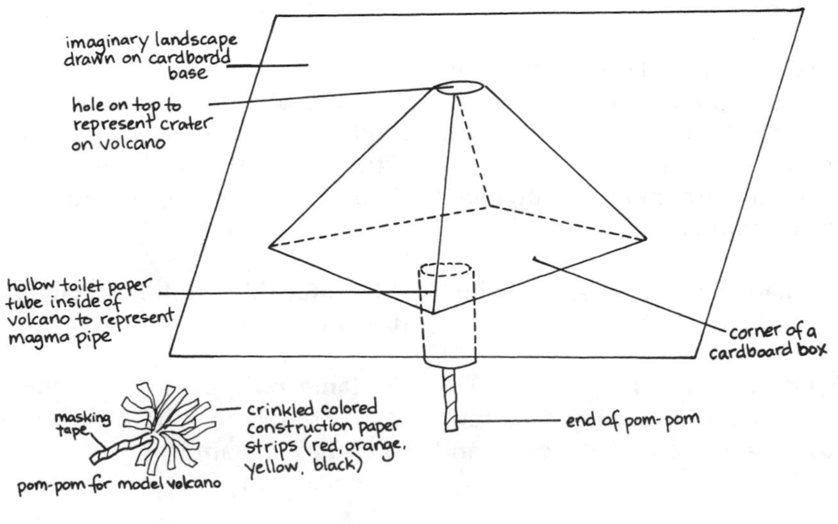

Crust for the piece of flat cardboard.
Magma for the pompom that is pushed up the paper tube. Push the pompom up the paper tube to demonstrate how the magma travels up the magma pipe.
Magma Chamber for the area directly underneath the magma pipe.

• As you push the model magma up the magma pipe, explain to the children that the magma rises up the pipe because of pressure that builds up inside of the Earth from gases that have warmed up and expanded. The magma is hot liquid rock. It is made up of rocks that become so hot they melt. The hot liquid rock causes gases to build up and expand. The pressure from the hot gases becomes so great and powerful that the gas cannot be contained. It has to escape. When these hot gases escape above the ground, an eruption occurs. It is called a volcanic eruption. The eruption continues until the built-up hot gases escape through the open crater holes on the volcano. When the gases have finished escaping, the volcano stops erupting. Volcanoes that do not erupt any more are called extinct. Those that have a lot of eruptions are called active, and those that stay asleep or dormant for many years are called inactive. When magma comes to the surface it is called lava. The lava is pushed out and continues to flow as long as the hot gases from deep inside are pushing up and escaping. Some of the lava forms into a fine volcanic dust which floats up with the escaping gas and forms large, black, smoky clouds.
• Hold the flat cardboard which represents the Earth's crust on your forehead so that your eyes are underneath the volcano. Explain that this is where the magma chamber is located. It is deep underneath the ground. Magma is made up of hot liquid rock and gases. It expands and pressure builds up and pushes magma out. The force for the push comes from pressures inside the Earth underneath the volcano.
• Have children make their own three-dimensional model of an erupting volcano with a magma pipe.

2. Breath

Materials None.

Procedure
• Have the children take a deep breath. Explain to them that the air we breathe in and out is gas. Have them feel their breath with their hands as they breathe out. Ask them the following kinds of questions:

How does the air feel that comes out of your mouth, warm or cool?
(Warm.)

How does the air feel before it enters your mouth?
(Cooler.)

What is the gas called that we breathe in?
(Oxygen—O_2)

What is the gas called that we breathe out?
(Carbon Dioxide—CO_2)

• Explain to the children that when we breathe in oxygen, it goes into our lungs and body. It is a fuel that gets burned up. When the oxygen is used or burned up it becomes carbon dioxide. The carbon dioxide becomes warm and expands. This causes pressure to build up in our lungs and to push out the used oxygen gas that has become carbon dioxide.

3. Holding a Breath

Materials None.

Procedure
• Ask the children to take a deep breath and to see how long they can hold their breath. They will discover that it is impossible for them to hold their breath indefinitely, because the medulla in the brain forces their bodies to let their breath out, thus allowing built-up hot gas to escape.
• Explain that our body is like an erupting volcano. When we hold our breath, gas builds up and our body forces us to open up or "erupt" and to take in a new breath of oxygen. When our body "erupts," it forces the built-up hot gas to escape, and new gas to enter our body. When we hold our breath and "erupt," we cannot continue to erupt. Like a volcano, we stop erupting when our gas supply runs out. We are like an active volcano. We continue to erupt as long as we breathe. If we stay perfectly still and quiet, we are like an inactive volcano. Inactive volcanoes are still able to erupt. Scientists can detect rumblings inside of the magma chamber and magma pipe with seismographs and other special instruments. Sometimes these instruments can help them predict when an inactive volcano will erupt and be active. But most eruptions are difficult to predict.

**Some of the instruments used by scientists to collect data on when a volcano will erupt are:

1. *Seismographs* for detecting earthquakes in the suspected area.

2. *Thermometers* for detecting increases in temperature in the suspected area.

3. *Tiltmeters* for detecting growth or expansion of a volcanic cone.

4. *Gas Detectors* for measuring increases in amounts of gas in the area.

4. Pictures

Materials Assorted pictures from *National Geographic* Magazine, *Life* Magazine or other pictorial source that depict volcanic islands, volcanoes erupting, crater lakes, and/or inactive volcanoes.

Procedure Show the children the pictures and discuss what volcanoes look like when they are erupting, inactive, and extinct. Explain what the word "extinct" means. It is when something was and is no longer. For example, dinosaurs were alive once, but are extinct now. No one has ever seen a living dinosaur. Sometimes when a volcano becomes extinct the old crater fills up with water and the crater becomes a lake.

5. How a Volcano Grows

Materials Flannel model of a volcanic mountain range; flannel pieces cut in assorted colors in various hues of brown to represent mountains and volcanic layers on the cone of the volcano; flannel in hues of red, gold, and orange to represent magma, magma pipe and lava; a large flannel board about 18 inches by 24 inches.

Preparation
- Create a mountain range out of flannel. Glue small pieces of brown flannel onto a larger piece about 18 inches by 12 inches to create a mountain range.
- Create a separate magma chamber in bright red, orange, and yellow to create a feeling of intense heat.
- Make a separate pipe-like shape that is able to slide up from the magma chamber underneath the flannel mountain range to the surface of the crust. Make the pipe about 24 inches long.
- Cut out numerous curved strips in assorted hot colors and lengths to represent lava flowing from the volcano. Also cut out several brown cone shapes in sequential size to represent the hardened volcano after a volcanic eruption. With each eruption the volcano's cone grows in size or volume.
- Hold the flannel board in a vertical position and place it upright. Place the pieces of flannel which represent the magma chamber and magma pipe underneath the mountain range, hidden from view on the flannel board. See diagram.

Procedure
- Show children the flannel board. Ask them what the picture looks like on the flannel board. (A mountain range.)
- Explain that a mountain range does not stay still. Change takes place gradually over a long period of time. Usually the change is so slight we cannot see the change take place because it happens so slowly. Some mountains become smaller because weather conditions erode them away. Sometimes mountains grow very quickly, almost overnight. This happens when a lot of hot gases build up underneath them and need to escape. Sometimes the top blows off the mountain and hot lava flows out. When this happens the mountain grows very suddenly and is called a volcano.
- Pull up the piece of flannel that represents the magma pipe so that just a little bit of it can be seen. Ask the children the following kinds of questions:

What might be happening to the model of the mountain range?
(A volcano is beginning to erupt.)

Where is the magma coming from?
(From deep beneath the ground under the volcano.)

Can we normally see underneath the ground?
(Normally, no.)

Is this a real volcano or a model of a volcano?
(A model.)

FLANNEL MODEL OF HOW A CINDER CONE VOLCANO GROWS

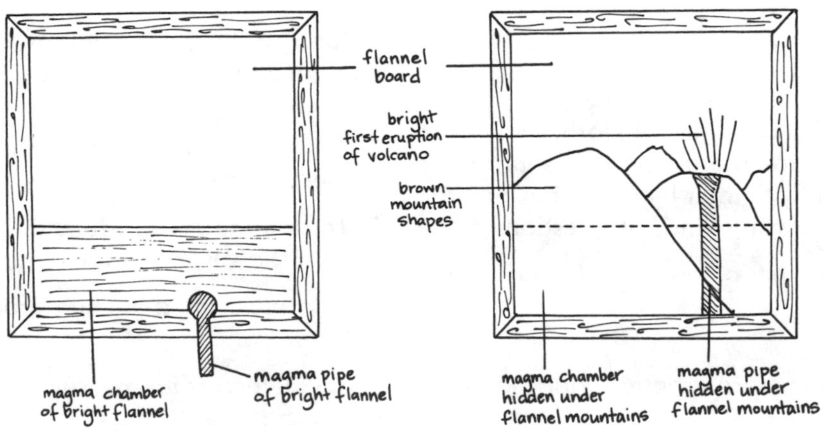

Is it possible to look underneath the ground of a model?
(Yes.)

If we lift up the mountain range and look underneath it, what might we be able to see?
(The magma chamber, magma pipe, and magma.)

• Lift off the mountain range by rolling up its right or left side. Explain to the children that the magma is coming from the magma chamber, rising through the magma pipe to the top of the volcanic cone called the crater.
• Place the mountain range in place again. Allow the volcano to erupt. Show the eruption by placing curved flannel strips on the flannel cone. Then cover the cone with a larger flannel cone, so that none of the lava or magma can be seen. Explain to the children that the volcano stays at rest or is inactive after it erupts. It stays that way until gas builds up again, and then it erupts again:

1. Pull the magma pipe up again.

2. Place lava strips on the cone again.

3. Cover the lava again with a larger sequential-sized cone.

4. Review what is happening each time by making the children describe what is happening using the appropriate vocabulary words.

5. Continue this four-step process for another three or four eruptions.* See diagram.

*Explain that scientists are able to find out about volcanoes by taking soil samples from them and by using low frequency sound waves that create X-ray-like pictures which give them information or data about the volcano, its age, the number of eruptions it had, and the kinds of eruptions it had.

• When the volcano is finished erupting, call it an extinct volcano. Peel off the entire volcano so that the inside layers can be seen. Count the layers and find out how many eruptions occurred. Each sequential cone should be cut out in different shades of brown flannel.
• Have children continue to use the flannel board model and simulate volcanic eruptions.

6. Building up Layers

Materials Black, brown, and yellow construction paper; clear Contact paper; a picture of a crater lake.

Preparation
• Cover the construction paper on both sides with clear Contact paper.
• Cut the brown and black paper into sequential-sized V-like shapes with a flat top. Also cut out one small cone shape.
• Cut out a yellow magma pipe and a yellow magma chamber.

Procedure
• Show the children the construction paper shapes covered with clear Contact paper. Ask them what they look like. (Layers of a volcano.)
• Show children how they can be arranged sequentially. Place the magma chamber down first. Slide the magma pipe underneath the magma chamber. Place the small cone on the magma pipe. Push the magma

FLANNEL MODEL SHOWING LAYERS INSIDE A CINDER CONE VOLCANO

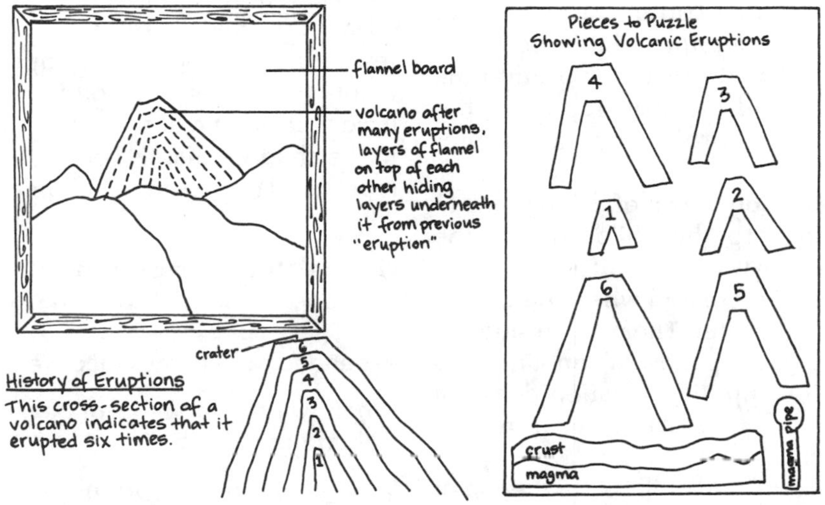

pipe up so that it sticks up above the cone. Add on a flat-topped V-shape over the cone to cover up the magma. Continue to push up the magma and to add new flat-topped V-shaped layers to the cone.

• Explain to the children that this kind of erupting volcano is called a composite volcano. It grows and expands by building up alternate layers of thin and thick lava. Thin lava flows quickly while thick lava flows more slowly. Volcanoes come in two basic shapes. They either have one crater and a cone-like shape that grows, or they are flat and have several craters or holes where hot lava shoots up and oozes out.

• Show children the picture of a crater lake. Explain that sometimes when all of the gas from inside escapes, the magma chamber becomes quite empty. It becomes a large empty hole. The hole collapses because of all of the weight from the earth on top of it. When this happens, the crater sinks inside of the extinct volcano and the crater's hole becomes quite large. The hole fills with water and becomes a natural lake.

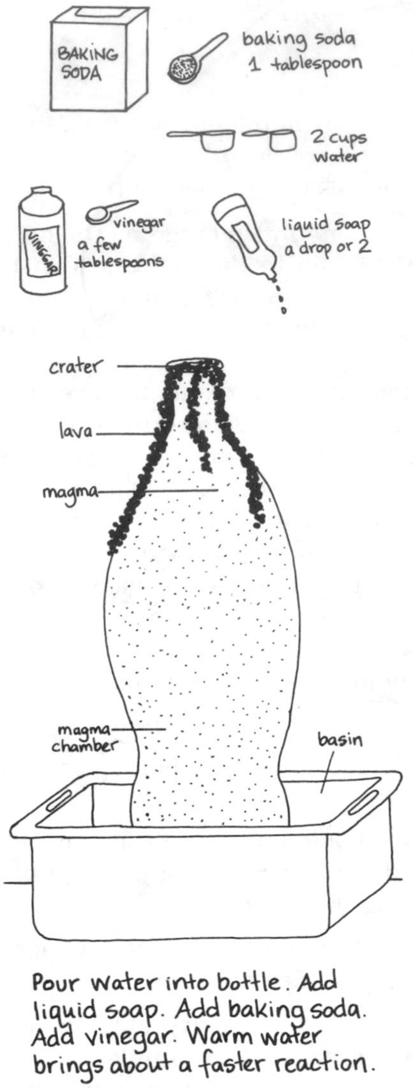

ERUPTION IN A BOTTLE

7. Bottle Model of an Erupting Volcano

Materials A basin; an empty salad dressing bottle (Wishbone bottles are perfect); warm water; liquid soap; baking soda; vinegar; a teaspoon; a measuring cup.

Procedure

• Place the bottle inside an empty basin. Explain to the children that the bottle is a model of the inside of a volcano. The inside of the bottle represents the magma chamber, the neck of the bottle represents the magma pipe, and the opening on top of the bottle represents the crater on top of the volcano where the lava flows out.

• Have a child add about one cup of warm water to the bottle, and then have another child add a few drops of liquid detergent to the water. Explain to the children that the water and the soap represent hot bubbly liquid magma inside of the magma chamber deep inside the earth.

• Have a child add a teaspoon or two of baking soda to the warm water. Explain to the children that the baking soda added to warm water sets off a reaction. A gas called carbon dioxide is created when the baking soda dissolves in the warm water. The water inside the bottle is warm and the gas expands. When air or gas expands, it tends to move up. (If a reaction does not occur, add a teaspoon or two of vinegar to the solution inside of the bottle.)

• When the reaction occurs, suds will rise to the top of the bottle and overflow down the sides. Explain to the children that when magma comes to the surface of the earth and flows out of the volcano it is called lava.

• Have the children repeat the steps to this procedure several times. After each eruption have the children empty the contents of the bottle into the basin, then have them fill the bottle with fresh ingredients. Explain to the children that the pool of liquid in the basin can represent lava before it solidifies into rock.

Fine points to discuss with children

Why does the model volcano stop flowing or erupting?
(The gas has expanded, and the energy has been expended. It becomes inactive as it runs out of steam.)

When will the model erupt again?
(When the gases build up again.)

What causes the eruption?
(Gases that heat up and expand cause the eruption to

occur. The eruption occurs because of internal pressure.)

8. Lava Rock

Materials A lava rock (can be purchased at a rock store, a natural history museum or at a drugstore as a pumice stone); a non-lava rock about the same size as the lava rock; a basin of water.

Procedure

- Show children the two rocks. Ask them if they can tell which one might weigh less by just looking at the two rocks. (The one that has lots of holes or bubbles on its surface will probably weigh less because it is not as solid-looking as the other rock.)
- Have the children feel both rocks and notice which rock feels lighter. (The lava rock will feel lighter.)
- Have the children smell each rock. Do they smell alike dry? (Probably.)
- Place the two rocks in the water and observe what happens to the lava rock. It will float. Smell the two rocks again and see if they have different odors when they are wet. (The lava rock will most likely smell like volcanic ash. It may have a very earthy and dusty odor.)
- Explain to the children that the lava rock is very light in weight because it is like a foam sponge that has hardened. It is full of air bubbles or holes like a sponge. It is not solid like other rocks, and it has a very rough texture.

9. Cross-section Model of an Erupting Volcano

Materials White construction paper; cross-section diagram of a volcano; colored pencils; a lift-off paper diagram of the outside of a volcanic cone; Contact paper; word labels; mounting board or tagboard for finished model; clear Contact paper; masking tape. See preparation instructions below.

Preparation

- Color in cross-section diagram of a volcano with colored pencils, mount on tagboard, label appropriate parts: crater, lava, magma, magma pipe, magma chamber, sedimentary rock, metamorphic rock, igneous rock, ash, volcanic cone. Make separate word labels for each part labeled on diagram. Cover diagram and word labels with clear Contact paper.
- Cut out a volcanic cone shape that fits on top of the cross-section model of the volcano. Color in the cone shape with colored pencils and cover with clear Contact paper.
- Mount the diagram of a cone on top of the cross-section diagram with a rolled piece of masking tape so that it acts like a hinge. The cone can then be lifted up to expose the cross-section diagram showing the interior of a volcano.

Procedure

- Show children the finished model covered with clear Contact paper. Ask the children the following kinds of questions:

What is the picture a model of?
(An erupting volcano.)

How can they tell it is an erupting volcano?
(Ash and lava are coming out of the crater, the opening at the top of the volcano.)

What is inside an erupting volcano?
(A magma pipe, with magma flowing up from a magma chamber.)

- Lift up the cone and let the children look inside to see the cross-section of the volcano. Point to various

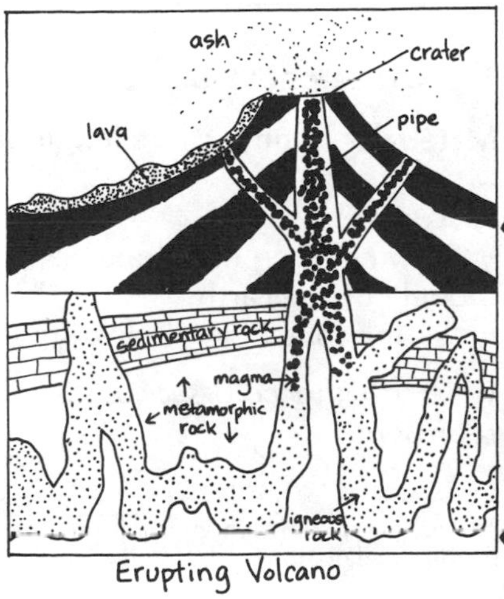

Erupting Volcano

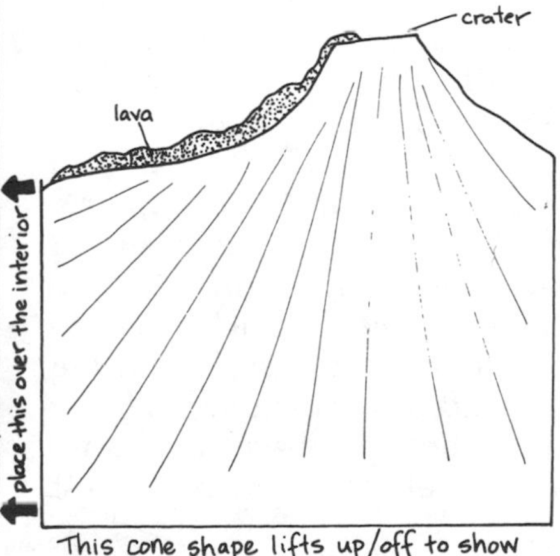

This cone shape lifts up/off to show (inside) cross-section view of volcano.

parts inside of the volcano and ask them to name the part you are pointing to. Explain that this is the way the volcano would look in the inside if we were able to slice the volcano open and look at a cross-section.

• Hold up the word labels and name them. See if the children can find the appropriate spot or place on the chart as you name it and if they can place the word on top of the same word on the chart.

• Have children make up their own cross-section model of a volcano with labeled parts.

10. Seismic Waves

Materials A globe or world map; a Slinky; 10 feet of rope; 2 wooden blocks; a ping-pong ball; a golf ball; a wooden table; a basin of water; newspaper to absorb possible mess from the water.

Procedure

• Explain to the children that over one million earthquakes occur every year on the Earth. Some of them are very destructive, while others are hardly even felt. Most of them occur along a belt called a fault line. A fault line is an area of the Earth's crust that is known to break apart and slip or slide. There are three major fault lines or tremor areas on the Earth where earthquakes and volcanoes are known to occur most frequently.

• Show children the globe or a map of the world. Point out to them where the three major fault lines or belts of unrest occur on the Earth's surface. (Refer to the information at the beginning of this chapter.)

• Explain that earthquake tremors usually start within the Earth under the surface and travel to the surface. These tremors are called seismic waves. Seismic waves can be measured by a seismograph machine. Scientists called seismologists study seismograph readings and the movements or vibrations caused by earthquakes. They interpret their findings and attempt to make predictions about when and where earthquakes will happen and when and where volcanoes will erupt.

• Explain that there are three types of seismic waves and tell them that you will demonstrate how seismic waves travel through the interior of the Earth and on the surface of the Earth.

a. *Primary wave with a Slinky.* Hand one end of a Slinky to a child to hold. Stretch the other end out and then let go of about 20 coils of the spring. Ask the children to observe the ricocheting or back and forth pushing and pulling motion that takes place in the Slinky. Explain that this kind of wave motion is like a primary seismic wave. It bounces back and forth, pushing and pulling as it penetrates through the crust of the earth.

b. *Secondary wave with a rope.* Give one end of a rope to a child to hold. Move the rope up and down or from side to side. Explain that this kind of wave motion is like a secondary seismic wave. It moves back and forth in a zig-zag pattern and arrives after a primary seismic wave.

c. *Surface wave with two wooden blocks.* Press the two wooden blocks together in your hands. Slide the wooden blocks up and down or from one side to another. Explain that this kind of sideways sliding motion takes place on the surface or crust of the Earth. This kind of motion causes the most damage on the surface during an earthquake. It makes buildings fall over.

d. *Primary and secondary waves with a ball in liquid.* Have a child hold a golf ball and a ping-pong ball about one foot above a basin filled with water. Tell the child to drop the golf ball into the water. Observe what happens. It sinks. Drop the ping-pong ball into the water and observe what happens. (It floats.) Explain that the golf ball penetrates through the water like a primary seismic wave. The ping-pong ball acts like a secondary seismic wave. It does not penetrate through the liquid. The ping-pong ball comes to a halt on top of the water.

e. *Primary and secondary waves with balls on solids.* Have a child drop a ping-pong ball and a golf ball onto a wooden desk and observe the way the two balls bounce. How many times does each ball bounce? Explain to the children that the golf ball acts like a primary seismic wave. It penetrates deeply and loses a lot of energy through the wood. The children can feel the wooden desk vibrate when the golf ball bounces on it. Like a secondary seismic wave, the ping-pong ball will penetrate less deeply and bounce up and down more frequently than the golf ball did.

II. Crust and Interior of Earth

1. A Globe of the Earth

Materials A physical relief globe on an axis.

Procedure

• Show children the globe. Explain to them that it is a model* of the Earth.

• Ask the following kinds of questions:

What do the colors of blue and brown and green represent?

*A model is a representation of the "real" thing. See Chapter 1 for further explanation.

(Blue represents water; brown represents mountains and land area; green represents low areas of land.)

Where are the areas of land?
(Have a child identify them.)

Where are the areas with water?
(Have a child find the oceans and the large inland lakes and seas.)

What is underneath the oceans and all of the water on the Earth?
(Land.)

What are the highest areas of the Earth called?
(Mountains.)

What are the large low areas of the Earth that are covered with water called?
(Oceans, seas, and lakes.)

What is underneath the land?
(Hot molten rocks.)

What is inside the Earth?
(Matter that is composed of many layers of solids, liquids, and gases.)

What is inside the globe?
(Air. It is hollow inside. The globe is only a model of the outside or skin of the Earth's surface. It's the part we can see with our eyes and from an airplane.)

2. Diagram of an Island and a Volcanic Island

Materials White paper; colored pencils; clear Contact paper; a sketch of an island, without water surrounding it.

Preparation

- Sketch a diagram of an island. Show it as a mountain with a flat top, or a mountain with several peaks and plateaus. Draw in water line to show where the water line would hit the mountain. Part of the island would be under the water, connected to the Earth. The island would be grounded, not floating.
- On a separate piece of paper create a width that is as deep as the water in the island picture. Color in this sheet of paper the color of the water.
- Color in the island picture with colored pencils so that it appears to be partially under water.
- Cover both papers with Contact paper. Attach the water picture to the larger picture so that the water can be lifted off the larger picture as if one could look underneath the water. See diagram.

Procedure

- Show children the picture of the island and the volcano.
- Ask the following kinds of questions:

What is underneath the water at the beach?
(Sand and land.)

What is a small area of land that is surrounded by water called?
(An island.)

Does the island float in the water?
(No, it is attached to the land underneath the water.)

If there were no water, what would the island look like?
(A tall mountain or a tall flat mountain.)

- Lift off the water and look at what is underneath the water. Have the children comment about the under-

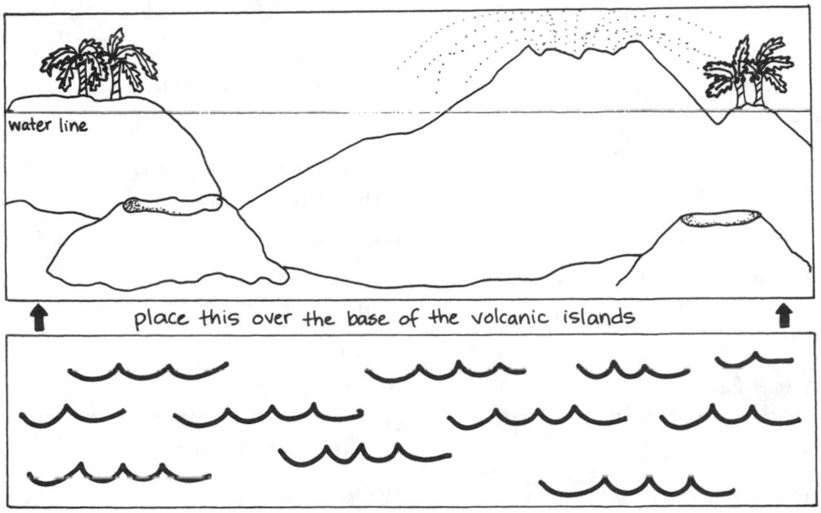
water line
place this over the base of the volcanic islands

water landscape, and about the connection to the Earth. Discuss how only the peak is above the water, and that the water usually occurs at the lowest altitudes of the Earth's crust. The crust is the outer surface of the Earth that we can see.

• Have children design their own lift-off model of the ocean floor surrounding a volcanic island.

3. Apple as a Model of the Earth

Materials Three apples; a sharp knife; a cutting board; paper towels.

Procedure

• Ask the children what is inside of the Earth. Listen to their responses. Discuss what they think is underneath the water and the land.

• Hold up an apple. Ask the children the following kinds of questions:

What is inside an apple?
(A solid area.)

What is on the outside of the apple?
(A skin.)

Are there any layers inside the solid area?
(Yes, the core.)

What is the core surrounded by?
(The fruit we eat.)

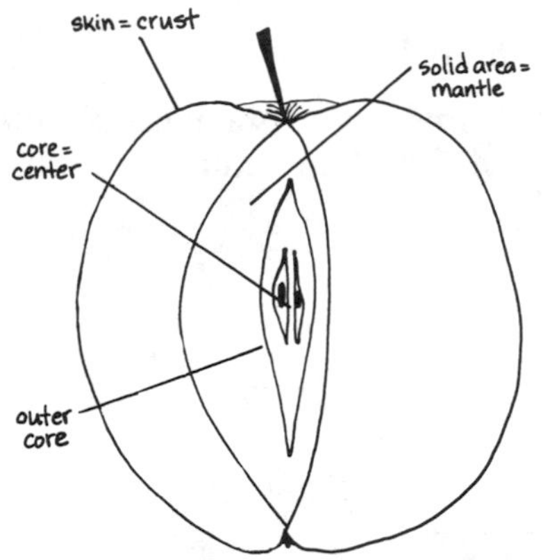

The apple, like the earth, is solid, not hollow.

• Cut the apple in half vertically, and cut another apple in half horizontally. Ask the following kinds of questions about the apples:

How are the apples like the Earth?
(They are round, surrounded by a skin or crust, and solid in the center.)

Can the apples be a model of the Earth?
(Yes.)

Is the skin on the model very thick?
(No, it is a very thin layer.)

Is the meat or fruit area very thick?
(Yes.)

What is in the center?
(A core.)

• Explain that scientists have never seen the inside of the Earth, but they believe that it is composed of many layers. They call the center of the Earth the core, and the area surrounding the core the mantle. The part that we live on is called the crust. It is very thin in relation to the mantle, just as the apple skin is thin in relation to the apple's meat. The apple's skin represents the Earth's crust. The meat of the apple represents the Earth's mantle layer.

• Cut a one-quarter section out of one of the uncut apples. Discuss the different appearance of the apple's inside when it is cut in half vertically, cut in half horizontally, and cut with a quarter removed. Explain that the same thing can look different when seen from different angles or from different points.

4. An Orange

Materials An orange; a knife; a cutting board; paper towels.

Procedure

• Cut the orange into quarters or into smaller sections. Have the children look at the surface of the cut sections. Peel the fruit away from the orange peel. Discuss the flatness of the section. It does not appear to be as round when it is a part of the whole. Small parts of an orange's peel appear flat rather than round.

• Ask the following kinds of questions:

If we pretend the orange is a model of the Earth, what part would the peel of the orange be called?
(The crust.)

What would the white inside of the peel be called?
(The inner crust.)

What would the orange part of the peel be called?
(The outer crust.)

Does the orange have a core?
(It is not as well defined as the apple's core, but is a hollow area in the center.)

Which fruit is a better model of the Earth, the orange or the apple?
(The apple is a better model of the Earth because it has a solid core in its center.)

Why does the Earth appear to be flat rather than curved where we live?

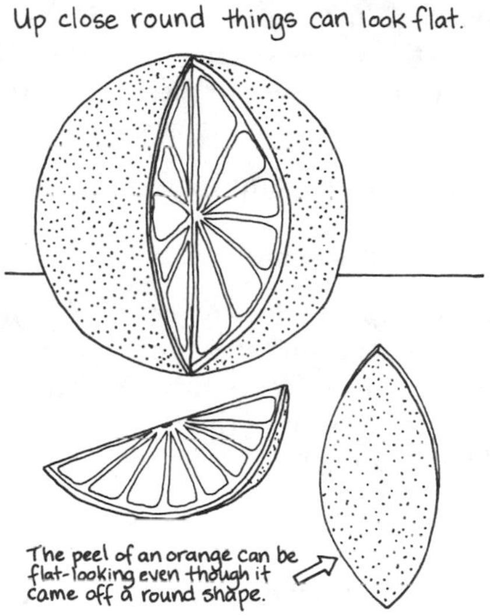
Up close round things can look flat.
The peel of an orange can be flat-looking even though it came off a round shape.

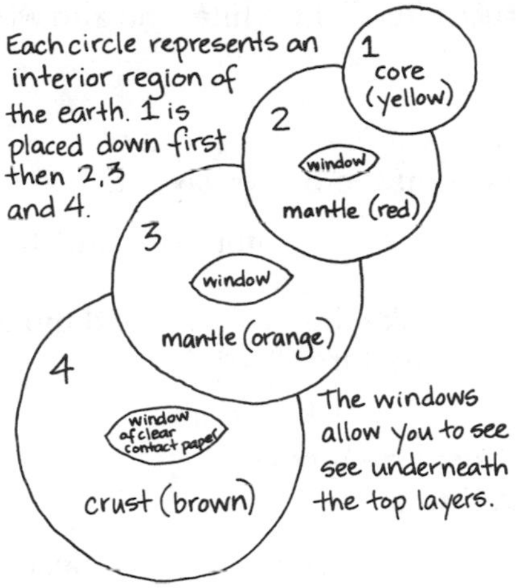

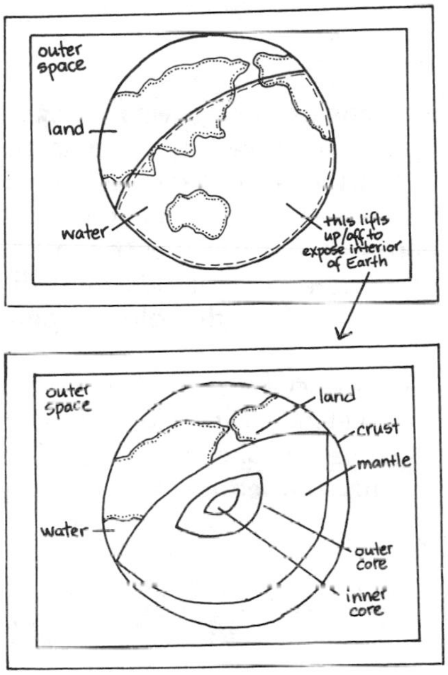

Each circle represents an interior region of the earth. 1 is placed down first then 2, 3 and 4.

core (yellow)

mantle (red)

mantle (orange)

crust (brown)

(We live on a small section of the Earth and we cannot see it in its entirety. We are too close to the ground to appreciate its roundness.)

Where do we have to be to observe that the Earth is round?

(High up in space in a space capsule or at the beach or desert we can see the roundness of the horizon line. It has a very slight curve.)

5. Model of the Interior Layers of the Earth

Materials White, dark blue, yellow, red, orange, and brown construction paper; a compass; a pencil; colored pencils; scissors; clear Contact paper; tagboard.

Preparation

- Cut out a series of graduated circles. Make two of each of the following circles: two small yellow circles, two red larger circles, two larger orange circles, and two brown circles (the brown circles should be the largest). Cut out one large white circle that is the same size as the large brown circles.
- On the large white circle draw in shapes to represent the continents and the oceans. Color in the shapes with the colored pencils so they will look like land and water areas.
- Glue one set of the graduated colored circles on to a piece of dark blue construction paper mounted to tagboard. See diagram.
- Cover the circles that are glued to the blue tagboard with clear Contact paper, and cover the individual circles with clear Contact paper.

Procedure

- Show the children the model of the interior layers of the Earth. Have the set of loose colored circles on top of the matching graduated circles that have been glued to the blue paper. The white circle that represents the Earth's outer crust should be the top circle and should be hiding or covering up the other circles.
- Ask the following kinds of questions:

What is this a model of?
(The Earth or a globe of the Earth.)

What is inside the Earth?
(Many layers.)

What surrounds the Earth?
(Outer space.)

If we were able to lift the crust off the Earth and look inside, what would be the first layer we would see underneath the water and the land underneath the water?

(The inner crust. Lift off the white land and water layer to see it.)

What is the next interior layer called?
(The mantle. Lift off the brown layer to see it.)

• Continue with the red outer core and the yellow inner core.
• Have children make their own labeled model of the interior layers of the Earth.

6. Lift-Up Landscape Model of Interior of Earth

Materials Paper; colored pencils; clear Contact paper; scissors; tagboard; masking tape.

Preparation
• Sketch a landscape drawing of a park or golf course, mostly flat rolling hills covered with grass and a few trees. Color in the sketch with colored pencils.
• Sketch the same scene again but in the middle of the paper draw in the interior layers of the Earth so that it will appear as a cross-section of the land with a slice in it. Color in the sketch with colored pencils. See diagram.
• Mount the cross-section sketch on tagboard, and cover the two sketches with clear Contact paper. Hinge the full landscape sketch on top of the cross-section sketch with a curled piece of masking tape.

Procedure
• Show the children the landscape with the lift-off land which reveals a cross-section underneath the land.
• Ask the following kinds of questions:

What is underneath the park under the grass?
(Layers of soil, then layers of bedrock. Then the mantle layer, then the core.) Listen to their responses, then lift up the landscape to see the layers.

What is underneath all landscapes on the crust of the Earth?
(The same kinds of layers.)

Do volcanoes erupt in all parts of the Earth?
(No, there are certain areas of the Earth where volcanoes erupt more frequently. Scientists are aware of these belts or sections of the Earth where volcanoes are most likely to occur. These belts are called fault lines.)

What is a fault line?
(A fault line is a weak section of the Earth's crust where an earthquake or a volcano might occur. When the movements inside the Earth cause movements to occur on the crust, sometimes the crust breaks apart and slides in two different directions. When this occurs it is called an earthquake.

• Have children create their own lift-up model of the layers of the Earth underneath their house or the school.

III. Distinguishing Rocks From One Another

1. Matching and Naming Rocks That Look Alike

Materials Two identical sets of store-bought rocks from a museum shop or lapidary store.

CUTAWAY MODEL OF EARTH'S INTERIOR

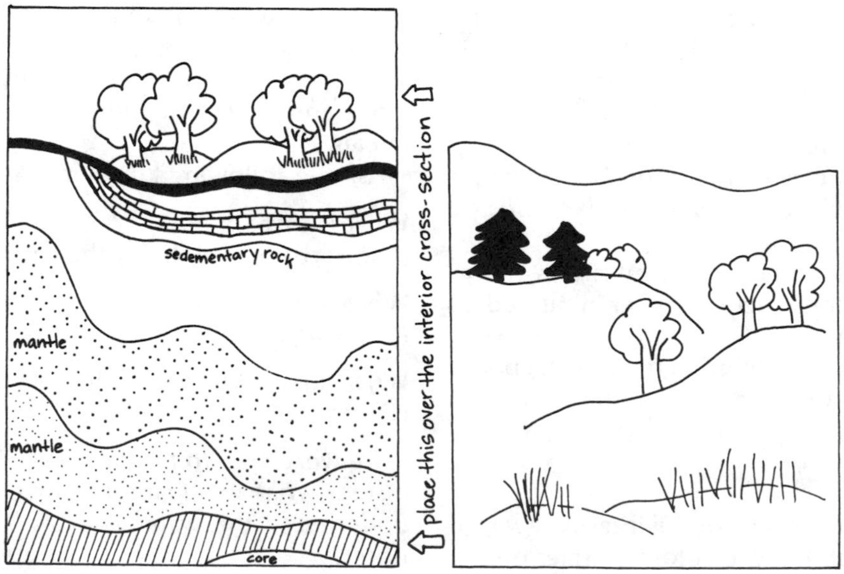

Preparation
• Mount each rock on a separate piece of cardboard about 2 inches by 2 inches. Label each rock in the set with a word label.

Procedure
• Show the children one complete set of mounted individual rocks.
• Discuss the properties of each rock and what the name of each rock is.
• Describe a rock and see if the children can find the rock you are describing; name the rock for them if they cannot.
• Show children the second set of identical matching rocks. Tell them that each rock has a matching pair and ask them to find the rock that matches each rock. The children can play a game with the rocks with one of their classmates by picking up one of the rocks and having their classmate find the matching rock, or guessing which rock is missing.

2. Cleavage

Materials A variety of broken rocks; two pieces or more from: a broken bar of soap, a split piece of wood, a broken rock.

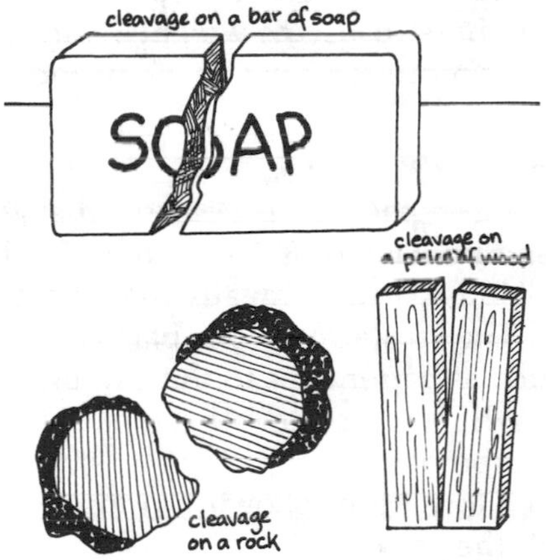

Procedure
• Show the children the piece of soap. Hold it so that the crack does not show so that it appears to be unbroken. Then split it open so the children can see the crack. Do the same thing with the piece of wood and with the rock.
• Explain to the children that when materials break they break differently. Some break in a jagged line like the soap, some break in layers like the wood, and some break in a smooth line like the rock. Not all rocks break in a smooth line, but some do. Cleavage is a word that refers to the way something breaks. A cleavage line can be rough, smooth, jagged, layered, etc. Many rocks and minerals have a cleavage pattern that is constant no matter how small the pieces are broken.
• Look at various rock samples and discuss the texture of the cleavage lines with the children.
• Give children a small (hotel courtesy type) bar of soap or a thin wood scrap to break or a piece of paper to rip. Then have them examine the texture of the cleavage line and fit the two pieces together along the cleavage line.

3. Luster

Materials A variety of rocks with and without luster mounted on 2″ × 2″ cardboard squares. (You may need to buy rocks or samples from a museum or a rock and mineral supply store.)

Procedure
• Show the children the rocks.
• Have the children describe what the individual rocks look like.
• Explain that the shine and sparkle of some of the rocks is called luster. Some rocks have luster, some do not. When a rock has the property of luster, the quality of the luster is used to describe the rock's appearance. (Luster can be pearly, dull, brilliant, glassy, metallic, etc.)

4. Hardness

Materials A variety of labeled rocks with varying degrees of hardness and softness that have been mounted on 2″ × 2″ cardboard squares (*i.e.*, talc, quartz, slate, sandstone, marble, sulfur, anthracite, limestone, calcite); a penny, a nail; a piece of glass; talc powder.

Procedure
• Show the children the variety of rocks.
• Explain to the children that rocks have different degrees of hardness. A very hard rock cannot be scratched by another rock. The hardest rock of all is a diamond. The softest rock of all is talc. Talc rubs off on any surface that rubs against it.
• Demonstrate with a talc rock how soft talc is. Let the children touch the talc to feel how soft the piece of talc feels. Ask them if they know where talc powder comes from. Talc powder is ground-up talc rock with scents of perfume added. Sprinkle talc powder out for children to see and smell.
• Explain that a man named Moh set up a testing scale for measuring the hardness of rocks. He discovered that materials such as a fingernail, glass, other rocks, nails, pennies, knives, etc., could be used to test the

hardness of rocks. He rated rocks with a number. The lower the number the softer the rock. The numbers range in a scale of 1 to 10. Number one is talc and number ten is a diamond.

• Tell children the numbers. Write them on a blackboard or prepare a chart ahead of time.

1—Talc (can be scratched by a fingernail)
2—Gypsum (can be scratched by a fingernail)
3—Calcite (can be scratched by a penny)
4—Fluorite (can be scratched by a knife)
5—Apatite (can almost be scratched by a knife and will scratch any other rock which has a lower number than itself)
6—Feldspar (will scratch a knife blade)
7—Quartz (will scratch a piece of glass)
8—Topaz (will scratch the quartz)
9—Corundum (will scratch the topaz and any other rock with a lower number than itself)
10—Diamond (will scratch any rocks that are softer than itself)

• Let the children experiment to see which rock scratches what, and to arrange the rocks in an order from softest to hardest.

5. Streak

Materials Assorted labeled rocks from a rock or mineral supply store that have been mounted on 2″ × 2″ cardboard squares and that either have streaks of color running through them or leave a colored streak when rubbed on a piece of unglazed ceramic tile; a wet sponge. (Suggested rocks to use for streaking on a ceramic tile are: magnatite, graphite, anthracite, shale, galena, olivine, hematite, talc, slate, obsidian, calcite.)

Procedure

• Show children the assorted rocks. Explain that some of the rocks will leave a streak of color when they are rubbed against a piece of unglazed ceramic tile. Demonstrate the streaking of the rocks on the tile. Compare the different textures and intensity of color that rubs off onto the tile from the different rocks. Not all rocks rub off a color; only some rocks do.

• Have children experiment making streaks of color by rubbing the rocks on a piece of tile.

• Discuss the streaks that run through some of the rocks and minerals. Explain that a streak is a line of color or luster that runs through a rock.

6. Density

Materials A piece of lava rock; a piece of granite rock about the same size as the lava rock.

Procedure

• Show children the two rocks.

• Ask the following kinds of questions:

Can we tell by just looking which rock weighs more?
(No, but one rock has more holes in it than the other one does. The one with holes looks less solid.)

What kinds of rocks have a lot of holes in them?
(Lava rocks. See Activity 1, Procedure 8, from this chapter.)

What kinds of rocks can float in water?
(Lava rocks.)

Which rock will weigh more?
(The non-lava rock will weigh more because it is more solid.) Let the children feel each of the rocks to experience the difference in their weights.

• Pass around the two rocks so the children can feel the difference between them.

• Explain to the children that rocks have different densities. Density refers to the solidness of a rock. The more closely packed the minerals are within the rock the more solid or dense the rock is. Solid rocks weigh more than less solid rocks. "Bigness" does not mean that a rock is heavier. Many rocks could be the same size and each rock could weigh a different amount.

7. Weight

Materials A simple balance scale with two pans; a set of plastic metric gram weights or paper clips; marbles; coins or washers to use as weights; various assorted labeled rocks mounted on 2″ × 2″ cardboard squares.

Procedure

• Show children the scale. Discuss what the scale is used for and how it works. When one side is high and the other side is low it means that the scale is not balanced. The scale can be balanced by adding weights such as paper clips to the pan until both sides are even. When the scale is balanced, items can be weighed in the pans.

• Ask the children the following kinds of questions as they weigh the rocks:

If I place a rock in the pan, what will happen to the pan?
(The pan will go down on the side the rock went into, and up on the other side.)

How can the scale be balanced if a rock is in the pan?
(By adding metric gram weights until the scale is balanced.)

If weights are added to the other pan and the scale is balanced what information will we find out?
(The number of weights we added to balance the scale will tell us how much the rock weighed.)

How many rocks can be weighed at the same time if we are trying to find out how many grams each rock weighs?
(One rock at a time.)

- Have the children determine the amount of weight that each rock has in grams.
- Have the children determine the order to place the rocks in so that they are arranged in a sequential order, either heaviest to lightest or lightest to heaviest.

8. Magnetic Test

Materials Assorted black and gray rocks including a piece of magnatite; a magnet; a paper clip.

Procedure
- Place all of the black and gray rocks including magnatite on the floor or on a table near each other.
- Show the children the magnet. Ask them if they think the magnet can pick up any of the rocks. Hold the magnet out over the assorted rocks and have the children observe whether any of the rocks are affected by the magnet. When the piece of magnatite is observed and singled out, pick up the magnatite and see if the magnatite will pick up a paper clip.
- Explain to the children that magnatite is a natural magnet found in nature. (Refer to Chapter 4, which deals with magnetism.)
- Let children experiment with the magnet to find the magnetite with a different mixture of rocks.

9. Test for Limestone

Materials Lemon juice or vinegar; limestone; marble; rock; chalk (natural); calcite; chalk board chalk; a toothpick.

Procedure
- Show the children the rocks. Tell them the names of each if they do not know what they are. Children will probably find it strange that chalk is a rock. Explain that the chalk we use in the classroom is chalk that has been pressed and molded into a solid cylindrical shape. It is helpful to compare natural chalk with man-made chalk.
- Have the children dip a toothpick into vinegar and drop a drop of vinegar onto each of the rocks. (The limestone, marble, calcite, and chalk will form little bubbles or fizz when the vinegar touches their surface. The other white rocks will most likely not have a bubbly or fizzy reaction unless they too contain traces of limestone, which the acid test is able to find out.) Explain that the bubbles are caused by carbon dioxide (CO_2) gas that forms when limestone is touched by vinegar or lemon juice, which are acids.

IV. Three Classes of Rocks

1. Igneous Rocks

Materials Assorted igneous rocks (for example, obsidian, pumice, granite, quartz, feldspar, biotite, scoria, basalt), a wet sponge; man-made cellulose; a dry sponge; wet, soft clay.

Procedure
- Explain to the children that when rocks form due to volcanic eruptions or from magma they are called igneous rocks or fire rocks. Rocks that form because of heat or fire all form from magma. Magma is hot liquid rock. It is made up of minerals and gases from deep inside the Earth.
- Explain to the children that when magma flows it is hot; as it begins to cool it hardens. If it cools quickly it looks different than when it cools slowly. If it cools quickly it looks glassy like obsidian, or full of holes like pumice. Show children a sample of obsidian and pumice. If the magma cools more slowly it forms granite. Show children a sample of granite. Granite is made up of small crystals of quartz, feldspar, and biotite. Show children samples of quartz, feldspar, and biotite. Ask them if they can find small flecks of the rock samples in the granite rock.
- Show children the wet sponge and the wet soft clay. Explain to them that the sponge and the clay are both models of igneous rocks that are still in a liquid form. They are not hot like liquid magma, but they are soft and malleable. The sponge can be squeezed and the clay can be shaped into forms. Ask the following kinds of questions:

When a sponge dries, what happens?
(It becomes very stiff and the shape remains the same. It cannot be squeezed easily, and the holes allow it to dry quickly.)

What happens to the clay when it dries out?
(It becomes very hard and brittle. It takes longer to dry than the sponge.)

Explain that the sponge is like pumice. It dries quickly. The clay is like granite. It dries slowly. Like magma, both the sponge and the clay become hard when they no longer contain a liquid and are not in a liquid form.

2. Metamorphic Rocks

Materials A candle; a match; a piece of waxed paper; samples of metamorphic rocks (for example, marble, slate, schist, gneiss, quartzite); the cross-section model of an erupting volcano (Activity I, Procedure 9 from this chapter).

Procedure

• Show the children the cross-section model of an erupting volcano from Activity I, Procedure 9 from this chapter. Have them notice that the area surrounding the magma under the ground continually heats and cools. The area near the magma is often surrounded by metamorphic rock. Explain that metamorphic rock is rock that changes. It changes due to extreme changes in heat or pressure. Metamorphic rocks are also called changing rocks. A rock that starts off as an igneous rock can become a metamorphic rock if it changes due to pressure or due to a temperature change.
• Light a candle with a match. Allow the drippings to fall onto a piece of waxed paper. Have the children observe how the candle becomes a liquid and drips, and that the drips become hard again.
• Ask the following kinds of questions:

Can the drips ever be made into a candle again?
(No, not unless they are all collected and molded into a candle again.)

Will the candle ever be the same again once it starts to drip?
(No, its shape will remain changed. The shape of the drips will also remain changed.)

How is the candle like a rock that has gone through metamorphosis and changed?
(The candle has a new shape. It can never be the way it was before.)

Can adults ever become small children again?
(No, once they grow up, they will remain adults.)

Can you stay the age you are for your entire life?
(No, we continually go through aging and changes while we are alive.)

How are metamorphic rocks like us?
(Once a change occurs, the change cannot be reversed. Like Toyland, "once you pass its borders, you can never return again.")

3. Opening up Rocks

Materials Assorted rocks picked up from outside on the playground or from the backyard; newspaper; a large paper bag; a hammer; an empty egg carton.

Procedure

• Show the children the rocks. Place one of the rocks inside a paper bag. Choose a child to place newspaper on top of the paper bag and on the bottom of the paper bag. Tell the children you are going to strike the paper bag with a hammer. Ask them what they think will happen to the rock.

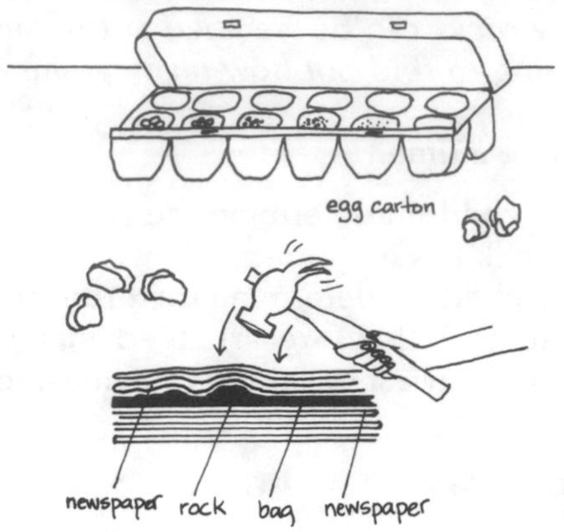

• Have a child strike the paper bag with the hammer and then have the children observe what happens to the rock. (The children will observe that the rock has broken into several smaller pieces of rock. The inside of the rock may look slightly different from the outside of the rock. The inside may have brighter colors, or may have a jagged cleavage line. The outside may be smooth and weathered compared to the inside, which may be brighter and rougher, or there may be no difference.)
• Continue to have the children break the rocks with a hammer and to observe whether some rocks are harder to break than others and whether some rocks form smaller pieces when struck.

Can the small rocks be made even smaller?
Can the rocks be turned into sand or dust?

• Have the children grade their small rocks and pieces of rock according to their size in an egg carton or other sorting container.

4. Crystals

Materials A variety of geodes* that have been cut open; rock crystals purchased from a rock supply store or from a museum shop; pictures of gemstones and crystals.

Procedure

• Show the children the geodes. First show them the complete geode by holding the two halves together so that it looks like one unopened rock. Ask the children what they think the inside of the rock will look like. Listen to their responses, then open the rock (geode) so they can see the interior. Explain that the inside has been polished. When some rocks are polished, they become very beautiful to look at. Harder rocks are

*A geode is a hollow rock with a crystal lining.

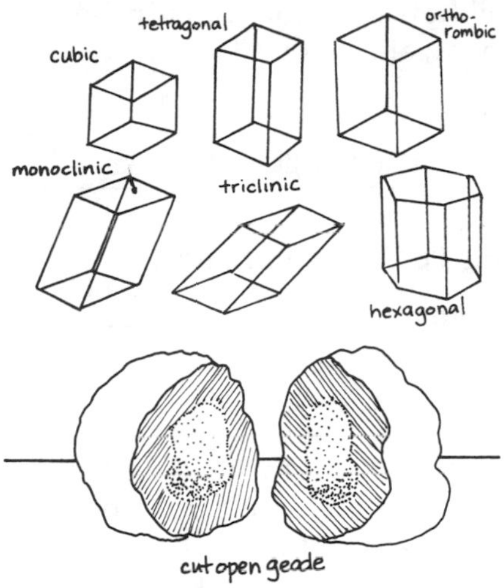
cubic
tetragonal
ortho-
rombic
monoclinic
triclinic
hexagonal
cut open geode

easier to polish and look beautiful when they are sanded down and made smooth.

• Show children pictures of gemstones and crystals. Explain that some stones are cut into gemstones and polished by people called lapidaries. Jewelers then mount stones with precious metals like gold and silver. Explain that minerals in rocks form crystals. Every mineral has its own unique crystal form. Some crystals are prettier than others and are treasured for their beauty and made into jewelry or displayed at museums. Suggest that children visit the local natural history museum to see the rock and mineral collection, and to observe shapes and forms of crystallized minerals.

5. Growing Sugar Crystals

Materials Clear or colored rock candy samples; boiling water; granulated sugar; food color; string; pencils; a teaspoon; clear plastic drinking glasses; salt.

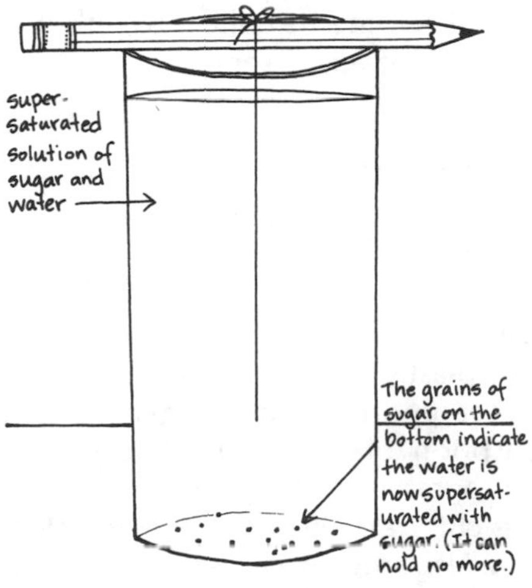
super-
saturated
solution of
sugar and
water
The grains of
sugar on the
bottom indicate
the water is
now supersat-
urated with
sugar. (It can
hold no more.)

Procedure

• Pass around the rock candy. Tell the children that even though the crystals look like rock crystals they are really candy. Break off pieces of the rock candy for the children to taste. Explain that the sugar is made up of minerals just as the rocks are made up of minerals. When minerals are exposed to moisture and then extreme temperature changes, crystals will frequently form or grow. Minerals are not alive; they grow larger from the outside by forming new layers on top of old layers. Materials that are alive like plants and animals grow from the inside out and all over, not just in layers on the outside.

• Explain to the children that you too can make sugar into crystals. Boil some water. Pour the water into a clear plastic drinking glass. Have the children add some sugar to the hot water. Stir the sugar until it dissolves. Continue to add sugar to the glass until the water becomes supersaturated. (It will be supersaturated when the water can no longer hold all of the sugar. Some of the sugar will sink to the bottom of the glass and will not dissolve in the water.) Have the children add food color for interest. Then have the children place a pencil across the top of the glass and tie a piece of string to the pencil so that the string is submerged in the sugar water. See diagram. Place the sugar water with the pencil and string in it on top of a high shelf. Let it sit undisturbed for a few days or a week. (Crystals will start to form and grow on the string. Eventually, all of the water will evaporate. If the water evaporates very slowly the crystals will be large. If the water evaporates fast, the crystals will be smaller.)

• Explain to the children that the same process takes place in minerals that form rocks. Crystals form when moisture is trapped inside and evaporates slowly.

• When salt water is boiled, it will form crystals too. Let the children experiment to see how different salt crystals look from sugar crystals.

6. Sedimentary Rocks

Materials Samples of sedimentary rocks with visible layers, plus store-bought samples of sandstone, shale, limestone, clay conglomerates (rocks composed of small pebbles that have been cemented together by mud that has become rock).

Procedure

• Pass around the sedimentary rocks. Have the children observe the layers that have formed. Lines or stripes of colors can be seen in the rocks.

• Pass around the store-bought rock samples. Have the children observe the granular look of the limestone and the sandstone. Have the children observe the way the conglomerate sticks together to form a large rock. Explain that concrete is a conglomerate. It is held together by cement. The little pebbles and stones in the sedimentary conglomerate are cemented together by hardened mud. Sedimentary rock is usually of a softer variety than igneous and metamorphic rocks.

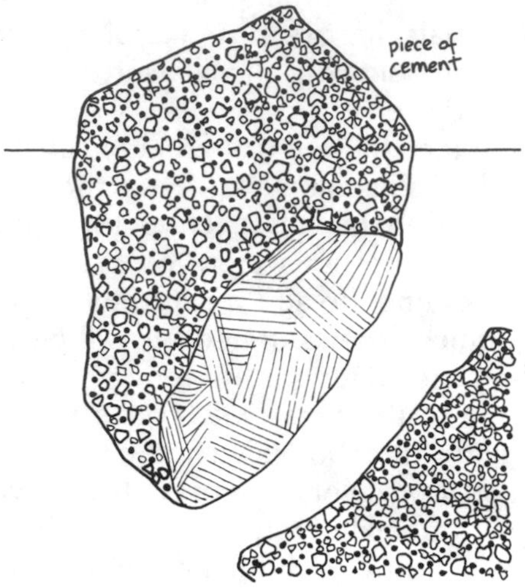

CONGLOMERATE

7. Pictures of the Grand Canyon

Materials Pictures can be obtained from *National Geographic* magazines or from the library.

Procedure Pass around the pictures of the Grand Canyon or other similar picture of sedimentary rock that has been built up over the centuries. Discuss the visible layers that can be seen in the rock along the canyon walls. Discuss how the water from the river keeps making the canyon deeper.

8. Uses of Rocks

Materials Samples of slate, coal, limestone, clay, gravel, granite, marble.

Procedure

• Show the children the samples of rocks. Discuss where the various rocks might be used. For example, slate is used outside for walkways, on roofs, and for blackboards. Coal is used for heat. Limestone is used in buildings and is mixed with cement. It is also ground up and used to put lines on soccer and football fields. Clay is used to make bricks, in pottery and ceramics. Gravel is used to build roads, paths, and driveways. Granite and marble are used in buildings, and are often used by artists to carve out statues or monuments.

• Have children look for rocks in buildings and on bridges, roads, and sidewalks.

V. Erosion and Formation of Rocks

1. Grinding Rocks and Erosion

Materials An empty can with a plastic cover; several small rocks.

Procedure

• Show the children the rocks. Place them in the empty can. Place a plastic cover over the end of the can. Ask the children what they think will happen to the rocks if they are shaken vigorously in the can. Have the children shake the can vigorously and observe what happens to the rocks as a result of the motion and shaking. (The rocks will hit against each other and break into smaller rocks and particles of rocks. Dust and sand will be present in the can.) Explain to the children that erosion takes place. Erosion means that the rocks are breaking apart. Erosion takes place because of a mechanical action such as being shaken up, rubbed or hit, or from a chemical action such as may occur when a volcano erupts.

• Ask the children the following kinds of questions:

What happens to rocks when they hit against each other?
(They break apart and become smaller and jagged; eventually they become smooth.)

What happens to rocks that travel in a river or are carried in a stream?
(The water erodes them. The water pushes the rocks around and the rocks are bounced around and off each other.)

Explain to children that sedimentary rock is made up of small fragments, or sediments. Sediments are tiny pieces of soil or particles that are often carried by water. When a lot of sediments collect together they form a layer of soil or a layer of rock.

2. Sorting Sediments

Materials Sand; gravel; pebbles; mud; a clear plastic glass; water; a teaspoon.

Procedure

• Fill a clear plastic glass with water. Drop in a teaspoon of sand, a teaspoon of gravel, a teaspoon of pebbles, and a teaspoon of mud. Stir all of the ingredients vigorously together in the glass.

• Have the children observe the color of the water. It will be brownish and hard to see through. Ask them the following kinds of questions:

What is another name for all of the dirt that is floating around in the water?
(Sediments.)

Will the water remain muddy-looking?
(No, the sediments will settle to the bottom of the glass.)

Will the water ever become clear again?
(Yes, the water will become clearer, but it will most likely not become as clear as it originally was unless it is filtered.)

If the sediments settle out and sink to the bottom, how will they settle out?
(The sediments will sink differently. The heaviest particles will settle to the bottom first. Layers will form. Sorting will take place as the sediments settle.)

• Let the muddy water sit for several hours or overnight and have the children observe what happens to it.

3. Separating Salt from Sand

Materials Sand; salt; a clear plastic container; a teaspoon; water; clear plastic glasses.

Procedure

• Show the children the sand and the salt. Have the children mix the sand in a glass of water and observe what happens. Then have the children mix the salt in the water and observe what happens. (The sand will sink to the bottom. The salt will mix in with the water and float.)

• Have the children mix the dry sand and salt together. Ask the children to think of a way to separate the salt from the sand. See if they suggest adding water to the dry sand and salt. Ask them what they think will happen to the salt when the water is added to the dry mixture of sand and salt. (The salt will separate itself from the heavier pieces of sand. The sand will sink. The salt will float. If the water with salt is poured into another glass, the salt will be separated from the sand. When the water evaporates the salt will remain.)

• Explain that when some things are dissolved and others are not it is called chemical erosion. Sometimes erosion is mechanical because rocks bounce against each other and break apart. When salt dissolves it is a chemical reaction that causes erosion.

• Have children continue to mix and separate the sand and salt. Also have them tumble rocks together in a closed container so that they can see and experience the difference between chemical erosion and mechanical erosion.

4. Soil Erosion Due to Water

Materials A rectangular pan; sand; a block of wood; a water-sprinkling can; water; dead leaves; Popsicle sticks; an eye dropper.

Procedure

• Create a miniature wet sand mountain inside one end of a rectangular pan. Place a wooden block underneath the side of the pan that has the sand mountain, so that the pan will be slightly elevated and tilted.

• Explain to the children that the wet sand mountain is a model of a mountain without any trees or grass. Ask them what they think will happen to the soil on the mountain when rain falls on it. Then choose a child to pour "rain" out of the sprinkling can. Ask the children to observe what happens to the mountain as the water hits the sand mountain.

• Have the children observe where most of the erosion takes place (at the top of the mountain). Also have them observe where the eroded soil went. (It will tend to flow down and be carried by the water.)

• Have the children rebuild the sand mountain. Place some dead leaves on the sand mountain. Ask the children what they think will happen when it rains if there are leaves covering the soil. Then choose a child to pour "rain" from the sprinkling can again and see if the dead leaves make a difference in the amount of soil that erodes away when it rains. (The leaves will control some of the erosion.)

• Have children build up the sand mountain again. This time add Popsicle sticks to the sand mountain. See diagram.

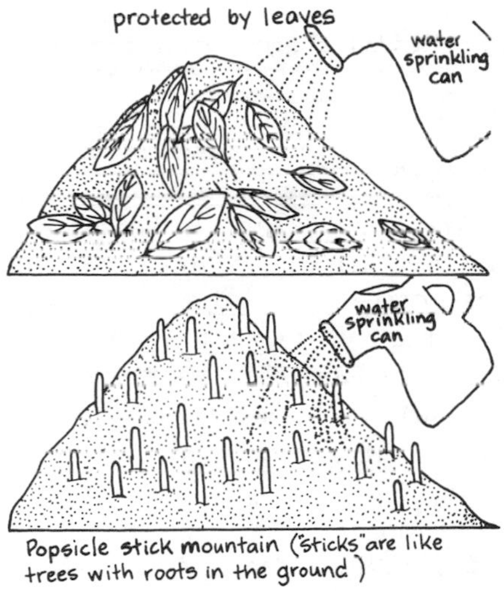

Explain that the Popsicle sticks are like trees. Ask the children how the trees might affect the way water flows down the sand mountain. Then choose a child to pour the "rain" from the sprinkling can and observe the results. (The children might notice the formation of streams, dams, fan formations of water flowing, and delta formations being formed from the flow of water down the mountain.)

• Have the children build up the sand mountain again. This time have the children use an eye dropper to drop water on the mountain. Have the children observe the erosion caused by a drop of water on the sand. Have them notice the effect that a drop makes when it is dropped from a point very high above the mountain, and when the drop falls very close to the mountain. Have them observe whether a drop causes more erosion when it falls at a slant or when it falls straight on. Most importantly, be sure they observe where the soil goes when it erodes away. (It flows downhill with the water and is deposited there, until it is moved again.) **A glacier of ice will do the same thing.

5. Soil Erosion Due to Wind

Materials A pile of dry sand; a drinking straw; a basin; some dead leaves; pictures cut from magazines showing wind erosion in the desert and on the plains.

Procedure

• Tell the children you are going to blow on the sand with the drinking straw. Ask them what they think will happen to the sand. Listen to their responses. Then blow through the straw and observe the holes the wind is able to create in the mountain.

• Observe the pictures of wind erosion cut from magazines. Discuss how the wind changed the landscape and blew sediments away causing erosion to take place.

• Give children their own straw to experiment with to see the effects of wind erosion on the sand.

6. After a Heavy Rain

Materials Access to puddles on a blacktopped area, to a flower bed, and to a run-off or stream caused by the rain.

Procedure

• Have the children observe puddles after a rain. Ask them to notice where puddles are found. Puddles are usually found where the soil is very hard, or where there is a low spot. Puddles are not usually found in flower beds, or in high places. Puddles are frequently found on sidewalks, on outdoor tennis courts, and on playgrounds. The water cannot be absorbed into the soil when the soil is very hard or when it is cemented over or blacktopped.

• Discuss what makes a puddle go away: filling in the low spot with an absorbent material like sawdust or woodchips, sweeping the puddle with a broom, or waiting for the air to evaporate the puddle.

• Have the children observe any streams that might have formed due to the rain, and any sediments that are being carried by the run-off of water from the land to the street.

7. Erosion Due to Freezing

Materials A plastic container with a lid; water; access to a freezer or freezing outside temperature.

Procedure

• Fill the container to the top with water. Cap the top with a lid. Tell the children you are going to place the filled container in the freezer. Ask them if they know what will happen to the water in the container when it is in the freezer. (They will probably respond that the water will freeze.) Place the container in the freezer.

• Have the children observe the container the next day after the water has frozen. The cap will be off or the container may be split open. Ask the children why the container has split open or why the cap has popped off. (You may have to explain to the children that when water freezes it takes up more space. It expands, and when it does, things around it may break.)

Fine points to discuss with children

Why do potholes form in roads?
(In the heat of day, the road expands; when it gets cold, the road contracts. But when the road freezes, it expands. The abrupt expansion and contraction of the roadway with uneven temperatures causes the road to break apart and potholes to form.)

Why do pipes burst when they freeze?
(Pipes burst when the water in them freezes and expands. The frozen water pops the pipe. If water is running, the water leaks out of the frozen pipe and much water damage may take place.)

Why do sidewalks have cracks between joints, and why do bridges have expansion joints?
(Cracks at joints in sidewalks and expansion joints in bridges help prevent possible damage due to expansion and contraction from changing temperatures and uneven temperature in the cement or steel.)

Why do railroad tracks have space between their joints and between railroad ties?
(For the same reason that sidewalks and bridges have space—to allow for expansion and contraction with the least amount of damage from freezing temperatures.)

8. Erosion Due to Glaciers

Materials Wet sand; a rectangular pan; small rocks frozen in water at the bottom of a cut-open quart milk container.

Procedure

• Explain to the children that in the far North and in the far South, the temperatures are very cold. In fact, the poles of the Earth are surrounded by ice and there are

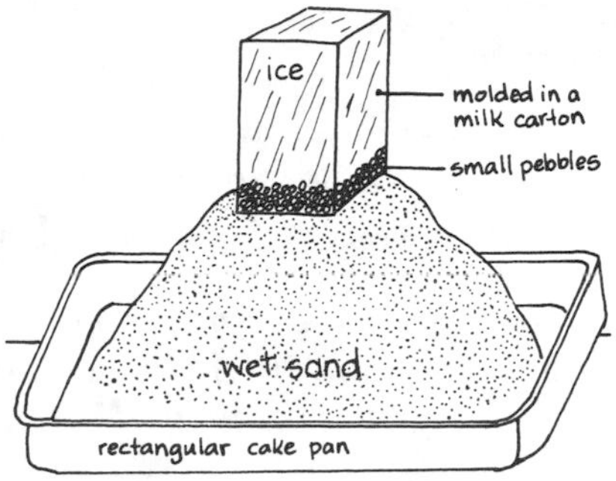

EROSION FROM ICE CUBE GLACIER

ice caps on both poles of the Earth. When water freezes inside of a valley, it is called a glacier. As a glacier melts, it moves and it carries rocks and sediments with it. When the dinosaurs died out there was a very cold time on the Earth known as the Ice Age. During the Ice Age, there were a lot of glaciers on the earth. The glaciers dug out pieces of land and formed lakes and valleys as they melted and moved.

- Have the children build a small wet sand mountain in the rectangular pan. Place the frozen water with small rocks in it shaped like a small rectangle on top of the sand mountain. Explain that the small block of ice with rocks frozen in it is a miniature model of a glacier. Glaciers often had rocks or boulders frozen in them. As the glacier melted, the rocks and boulders that were carried by them broke off or became loose.
- Ask the following kinds of questions:

What will happen to the rocks in the frozen ice as the ice melts?
(They will come loose.)

Where will the rocks move to?
(It is not clear, but they will most likely fall off or roll down the sand mountain.)

What will happen to the sand mountain as the ice melts?
(The mountain may have a change in its appearance due to the action of ice and the water that runs off from the melting.)

9. Falling Sediment Chart

Materials White paper; colored pencils; clear Contact paper; a sketch of horizontal lines showing different depths of the ocean and the ocean floor; a strip of paper covered with spots; masking tape.

Preparation

- Sketch a picture of the sky, the ocean, and the ocean floor—a sketch with a lot of straight horizontal lines. Another piece of paper should be colored all blue to represent the top of the ocean. See diagram.

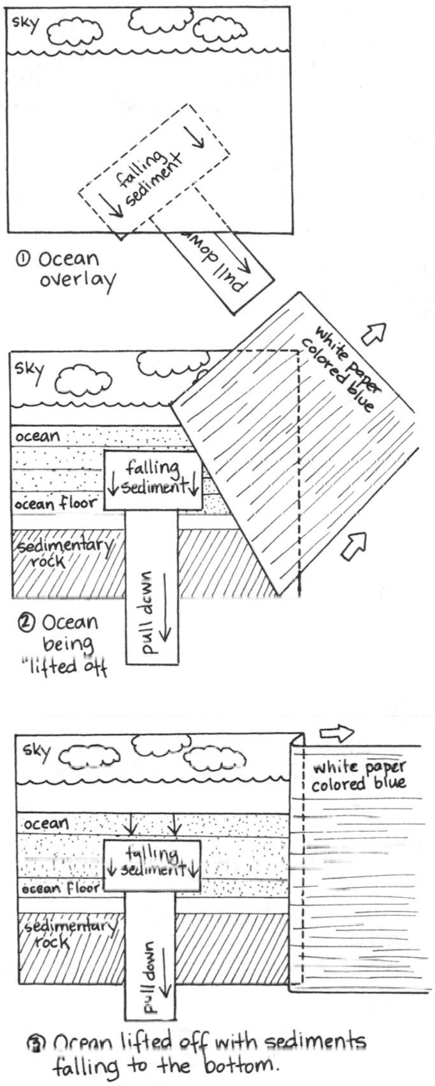

- Color in the sketch with blues to represent the sky and the ocean, and browns to represent the ocean floor. Write labels for the sky, the ocean, and the ocean floor. Attach the labels to the sketch at appropriate places.
- Cover the blue piece of paper and the sketch of the sky, ocean, and ocean floor with Contact paper. Cover the strip of paper covered with spots with Contact paper too. Label the sediments before covering it with Contact paper.
- Use masking tape to form a hinge for the top of the ocean to connect to the sketch.

Procedure

- Show the children the model of the ocean and the ocean floor. Lift off the top of the ocean to expose the layers of water inside of the ocean at the different depths and the ocean floor.

• Explain that when it rains, water runs into streams and rivers and eventually much of the water that falls runs into the ocean. The water that flows into the ocean is loaded with sediment. Show the sediment falling through the water. It eventually settles onto the ocean floor. When a new layer of sediment falls, a new layer of soil is created and the bottom layer of soil gets pushed down and forms a new layer of sedimentary rock.
• Have children make their own model of the ocean floor and falling sediment.

10. Model of Sedimentary Rock Formation

Materials Several clear plastic glasses; sand.

Procedure
• Fill several clear plastic glasses with a quarter of an inch of sand. Place one glass inside another. Several layers of sand will be seen through the clear plastic glasses.
• Explain to the children that the sand in the glasses is like a layer of sediment that settles out. Each glass of sand is like another layer of sediment that settles out. The layers fall on top of one another. Each glass holds a different layer of sediment. All of the layers are pressed together and form a piece of sedimentary rock. Sedimentary rock is made up of small particles or fragments that once belonged to another rock before it began to erode.
• Let children make their own model showing layers of sedimentary rock.

Model of Sedimentary Rock Formation

A series of plastic glasses on top of one another. Each glass contains some soil or sand and represents a layer of sediment.

11. Folds and Faults on the Earth's Crust

Materials Three towels in three different colors; three colors of clay; a butter knife.

Procedure
• Fold the towels in strips lengthwise. Place the three towels on top of each other. Press in on the sides so that the towels slide toward the center and form folds. See diagram.

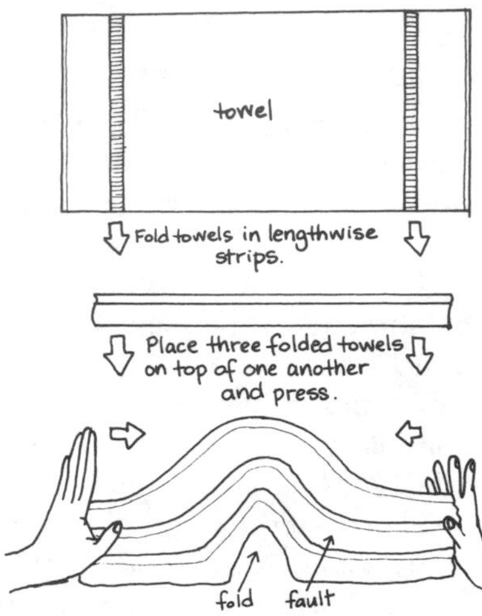

MODEL OF A FOLD AND FAULT

• Explain to the children that the layers of sedimentary rock and the layers of rock on the earth's crust form layers just as the towels do. Pressures from inside or outside of the crust force the layers to fold up. When the layers fold up or to the side, different land forms are formed. When the folds go up and down, mountains are formed. Mountains can be folded or can look like blocks if they were formed by breaks or faults.
• Repeat the same procedure with the clay. Place the three different colors on top of each other in flat strips. Press in on each of the sides so that the clay folds up due to the external pressure. Observe the folds and the formation of the layers. Explain to the children that the layers of the rocks get all mixed up when the folds occur. Parts that were on top can be buried beneath in a fold. Parts that were on the bottom can come up to the top surface after a fold occurs.
• Slice the clay with a bread knife to separate it. The clay will break. Place the two pieces of clay near each other, but do not align them evenly. This is what a fault looks like. A fault occurs when a break occurs in the earth's crust and the land shifts up or down along the crack or sideways along the crack. This occurs during an earthquake. See diagram on next page.
• Let children create a "fold" with a towel and with clay.

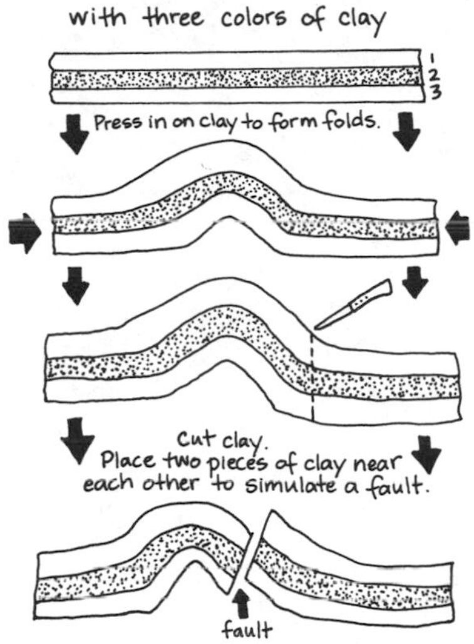
with three colors of clay
1
2
3
Press in on clay to form folds.
Cut clay.
Place two pieces of clay near each other to simulate a fault.
fault

MODEL OF FAULT

Further Resources

Suggested Books for Children

Dewey Decimal Classification Number for rocks is 550; for volcanoes, 551.

Baylor, Byrd, *Everybody Needs a Rock.* New York: Charles Scribner's Sons, 1974. (A story about a child's way to hunt for rocks.)

Boltin, Lee, and T. S. White, *Color Under Ground, The Mineral Picture Book.* New York: Charles Scribner's Sons, 1971.

Challand, Helen, *A New True Book, Volcanoes.* Chicago: Children's Press, 1983.

Coldin, Augusta, *Salt.* New York: Thomas Y. Crowell, 1965. (Tells where salt comes from and how it is used, and how to grow a salt crystal.)

Heavilin, Jay, *Rocks and Gems.* New York: Macmillan, 1964. (Large picture book.)

Podendorf, Illa, *The True Book of Pebbles and Shells.* Chicago: Children's Press, 1972.

Podendorf, Illa, *The True Book of Rocks and Minerals.* Chicago: Children's Press, 1972.

Ruchlis, Hy, *How a Rock Came to Be in a Fence on a Road Near a Town.* New York: Walker, 1973. (Story of a rock and its travels over millions of years.)

Severy, O. Irene, *The First Book of the Earth.* New York: Franklin Watts, 1958.

Shaffer, Paul, *The Golden Stamp Book of Rocks and Minerals.* Racine, Wisconsin: Western Publishing, 1968.

Simon, S., *The Rock Hound Book.* New York: Viking Press, 1973.

Updegraff, Imelda and Robert, *Earthquakes and Volcanoes.* New York: Penguin Books, 1982.

Updegraff, Imelda and Robert, *Mountains and Valleys.* New York: Penguin Books, 1982.

Zim, Herbert, *Caves.* New York: Morrow, 1978.

Resource Books for More Ideas

Asimov, Isaac, *About Volcanoes.* New York: Walker, 1981

Blackwood, Paul, *The How and Why Wonder Book of Rocks and Minerals.* New York: Grosset and Dunlap, 1976.

Burt, Olive W., *Black Sunshine, the Story of Coal.* New York: Julian Messner, 1977.

Raymo, Chet, *The Crust of the Earth, An Armchair Traveler's Guide to the New Geology.* Englewood Cliffs, New Jersey: Prentice-Hall, 1983.

Shuttlesworth, Dorothy, *The Story of Rocks.* New York: Doubleday and Co., 1966.

Suttan, Felix, *The How and Why Wonder Book of Our Earth.* New York: Wonder Books, 1960.

White, Anne, *Rocks All Around Us.* New York: Scholastic Book Services, 1959.

Wyler, Rose, *Exploring Earth Science.* Racine, Wisconsin: Western Publishing, 1973.

Wyler, Rose, and Gerald Ames, *Secrets in Stones.* New York: Four Winds Press, 1970.

Zim, Herbert, and Paul Shaffer, *Rocks and Minerals, A Golden Nature Guide.* New York: Golden Press, 1957.

11
ANIMALS

Objectives

- For children to understand that the world is made up of living and nonliving things.
- For children to become aware that most living things are either plants or animals.
- For children to develop an awareness that animals live in many places.
- For children to understand that all animals need food and water.
- For children to understand that each animal needs its own kind of food.
- For children to develop an awareness that animals are mobile.
- For children to understand that animals can move in different ways (crawl, jump, slither, walk, run, etc.).
- For children to become aware that most animals move, eat, and grow.*
- For children to develop an awareness that animals adapt to their environment in different ways to aid their survival.
- For children to become aware that animals kept in captivity need to be taken care of.
- For children to develop an appreciation and respect for life and living things.

*With the exception of animals like sponges that do not move at all (except to grow); certain coelenterates, such as sea anemones, which seldom move about; and barnacles, as adults, which stay anchored on their rocks, most animals do move.

- For children to develop an awareness of how to group or classify animals with similar characteristics or attributes.
- For children to develop an awareness of the meaning of the following terms: skeleton, exoskeleton, segmented, backbone, vertebrate, invertebrate, characteristic, group, classify.

General Background Information for Parents and Teachers

Use of magnifying glass A good way for young children to use a magnifying glass is to place the magnifying glass next to the eye the way a jeweler does. Then move the object closer or nearer to the eye. This helps reduce the field of vision and eases the focusing problem young children might encounter.

Note: If you hold the magnifying glass too far away from the eye, everything will look upside-down.

Observe To actually see, feel, smell, taste, or hear something.

Inference An interpretation of an observation we have made by using our senses.

Vertebrates Animals with backbones.

**Items marked by two asterisks indicate that the information is too abstract and too complicated for young children to understand or comprehend. It is included to enhance parent or teacher background only.

Invertebrates (small creatures) Animals without backbones.

Zoo A place where animals are cared for in captivity.

Camouflage Protective coloration to aid an animal to survive in its environment.

Environment The natural world that surrounds an animal and influences its growth and development.

Domestic animal An animal that is raised and cared for by people.

Wild animal An animal that lives in the wild on its own and fends for itself.

Classify To arrange or organize according to a general or specific class or category.

Dichotomous classification To divide into two parts or classifications on the basis of one characteristic by only allowing two choices. Branching occurs through successive forking of two approximately equal divisions. For example: This animal has a backbone, or this animal has no backbone; this animal has six legs, or this animal has more than six legs; this animal has a segmented body, or this animal does not have a segmented body.

Classification scheme An orderly plan for classifying.

Method of classification Move from general to specific.

Scientific scheme for classification of animals Moves from a broad, general division to a more specific division that narrows the field of animals to one animal species. See chart below.

• In studying animals with children, emphasis should be placed on gathering experiences and on developing a child's understanding of likenesses and differences between animals. It is a wonderful opportunity to help children become familiar with descriptive words to describe these likenesses and differences, and to develop the ability to make inferences about these observations.

• It is also a great opportunity to help children develop their ability to skillfully sort and group animals, and to work out a dichotomous classification scheme.

• Actually observing live animals gives children an opportunity to use their senses and to learn from the sensory input. Use live specimens or pictures of animals. Avoid doing mental activity without any materials. Telling does not work as well as real experiences with tangible materials. Encourage children to do something with the materials. Also avoid having children memorize trivia and vocabulary for the sake of enriching their vocabulary.

• Ask as many questions as possible to arouse children to become even more astute as observers. Help children find answers to your questions, listen to their responses and questions, and continue to ask more questions.

• Remember that the world is new to children. Help guide them to see things that are evident to us as adults, but not evident to them.

• When experimenting with animals, five criteria for good investigations are:

1. The animals should be respected and not harmed.

2. In order to know if the animal is doing something different when it approaches an obstacle or is disturbed, we first must know what its usual behavior is.

3. An animal must be given a choice if it is going to show a preference for doing one thing instead of another.

4. Before reaching a conclusion, the same experiment should be done more than once.

		Human Being	*Dog*	*Squirrel*	*Monarch Butterfly*
General	Kingdom:	Animal	Animal	Animal	Animal
↓	Phylum:	Chordate (or vertebrate)	Chordate (or vertebrate)	Chordate (or vertebrate)	Arthropod
	Class:	Mammal	Mammal	Mammal	Insect
	Order:	Primate	Carnivore	Rodent	Lepidoptera
	Family:	Huminidae	Canidae	Sciurus	
	Genus:	Homo	Canis	Tamiasciurus	Danaus
Specific	Species:	Sapiens	Familiaris (or domestic)	Carolenis	Plexippus

**Note:* Scientific name includes genus and species written as follows: *danaus plexippus* (Monarch butterfly).

5. The animal should be returned to its natural environment when the experiment or investigation is finished.

• When studying and observing animals, try to start with living things. Then after careful observation, have the children try to build models of the animals. If live specimens are not available, then use high-quality color photographs. These kinds of animal photographs are abundant in publications like *National Wildlife, Ranger Rick* Magazine, and *World* Magazine. There are also many recently published books with good quality color pictures at the library.

Activities and Procedures

I. Introduction to Animals

1. What Is an Animal?

Materials Assorted living and nonliving things, such as: various house plants; small pets like a goldfish, canary, kitten, puppy, hamster, guinea pig, rabbit, turtle; smaller animals such as insects (grasshopper, beetle, cricket, ant), millipede, spider, snail; rocks, sea shells, etc.

Procedure

• Show the children the assorted living and nonliving things. Have them observe at least two or three animals that are alive. Ask them to compare the animals to one another.

• Ask them the following kinds of questions:

How are the animals different?
(They have different features such as: different skin coverings and colors, and different sizes and shapes. They make different kinds of sounds or none at all. They move differently from one another. Some move faster or slower than the others, etc.)

How are they alike?
(They are all alive. They each have a way to eat and a way to move.)

How are animals different from plants?
(Plants cannot walk or move from where they are planted unless someone moves them. Animals are mobile.)

What makes plants and animals alike?
(They are both living things.)

Are we living things?
(Yes.)

Are we plants or animals?
(Animals. We are mammals. A mammal is an animal that has hair.)

What is the largest animal you can think of?
(The blue whale is the largest animal alive today, but whatever answer they give is the largest they can think of.)

What is the smallest animal you can think of?
(One-celled animals like the amoeba are the smallest animals; however, these animals are probably not in a small child's experience so whatever animal a child names as the smallest is the smallest for that child to think of.)

• Ask the children to find or make pictures of living things and nonliving things. Have the children sort the pictures into piles of living and nonliving things, and then to further sort the pictures of living things into plants and animals.

2. Where Do Animals Live?

Materials Assorted pictures of various terrains and environments; assorted pictures of animals, at the zoo or in their natural environment.

Procedure

• Show the children the pictures. Discuss where the various animals live.

• Ask the following kinds of questions:

Can polar bears live in warm climates?
(No.)

Can seals live on land away from water?
(No.)

Can turtles live in the Antarctic?
(No.)

Can tropical birds from warm areas live outdoors during the winter if it snows?
(No.)

Where do earthworms live?
(Under the ground in moist soil.)

Do earthworms live in deserts?
(Not usually; it is too dry for them.*)

Is there any place animals do not live on the Earth?
(Animals live almost every place on the Earth, unless the conditions are too extreme for them to live.)

When animals are alive at the zoo, do they all have the same kinds of surroundings?
(No. Zookeepers make the homes and environments of the animals they care for as much as possible like the environment the animals are accustomed to in their natural environment.)

*"Earthworms live in most lands of the world, including oceanic islands and subarctic regions. They are scarce in poor, acid, sandy, or dry situations." (Storer, T. I., *General Zoology*, pp. 517–18. See Bibliography.)

Are all animals at the zoo fed the same thing?
(Probably not. This can be found out by visiting the zoo at feeding time.)

Is your backyard a natural environment?
(Yes.)

Where can you find animals in your backyard?
(In the soil, under logs and rocks, in trees, on flowers, in the grass, in puddles, under lawn furniture.)

Are the animals you would find in your backyard larger or smaller than you are?
(Most of the animals would be smaller than you are.)

II. Small Creatures

1. Looking for Small Creatures

Materials Magnifying glass; flashlight; shovel; hand trowel; strainer.

Procedure
• Take the children outside and look for small creatures with them. Have them gently turn over large rocks, roll logs over, look under dead leaves, examine tree bark, and inspect different parts of plants for small creatures. If there is a pond in your vicinity, go to it and look for small creatures along the edge of the pond, on the banks, and in the long grasses.
• Use the flashlight to see better under rocks and logs. Small creatures are often the same color as the soil and are hard to see. Once you find them, look at them through the magnifying glass. To find small creatures, you may have to turn the soil over with a shovel or a small hand trowel and sift loose soil with a strainer.
• Help children come to the understanding that the soil, plants, and ponds are filled with animal life. Have children notice the colors of these small animals, how they move, where they live, what they appear to be doing, and what they appear to be eating. Have the children observe the small creatures in their natural environment. Have them notice how many different kinds of small creatures are on one plant and how many of the same kind of small creatures are on the plant or under one rock. Have the children observe how many flying insects visit one flower, or how many bees visit the same flower.
• Help children observe the physical surroundings where the animal lives. Does the animal appear to like light or dark places? Does it appear to like moist or dry places?
Note: Additional trips outdoors would be useful for observing where small creatures can be found on a sunny day, and where they can be found on a rainy day. Also, to observe whether the time of day or season of the year makes a difference as to where animals are found, and as to whether or not the animals are found at all.

2. Creating a Zoo for Small Creatures

Materials Magnifying glasses; nature guidebooks about invertebrates; a large number of clear plastic shoeboxes or empty one-quart jars with wide mouths (peanut butter and mayonnaise jars are excellent); aquarium tanks; soil; compost; dried food; cut-up fresh fruits and vegetables; dead leaves; cotton balls; black construction paper; cheesecloth or nylon mesh from old pantyhose; rubber bands; cardboard boxes; marking pens; index cards; Scotch tape.

Procedure
• Explain to the children that it is possible to collect a large variety of small creatures and that by doing so, it is possible to create a zoo of small creatures.
• Ask the children the following kinds of questions:

What is a zoo?
(A place where animals live.)

What do zoos have?
(Animals, zookeepers, cages or houses for animals, benches, trash cans, trees and grass and flowers, food stands for visitors.)

How does a zoo keep animals?
(By taking care of the animals that are living there, by providing the animals with the kind of environment and foods that keep them healthy.)

How do zookeepers know how to take care of the animals in the zoo?
(By observing them in their natural environment before they are captured, and by observing the way the animal acts in captivity.)

Why do people enjoy visiting zoos?
(Probably because they enjoy observing animals, enjoy watching the way the various animals move and eat and play. Also because they want to learn about other animals.)

What could we find out if we created a zoo for small creatures?
(We could compare the small creatures. We could observe the ways they move and eat. We could observe the way they live.)

What would we have to do to run a small creature zoo?
(Keep the animals safe, well fed, and comfortable.)

• Show the children the various materials and ask them to suggest how these materials could be used to create cages or houses for the animals, and labels or instructions about caring for the animals.

3. Collecting Small Creatures for a Classroom or Home Small Creature Zoo

Materials Assorted empty jars with lids; a sturdy butterfly net (can be used in a pond as well as in the air); flashlight; magnifying glass; hand trowel; rectangular plastic basin or cardboard box to carry everything in and to keep the jars safe; masking tape; marking pen; nature guidebook about invertebrates.

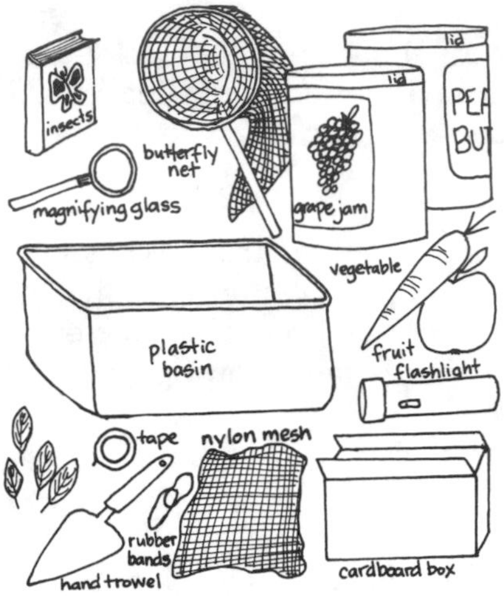

Procedure

- Follow the same procedure as in Activity II, Procedure 1, but this time when you find the small creatures try to catch them. This is not always so easy. Some of them move very fast. It is their ability to move quickly that often saves their lives.
- After you capture a small creature, place it in a jar and close the lid. Then observe what it looks like and have the children thumb through the nature guidebook until they find an animal that looks like the one you just captured. Read about it. Find out what kind of food it likes to eat. If there is no mention of the food the animal eats, then place a sample of soil or leaves in the jar with the animal after it is captured so that it will not starve. Place a piece of masking tape on the jar and use a marking pen to write the identity of the kind of creature that is in the jar. Do not worry about putting holes in the jar lid. There is enough air in the jar for the animal to live for several hours. If you open the jar lids every few hours for a few seconds, the small creatures will have enough air. If you poke holes in the metal lids, the sharp points on the lids could injure the small animals inside the jars and/or the animals might be able to escape out of the holes.
- Emphasize to the children that they should leave the places they have looked for small creatures as undisturbed as possible. They should replace rocks and logs that they have lifted. Remind them that it is necessary to capture only a few of the small creatures they have seen, not everything that moves. Stress the care of living things and a respect for life. Animals should not just be collected. Children should understand that the animals are being collected so they can be observed. The animals should be provided with a suitable place to live for a few days while they are being observed. After they are observed they should be returned to natural surroundings outside. Children can watch them return to the soil when they are brought back outside.

4. Suitable Temporary Housing for Small Creatures

Note: The small creatures are listed in alphabetical order. Most of them require similar housing with slight variations. Read on for specifics. An adult needs to supervise the capturing of small creatures and also needs to carry any glass container. The glass container could be hazardous for a small child to carry.

Ants

Materials An empty one-quart jar; a pie pan filled with water; a piece of black construction paper; a rubber band; a small piece of cardboard with a hole in the center to rest on top of the jar; soil containing ants; a hand trowel; a piece of cotton soaked with sugar water.

Procedure Have a child place the soil containing the ants in the jar with the hand trowel. Then have him or her place the jar in the pie pan filled with water. (The water will prevent the ants from escaping.) Have a

ANT HOME

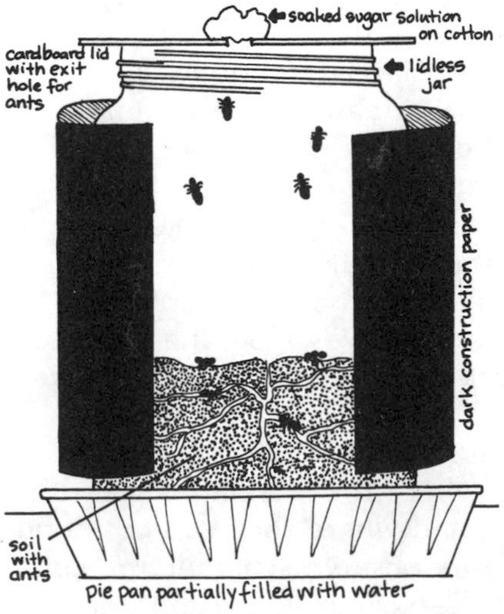

child place a piece of cotton soaked in sugar water on top of a piece of cardboard with a hole in the center. (The ants will come to the surface to feed. You might want to add a piece of dark-colored construction paper to the outside of the jar since the ants will feel more at home in a dark environment. Then you can lift off the paper to see the activity along the sides of the jar.) See diagram.

Caterpillars

Materials An empty one-quart jar or clear plastic shoebox; a small container for water; a small twig from the tree or plant where the caterpillar was found; some moist soil; a piece of bark; nylon mesh; a rubber band to secure the mesh as a lid.

Procedure Place the soil on the bottom of the jar and a piece of bark at a slant against the jar. Place the twig in the water on top of the soil so that the leaves will stay alive longer. Place the caterpillar on the twigs. Caterpillars are very fussy about what they munch. They have very specific kinds of leaves they enjoy eating. So be sure you take a twig with you that the caterpillar was crawling on when you caught it. See diagram.

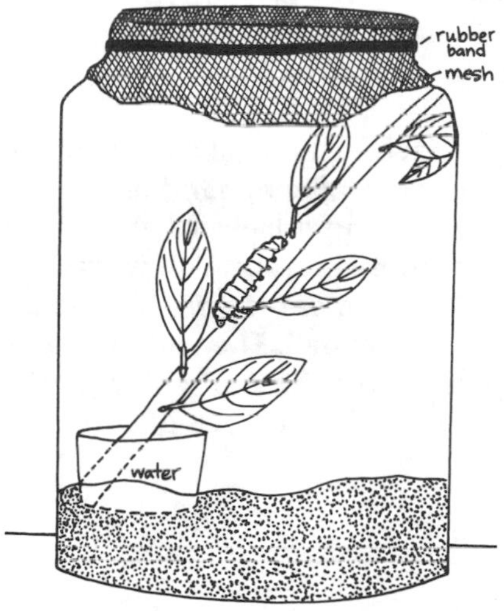

CATERPILLAR HOME

Note: The soil and the bark are in the cage in case the caterpillar decides to pupate while it is in captivity. Different species pupate in different kinds of places, so allow for all possibilities.

Crickets

Materials An empty one-quart jar or clear plastic shoebox; soil; clumps of grass or dead leaves; a medium-size rock to hide under; raisins; dry cereal; bread or cake crumbs; lettuce; a few drops of water shaken from your hands.

Procedure Have a child fill the bottom of the container with soil and add a layer of leaves or grass clumps to the top of the soil. Have another child place a rock on top of the soil so the cricket can hide under it. Then have another child place some food for the cricket to eat on top of a large leaf, and add the cricket or crickets to the container. Remember to have the children sprinkle a few drops of water into the container every day.

Earthworms

Materials An empty jar or clear plastic shoebox; moist soil taken from where the earthworms were found; pieces of grass or dead leaves; dark construction paper; a rubber band or Scotch tape; dry oatmeal; coffee grounds or cornmeal.

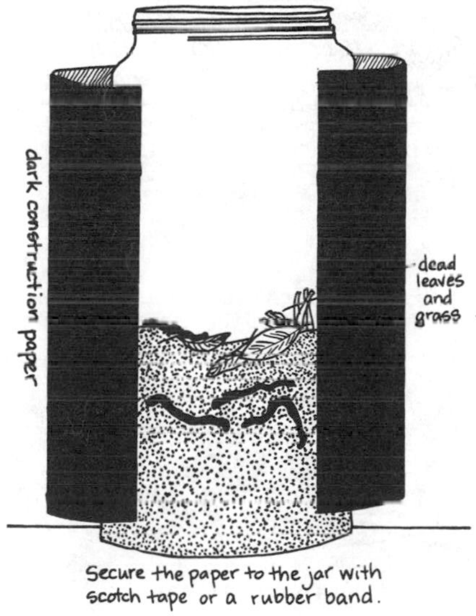

EARTHWORM HOME

Procedure Have a child fill the jar about three-quarters full with moist soil. Have another child sprinkle some dry food and grass or dead leaves on top of the soil. Choose another child to mix the soil lightly so that the food matter is in the soil. Then have children add the worms to the jar. Cover the sides of the jar with dark construction paper. Secure the paper with Scotch tape or a rubber band. Be sure to have the children sprinkle the soil with water every day so that it stays moist. Remind the children *not* to make the soil too moist or the worms will drown.

Fireflies

Materials An empty jar with a lid; nylon mesh; a rubber band; a wet cotton ball; pieces of grass to cover the bottom of the jar.

Procedure Have a child place some pieces of grass at the bottom of a jar. Take the children outside at twilight in spring or summer. Instruct the children to use a butterfly net or their two hands to catch some fireflies. Place the caught fireflies inside the jar. Quickly place the lid on top so they will not fly away. Put a wet piece of cotton in the jar so that they will have some water. Replace the metal lid with a mesh lid and a rubber band so they can receive air. Keep them in captivity only a day or less. They do not eat much. They live only to mate. Both the male and the female light their light to attract each other.

Note: It is not respectful to the firefly to keep it in captivity. Captivity prevents fireflies from finding a mate and from allowing the female to lay her eggs.

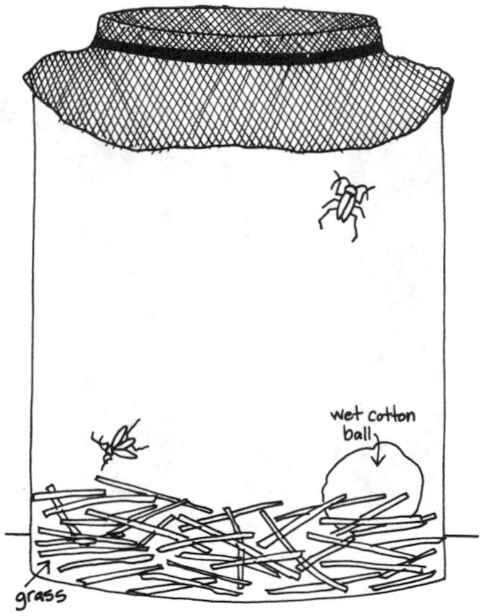

FIREFLY HOME

Flies

Materials An empty one-quart jar; cheesecloth or nylon mesh obtained from an old pair of cut-up pantyhose; a rubber band; a piece of string with a small piece of raw meat tied to one end, or a cotton ball soaked in sugar water or honey; moist sawdust.

Procedure Have a child place moist sawdust at the bottom of the jar. Have another child place a string with meat or a cotton ball soaked with honey or sugar water so that it dangles inside the jar. Place the fly or flies in the jar. Cover the jar with the cheesecloth or nylon mesh. Secure the mesh to the top of the jar. (The transfer will be easier if it is possible to place the fly in a freezer for a few seconds to slow it down.) See diagram.

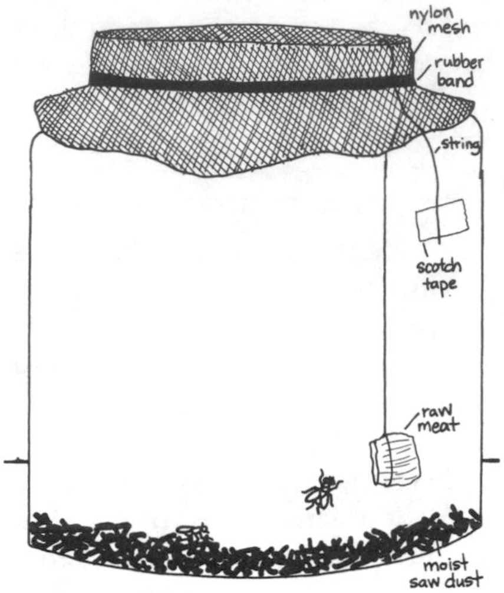

HOUSEFLY HOME

Grasshoppers

Materials An empty clear plastic shoebox or other clear container; sand or soil; nylon mesh; a rubber band or a piece of string; wheat; raw corn cob; grasses; a wet cotton ball.

Procedure Have a child make the container ready for the grasshopper by placing sand or soil on the bottom of the container and a layer of grasses on top of the soil. Have another child sprinkle wheat grasses or part of a corn cob in the container. Choose another child to add a wet cotton ball. Then add the grasshopper or grasshoppers. Cover the top with a mesh lid secured with a rubber band or a piece of string tied together.

Ladybugs

Materials An empty one-quart jar; a piece of cheesecloth or nylon mesh; a rubber band; a cotton ball soaked in water to create dampness inside the jar; a piece of a rose plant containing live aphids.

Note: Aphids are insect pests. They often live on rose plants. Aphids attack the young shoots and buds of the plant.

Procedure Have a child place a wet cotton ball inside a jar. Add a piece of rose plant infested with live aphids and add the ladybugs to the jar. Secure the piece of cheesecloth or nylon mesh over the opening of the jar with the rubber band.

Mealworms

Materials An empty clear plastic shoebox; oatmeal or a bran cereal; a piece of cut-up apple or a moist cotton ball; a small bottle cap.

Procedure You do not need to place a lid on top of the mealworms. They cannot climb out of the container. Have a child fill the bottom of the container with oatmeal. Have another child place a piece of cut-up apple inside the container for moisture, or add a moist cotton ball to a small bottle cap. Mealworms are the larva form of a beetle. They can be purchased at a pet store. Pet stores usually sell mealworms as food for other animals like lizards and fish.

Millipedes

Materials Damp earth; soft green leaves or small pieces of cut-up apple, banana or orange; an empty one-quart jar with a mesh lid secured by a rubber band.

Procedure Have a child place a layer of moist soil on the bottom of the jar. Then choose another child to place a layer of soft green leaves and a layer of small cut-up fruit pieces inside the jar. Then place the millipedes inside and cover the jar with nylon mesh secured with a rubber band.

Slugs

Materials A small cardboard carton; an empty one-quart jar; moist compost soil; a cut-up carrot, apple, potato or pear; nylon mesh and a rubber band.

Procedure Have a child fill the bottom of the jar with moist soil and dead leaves. Have another child place a cut-up fruit or vegetable on top of the soil. Have the children put slugs into the jar and cover the lid of the jar with nylon mesh and a rubber band. Put the jar into a cardboard box so that it will seem dark to the slugs. They prefer a dark, damp environment.

Land Snails

Materials An empty one-quart jar; moist soil; dead leaves; a small dish sunk into the moist soil and filled with food, which should consist of raw vegetables or oats.

Procedure Set up an aquarium filled with moist soil for the snails.

Pond Snails

Materials An empty one-quart jar; some sand; a water plant from an aquarium supply store; water. Pond snails can also be bought at the aquarium supply store if you cannot find your own.

Procedure Set up an aquarium filled with water for the snails.

Sow Bugs

Materials An empty one-quart jar or shoebox; damp soil; a thick piece of bark; moist dead leaves; mesh netting, a rubber band.

Procedure Have a child fill the bottom of the jar with the damp soil. Have another child place a layer of moist dead leaves on top of the soil. Choose another child to place a piece of bark on top of the leaves as a shelter for the sow bug. Add the sow bug, cover the jar with mesh, and secure it with a rubber band.

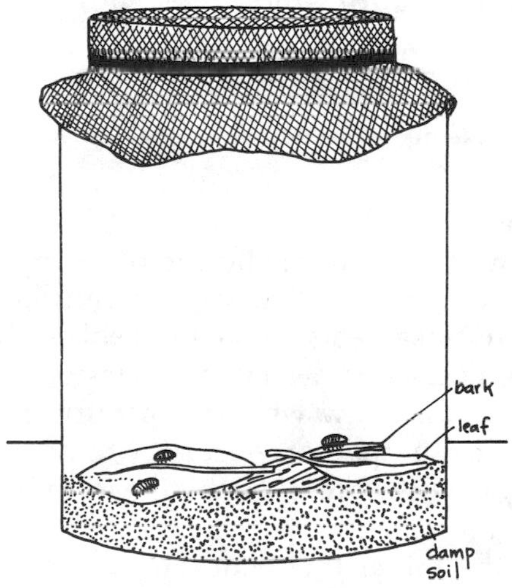

SOWBUG HOME

Spiders

Materials An empty aquarium; sand; twigs planted in the sand to supply supports for a possible web that might be spun; a dish of water; a toilet paper tube (for spider to hide in); a nylon mesh covering; a string to secure nylon mesh covering as a lid; flies to eat. See diagram.

Procedure Obtain a spider from your house or from the garden outside. After the jar has been made ready for it, place the spider inside the jar. Do not worry

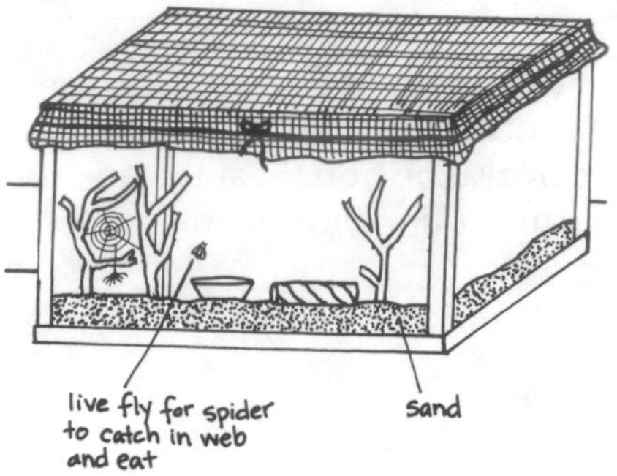

SPIDER HOME

about catching flies for it right away. Spiders can live several days without food.

Note: The black widow spider is dangerous. Black widows are not found in most houses. They are usually found in low, dark places under logs and in basements. They have a shiny black body with a red spot shaped like an hourglass on their abdomen. There are very few around, but children should be warned about them.

5. Creating General Guidelines with Children for Observing and Investigating Small Creatures in Captivity

Materials None.

Procedure

- Discuss with the children how to observe and handle the small creatures. "Observe" means to use our senses—our noses, ears, and eyes. Explain that taste is not used unless we know it is safe to taste. Touch is not used unless we know we are not hurting the small creature. Explain that it is necessary to be gentle with our touch when we feel a small creature because we can hurt it.
- Discuss the things that children can be looking for when they make observations. The following is a partial list of the kinds of things children can be looking for and thinking about when they observe the small creatures in the small-creature zoo.

How does it use its body to move?

How does it use its body to eat?

How does it find its food?

Does it have legs? How many?

Does it have wings? How many?

Does its color help camouflage it? How?

How steep a slope can the small creature climb?

How does the small creature react to water?

How does it react to obstacles in its path?

How does it react when it meets another small creature?

What does it do when it is disturbed?

Can it be made to back up?

What does it have in common with other small creatures?

Which of all the small creatures seems to be able to move the fastest?

Which of all the small creatures seems to move the slowest?

Which small creatures appear to like well-lit places? Why?

Which small creatures appear to like dark places? Why?

Does the creature prefer to be on top of things or hidden underneath?

Which animals prefer dry places? Which prefer moist places? Why?

Which animals appear to be helpful to us? Why?

Which animals appear to be pests to us? Why?

6. Materials for Observing and Investigating Small Creatures in Captivity

Materials Magnifying glass; eye dropper; water; a clear plastic container; a plastic lid; toothpick; a twig; a ruler; a piece of black construction paper and a piece of white construction paper taped together so that they lie side by side with a common border; a moist paper towel; a cellulose sponge.

Procedure

- Show the children the materials. Discuss how each of the items can be used to observe and find out more about each of the animals in captivity.
- *Magnifying glass*—Can be used for observing the small creature's body, its parts, its color and texture, and for taking a closer look at how the animal moves or eats.
- *Eye dropper*—Can be used for lifting and dropping water in the small creature's path, and for creating a small puddle of water. Also used for touching and lifting the small creature.
- *A clear plastic container*—Can be used for observing the small creature in a small space.
- *A plastic lid*—Can be used as an obstacle in the small creature's path, or for a closer look at the way the small creature behaves in a small space.

• *A toothpick or a twig*—Can be used as an obstacle, or as a touching and lifting tool, and as a tool for making the small creature back up or climb.
• *A ruler*—Can be used for measuring the length of a small creature. It can also be used as an incline to see how steep an incline the animal can climb up or down.
• *Black and white construction paper taped together*—Can be used for finding out whether an animal prefers to be on light or dark surfaces, or under light or dark surfaces.
• *A moist paper towel*—Can be used to find out if the creature prefers to be on top of or underneath moist surfaces.
• *A moist cellulose sponge*—Can be used as an obstacle in a small creature's path and as an item for a small creature to crawl under.

7. Investigations and Observations of Specific Small Creatures While in Captivity

Note: The animals are listed in alphabetical order. Activities are suggested for each animal. The choice should be up to the individual child as to whether or not the child wishes to participate. Some children and adults are squeamish around crawly small creatures. If, as an adult, you do not feel comfortable, your attitude will be felt by the children. If you do feel uncomfortable, try to get over it by dealing with your fears. Discuss your fears and the fears the children have with them. Remember that the animals are much smaller than you are and that they have more to fear than you do. They do not inflict death if they bite you. If they do bite you, it will feel like a slight pinch. Unless there is an extremely allergic reaction, the bite would be no worse than a mosquito's bite. If you use a twig, toothpick, or eye dropper to gently handle the small creature, there is less chance of being bitten and/or damaging the small creature's body.

*Ants

Materials A magnifying glass; a small plastic container; cookie or cake crumbs; ants in a jar filled with soil and covered on the outside with dark construction paper; water; eye dropper.

Procedure
• Have a child remove the dark paper from the outside of the jar. Are there any visible tunnels? Are ants in the tunnels? How many ants come to the surface of the lid at one time to eat the sugar water in the cotton ball? How do the ants move in the light and in the dark? What do two ants do when they meet each other? How do ants use their feelers or antennae on top of their heads? After you have observed them, cover the jar with the dark paper again. Next time you look, see if there are more tunnels.

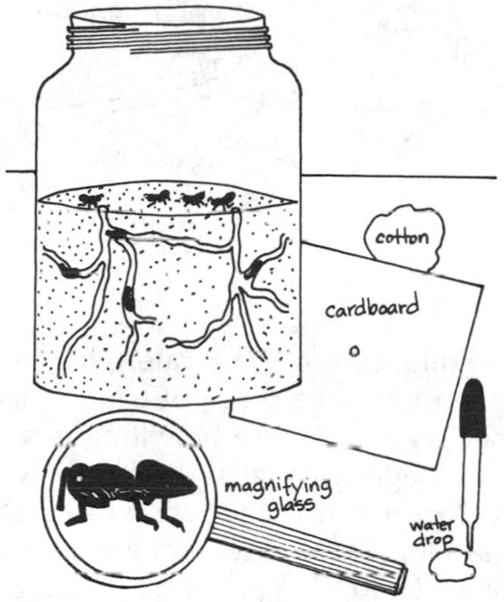

• Remove from the lid of the jar a few ants that are feeding on the cotton soaked with sugar water. Place them in a small container. If you place the container in the refrigerator with a cover, it will slow the ants down a little so that it will be easier to observe them. Look at the ants through a magnifying glass. How many legs do they have? (Six.) How many sections do their bodies have? (Three.) How many antennae do they have? (Two.) What colors are they? (Brown, red, or black.) Place a few drops of water in the container. What do ants do when they feel water? Drop a few food crumbs into the container. What do the ants do? (Place the ants back in the jar with the other ants or put them back outside when you finish with them.)

Caterpillars

Materials Magnifying glass; jar of caterpillars with the food they like to eat; a piece of paper; a ruler; eye dropper; water.

Procedure
• Have the children observe the caterpillars in the jar. What are they doing? Where are they located? How much have they eaten? What do the leaves that they have been on look like? Has the caterpillar built a cocoon?

*One asterisk indicates the animal is an adult insect. All adult insects have six legs and three body regions (the head, thorax, and abdomen). All six legs and the wings are connected to an insect's thorax, which is in the middle of its body. Not all insects have wings.

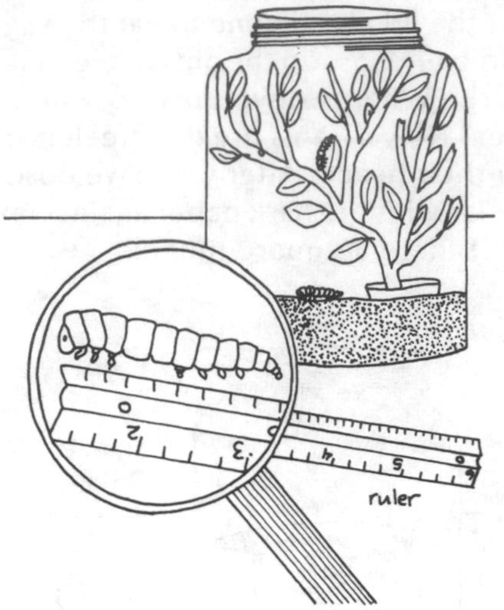

• Have the children remove a caterpillar or two from the jar. Place them on a piece of paper. Place a ruler next to one. Try to measure how long it is. Look at it through the magnifying glass. How many segments does it have? How many legs does it have? Does every segment have legs? How does it move? Does it slide or hump along? Hold the paper at a slant. Can the caterpillar crawl up a steep slope? How steep? What happens when the caterpillar comes to water? What do two caterpillars do when they meet?

Note: Caterpillars are the larval form of moths and butterflies. Most of them are considered pests because they eat a lot.

•Crickets

Materials Crickets in a plastic container with soil, bark, and dead leaves; magnifying glass.

Procedure

• Have the children observe the crickets in captivity. What do they do? Where do they go to? What do they do when they meet? Do they all chirp? Where does the noise come from? How many legs do they have? Why do they make noise? Do all of the crickets look alike?

Note: Only male crickets make noise or chirp. They chirp to attract a female mate. The noise is made when the male cricket lifts its wings and rubs them together. Male crickets can be easily distinguished from female crickets; female crickets have a long-looking spike at the end of their abdomen. The spike is called an oviposter. An oviposter is used to store eggs and to bury eggs under the ground.

• Have the children find a female and a male cricket. Place the male cricket in a jar. When the male chirps, what does the female do? Move the jar a little bit away from the female. What does the female do? If you move the male cricket into another room so that the female can no longer see the male cricket, what does the female do when the male chirps? How can you tell if the female can hear the male? (When the female hears the male, she turns toward the male, or she hops in his direction.)

• Place a cricket in a small box. Examine the cricket with a magnifying glass. See if children can locate the following parts: head, thorax, abdomen, four wings, eyes, antennae, palpi, feet, ears (located on each of its front legs under the knees), cerci (the two short spikes), spiracles (along the abdomen, for breathing). See diagram of a cricket's body, with its parts labeled.

• Locate the abdomen on the cricket. Watch the abdomen move in and out as the cricket breathes. Who breathes faster, you or the cricket?

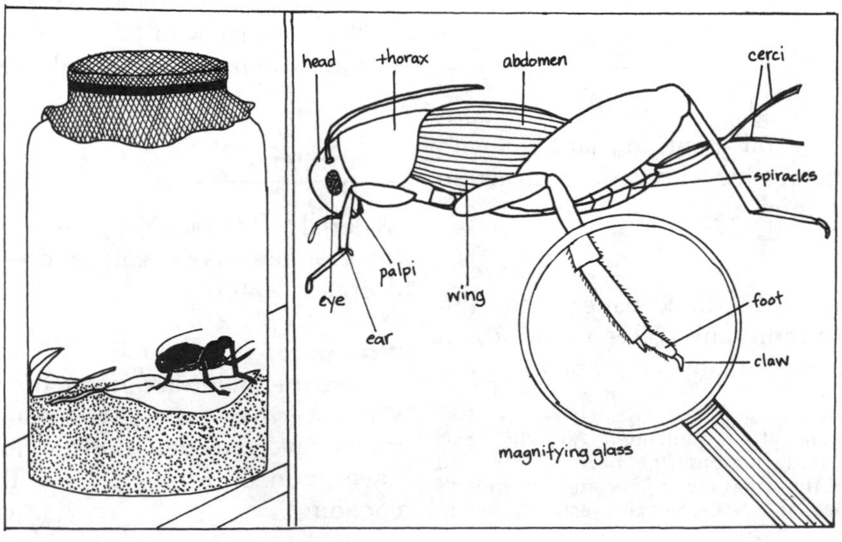

Earthworms

Materials Magnifying glass; container with worms in soil; black or brown construction paper; white construction paper; an eye dropper; water; moist paper towel; plastic lid; cellulose sponge; a toothpick.

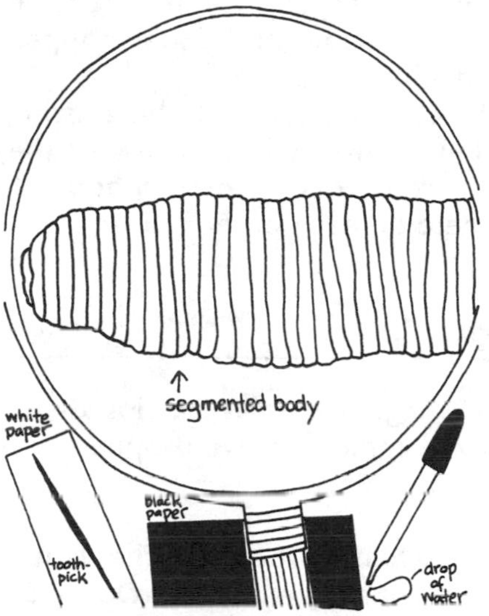

Procedure

• Have a child lift the cardboard box off the container. Have the children observe the tunnels that the worms may have made in the soil. What do they appear to be doing in the soil? Do they stay still or move?

• Have a child place a worm on top of the soil. What does it do? How does it move? How long does it take to bury itself in the soil?

• Have a child place a worm on a table. Put a piece of black paper and a piece of white paper alongside of each other on the table. Place the worm on the two pieces of paper so that its body is touching both pieces of paper. Does the worm prefer to be on the black or the white piece of paper? Try it several times and see if there is a preference. (Worms usually prefer to be on lighter colors. Worms cannot see, but their bodies can sense the warmth from darker colors. Darker colors absorb more heat. They need to keep their bodies cool and moist. If worms become too hot and dry, they die. They stay alive when it becomes too hot or too cold by burrowing deeper in the soil.)

• Have a child place an earthworm on a moist paper towel on a table. Have the children look at its body through a magnifying glass. Which end of its body is its head and which end is its tail? How can you tell which is which? Does it have a top and a bottom? Roll the worm over and see what it does. What does its skin feel like? Does it have any legs or feet? Gently have a child touch the worm's tail or head with a toothpick. How does it respond? Drop water on the worm with an eye dropper so that its skin does not dry out. Drop a small drop of water near its head. How does it respond to the drop of water?

• Have a child place a wet sponge next to the worm. What does it do when it feels the sponge? Have another child place the worm on a plastic lid. Put a small amount of water in the lid. How does the worm react to water? Place the worm next to the lid. Does the worm try to go under the lid? Place the worm on top of a rolled piece of paper so that it is elevated.

How does the worm move from one height to another?

What do worms do when they meet?

Can you hear a worm move on a piece of paper?

As the worm moves like a Slinky, stretching and shrinking as it moves, can you see the intestinal tract inside the worm?

Does the worm appear to prefer moving forward or backward?

Can it move as well in both directions?

• Be sure to have children place the worm back with the other worms when they are through investigating its reactions and movements. The worm will need to rest after so much excitement and activity.

Fireflies

Materials Magnifying glass; fireflies in a clear closed container.

Procedure

• Have children observe the fireflies in the jar.

Are their lights always on? What do fireflies look like? Are they really flies?
(No, they have four wings, not two.)

How are their two sets of wings different from one another?
(The outside wings are hard, the inner wings are hidden and transparent.)

What colors are fireflies? Do they all look alike?

Do they blink their lights or do they stay lit for awhile?

Are the colors of the lights the same?

If one firefly blinks, do others blink in response?

• Have the children use a magnifying glass to take a better look at the body of the firefly, and at the light when it goes on. How many legs does it have?

*Flies

Materials Magnifying glass; container with a fly or flies.

Procedure

- Have the children observe the fly in captivity. What does it do? Does it buzz? When does it buzz? Does it stay on its food or prefer another place to rest? How does it eat? (Look for its proboscis [sucking tongue].) Does the fly clean itself? Does the fly stay still or move around a lot? What do the fly's legs look like? Can the fly's legs bend? How many wings does a fly have? What color is the fly? What color are the fly's eyes? Why can the fly walk on a ceiling or along the side of a jar? Do flies have claws or suction cups on their feet?
- Have the children observe the fly with a magnifying glass while it is at rest on the side of the glass jar. Look at its eyes and its feet. Can they see hair on the legs? Can they see the parts in the surface of the compound eye? Look at its wings. Can they see the veins running through its transparent wings? How many legs does it have? (Six.)

Note: A fly is an insect that has two wings. Other insects that fly and are not flies have four wings. Dragonflies and butterflies have four wings and are not flies.

*Grasshoppers

Materials Magnifying glass; a container with one or more grasshoppers.

Procedure

- Have the children observe the grasshoppers in the container. How do they eat? Can they fly in the container? How many wings do they have? Are they easy to see in the grass? How does their color help protect them? How does the grasshopper move? Does it walk, hop, or jump? Why can the grasshopper jump high? Are all of its legs the same length? How many legs does the grasshopper have? Can the grasshopper's legs bend? How many joints does each leg have? What section of the body do the wings grow from? (The middle part called the thorax.)
- Have the children use the magnifying glass to find the simple eye, the ear, the spiracles on the abdomen, the palpi near its mouth, and the claws on its feet for gripping. See diagram of the grasshopper to find the parts listed above.
- Have the children compare the grasshopper to the cricket. How are they alike and how are they different? How do the colors of each of their bodies help protect them? Where do each of them live?

Ladybugs

Materials Magnifying glass; a closed container with ladybugs and aphids; an eye dropper; water.

Procedure

- Have the children observe the ladybugs in the container. What are they doing? Do all ladybugs look alike? Are they all the same color? Do they all have the same number of spots on their back? How do the ladybugs move? Do they fly? Can you see them eating aphids?
- Have a child take a ladybug out of the container and then watch it walk on a table. Does it walk in a straight line, or zig-zag? If you hold the ladybug between your thumb and your index finger and then smell your finger, does it have an odor? Look at the ladybug's body with a magnifying glass. How many legs does it have? Do the legs have joints? Are the legs different sizes? What does it do when it is flipped over on its back? How many wings does it have? Which wings are hard? Which wings are transparent? Drop a drop of water in its path. How does it react to the water?

Note: Ladybugs are helpful insects because they eat aphids and other insect pests.

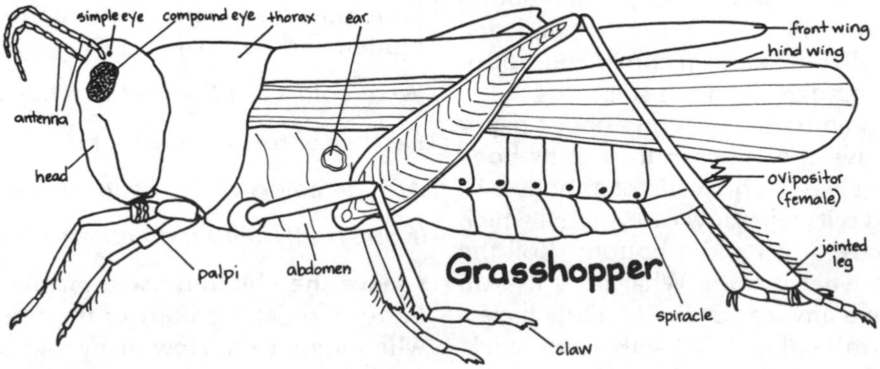

Mealworms

Materials Container with mealworms; dried cereal and a piece of cut-up apple; plus all of the materials listed for earthworms.

Procedure

• Have the children observe the mealworms in the cereal inside the container. How do the mealworms move? How do they know where to go? Where do they walk most of the time? What does a mealworm do when you put something in its way?

• Have the children experiment with a mealworm on a table. What does a mealworm do when you put something in its way? How can you make it back up? How does the mealworm move? How many legs does it have? Which end is its mouth on?

• Have children do all of the activities they did for earthworms. Have children compare the responses of the mealworms to those of the earthworms. Do they respond the same or differently? How are mealworms like earthworms? How are they different from earthworms?

Note: Mealworms are insect pests that live in ground grain. They are the larval form of beetles. They are called mealworms because when grain is ground, it is called meal.

Millipedes

Materials A container with a millipede; a magnifying glass; a toothpick; an eye dropper; some water.

Procedure

• Have children observe the millipede. Does it like light or dark places? Have a child place the millipede out on a table. How does it move? How many legs does it have? (Two on each segment of its body.) What does it do when it is disturbed? (Roll up.) How does it react to a drop of water in its path? How can you make it back up? Ask the children to observe its body through a magnifying glass. Can they find its head? Does it make any noise when it moves? How does it react to noise?

• Compare the millipede to the earthworm and the mealworm. How are these animals alike? How are they different? Which of these animals moves the fastest? Which moves the slowest? Which animal has a dry body? Which animal has a moist body? Which animal has no legs? Which animal has the most legs? Compare the colors of their bodies and discuss their individual environments and how their colors protect them. Which animal can climb along the sides of a container the best?

Slugs

Materials A clear covered container with slugs covered with a cardboard box; a magnifying glass; a toothpick; sand; an eye dropper; water.

Procedure

• Have a child observe the slugs. When the container is uncovered by lifting the cardboard box, what do they do? Do they like to be in dark or light places? How do they move? Have a child remove a slug from the container and place it on a table. Can the children tell by looking where it has crawled? (Yes, slugs leave a slime trail wherever they move.) How does the slug react to a drop of water in its path? How does the slug react to a small puddle of water? How does a slug react to the end of a toothpick? What color is the slug? How does it feel when you touch it? Place sand in its path. Does the sand stick to the slug's body as the slug moves over it?

• Have the children look at the slug through a magnifying glass. What does it have on its head? What does its skin look like? What does the slug do when it is flipped over? Can you make the slug back up?

Snails

Materials A clear container with land snails; an aquarium with pond snails; a magnifying glass; a toothpick.

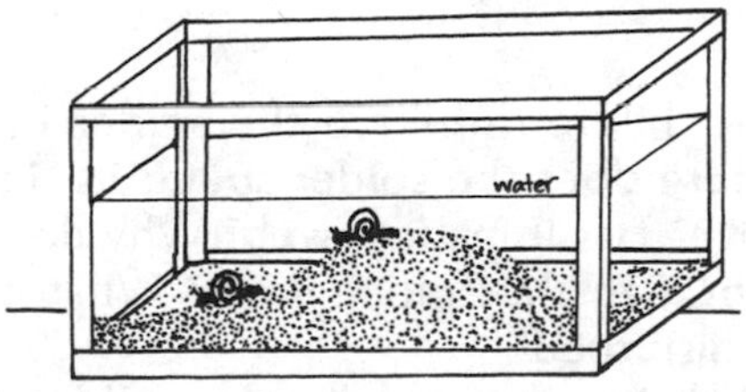

Procedure

• Have the children observe the two kinds of snails. How are they different from each other? How are they the same? How do they move? What does the land snail leave behind as it moves? What happens to the green algae along the sides of the aquarium as the pond snail moves over it? Which moves faster, the pond snail or the land snail? When does the snail go into its shell? When does it come out of its shell? Can the children make it back up?

• Have the children look at the snails through a magnifying glass. What do their heads look like? Compare the way a snail's head looks with the way a slug's head looks. How are they alike? How are they different?

Sow Bugs

Materials A container with sow bugs; a magnifying glass; a toothpick; an eye dropper; some water; dry sand and wet sand; dark paper and white paper.

Procedure

• Have a child observe the sow bugs in the container. Are they easy to find? Are they underneath something? What are they doing? Have a child take one out of the container and place it on a table. What does it do when you pick it up? What does it do when it feels the table? What does it do when it is flipped over? How many feet does it have? Have another child drop a drop of water in its path. How does it respond to a drop of water? How does it respond to a small puddle? Does it prefer light or dark places? Does it prefer dry or moist places? Can it climb up the side of a jar? What does it do when a toothpick touches it?

• Have children observe the sow bug through a magnifying glass. How many scales does it have? Does it have any antennae? What else can they see about the sow bug through the magnifying glass?

Spiders

Materials A clear plastic covered container with a spider; a magnifying glass; a toothpick.

Procedure

• Have the children observe the spider in the container. Where does the spider spend its time? Is the spider active? Has it made a web? Why does a spider spin a web? Can the spider jump? What does it do when it is disturbed?

• If the spider has spun a web, ask a child to touch the web with a toothpick. What happens to the web? Is the web sticky? What kinds of creatures do spiders catch in their webs? What do they do to creatures they catch? What does a spider do to its legs when it spins silk for its web?

• Have the children look at the spider through a magnifying glass. How many sections does it have on its body? How many legs? Does it have eyes? Are its legs jointed? What color is its body? How does it move? Do all of its legs move at the same time? Can they find the spinnerets on the underside of the abdomen? (Spinnerets are used in web making. Only females have them. See the diagram of the spider to identify its body parts.)

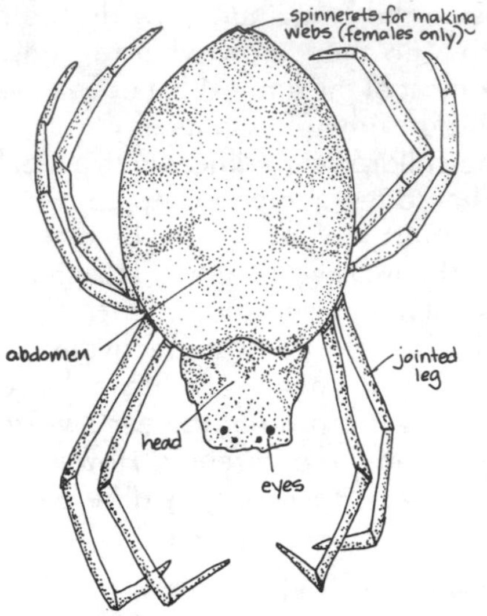

A spider has eight jointed legs.

III. Observing How Small Creatures Develop and Grow

1. Small Creatures Zoo

Materials Small creatures in captivity.

Procedure If you are lucky the animals that are in captivity will cooperate and supply you with eggs, larvae, and pupae so that the children can see the four stages of a complete metamorphosis take place. If not, purchase mealworms.

2. Mealworm Colony

Materials Mealworms; a shoebox with a lid; bran cereal; apple slice or carrot; chart paper and a marking pen.

Procedure

• Mealworms can be purchased at a pet store. They are used as food for fish and lizards. Once a day have the children look in the box to count the number of larvae, pupae, and adults. At first, only larvae will be seen. Keep a simple chart with the children of what is seen. Record results.

• After several weeks there should be some obvious changes. The larvae begin to turn a darker color before they are ready to pupate. Pupae will look dead. Explain to the children that they are growing while they appear to be resting. Eventually they will emerge as adult beetles. Explain to the children that when an animal changes its form the way the larva does to become an adult beetle, this is called metamorphosis.

• Explain to the children that not all insects have a complete metamorphosis like the beetle. Some just have a gradual change or an incomplete metamorphosis. Ask the children if our bodies grow gradually or whether we have a metamorphic change. (We grow gradually.)

3. Create a Fruitfly Culture

Materials An empty jar; a funnel with spout down; an overripe banana; cotton; wool; a magnifying glass.

Procedure

• A fruitfly culture can be created by attracting fruitflies to a jar. Place a piece of overripened banana into a jar to attract them. Place a funnel on top of the jar so that they can fly in but will have trouble flying out.

• After several fruitflies have been captured, stuff the top of the jar with cotton so that air can still come in but the fruitflies cannot come out. If the weather is warm, the container can be placed outside.

• With luck, eggs will be deposited. The eggs will hatch into hungry larvae. The larvae will grow, pupate, and complete their metamorphosis. Eventually, they will emerge as adult fruitflies. Fruitflies are very small. Their larvae are harder to see than the mealworm's. Children will need a magnifying glass.

4. Growing New Parts

Materials A living or dead crab or crayfish with two different-sized claws; a starfish alive or dead with one short foot; an earthworm that is alive.

Procedure

• Show the children the animals. If the animals listed cannot be found, then a picture or diagram can be substituted. Ask the children how an animal like the crayfish or crab could have one large claw and one small claw. Discuss with the children how this could happen. Some animals can grow new parts when their body parts are broken off. It takes time for the part to grow back and that is why they look unbalanced for awhile. When the new claw grows back, it will remain slightly smaller than the old claw. If we lose a finger, an arm, or a leg, we cannot grow a new one. If a starfish is cut into several pieces, each piece can become a new starfish.

• *Explain:* A lobster, crayfish, or crab can grow a new claw, but if a lobster, crayfish, or crab is cut into pieces, it will die. Only very primitive animals can be cut into pieces and continue to live and grow. When an animal is able to grow a new body part, it is called regeneration. Regeneration helps an animal grow back a lost part.

• Show the children the earthworm that is alive. Explain to the children that if the earthworm is cut into two different pieces at certain places, both parts will continue to live. But only one part will have a mouth. So, one part will live longer than the other part and grow a new tail. Ask the children why a mouth is important to the animal. Would we be able to live long if we could not eat? What would happen to us? (We would starve to death if we could not eat.)

**It is suggested that you not cut the worm in half, as it may upset the children.

Why do animals need to be able to eat?
(So they can have energy to grow and move. Food gives animals energy.)

IV. Learning to Classify Small Creatures

1. Distinguishing Small Creatures from One Another

Materials Small-creature zoo; nature guidebooks on invertebrates with lots of large photographs of animals in color.

Procedure

• Discuss with children how we can tell one animal from another. What makes each animal in the small-creature zoo unique or special?

• Ask the following kinds of questions:

Do some of the animals look alike? Which ones?

What do they have in common?

Which animals have no legs?

Which animals have one foot and a hard shell?

Which animals have six legs?

Which animals have eight legs?

Which animals have many legs?

Which animals have antennae?

Which animals have segmented bodies?

**All items marked by double asterisks indicate that the information is too abstract and too complicated for young children to understand or comprehend. It is included to enhance parent or teacher background only.

Which animals have a head, a thorax, and an abdomen?

Which animals have a head and an abdomen?

Which animals have soft bodies?

Which animals have hard outer coverings or exoskeletons made up of several shell-like pieces?

Which animals have wings? Are the wings hard, soft, or transparent?

What makes an animal an insect?
(Three body parts, six legs, exoskeleton.)

What makes an animal a spider?
(Two body parts, eight legs.)

What makes an animal a snail?
(Soft, unsegmented body with a shell.)

What makes an animal an earthworm?
(Soft, segmented, round body.)

*What makes an animal a larva?**
(Usually a soft, segmented, round body with a few sets of legs, but not a pair of legs on every segment.)

What makes an animal a millipede?
(A soft, segmented, round body with a pair of legs on each segment.)

2. Distinguishing Insects from One Another

Materials A variety of live insects from the small-creature zoo to observe, and/or nature books about insects with large photographs in color of insects like *A Golden Guide to Insects,* and/or *The How and Why Wonder Book of Insects.*

Procedure
- Observe the live insects and browse through the insect nature books.
- Ask the following kinds of questions:

Which of the animals in the small-creature zoo are insects? How can you tell? Can you find their picture in the insect guidebook?

How many insect groups are there in the insect guidebook?
(About sixteen.)

What are the major groups?
(Grasshoppers and their relatives; dragonflies; termites, earwigs, and lice; true bugs; beetles; moths and butterflies; flies; ants, bees, and wasps.)

*A larva is the young of an insect that undergoes a complete metamorphosis. Larvae do not always have soft bodies and some have no legs at all. (Also, young frogs and toads are called larvae.)

Which groups would the insects from the small-creature zoo fit into?

- Have the children take a closer look at their insects, or at the pictures of the insects in nature guidebooks. Ask them the following kinds of questions:

What kinds of wings do beetles have?
(An outer set of hard wings, and an inner set of transparent, soft wings.)

What are the differences between moths and butterflies?
(The antennae of moths are usually full and feathery, and their abdomens are thicker. Also, the colors of moths tend to be drabber, whereas butterflies usually have brighter colors, thinner abdomens, and knobs at the ends of their antennae. Butterflies rest with their wings held vertically and moths tend to rest with their wings held horizontally.)

What insects are true bugs?
(Insects that have a beak on their mouth with joints for sucking.)

How are ants, bees, and wasps alike?
(They each have transparent wings [when they have wings] and "wasp waists.")

How are flies different from other flying insects?
(Flies have two wings. Other kinds of flying insects have four wings.)

Which insects undergo an incomplete metamorphosis (a gradual change) when they grow?
(Grasshoppers, dragonflies, termites, earwigs, lice, and true bugs.)

Which insects go through a complete metamorphosis when they grow?
(Most flies, beetles, butterflies, moths, ants, bees, and wasps.)

What is a difference between a larva and an adult insect?
(Insect larvae cannot lay eggs, but usually eat a lot.*)

3. Creating Models of Insects, Spiders, and Worms

Materials Pipe cleaners; scissors; construction paper; crayons; glue; cellophane; tissue paper; large sequins; Play-Doh or modeling clay; colored pencils; marking pens.

*A larva is a young insect that does not resemble the adult. From a human point of view some insect larvae cause damage, but not all larvae cause damage. Bee larvae do *no* damage. Some larvae are even helpful, such as the larval flies or maggots, which eat decaying material.

Procedure

- Show the children the materials. Tell them to design a model of an insect, spider, or worm using the materials. They can use the materials for any part of the animals they create.
- Discuss with the children what parts each of the animals would need to have in order to be a worm, an insect, or a spider. For example, if an insect model were being made, it would need to have six jointed legs, three body parts (head, thorax, abdomen), two antennae, possibly wings.
- Have the children notice where the legs and wings are attached to the body of an insect (on the thorax), where the legs are connected on a spider's body (between the abdomen and head), and where the legs are on a larva's body. Remind them to design their model with these proper body connections in mind.
- Have children utilize cellophane for transparent wings, sequins for compound eyes, tissue paper for opaque wings, pipe cleaners cut at different lengths for legs and antennae. Remind children that sometimes we cannot see all of the body parts on an insect because the parts are hidden by the wings, but ask them to put in all of the parts even if they cannot be seen. For example, a beetle model can be designed so that the wings can be lifted off to expose the hidden abdomen and the hidden transparent wings.

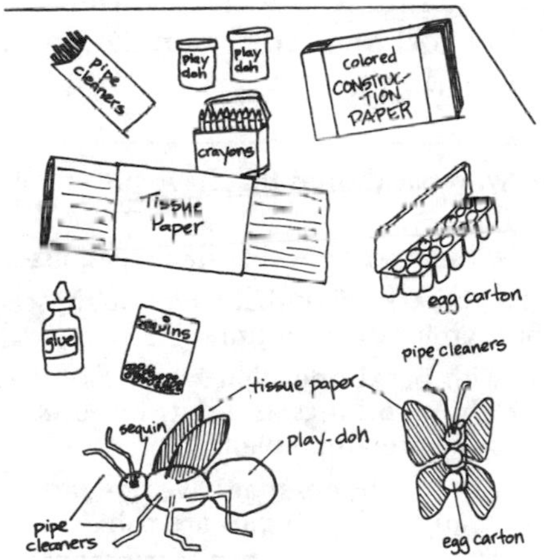

4. Mounting Dead Insects

Materials Straight pins; cardboard; marking pen; plastic wrap; cotton balls; jar lids.

Procedure

- If an insect dies and the children find it, the insect can be mounted. There are two easy ways to mount a dead insect. One way is to place the dead insect on a cotton ball inside of a jar lid and cover it with plastic wrap. The other way is to stick a straight pin through its thorax and mount the pin on a piece of cardboard.*
- To make a nice-looking mounting, it is advisable to freeze an insect while it is alive by placing it in the freezer in a closed jar. It will freeze to death. Then the insect can be thawed out quickly. The body will still be moist and soft. It will be easier to stick a straight pin through its thorax, and to mount it for stretching. The wings of the insect can be opened to a flying position by placing pins in the opened wings. The legs can also be stretched out and positioned as you want them to be. They will also need to have additional pins placed around them to hold them in position. When it dries out, the insect will remain in the position it is pinned and stretched to. The pins can be removed.

Note: Show the children the mounted insects after they have been pinned and stretched. Do not ask young children to freeze, thaw, stretch, and pin insects for mounting. Their muscular coordination is not developed enough and it does not engender a respect for life. Mounted insects are easier for children to study and observe. If a magnifying glass is used, a butterfly's proboscis can be seen, veins on a wing can be looked at, hairs on legs can be seen, compound eyes can be looked at up-close, and other features can be observed. Obviously, it is easier to keep a still object in focus than a moving one. When animals are alive and moving, it is harder to observe their parts. A lot can be gained by studying the insects that have died, and by creating mounts on 2" × 2" cardboard squares of insects that have been frozen and stretched.

V. The Animal Kingdom

1. Classifying Animals

Materials A picture or a rubber model of a human skeleton; a cleaned crab or lobster exoskeleton left over from dinner; snail and clam shells.

Procedure

- Explain to the children that there are many kinds of animals. Scientists called zoologists study animals. Zoologists have created classification groupings to understand and study animals. Animals can be grouped into two large groups—those that have a backbone and those that do not. Animals with backbones are called vertebrates. Those without backbones are called invertebrates.

*When insects die, their bodies tend to dry out quickly. They become brittle. It is hard to stretch their legs and their wings out without breaking them. Usually their legs are all bent up. If the insect is frozen to death, it can be mounted more easily for observation. The legs can be straightened out and the wings can be opened without being broken.

• Ask the children what kind of animal they think they are, one with or without a backbone. Have them feel their backbone or another child's backbone. Have them feel their ribs and follow their rib bones around to their backbone. Show the children a picture or a model of a human skeleton. Ask the following kinds of questions:

Is this a real skeleton?
(No, it is a model of a skeleton.)

Do the bones in our bodies connect to each other?
(Yes, they are all connected to our skeleton.)

Can we see our bones?
(No, not unless they are photographed by an X-ray machine but we can feel them under our skin.)

What do our bones do for our body?
(They provide a frame for our body to rest on and they protect our lungs and our heart. Our skull protects our brain.)

What would your body look like without bones?
(Probably it would look like a deflated balloon.)

• Explain to the children that some animals do not have backbones. They have hard shells or they have exoskeletons made up of many thin shell-like pieces to protect their bodies. Animals with exoskeletons or hard outer shells do not have bones inside their bodies. Show children the crab and lobster exoskeleton, snail and clam shells. Explain that these animals belong to the group of animals without backbones called invertebrates. Invertebrates are animals that do not have a backbone. Ask the following kinds of questions:

Are the exoskeletons and hard shells real or are they models?
(They are real. They came from animals.)

Can we feel the exoskeleton and hard shell on these animals?
(Yes, they are an outer covering on the animal's body.)

How does an exoskeleton or hard shell protect an animal?
(An exoskeleton protects the soft parts of an animal. The soft parts are in an armorlike coat. The hard shell[s] on mollusks protect the animals' soft parts when the animal withdraws inside its shell[s].*)

• Show the children the assorted pictures of animals. See if they can create two piles of pictures—one pile to contain pictures of vertebrates, the other pile to contain pictures of invertebrates.

*Arthropods have exoskeletons; mollusks have one or two hard shells.

2. Dividing Vertebrate Animals into Smaller Groups

Materials Pictures and small rubber models of assorted vertebrates.

Procedure
• Have the children study the pictures and/or models of assorted vertebrates. Ask them what makes each of the animals look different from the others. Ask the following kinds of questions:

Do any of the animals have hair or fur?

Do any of the animals have feathers?

Do all of the animals have feet?

Do any of the animals have rough, scaly skin?

Do any of the animals appear to have a smooth, moist skin?

• Suggest to the children that the pictures and models of animals can be further divided by the kind of skin the animals appear to have. Explain that zoologists have divided the animals that have backbones into five large groups or classes of animals. Ask the children if they can guess what the five groups or classes of animals with backbones might be. Listen to their ideas and then tell them the five classes. The five classes of animals with backbones are: mammals, birds, reptiles, amphibians, and fish.

All animals with backbones that have fur or hair are mammals.*

All animals with backbones that have feathers are birds.

All animals with backbones that have rough, scaly skin and breathe through lungs are reptiles.

All animals with backbones that have smooth, moist skin and breathe through lungs as adults but breathe through gills when young are amphibians.†

All animals with backbones that have fins and scales, live in water, and breathe through gills are fish.

• Ask the children to sort the pictures and models of vertebrates into piles of mammals, birds, reptiles, amphibians, and fish.

*A main characteristic of mammals is that female mammals have mammary glands to feed milk to their babies. Mention should be made of this fact. However, it is easier for young children to see fur or hair in pictures and in models than it is for them to see teats, nipples, or breasts giving milk.

†The most important feature about amphibians, as their name suggests, is that they have "two lives" (larval and adult). Tadpoles are the larval stage of frogs and toads. Frogs and toads go through a metamorphosis.

3. Dividing Invertebrate Animals into Smaller Groups

Materials Pictures and rubber models of assorted invertebrates, and animals from the small-creature zoo.

Procedure

• Have children look at the pictures, models, and the animals from the small-creature zoo. Ask them how the small creatures could be grouped into smaller groups. Discuss what the characteristics are that make each of the animals alike or different. Allow children to come up with ways to group the animals. For example, the animals in the small-creature zoo could be divided into animals with shells and animals without shells. They could be further divided into animals with segmented bodies and animals without segmented bodies. Or they could be divided into animals with many legs, eight legs, six legs, or no legs.

• Ask the children if they can guess what some of the animal groupings are that zoologists have come up with for animals without backbones. Listen to their ideas and then help them see the differences that zoologists have used or found for grouping the animals they have collected in their small-creature zoo.

• Explain that the animals in the small-creature zoo do belong to different zoological groups. Earthworms belong to a zoological group known as annelids. Annelids have segmented bodies. Slugs and snails are members of the mollusk family. "Mollusk" means soft bodies. Mollusks have bodies that are not segmented. Most mollusks have well-developed heads with eyes, tentacles, and a muscular foot. Spiders, millipedes, sow bugs, and insects are all arthropods. All arthropods have jointed feet, and most except the spider have a segmented abdomen, an exoskeleton, and antennae.

4. Subdividing Invertebrates into Smaller Groups

Materials Assorted models and living or nonliving specimens; pictures of arthropods from the five classes of arthropods.

Note: There are five classes of arthropods. The five classes are: crustaceans, like lobsters and crabs; centipedes; millipedes; spiders; and insects.

Procedure

• Explain to the children that each of the large zoological groups of animals can be further divided into smaller groups and that each of those groups can also be further subdivided into even smaller groups of animals with specific characteristics. Show children the assorted models, pictures, and living and nonliving specimens of arthropods. Have them observe them closely. Ask them to think of ways to group them into smaller groups. Allow the children to come up with ways to divide the arthropods into groups.

Note: Zoologists do not always agree on the ways to classify animals into groups.

Spiders are another group or class of arthropods. Mites, ticks, horseshoe crabs, and scorpions are grouped with spiders. They are called arachnids. Arachnids have eight legs, no antennae, and two body regions. The largest group of arthropods, and the largest group of animals in the animal kingdom, are the insects. Insects can be further subdivided into about 16 or more major groups. All insects have six legs, three body regions, and two antennae (see Section IV, Activity 2, in this chapter). There are over 800,000 known insect species that are unique.

• Ask the children to sort out the pictures, models, and specimens into groups of animals the way a zoologist might divide them.

5. Subdividing Mammals into Groups

Materials Mammals to observe (like a dog, cat, rabbit, guinea pig, hamster); or a field trip to a pet store that stocks mammals; or a trip to a farm or zoo.

Procedure

• Have children observe mammals that are alive. If it is possible, encourage the children to touch or pet the mammals gently, and to use their five senses to observe the mammals.

• Ask the following kinds of questions as they observe each mammal:

What kind of animal is this?

Does it have a backbone?

Can you feel the backbone?

How is this animal different from the invertebrates that were observed?

Does the animal feel warm or cold when you hold it?

Does your own body feel warm when you touch it?

What covers the animal's body?
(Hair or fur.)

Does the animal have toenails or fingernails?

What are some of the body parts the animal has that you have on your body?
(Eyes, ears, nose, mouth, legs, hair, teeth, tongue, nails, etc.)

How does the animal move?

Does the animal make noise?

How does the animal eat?

What kind of food do you think this animal eats? How can you tell?

Does the animal have teeth?

Do the animal's teeth look like your teeth?

• Explain to children that mammals can be divided into three large groups based on what they eat. If they eat only plants, they are called herbivores. If they eat only other animals, they are called carnivores. If they eat both plants and animals, they are called omnivores. Usually you can tell what kind of diet a mammal has by the way its teeth look. If the teeth are sharp and jagged-looking like those of a dog or wolf, then it is obvious that it uses its teeth to rip apart other animals. If the teeth are mostly large and flat and the front incisor teeth are sharp, with a large space between them and the molars with no canine teeth, it means that the mammal eats plants. If the teeth look like our teeth with incisors, canines called cuspids, and molars, then the animal can eat both plants and animals.

6. Subdividing Mammals into Smaller Groups

Materials A mammal like a cat, dog, rabbit, guinea pig or hamster to observe; assorted small rubber models and/or pictures of mammals.

Procedure

• Show children the assorted models and pictures of mammals. Explain to them that when animals have mammary glands to feed milk to their babies, have fur or hair and feel warm to touch, they are called mammals. Mammals can be grouped by the way they look. Ask the children if they can think of ways to sort the pictures and models of mammals into smaller groups. Allow the children to come up with ways to group the mammals, and to sort the pictures and models of mammals into groups by the way the mammals look: by their color, size, body covering, or other characteristics or attributes.

• After the children have grouped the pictures and models of mammals, explain the characteristics that zoologists have used to sort or separate mammals from one another. As you describe the various groupings, show the children an example (a model or a picture) of each of the major orders or groupings of mammals listed. The zoological groupings which include most mammals are:

1. *Egg-laying Mammals.* They are almost extinct. They are the only mammals that lay eggs. Examples are the platypus and the spiny anteater.

2. *Marsupials.* Marsupials are mammals that have pouches. The females have pouches that they carry their babies in. Examples are the kangaroo, opossum, and koala bear.

3. *Toothless Mammals.* These are mammals that either lack teeth or have no front teeth. They are protected with an armor. They burrow in the ground. Examples are the anteater, armadillo, and aardvark.

4. *Insect-eating Mammals.* These are mammals that eat insects. They are usually animals that live underground, sleep during the day, and roam around at night. Examples are shrews, moles, and hedgehogs.

5. *Marine Mammals.* These are mammals that live in the water and breathe with lungs. They have two front limbs that look like paddles, and no back limbs. Examples are whales, dolphins, and porpoises.
Note: Unlike fish, their babies are born alive. They do not have scales, and they do have some hair on their bodies.

6. *Carnivores.* These are mammals that eat other animals. They have strong jaws, sharp canine teeth, and sharp claws for ripping the flesh of other animals. Examples of water or aquatic carnivores are sea lions, seals, and walruses. Examples of carnivores that live on the land are bears, cats, dogs, raccoons, and minks. Land carnivores have keen senses for hearing, seeing, and smelling.
Note: Some carnivores like bears and raccoons also eat plants.

7. *Rodents.* These are mammals that gnaw their food with their two front incisor teeth. Their two front incisors continue to grow throughout the animal's life. They continually wear down from gnawing at things. Rodents eat only plants. Examples are beavers, rabbits, squirrels, mice, rats, and porcupines.

8. *Hoofed Mammals.* These are mammals with hooves on their feet. They are all plant eaters. They use their teeth for grinding grasses. Hooved mammals can be further divided into mammals with single toes, those with an odd number of toes on their feet, and those with split hooves. Examples of hoofed mammals are horses, sheep, cattle, hogs, pigs, camels, deer, and hippopotamuses.

9. *Elephants.* These are mammals that have long incisor teeth that have been modified to form tusks, large flat teeth for grinding plants, and a long modified nose or proboscis which is used for grasping.
Note: Butterflies and moths have a proboscis also, but obviously it is a more delicate one.

10. *Flying Mammals.* These are mammals that can fly. They have a web of skin between their fingers and limbs for flying. They eat insects. Examples are bats.

11. *Monkeys, Apes, and Humans.* These are mammals with flexible fingers, opposable thumbs, and long toes used for grasping. They can walk erect or semierect, and have brains that are well developed.
Note: People are grouped with the primates along with monkeys and apes. Humans belong to the family of Homo sapiens. They walk erect, have well-developed brains, and are the most intelligent form of life in the animal kingdom. They can eat both plants and animals.

VI. Vertebrates—Animals with Backbones

Comparing Backboned Pets

Materials Live horse, cat, dog, rabbit, bird, fish, turtle, guinea pig, hamster, or other available animal with a backbone.
Note: It may be necessary to visit a farm, zoo, pet store or aquarium with the children.

Procedure As the children observe the animals, help them to compare two animals to each other. Ask the following kinds of questions:

How are they alike?

How are they different?

Where do they usually live?

How does their color help protect them?

How does the texture of their skin help protect them?

What kind of teeth do they have?

Can you tell by looking at their teeth what kind of food each animal might eat?

Do the animals leave a footprint when they walk?

Do the footprints of the two animals look alike?

How can you tell which footprint belongs to which animal?

Do the animals feel warm or cold to touch?

Do these two animals prefer living on the land or in water?

How active are these two animals—do they move around a lot or rest a lot?

What kinds of noises do these two animals make?

If they make noise, when do they make the noise?

If these two animals have front legs, how do they use them?

How do these two animals keep clean?

Where are each animal's eyes located, on the front of its face or on the sides of its face?

Where are the mammary glands located?

Note: Fish and horses have their eyes located on the sides of their face. This allows them to see on each side of their head at the same time. They can look in two different directions at once.

What does your pet animal do to get attention?

Can you tell how your pet feels?

How does it talk to you?

Further Resources

Suggested Books for Children

Dewey Decimal Classification Number for animals is: 590 to 595.

Althea (Brathwaite), *Animals at Your Feet.* Cambridge, England: Dinosaur Publications Ltd., 1980.

Althea (Brathwaite), *All About Squirrels and Moles and Things.* Cambridge, England: Dinosaur Publications Ltd., 1980.

Brenner, B., *If You Were an Ant.* New York: Harper, 1973. (The perception of the world from an ant's point of view. What is small to us appears huge to the ant.)

Clarkson, J. N., *Tricks Animals Play.* Washington, D.C.: National Geographic Society, 1975.

Cooper, Gale, *Inside of Animals.* Boston: Little, Brown, 1978. (Anatomical sketches of a variety of vertebrates.)

Daly, Kathleen, *Hide and Defend.* New York: Golden Press, 1976. (A book about adaptations animals have made in order to hide and to defend themselves.)

Dutton, George, *All Upon a Sidewalk.* New York: Dutton, 1974. (The perception of the world from an insect's point of view.)

Freedman, Russel, *When Winter Comes.* New York: Dutton, 1981. (How animals prepare for winter.)

Friedman, Judi, *Noises in the Woods.* New York: Dutton, 1979. (Animal sounds in the woods.)

Gallant, R. A., *Me and My Bones.* New York: Doubleday, 1971. (A comparison of our skeleton to that of other animal skeletons.)

Goldin, Augusta, *Spider Silk.* New York: Thomas Y. Crowell, 1964. (All about the habits and lives of spiders.)

Green, I. E.; photography by George A. Smith, *Hatch and Grow—Life Stories of Familiar Insects, Shown in Close-Up Photographs.* New York: Abelard, 1967.

Hawes, Judy, and Aliki, *Bees and Beelines.* New York: Thomas Y. Crowell, 1964. (All about bees.)

Heller, Ruth, *Chickens Aren't the Only Ones.* New York: Grosset and Dunlap, 1981. (A picture book about the variety of animals that hatch from eggs.)

Henrie, F., *Cats.* New York: Watts, 1980. (How to care for cats.)

Kohn, Bernice, *Chipmunks.* Englewood Cliffs, New Jersey: Prentice-Hall, 1970. (Picture book about chipmunks.)

McClung, R. M., *How Animals Hide.* Washington, D.C.: National Geographic Society, 1973. (All about animal camouflage.)

Newing, F. E., and Richard Bowood, *Animals and How They Live.* Loughborough, England: Wills and Hepworth, Ltd. 1965.

O'Hagan, Allan, Judith, and Caroline, *It's Easy to Have a Caterpillar Visit You.* New York: Lothrop, Lee and Shepard, 1980.

O'Hagan, Allan, Judith, and Caroline, *It's Easy to Have a Worm Visit You.* New York: Lothrop, Lee and Shepard, 1980.

O'Hagan, Allan, Judith, and Caroline, *It's Easy to Have a Snail Visit You.* New York: Lothrop, Lee and Shepard, 1980.

Piecewicz, Ann Thomas, *See What I Caught!* Englewood Cliffs, New Jersey: Prentice-Hall, 1974. (All about how to catch and care for small creatures like insects, reptiles, and amphibians.)

Pluckrose, Henry, *Lions and Tigers.* New York: Glouster, 1979. (Large colored sketches.)

Pluckrose, Henry, *Apes.* New York: Glouster, 1979.

Pringle, Lawrence P., *Twist, Wriggle and Squirm, A Book About Earth Worms.* New York: Thomas Y. Crowell, 1973.

Selsam, Millicent. *A First Look at Birds.* New York: Scholastic Books, 1981.

Selsam, Millicent, *A First Look at Animals Without Backbones.* New York: Walker, 1976.

Selsam, Millicent, *Backyard Insects.* New York: Scholastic Books, 1981.

Selsam, Milicent, *Hidden Animals.* New York: Harper and Row, 1969. (Camouflage.)

Selsam, Millicent, *How to Be a Nature Detective.* New York: Harper and Row, 1963.

Simon, Seymour, *Discovering What Earthworms Do.* New York: McGraw-Hill, 1969.

Stevens, Carla, *The Birth of Sunset's Kittens.* New York: Wm. H. Scott, 1969. (Black and white photographs of the birth of kittens.)

Tarrant, Graham, *Butterflies.* Los Angeles: Intervisual Communications, Inc., 1983. (A pop-up book that describes and illustrates metamorphosis.)

Tarrant, Graham, *Frogs.* Los Angeles: Intervisual Communications, Inc., 1983.

Van Gelder, Richard George, *Whose Nose Is This?* New York: Walker, 1974. (Close-up pictures of animals' noses. Reader has to guess what animal the nose belongs to.)

Waters, John, *A Jellyfish Is Not a Fish.* New York: Thomas Y. Crowell, 1979. (All about jellyfish.)

Resource Books for More Ideas

Buck, Margaret, *Where They Go in Winter.* New York: Abingdon Press, 1968. (Tells where insects and animals with backbones go during the winter.)

Civardi, Anne, and Kathy Kilpatrick, *How Animals Live.* London: Usborne; 1978.

Farb, P., *The Insects.* New York: Time/Life, 1977. (Large close-up colored photographs.)

Ford, B. G., *Do You Know?* New York: Random House, 1979.

Hussey, L. J., and C. Pessino, *Collecting Cocoons.* New York: Thomas Y. Crowell, 1953. (Sketches of how to care for cocoons so they will produce butterflies or moths. Good background for an adult.)

Keen, Martin, *How and Why Wonder Book of Wild Animals.* New York: Grosset and Dunlap, 1962.

Kots, A. and E., *Insects of North America.* New York: Doubleday, 1971. (Contains colored photographs, appropriate for an adult to share with a child.)

Rhine, Richard, *Life in a Bucket of Soil.* New York: Lothrop, 1972.

Rood, Ronald, *How and Why Wonder Book of Insects.* New York: Grosset and Dunlap, 1981.

Shuttlesworth, Dorothy, *The Story of Ants.* New York: Doubleday, 1964.

Simon, H., *Insect Masquerades.* New York: Viking, 1968. (Good background material for an adult, describes camouflage, tricks, traps, and gimmickry practiced by some insects.)

Simon, Seymour, *Pets in A Jar, Collecting and Caring for Small Wild Animals.* New York: Penguin Books, 1979.

Sisson, Edith, *Nature with Children of All Ages.* Englewood Cliffs, New Jersey: Prentice-Hall, 1982.

Stevens, Carla, *Insects as Pets: Catching and Caring for Them.* New York: Morrow, 1977.

Storer, Tracy I., et al., *General Zoology,* 5th edition. New York: McGraw-Hill, 1972.

Thompson, Ruth, *Understanding Farm Animals.* London: Usborne, 1978.

Zim, Herbert, *Insects, a Golden Guide.* New York: Golden Press, 1976.

Zim, Herbert, *Mammals, a Golden Guide.* New York: Golden Press, 1955.

12
ALL ABOUT SEED-BEARING PLANTS

Objectives

- For children to be able to distinguish living from nonliving things.
- For children to become aware that seeds house dormant baby plants.
- For children to understand that each plant has its own unique seed that can only grow into the kind of plant that produced it—for example, tomato seeds can only grow into tomato plants.
- For children to understand that if seeds are planted in soil and are kept moist and receive sunlight, they have the potential to become mature plants.
- For children to become aware that gravity, moisture, and sunlight affect plant growth.
- For children to become aware that roots, stems, and leaves have tubes or veins running through them that carry liquids to and from the leaves and to and from the roots.
- For children to be able to distinguish a simple leaf from a compound leaf, a monocot leaf from a dicot leaf, a pinnate midrib from a palmate midrib, and a deciduous leaf from an evergreen leaf.
- For children to develop an awareness that the fruit of a plant is where the seeds for the plant are produced and found.
- For children to become aware that dead flowers left on plants grow into fruits that will eventually contain seeds.

General Background Information for Parents and Teachers

Plants

Plant Everything that grows in the ground is a plant.

Botany The biological science of plants.

Botanist A scientist who specializes in the study of plants.

****Classification of Major Plant Groups**

Simple Plants—Plants lacking roots, stems, and leaves.

Seedless Complex Plants—Plants with tubes that run through stems to and from leaves and to and from roots (ferns, horsetails, and club-mosses).

Complex Plants With Seeds—Plants that are divided into two categories: those that have cones such as pine, fir, and spruce, and those that have flowers. Flowering plants are divided into two main categories: those that belong to the monocotyledon and those that belong to the dicotyledon family of plants.

Cotyledon Part of the embryo of a seed. Plants with seeds have either one cotyledon or two cotyledons.

Monocotyledons Are called monocots for short. They have one cotyledon. Monocot seeds grow into

**All items marked by two asterisks indicate that the information is too abstract and too complicated for young children to understand or comprehend. It is included to enhance parent or teacher background only.

plants that have a fibrous root system and leaves with parallel vein patterns, and they bear flowers that grow their parts in threes. Examples are: tulips, irises, lilies, and orchids. All of the grasses including corn, rye, wheat, and trees such as the palms and bamboos are monocots.

Dicotyledons Are called dicots for short. They have two cotyledons. Dicot seeds grow into plants that have a taproot system, a webbed vein pattern, and bear flowers that grow their parts in fours and fives. Examples are: roses, pear trees, geraniums, beans. Most of the flowering trees, herbs, and shrubs as well as the composite flowers are dicots.

Composite flower Flowers that appear to be one flower, but actually consist of many tiny flowers. Examples are: a daisy, a sunflower, and a dandelion.

Vegetable Roots, stems, leaves, and flowers that are grown to be eaten are usually called vegetables. However, a vegetable in the botanical sense is any organism that is classified as a plant. All plants are members of the vegetable kingdom.

Fruit The ripened ovary or ovaries of a seed-bearing plant. Examples are: tomatoes, eggplant, squash, apples, and bananas.

Weed A plant that is considered undesirable or troublesome. It grows where it is not wanted.

Coniferous trees Nonflowering evergreen trees that produce cones that have seeds. Examples are: pine, spruce, hemlock, and redwood.

Evergreen plants Plants that do not lose their leaves all at once, but lose them gradually all year. Most coniferous trees are evergreens. Examples are: ivy, holly, boxwood, yew, rhododendron.

Deciduous plants Plants that lose all of their leaves in the fall and stay dormant during the winter.

• The leaves of many deciduous plants change colors in the fall. The green color in leaves comes from chlorophyl, a pigment in the chloroplast cells. The green hides or covers up the other colors that are there. When the leaf begins to die in early fall because the days are shorter and the temperature is cooler, the other colors that were hidden but "there" begin to show. In addition, new colors are formed.

****Seasonal color change in leaves** Is caused by pigments (colorations) that are in the leaf. During the growing season, leaves appear to be different shades of green due to the different amounts of colored pigment present underneath the chlorophyl pigment.
**Green comes from *chlorophyl* pigments.
**Yellow, brown and orange come from *cartenoid* pigments.
**Red and purple come from *anthocyanin* pigments.
***Anthocyanin pigments* occur in the sap of cells and are not present during the growing season of the leaves as are the chlorophyl and cartenoid pigments.

****Perennial plants** Are plants that bloom year after year. They have a set time to bloom, then they lose their leaves and lie dormant the rest of the year.

****Annual plants** Grow from seeds each year. They only live and grow for one year or season.

Flowers

Flower A flower is the reproductive structure of a seed-bearing plant. Flowers usually have specialized male and female organs. The stamen is the male part and the pistil is the female part of the flower. Usually, the pistil and stamen are in the center of the flower and are surrounded by colorful petals and sepals. See diagram.

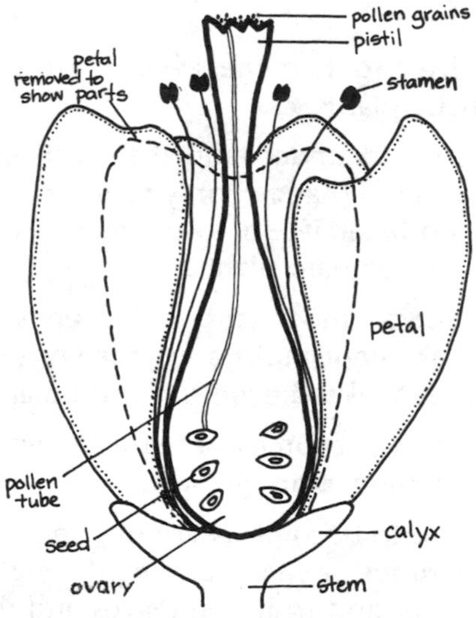

PARTS OF A FLOWER

Stamen The specialized male organ on a flower. It is the part of the flower that produces pollen. It usually consists of a filament and an anther. The pollen grows on the anther.

Pistil The specialized female organ on the flower. It is the part that produces the seeds for a plant. It includes a stigma, style, and ovary. The stigma is a hollow sticky opening at the top of the style tube that connects to the ovary at the base of the style tube. The pistil is usually in the center of the flower inside the petals and sepals.

Pollination Pollination occurs when the pollen from a flower's stamen comes in contact with the pistil of the flower.

Cross-pollination Occurs when the pollen from one flower comes in contact with the pistil of another flower of the same species. Bees, other insects, and the wind are responsible for pollination and cross-pollination.

Fertilization When the pollen comes in contact with the pistil, a tube begins to grow down the style to the ovary. When the pollen attaches itself to an ovule in the ovary, the ovule begins to develop into a seed. The seeds in the ovary are not capable of growing into new plants unless fertilization occurs. Flowers often have eye-catching colors or aromas. The colors and aromas help attract insects. The insects help fertilization occur by pollinating flowers.

Seeds

Seed The fertilized and ripened small body produced by a flowering plant. It contains an embryo capable of germinating to produce a new plant. Seeds remain dormant until conditions are right for them to sprout.

Embryo The minute rudimentary plant contained within a seed.

Germinate To begin to grow. When a seed sprouts, it has germinated.

Seedling A seed that has germinated and become a young plant. The cotyledons are still attached to a seedling.

Sapling A very young tree that has lost its cotyledons.

Roots

Roots The portion of a plant that is usually underground. Roots serve as a basis for support, to draw food and water from the surrounding soil, and to store food. Rhizomes, corms, and tubers are often classified as roots because they grow under the ground, but they are really special kinds of stems.

Fibrous root system Found on monocot plants. It is a system of roots that consists of many branching roots. The branching roots grow from the bottom of the stem. See diagram.

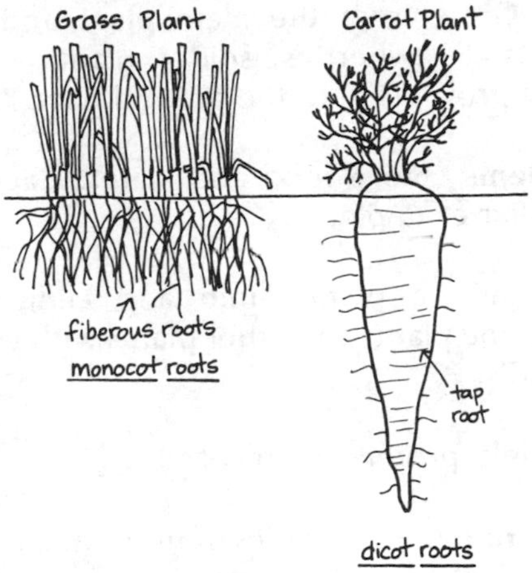

Taproot system Found on dicot plants and coniferous trees. It is a system of roots that consists of a main or taproot growing straight downward with other roots branching from it. See diagram.

Stems

Stem The part of a plant that has leaves and buds. The function of the stem is to supply a support system for the production of leaves and flowers, to store food, and to conduct liquids up and down the stem to different parts of the plant. Most stems grow above the ground, but some specialized stems grow under the ground.

Specialized stems that grow under the ground Rhizomes, tubers, bulbs, and corms.

Rhizomes Horizontal stems that grow under the ground. They are perennial plants and grow new shoots year after year.

Tubers Tubers store a lot of food. Potatoes are tubers. The "eyes" on the potato are buds. The "eyes" or buds are capable of growing into stems that grow above the ground. A new potato plant can be started with a tuber that has one or two eyes.

Bulb A bulb is a perennial bud that has a small stem, and many overlapping leaves. Tulips and onions are bulbs. A bulb is mainly leaves.

Corm A corm is a perennial stem with thin, papery leaves. A corm is mainly stem.

Specialized aerial stems Runners, storage stems, tendrils, and thorns.

Runners Grow from the main plant and produce new plants. Strawberries, spider plants, and other plants that grow close to the ground have runners.

Storage stems Store food and water. Cactus plants are a familiar example.

Tendrils Help a plant climb and cling to other objects. Grape plants and other plants with vines often have tendrils.

Thorns Help protect the plant.

****Vascular bundles** Bundles of tubes that run up and down the plant from the root system to the leaves. In the leaves, they form a network of veins.

****Xylem** The part of the vascular system that moves liquids from the roots to all parts of the plant including the leaves. Xylem tubes move liquids to the sides and up. (⬆)

****Phloem** The part of the vascular system that moves liquids from the leaves to all parts of the plant including the roots. Phloem tubes move liquids to the sides and down. (⬇)

Leaves

Leaves Green leaves make food for plants and oxygen is released into the atmosphere as a by-product. (This process is called photosynthesis.)

• Leaves are an excellent and inexpensive tool for sharpening observation skills and for learning to group like items into sets (and for learning rudimentary classification skills).
• Every kind of plant with leaves has its own distinct and unique leaf. Plants can be identified by their leaves.
• Leaves come in a great variety of shapes and patterns. They can be studied, identified, and sorted into groups by their edge, their vein pattern, their shape, the length of their leafstalks or stems, and their color.
• Edges or margins of broadleaf plants can be smooth, serrated, lobed, serrated and lobed, wavy, fine-toothed, double-toothed, dissected, or can have a combination of several edge types.

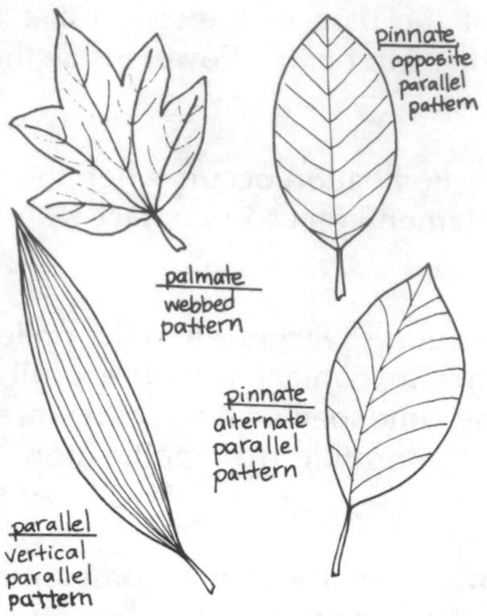

Vein patterns Vein patterns can be parallel or webbed. See diagram.

• Most leaves can be divided into three large groups: broad leaves, needle leaves, and narrow leaves.

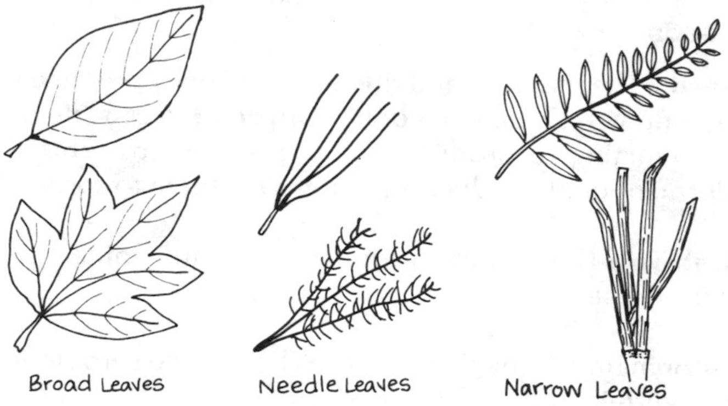

****Veins of a leaf** The veins of a leaf have two kinds of tissue flowing through them: xylem and phloem tissue.
**Xylem tissue carries water up to the leaves from the roots. This water is called sap.
**Phloem tissue carries food (sugar which is converted to starch) away from the leaves toward the roots. It also carries food up to flowers and fruits.

Leaves have many parts Each part serves a purpose for the leaf's health and well-being (as does each of

---

Broad Leaves
Most are deciduous, which means they lose their leaves in the fall. See diagram.

Needle Leaves
Are evergreens, which means they do not lose their leaves all at once, but appear green all year. See diagram.

Narrow Leaves
Are mainly grasses and palms with parallel veins. See diagram.

our own body parts). The important concept for children to become aware of is that many parts make up a whole; all parts are needed to make a "whole."

Leaves from deciduous trees can be grouped according to their growth patterns Some leaves are simple, some are compound, and some are double compound.

A simple leaf A simple leaf is composed of one leaf blade and a leafstalk, which connects directly to a woody twig. There is often a bud on the twig at the base of the leafstalk.

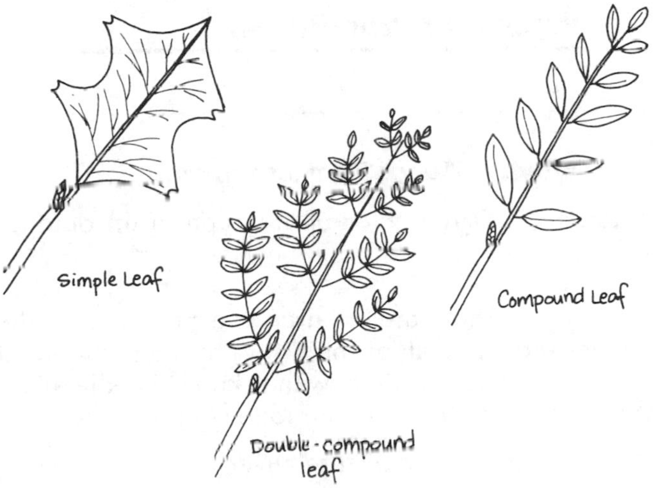

A compound leaf A compound leaf is composed of many leaflets on a stem. The leaflets connect to a nonwoody leafstalk that connects to a woody twig. There is often a bud on the twig at the base of the leafstalk.

Opposite and alternate Leaves can grow on the woody twig of a tree in an opposite or in an alternate pattern. See diagram.

****Photosynthesis** Photosynthesis is the process by which sunlight is turned into energy for the plant by the leaf. The leaves are food factories for the plant. The chlorophyl in the chloroplast cells allows water and carbon dioxide from the stomata cells to combine to form a molecule of sugar. Energy is stored in the sugar molecule for the plant.

- Oxygen is a by-product of the photosynthesis process and is released into the atmosphere. (The energy from the sunlight splits the water molecule into hydrogen and oxygen atoms. The hydrogen atoms combine with carbon dioxide, which forms a sugar, thereby leaving oxygen atoms over as a by-product.)
- Chloroplasts are the green cells in the green leaves. Chloroplast cells contain chlorophyl. These cells are usually located on the top surface of leaves and are exposed to sunlight. The chlorophyl stores and holds the energy from the sunlight.
- Stomata Cells—Most of the stomata cells are located on the underside of a leaf, the side not facing the sun. Stomata cells regulate evaporation. Air and water vapor come in and out of the leaf cells through the stomata cells.

Note: The concept that a leaf needs to breathe can be demonstrated by covering the surface of a leaf with Vaseline. The leaf will not be able to breathe and will become limp.

****Transpiration** The loss of water vapor from plants. Most of the loss occurs through the stomata cells.

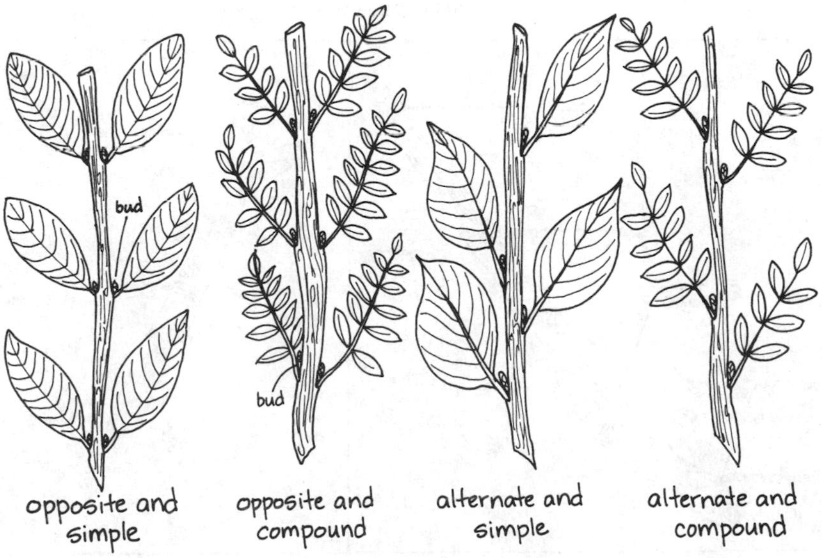

Twigs

Twigs Twigs tell stories if you can read their markings. Leaves leave a scar when they fall off. Also, each year of growth a new scale scar grows on the bark. It is possible to tell the age of a twig by counting the scale scars on its bark. It is also possible, if the twig has been cut, to count the rings on the inside. Each ring indicates a year of growth. The darker ring in the center is the heart wood. The lighter circles are the sap wood. The outer layer is the bark. Twigs are smaller versions of tree trunks.

• Twigs should be examined closely. They are easy to find and are often overlooked, and they are a good way to begin a study about trees. Twigs are miniature trees; they lack roots, but otherwise have all the parts of a tree. It is easy to bring them inside. Some twigs can even grow roots if they are allowed to soak in water. It is interesting to experiment with them.

Leaf growth patterns Leaf growth patterns can be identified by observing leaf scars on twigs. It can be ascertained whether a leaf grows in an opposite or in an alternate pattern. Most common trees have an alternate growth pattern. Most scrubs have an opposite growth pattern. **According to *A Field Guide To Trees and Shrubs,* by George A. Petrides, Houghton Mifflin, 1958, there are only four common trees with opposite leaves and twigs. They are maple, ash, dogwood and horse chestnut.

Buds on deciduous trees When deciduous trees lose their leaves in the fall they leave a bud behind. The winter buds are usually larger than the spring and summer buds. Winter buds have an extra layer of scales to protect them from the cold of winter.

• They also enclose embryonic leaves and flowers for the spring. Winter buds contain not only leaves and flowers but also beginnings of new twigs. These twigs eventually become new branches.

• There are two kinds of buds on a twig—the terminal ones at the end of the twig and the lateral ones which grow from the sides of the twig. The terminal buds are the ones that grow the most. Lateral buds act like terminal buds when terminal buds are damaged or pruned. Every year in the fall, when the growing season ends, the plant produces new terminal and lateral buds.

Activities and Procedures

I. Seeds

1. Identifying Things That Are Alive

Materials A large color photograph of an outdoor scene.

Procedure Show the children the picture. Ask the children to name all of the things in the picture that are alive, and to explain how they know that the things they name are alive. Ask the following questions:

Are the plants in the picture alive?

How can you tell that the plants are alive?
(They look healthy and full of color.)

How are plants and animals alike?
(They each grow and change and adapt to their surroundings, and they are able to reproduce their own kind.)

TWIGS AND BUDS

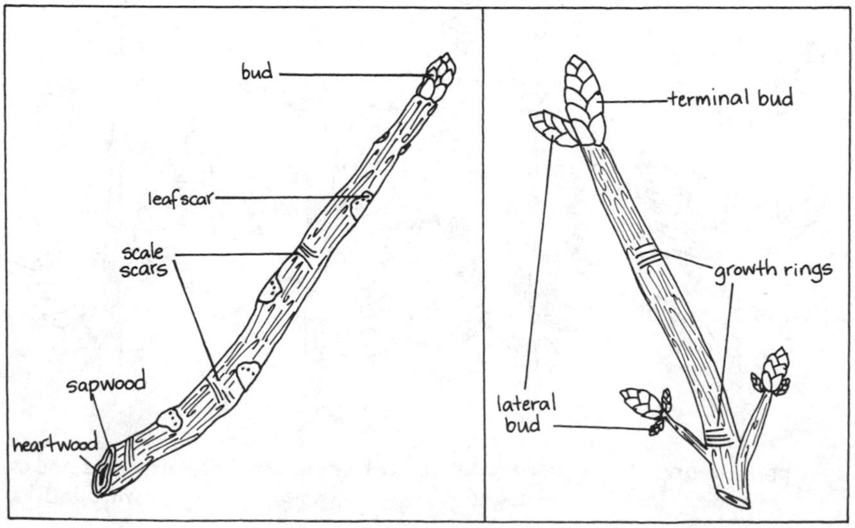

How are plants different from animals?
(Plants are not mobile. They are anchored to the ground where they grow, unless they are transported and moved by something or someone. Animals have to find food to eat or be fed. Plants are able to make their own food.)

Are there any things in the picture that are not alive?
(The sky, rocks, soil, water, roads, sidewalks, buildings, machines, the clothes people are wearing, etc.)

How are the plants in the picture alike?
(They have leaves.)

Note: Not all plants have leaves.

How are the plants in the picture different?
(The plants come in lots of different shapes and sizes. Trees are big plants, grasses and flowers are small plants. The colors of the plants are different.)

2. Seeds and Pebbles

Materials Lima beans; small pebbles the size of lima beans; water; two equal-size plastic containers.

Procedure
• Show the children the lima beans and the small pebbles. Ask them which of the two things is alive and which is not. Have the children sort out the lima beans from the pebbles.
• Have the children count out ten lima beans and ten pebbles. Have a child place the ten pebbles in a plastic container, and place the ten lima beans in another plastic container. Have another child fill each container with water. Leave the pebbles and lima beans in water overnight. Ask the children if they think any change will occur to the pebbles or the beans overnight. After the pebbles and beans have soaked in water overnight, have the children observe the change. (The beans will be larger. They will have absorbed water. Their skins may have popped, and they will feel soft. The pebbles will have remained the same.)

3. Looking Inside a Seed

Materials Pebbles and lima beans soaked in water overnight; a toothpick or pin; a magnifying glass.

Procedure
• Have children use a pin or a toothpick to peel the outer skin off of the bean. Then have them open up a soft, water-soaked lima bean. Have the children examine the inside of the seed with a magnifying glass. Discuss the difference between the pebbles and the hard and soft lima beans.
• Ask the following kinds of questions:

What happened to the seed while it soaked in the water?
(It absorbed water.)

How did the water get inside the seed?
(It seeped in.)

Can you find a baby plant?
(You may need a magnifying glass for this. Help the children find the tiny plant inside the bean.)

What does it look like?
(A baby plant.)

• Explain to the children that the small plant inside the seed is called an embryo. The two halves of the seed are called the cotyledons and store food for the embryo.

4. Water Enters Seeds

Materials A colored candle; a match; 20 lima beans with unchipped skins; a plastic container; water.

Procedure
• Have the children examine the lima beans to see if they can find any marks or cracks on them other than the scar mark on one side. The scar on the side will have one tiny spot on one of its ends.
• Light a candle and allow some wax to drip on the scar and the tiny spot on the scar. Do this to ten lima beans.

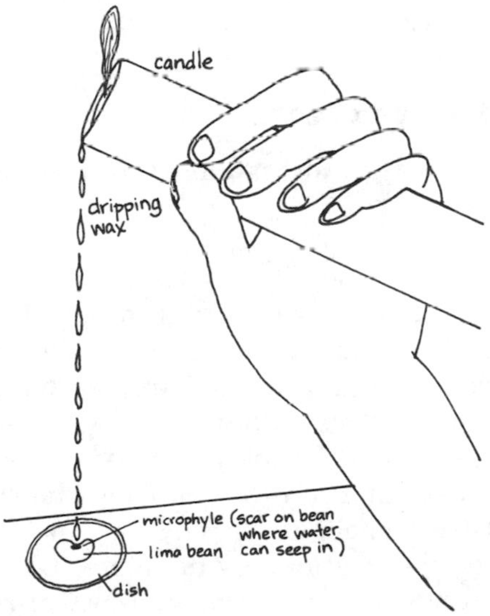

• Have the children count out another ten lima beans that have unchipped skins. Have a child put both sets of ten beans in a container filled with water. Let them soak overnight. Have the children examine the beans the next day. Ask the following kinds of questions:

Do all of the beans look alike?
(No, some are swollen, and some are unchanged.)

Which beans are swollen or have wrinkled skin?
(The ones without the wax.)

How does water seep into the seed?
(Water seeps into the seed through a little opening on the side of the seed where the scar is.)

How come the seeds covered with wax drops did not swell?
(The wax prevented the water from entering the opening.)

**The opening on the seed is called the *microphyle.*

5. Seeds Absorb Water

Materials Assorted beans; dry peas; an empty plastic spice jar with a lid; water; a plastic bag; a rubber band.

Procedure
- Fill the jar to the top with the beans and peas. Force as many seeds as you possibly can into the container by shaking it or tapping it to create more space. Then add as much water as the container will take and screw the top on tightly. Place the container inside a plastic bag, and close the plastic bag with a rubber band. Let the closed jar sit overnight.
- Have the children observe the container the next day. (Usually, the container has burst open because as the seeds absorb water they swell and create pressure inside of the container.)

6. Sprouting Lima Beans

Materials Lima beans; paper towel; water; clear plastic bag.

Procedure
- Moisten a paper towel. Fold it in half three times. Place several beans on the paper towel. Then place the paper towel with the beans on it inside a plastic bag so that the paper will stay moist.
- Let the seeds stay on the moist paper towel inside the plastic bag for a day or two. Then check to see if the seeds have changed. If they have not sprouted, continue to check until they do. *Note:* Do not make the paper towel too wet or the seeds will grow mildew and rot.

7. Seed Hunt

Materials Assorted fresh fruits and vegetables (cucumber, tomato, orange, apple, cantaloupe, peas, green beans, etc.); a knife; a cutting board; paper plates; paper towels; a magnifying glass.

Procedure
- Ask the children where seeds come from. Listen to their responses. Then show the children the assorted fruits and vegetables. Ask them what is inside the fruits and vegetables. Cut the fruits and vegetables up and remove the seeds.
- Have the children place the seeds from each kind of fruit or vegetable on a different paper plate. Allow the seeds to dry out. Have the children look at them through a magnifying glass.
- Have the children count how many seeds came from each fruit or vegetable.

Ask the following kinds of questions:

Which fruit or vegetable had the most seeds?

Which fruit or vegetable had the least number of seeds?

Which had the largest seeds?

Which had the smallest seeds?

Can these seeds grow into new plants?
(Yes.)

How many plants could one tomato start?
(It depends on the number of seeds.)

If an apple has ten seeds, how many new apple trees could be started from the seeds?
(Ten.)

Which can produce more new plants from one piece of fruit?
(The fruit or vegetable that produces the most seeds.)

Do all of the seeds grow into new plants?
(No.)

Why not?
(They are eaten by animals; only some of the seeds are used to produce new plants.)

- Dry out some of the seeds for a week. Observe how they change as they dry out. Then place them on a moist paper towel inside of a clear plastic bag for a few days to see if they will sprout. Explain to the children that when a seed sprouts, it is called "germination." Germinate means that the seed has begun to grow into a plant.

8. Sorting Seeds

Materials Assorted seeds; an empty egg carton; a small plastic container.

Procedure Place the assorted seeds inside the plastic container. Then show the children the assorted seeds and the egg carton. Ask them to sort the seeds into the egg cups in the egg carton. Ask them if they can guess what plants the different seeds will grow into.

9. Monocot and Dicot Seeds

Materials Corn kernels; lima beans; water; paper towel.

Procedure

• Place the two kinds of seeds on a moist paper towel. Let them sit overnight so they will be soft and easy to open the next day. Explain to the children that both the corn kernels and the beans are seeds. They are very different from each other; not only do they look different, they also grow quite differently.

• Have the children open up both the corn kernels and the bean seeds. Have them observe how different the two kinds of seeds look from each other. The bean seeds have two parts and split open easily. The corn kernels do not split open easily, and they have one part. Bean seeds belong to the dicot family of plants because they have two parts that become two cotyledons. The corn kernel belongs to the monocot family of plants, because it has only one cotyledon. "Mono" means one; "di" means two. Monocot seeds grow into grasses, palm and bamboo trees, and flowers with three to six petals like daffodils, tulips, and lilies. Dicot seeds grow into flowering trees, shrubs, herbs, and flowers that have four or five petals or multiples of four and five like roses or complex flowers that contain many tiny flowers inside a flower like a sunflower or a daisy.

10. How Seeds Spread

Materials Dandelion puff; seed with burrs; a wool mitten or sock; maple seeds (shaped like helicopter propellers and twirl when they are thrown in the air); pine cone with seeds; an exploding seed in a pod; dried seeds found anywhere outside, like acorns, catkins, or grass seeds.

Procedure

• Show children the dandelion puff. Ask them how new dandelions get planted. Take one of the seeds off the puff and let it fall. If there is a rug on the floor, it will probably land straight up on the rug. The seed plants itself in the ground.

• Show children the burr. Ask them how the stickers on the seed help it get moved. Discuss how seeds with burrs can travel from one place to another by sticking to animal fur as an animal goes by or by sticking to our clothes when we walk through a field. Have children put a wool mitten or sock on their hand and rub it next to the burr. Have them observe how the burr clings and attaches itself.

• Demonstrate how a maple-seed hovers through the air like a helicopter. Hold the seed above your head, then let it go and it will hover and spin till it lands on the ground. The design of the seed allows it to twirl and hover in flight.

• Give each child a maple seed to experiment with so that he or she can become familiar with how maple seeds and other similarly shaped seeds travel.

• Discuss how the other seeds on display are dispersed from the plants they grow on, and how animals such as squirrels and birds also help distribute seeds.

II. The Parts of Green Plants

1. The Parts of a Dandelion Plant

Materials A fresh dandelion flower; a hand trowel; a dandelion weed tool to dig up dandelion roots; newspaper.

Procedure

• Take the children outside to dig up a dandelion. Dandelions are easiest to dig up after a heavy rain. Show the children how to use the weeding tool. Ask the children why it is easier to dig up a plant after it rains. (The soil is easier to dig because it is diluted from the rain.)

• Show the children a dandelion flower. Explain that it is a wild flower. It is also a weed. All weeds are wild. A weed is a plant that grows someplace where you do not want it to grow.

• Find a dandelion plant in the grass. Have the children notice the way the dandelion grows in the grass. The leaves spread out flat and close to the ground. Explain that a dandelion is a very sturdy plant. It can be stepped on directly and it will not die. The leaves grow in a circular pattern off a very short stem. It grows in a rosette pattern.

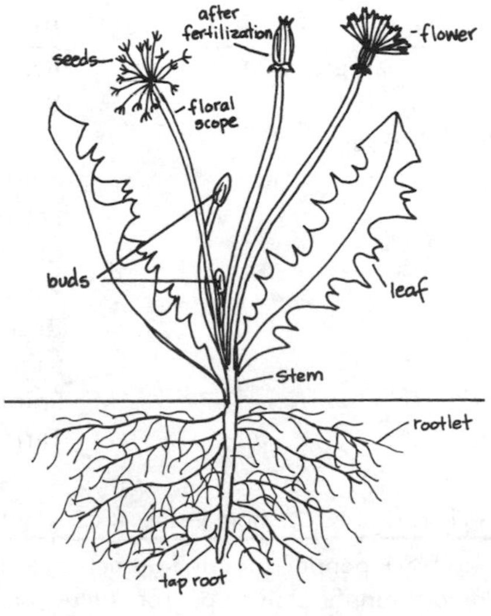

• Have the children look at the plant and ask children the following kinds of questions as they examine the dandelion plant growing in the ground:

Can you find the leaves? What do they look like?
(They look like jagged teeth.)

Can you find the flower? How is the flower attached to the plant?
(The flower is attached to the plant on a long hollow scope.)

Note: Pick a dandelion flower and then remove the scope from the flower to see what the scope looks like. (It is hollow.)

Can you find a bud? What is inside of the bud?
(A baby flower that is undeveloped.)

How many buds are there? How can you tell which buds are going to blossom soon?
(The larger buds with the longer scopes are going to blossom the soonest.)

What happens to the flower after it blossoms?
(It shrivels up and stays closed until it opens to become a seed puff.)

How can you tell which of the dead flowers is going to be a seed puff?
(It has a white tip rather than a yellow tip.)

How many seeds are on each seed puff?
(Too many to count.)

What happens to the seeds on the seed puff when the wind blows on it?
(The seeds come off and blow in the wind.)

What happens to the flower when the sun goes down?
(The flower closes up. It reopens when the sun shines on it.)

• Dig up the dandelion. Try to get the complete root. Have the children observe how long the root is. The main root has little rootlets on it. The main root is called a taproot. Soil clings to the roots and rootlets. Show children where the stem is located. The stem on the dandelion plant is very short because the leaves grow off it in a rosette pattern close to the ground. See diagram on previous page for location of stem.

2. Fruits and Vegetables (the parts of a plant we eat)

Materials Fresh fruits and vegetables; a knife; a cutting board; a paper towel or paper plate.

Procedure
• Show children the fresh fruits and vegetables. Explain that we eat plants and that when we eat fruits and vegetables we are eating plants or parts of plants. All things that grow in the ground are plants and are members of the vegetable kingdom. Flowers and fruits, grasses and trees, bushes and ferns are all plants. Introduce a few fruits or vegetables to the children each day. Discuss with them what part of the plant they are looking at or about to eat. See the chart at the bottom of this page for the parts of a plant you are eating.
• Explain to the children that when they taste roots sometimes the roots taste sweet. Roots store food in the form of sugar and/or starch for the plant to use to grow more new leaves and flowers. Roots like carrots are pulled from the ground before more leaves and

Roots	*Stems*	*Bark*	*Leaves*	*Flowers*	*Ovaries or Fruits with Edible Seeds*	*Ovaries or Fruits Without Edible Seeds*	*Seeds*
Beets	Asparagus	Cinnamon	Basil	Artichokes	Allspice*	Apple	Caraway
Carrots	Celery		Bay leaf	Broccoli	Banana	Cherry	Corn kernels
Garlic	Rhubarb		Cabbage	Cauliflower	Black Pepper*	Orange	Dill
Ginger			Kale	Cloves	Corn	Peach	Dried Beans
Onions			Lettuce	Saffron†	Cucumber	Plum	Mustard
Potatoes			Oregano		Eggplant		Nutmeg
Radishes			Parsley		Green beans		Nuts
Turnips			Rosemary		Hot pepper		Peas
			Sage		Peas		Poppy Seeds
			Spinach		Squash		Sesame Seeds
			Tarragon		Strawberry		
					Tomatoes		

Note: This chart is only a sample listing. It does not include all edible plants and parts of plants.

*Allspice and black pepper are dried-up berries.
† Saffron comes from the stamen of crocus blossoms.

flowers are produced by the plant. When we eat the roots, we are eating the food that the plant has stored for itself.

• Explain to the children that botanists are scientists who study plants. Botanists classify many of the fruits and vegetables we eat as fruits. A botanist classifies the part of a plant that contains its seeds as the plant's ovary or the fruit of the plant. So things like tomatoes, eggplants, cucumbers, and squash are each classified as fruits. A plant's ovary or fruit is the place where seeds develop and are nourished by the plant. The fruit or ovary supplies food to the seeds until the seeds germinate and grow into new plants able to make their own food.

III. Leaves

1. A Leaf-collecting Walk

Materials A paper bag; newspaper.

Procedure

• Take the children out on a walk around the backyard or the schoolyard. Have the children collect leaves. Have them take one sample of all of the leaves they find. The children should look in the grass for a variety of growth there. They should also take a sample from the shrubs and the flowers and the trees.

• Place all of the leaves in the paper bag. Bring the leaves inside and spread them out on a piece of newspaper. Have the children examine the leaves. Ask the following kinds of questions:

Do any of these leaves look alike?

How are they alike?
(Color, size, shape, edge, length of stem, vein pattern, texture of surface.)

Do any of the leaves look exactly alike?
(Only if they come from the same plant will they look exactly alike, but even then, no two leaves are ever exactly identical. Every individual leaf is unique. Fingerprints on people's hands are also unique. Even though fingerprints fall into general patterns, each individual has a unique set of fingerprints.)

Can you find two matching leaves from the same plant?

Can you find a group of leaves that have a smooth edge?

Can you find a group of leaves that have a jagged edge?

Can you find a group of leaves that have a combination of smooth and jagged edges?

How many different ways can you think of to group the leaves that were collected?

• Give each child a part of the leaf collection and ask each child to sort or group the leaves they have been given into two different piles based on a way that they can think of for separating the leaves. Then let each child share how they divided their leaves into piles and why.

2. Taking a Closer Look at the Edges of Leaves

Materials Leaves from leaf-collecting walk; newspaper; a knife with a serrated edge; a knife with a smooth edge.

Procedure

• Ask the children to find a leaf with a smooth edge and one with a jagged edge. Hold up both leaves after they are identified by the children. Explain that the edge that is jagged is called a serrated edge. When a leaf has an edge with many points, it is called a serrated edge. The edge looks like the edge of some kitchen knives. Some kitchen knives have a smooth edge and some have a serrated edge. Knives are hard and very sharp. They can cut you, but leaves which are soft cannot cut you.

• Hold up a leaf with a lobed edge. Explain that when a leaf has an edge that looks as though a part of it was cut out, it is called a lobed edge, and that the leaf you are holding has a lobed edge.

Point to the lobes and count them. The number of lobes will vary on different leaves from different plants. Ask the children if they can find another leaf with a lobed edge from the collection of leaves.

• Hold up another leaf that is both serrated and lobed, like that from a maple tree. Explain that leaves sometimes have a combination of edges. They can have an edge that is both smooth and serrated or serrated and lobed, or another combination. Ask them to find other leaves from the collection that have a combination of two patterns for an edge.
• Have children make a paper model of what a smooth-edged and serrated-edged leaf look like.

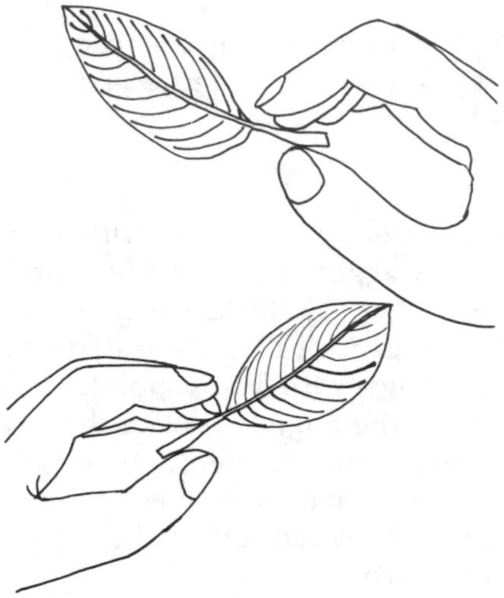

SETS OF LEAVES

3. Find Matching Real Leaves

Materials Leaves that came from the backyard or schoolyard.

Procedure Show children the leaves and give each child a set of leaves. Have them find a matching pair for each of the leaves outside, or have each child find another child with a set of leaves that matches his/her set of leaves. Discuss the edge of each leaf when its pair is found.

4. Monocot and Dicot Leaves

Materials Assorted leaves from monocot and dicot plants; a magnifying glass. (Most grasses have monocot leaves, most trees and shrubs have dicot leaves.)

Procedure
• Have the children see the difference between the monocot vein pattern and the dicot vein pattern. Monocots have veins that run parallel to the midrib. Dicots have veins that form a webbed or branched pattern from the midrib. Have the children look through the magnifying glass at the vein patterns, and sort the leaves into two piles, one with monocot leaves, the other with dicot leaves.
• Have children make a model of a monocot leaf and a dicot leaf.

5. Taking a Closer Look at Veins on Leaves

Materials Cardboard shapes of leaves and real leaves with the same shapes (example: oak, tulip, elm, willow); a pencil; paper.

Procedure
• Show the children the cardboard leaf shapes and the real leaves that match the shapes. Have them find the cardboard leaves that match the real leaves.
• Have children use a pencil to trace around a cardboard leaf shape. Ask the children what is needed to make the leaf shape look more like a real leaf. If they do not suggest adding the midrib and veins, then show them the midrib and veins on the real leaf, and then have them add these lines that represent midribs and veins to their leaf tracing.
• Explain that the line in the center of the leaf is called the midrib. It is the main vein. Smaller veins are connected to the midrib. Liquids flow through the midrib and veins of the leaf. Veins help move food or energy from one part of the leaf to another. The midrib of a leaf connects to the leafstalk or stem and the leafstalk connects to a branch of the plant. See diagram.
• Have the children trace around the remaining cardboard leaf shapes and add lines to the shapes to represent a midrib and the veins. Ask the following kinds of questions:

What do the veins look like on the real leaf?

Are the veins straight and parallel to each other or wavy looking?

What does the midrib look like?

Does the midrib go straight up and down like a straight pin, or does it appear to have branches like the fingers branching off your palm?

Do the lines you have added to your leaf shape look like the kind of pattern that the veins have on the real leaf that matches the leaf shape?

• Explain to the children that the midrib of a leaf can be either pinnate or palmate. If it is pinnate, it will be straight like a pin. If it is palmate, it will appear to have several branches. The veins on a leaf can be webbed and wavy or be very straight. The smallest and thinnest veins on a leaf are called capillaries. They are usually wavy looking.
• Explain that our bodies also have veins in them that carry liquid. Our veins also carry food or energy. The food is in the blood. Our tiniest veins are called capillaries, and our major veins are called arteries. Have the children locate a vein on their body. Ask them how their body is like that of a leaf. (We each have veins to carry liquids in our body from one place to another.)

6. Parts of a Simple Leaf

Materials A leaved twig from a shrub with a simple leaf.

Procedure
• Show the children the leaved twig. Take off a leaf from the twig and have the children notice the bud on the twig next to the leafstalk, and the scar that is left on the twig from where the leaf was pulled off. Explain to the children that when a leaf has one blade and a leafstalk that connects directly to a wood twig, it is called a simple leaf.
• Give each child a leaf from the twig. As you rip off each leaf from the twig, have the children notice where the scar is from the leaf on the twig and where the new leaf bud is on the twig.
• Teach each child to touch the midrib on their leaf. Then tell them to hold their leaf by its leafstalk. Next have them place their index finger on the edge of their leaf. Then have them point to a vein on their leaf. Explain to the children that the leaf is called a blade and that the bud of a leaf is often protected by a stipule. Sometimes stipules are hard to find, because they often wither and dry up early in the season.

7. Parts of a Compound Leaf

Materials Samples of real compound leaves on a twig, and of double compound leaves on a twig; a pencil, crayons and paper.

Procedure
• Show children the samples of compound and double compound leaves. Show them how these leaves are quite different looking from the simple leaves. Remind the children that simple leaves often have a bud on the twig at the base of their leafstalk. The compound leaf also has a bud on the twig at the base of its leafstalk, but it appears to be more than one leaf. The compound leaf is made up of several leaflets. All of the leaflets combined make up one leaf. There is only one bud on the twig at the base of the leafstalk, therefore

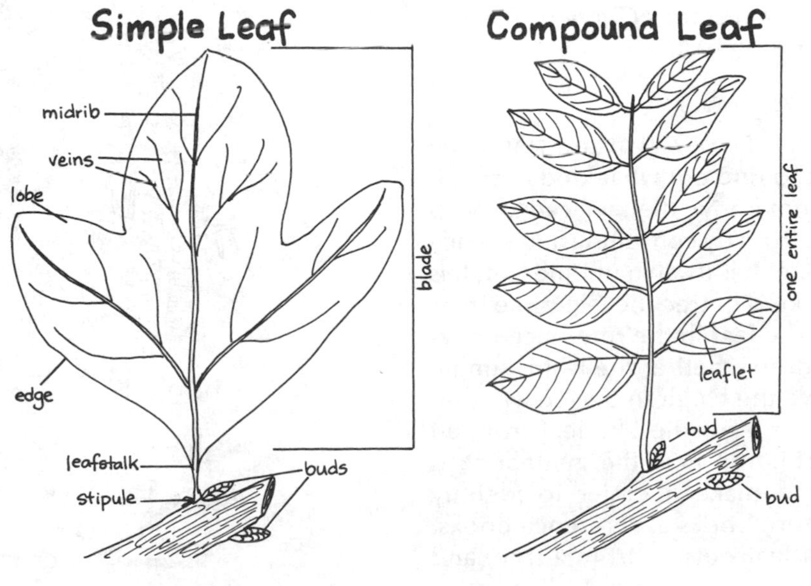

botanists classify it as a single leaf even though it looks like several leaves.

• Have children examine a compound leaf and a double compound leaf. Explain that simple leaves grow in an opposite or alternate pattern on a twig. Leaflets on a compound leaf grow opposite each other on a leafstalk. Demonstrate with your fingers what opposite and alternate patterns look like and show children an opposite and an alternate growth pattern on a twig. Then have them draw a sketch of what a simple, a compound, and a double compound leaf look like. See diagram.

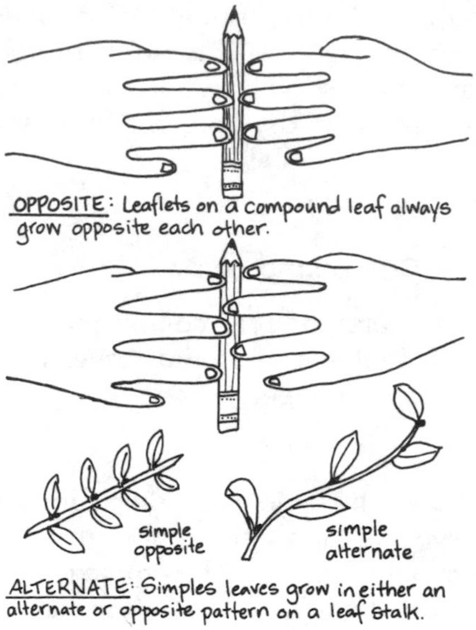

OPPOSITE: Leaflets on a compound leaf always grow opposite each other.
simple opposite
simple alternate
ALTERNATE: Simples leaves grow in either an alternate or opposite pattern on a leaf stalk.

8. Finding out the Names of Plants That Leaves Grow on

Materials A sample of a leaf from a tree; a nature guidebook about trees. For example: *Trees, A Golden Guide,* by Herbert Zim, or *Spotter's Guide to Trees of North America,* by Alan Mitchell.

Procedure

• Show children the leaf. Explain that the leaf came from a tree. If we want to find out what kind of tree it came from and we do not know, then we can look up the kind of tree it came from by consulting a reference book. Every tree and plant has its own unique leaf. It is possible to identify the kind of tree the leaf came from by finding a picture of the leaf in the reference book.

• Decide with the children whether the leaf is simple or compound. Also have the children decide whether the leaf is a broadleaf or a needle-like leaf from an evergreen. Show the children how the guidebook is divided into sections to make it easier to identify plants. Refer to the nature books as reference books. Have each child find a leaf outside from a tree, and then consult a nature book to find out what kind of tree it grew on.

9. Deciduous and Evergreen Leaves

Materials Gather assorted twigs with leaves from evergreen trees and deciduous trees.

Procedure

• Show the children the assorted twigs with leaves. Explain that the leaves that look like needles are from evergreen trees. Each evergreen tree has its own distinct needle leaf. Trees can be identified by the way the needles grow on the twigs. Some of the needles grow in clumps of three or five, or in pairs; some have short, single, stubby needles; some have long needles; some have white stripes on them; and some feel prickly. Some evergreens have broad, leathery leaves. There is a great variety of evergreens and needle-leaf evergreens.

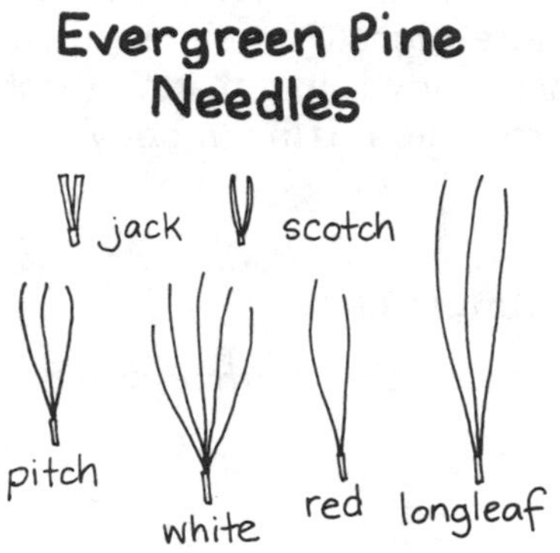

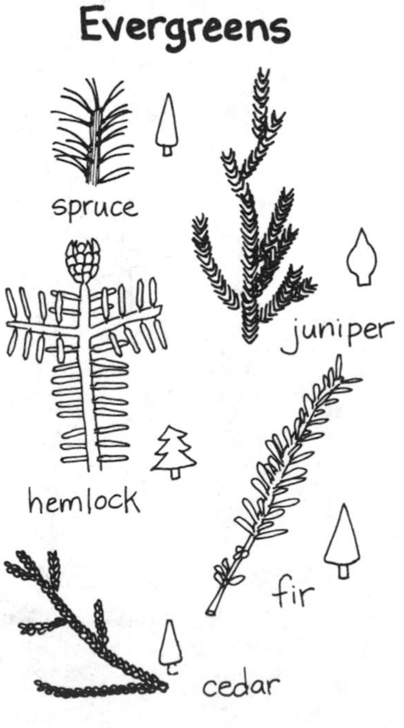

• Have the children sort out which twigs with leaves came from evergreens and which twigs are not from evergreen trees. Then have them try to identify which twigs with leaves came from which evergreen. Have them check a nature guidebook on trees to identify the needles they are looking at. Help them understand the difference between a pine, a fir, a spruce tree, and a cedar tree. Show them the difference between the scales on a cedar leaf and the short, stiff needles on a spruce tree. Show them the long, flexible needles that a pine tree has as opposed to the shorter needles on spruces and firs.

• Explain to the children that if a tree is an evergreen that means it does not lose its leaves in the fall. It stays green all year. The leaves of evergreens are usually tough and waxy. Instead of losing all of their leaves at once in the fall, evergreen trees lose their leaves all year, a few at a time, and continually grow new leaves. A deciduous tree has leaves which fall off every fall. Evergreens and deciduous trees are perennial plants. A perennial plant is any plant that continues to live for many seasons, even though it may die back to the ground in the fall.

• Have the children check the vein pattern on a pine tree needle with a magnifying glass. A pine tree is not a flowering tree. It grows cones, but not flowers. The needle leaves have parallel veins like monocot plants. Plants with needle leaves that grow cones are called conifers or cone-bearing plants, and are classified as gymnosperms, or plants without flowers.

IV. Roots and Stems

1. A Closer Look at a Carrot

Materials Freshly picked carrots with green tops still on; a knife; a magnifying glass.

Procedure

• Show the children a carrot. Ask them if they know what part of the plant a carrot is. It is a root. Look at the outside of the carrot. Observe how long the greens are on top of the carrot. If the carrot has been freshly picked, the children may be able to see the fine root hairs that are on each of the rootlets. Use a magnifying glass to look at the rootlets. (If the rootlets are not still attached, there will be small scars on the sides of the carrot root.) The carrot itself is called a taproot. A taproot is a long, thick root that grows down deep and straight.

• Slice two carrots with a knife. Slice one carrot crosswise and the other one lengthwise. Have the children notice the three parts on the inside of the root. There is an inner layer or circle of fibers in the middle of the carrot and another layer that surrounds that layer.

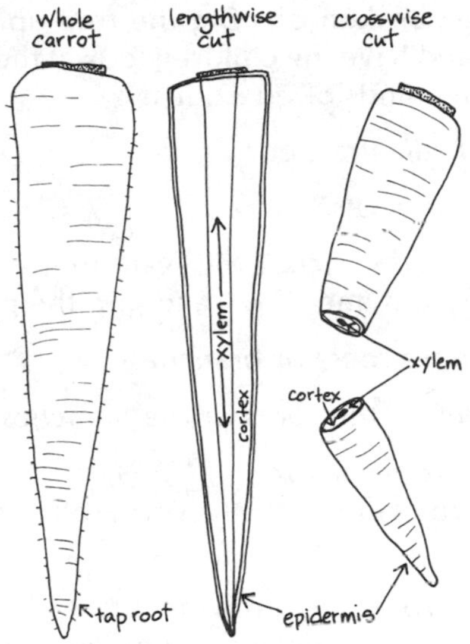

The entire carrot is surrounded by a thin layer of skin. Each layer inside of the root appears to be a different shade of orange. The lengthwise cut shows that the layers extend from the top of the root to the bottom of the root. They are long fibers. The fibers look like circles in the crosswise cut.

• Explain to the children that the outer skin on the carrot is called the epidermis. Our body is surrounded by an epidermis. We usually call our epidermis "skin." Inside the epidermis is the cortex. The cortex is the part of the carrot root where food is stored for the plant. The cortex of the root usually tastes sweet because it contains a lot of stored-up sugar for the plant made by the leaves. The very center of the carrot root is made up of tissues or tubes that transport food up and down the root. The food is absorbed from the soil in the form of moisture and minerals and travels to and from the leaves and to and from the roots in a circular path. The blood in our body also travels through tubes in a circular path.

• Have the children draw a model of a carrot slice and label the parts of the slice.

2. Looking at the Roots of a Tree Sapling

Materials An acorn; a dug-up oak tree seedling or oak tree sapling (or any other seedling of a tree) replanted in a large flower pot; a hand trowel.

Procedure

• Show the children the acorn. Explain that when an acorn sprouts, an oak tree begins to grow. Show the children the oak tree seedling or sapling in the flower pot. Explain that it is a baby tree. If the oak tree is a seedling you will probably still be able to see the acorn attached to the tree roots. If it is a sapling, the acorn will have already broken off. Dig the tree up out of the flower pot and have the children look at the roots. Ask the following kinds of questions:

Is the acorn still attached?

Where are the roots?

How do the roots anchor the plant to the ground?
(They spread out and down and grip the ground.)

Are there more roots or branches?

Which is longer, the roots or the branches?

How do the roots grow?
(One root grows down, the rest grow off of the main or taproot.)

Do all of the roots grow down?
(Some grow to the side and are called lateral roots.)

What color are the roots?

Do the roots look different from the bark?

Will this tree be able to continue to grow?
(Yes, if it is replanted and the roots do not dry out.)

• Have the children replant the tree in the pot and transplant it to a place the children choose to replant the tree outside. Explain that the tree will grow to be a very large plant. Trees need a lot of space to grow. Have the children use a hand trowel to break up the soil and to dig a hole for the tree seedling or sapling.

3. Cross-Section of a Log

Materials An unsplit firewood log, or a tree stump.

Procedure
• Show the children an unsplit firewood log. Explain that it used to be part of a living tree. The tree it was growing on either died or is still alive. Ask them what part of the tree they think it came from. It could be from the tree's trunk or from a branch on the tree. Have the children examine the bark on the outside. Then have the children look at the rings on the inside of the log. Explain that the bark is the epidermis or skin that protects the tree. Bark helps keep moisture inside of the tree and it protects the tree from insects and diseases. As the tree grows thicker each year, the bark splits or peels and new bark forms underneath the old layer of bark. The center of the log has a darker color to it. This center wood is called heartwood. It is the oldest wood. It is also harder than the outer wood. In the spring, the tree grows new wood. The new wood is called sapwood. The sapwood is lighter in color than the heartwood. Heartwood is dead sapwood. It acts as a support for the tree. Heartwood does not transport any liquids. If you count the rings from the center out you

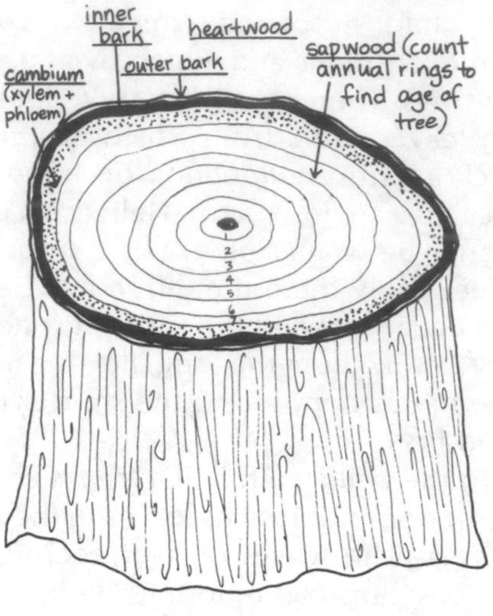

SEVEN YEAR OLD LOG

can find out how old the log was when it was cut from the tree. Each year the tree forms a new circle. Each circle represents a year's growth.
• Explain to the children that the trunk of a tree is connected to the roots. The trunk is really the stem of the plant. Trees are very large plants. They are the largest plants in the world. The trunk of a tree has branches that grow off it, and the branches have smaller branches that grow off them. All of the branches are connected to the stem and the root system through tubes that run up and down the tree. Food is transported from the leaves to other parts of the tree, and minerals and water are transported up to the leaves from the roots. The tubes that move foods and liquids up the tree are called xylem tubes. The tubes that move liquids down the tree are called phloem tubes.
• Have the children compare the carrot root's cross-section with the tree's cross-section. Explain that the carrot root's xylem tubes were in the very center, and were surrounded by phloem tubes. The xylem and phloem tubes in the carrot were surrounded by the cortex or stored food for the plant. In trees, the central part of the stem or trunk is dead. The heartwood merely supports the tree and keeps it from falling over. The xylem and phloem tubes in the tree are located near the bark layer and in the sapwood.
• Have children draw a model of a cross-section of a log and label the parts of the cross-section.

4. How a Twig Grows

Materials Fall or winter* twigs from a tree with buds; a magnifying glass.

*This activity is best done in the fall or the winter after the buds have had a chance to develop and be visible.

Procedure

• Show the children a twig from a tree. Explain that it was once a branch on a tree. It cannot continue to grow because it was cut from the tree it grew on. Sometimes twigs fall from trees when the wind blows hard. Sometimes twigs fall from trees because they are old. And sometimes twigs are picked off or cut off, as this twig was.

• Have the children examine a twig from a tree. Show them that you can count how old the twig is by looking at its cross-section and by counting its rings or by counting the circle scars along the twig that indicate a year's growth. Show the children a growth ring. Notice how much a twig can grow in one year. Ask the children which appears to grow more in length each year, them or the tree. Have the children notice the buds on the twig. The one at the tip of the twig is called a terminal bud. The twig grows longer at the terminal bud. When the bud opens and the growth takes place, a new growth ring is left on the twig. The buds on the side are called lateral buds. Lateral buds or side buds grow new shoots or tiny branches off the main branch.

• Pull a leaf off the twig. Have the children notice the scar or mark left on the twig when the leaf is taken off. Also, have them notice the new bud that is next to the leafstalk that was pulled off. Have them notice the protective covering that covers the new buds on the twig. Pick a bud apart and see if they can find tiny leaves all folded up inside.

• Twigs are like small tree trunks. Trunks of trees have heartwood, sapwood, and bark, just like twigs. But instead of leaf scars, tree trunks have scars or knots at places where twigs once grew.

• In the spring take the children outside to find a tree full of large buds. Have the children examine a twig from a tree and pick a bud apart to see if they can find tiny leaves all folded up inside.

V. Flowers and Fruits

1. A Closer Look at Flowers

Materials A variety of large, fresh, simple flowers like a tulip, lily, daffodil, poppy, buttercup, azalea blossom, apple or cherry blossom, pansy, etc.

Procedure Have children observe the flowers. Ask the following kinds of questions:

How are all of the flowers alike?

How are all of the flowers different?

Does each of the flowers have an aroma?

Does the aroma of each flower smell the same?

Which flowers look flat, which look like bells, which look like cones?

Which flowers have more than one color on them?

What is underneath the flower?
(A calyx made up of sepals which protected the flower when it was a bud.)

What is the flower attached to on the plant?
(A long stalk or part of the stem.)

Why do plants grow flowers?
(To produce seeds.)

What can you see inside the flowers?
(Stamens and pistils.)

Do all of the inside parts look alike?
(No, they look different from each other.)

How does the tallest part in the center feel at its tip?
(Sticky.)

2. Dissecting a Simple Flower

Materials A large simple flower like a lily or a tulip (or large azalea) blossom; pieces of paper; magnifying glasses; toothpicks.

Procedure

• Give each child a flower and a piece of paper. Have the children locate the petals on the flower. Have the children count the petals. Then have the children remove the petals. All of the petals are attached to each other on an azalea blossom; on a tulip the petals are each attached separately. Explain that all of the petals together are called the corolla. Place the entire corolla on a piece of paper. After the petals are off, it is easier to see the insides of the flower. The insides consist of the

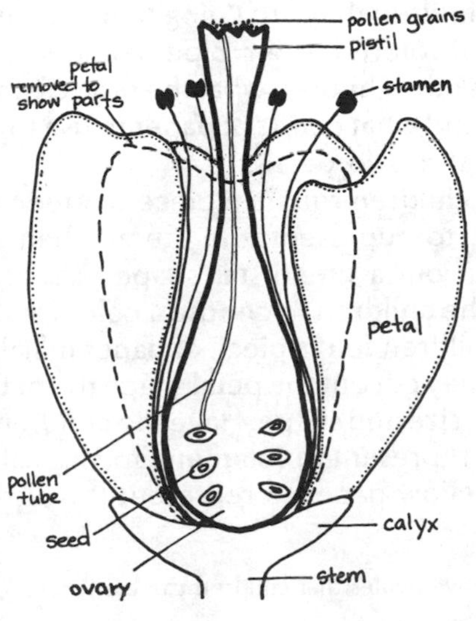

pistil, which has a sticky end and the stamens, which have pollen grains on their ends. Have the children feel the sticky end of the pistil. Explain that this sticky end is called the stigma.

• Have the children take off a stamen and look at the pollen grains with a magnifying glass. Then have them rub a stamen on the pistil and observe what happens to the pollen grains. (Some of the grains will stick to the pistil's stigma.) Explain that when the pollen from the stamen touches the stigma (sticky end) of the pistil it is called pollination. Have the children place the stamen on their paper.

Note: Not all flowers are complete. Some flowers only have pistils. Some flowers only have stamens. Bees, other insects, and the wind help pollinate flowers. See diagram.

• Have the children locate the ovary* at the base of the pistil. Have the children split the ovary open with their fingernail or a toothpick. Ask the children to count the eggs inside of the flower's ovary. The eggs are called ovules. Explain to the children that after pollination takes place, fertilization follows. The pollen grains grow tubes down the pistil into the ovary and into an ovule. When this occurs, a seed begins to develop and grow. The pistil grows larger and the ovary grows and develops into a fruit. The mature fruit holds seeds for new plants.

Note: Not all flowers are simple. Some, like the sunflower or daisy, are called compound and are a composite of hundreds of little flowers. See Activity IX, Procedure 1, of this chapter for more information about compound flowers.

3. Making a Model of a Simple Flower

Materials Colored construction paper; pipe cleaners; paper fasteners; scissors.

Procedure

• Tell the children they are going to make a model of a flower out of colored paper, pipe cleaners, and a paper fastener. Ask the children what the pipe cleaners could represent, and what colors of paper to use to represent the stem, calyx, and petals.

• Have the children roll up a piece of green construction paper to represent the stem. Then have the children cut out a green star shape to represent the calyx. Ask the children to choose a color for the petals. Have the children fold a piece of paper in half twice so that when they cut out the petal shape the petals will all be the same size and shape. Have the children use pipe cleaners to represent the stamens and a small piece of rolled-up yellow paper to represent the pistil.

*Lily flowers have ovules that children can easily see.

• Ask the children how they should begin the construction of the model flower. Suggest to them that it be constructed from the inside out. Begin by attaching the pistil (the hollow yellow paper tube) to the stamens (the two pipe cleaners) with a long paper fastener. Then have them push the paper fastener through the petals (the colored pieces of paper), then through the calyx (the green paper star), and finally have them attach the flower to the long green paper stem. See diagram.

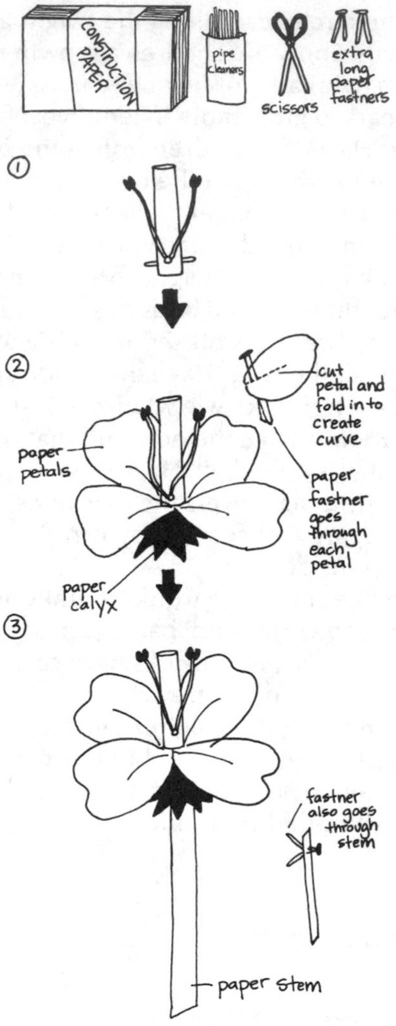

Fine point If children are older, just show them the materials and ask them to tell you how each of the materials could be used and what each of the materials could represent when the children make the model of a flower, rather than telling and giving them so much information.

4. Dissecting a Piece of Fruit

Materials Two apples; a knife; a cutting board.

Procedure

• Show the children the apples. Explain to them that the apple is a fruit of a plant. It grows on an apple tree and it holds seeds inside for new apple trees. Have children observe the outside of the apple. Ask them to locate the stem. The stem is where the apple was attached to the tree. Then have them notice the bottom of the apple. There are lots of little leaves and dead parts. Explain that this part of the apple is the old part of the flower blossom that died. The green is the old calyx, and the dead flower parts are the stamens of the dead apple blossom. The apple meat that we eat is the swollen old flower stem. Inside of the apple meat is the core. The core contains the ovary that has ripened into a fruit with mature seeds.

• Slice both apples in half. Slice one apple crosswise and the other apple lengthwise. Both cuts will produce different views of the inside of the apple. The crosswise cut will look like a star exposing all of the sections of the ovary. The lengthwise section will expose the new stem and the old calyx in relation to the fruit. See diagram.

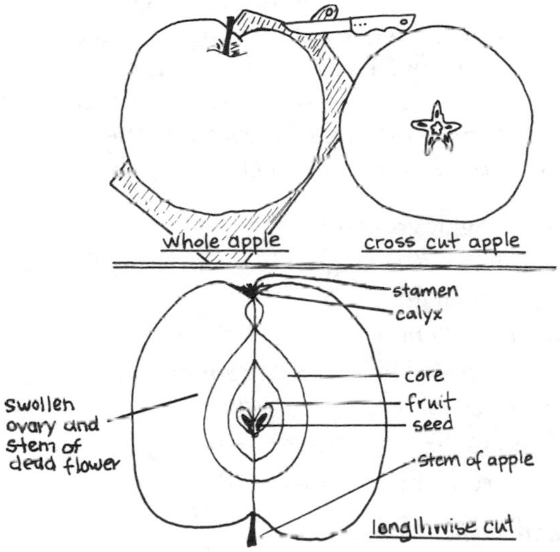

• Explain to the children that when the apple first starts to grow on the tree, it grows up and the stem is on the bottom of the apple. As the apple matures, it becomes heavier and the apple begins to hang as it grows. When the apple is mature, it becomes very heavy and if it is not picked from the tree, it will fall off by itself. When the apple falls off and eventually rots, the seeds will be free to begin to grow into new apple trees. Most apples get eaten by other animals after they fall to the ground. But a few apples grow into new apple trees. Have the children notice how many apple trees could grow from the seeds in one apple.

VI. Experiments with Seeds

1. Seeds Have Air in Them

Materials A bag of dried lima beans; warm water; a container.

Procedure Pour some beans into the container. Pour warm water on top of the beans in the container. Have the children observe the small bubbles of air that come from the seeds and that stay on the seeds. Have the children notice that most of the bubbles come from the tiny hole on the seed through which water will pass when the seed germinates. Explain to the children that all living things need air, even seeds.

2. Germinating Seeds

Materials Lima beans and other seeds (possibly bird-seed); paper towels; water; an empty pie tin; plastic wrap or newspaper to keep the water in the paper towels from evaporating.

Procedure

• Show children the seeds. Tell them you are going to germinate the seeds by placing them between moist paper towels. Explain that when a seed germinates, it begins to grow. Ask the children what they think the seeds need to have in order to germinate. Set up some experiments and find out what conditions are best for the seeds to germinate. See diagram.

• Possible things or conditions that the children might want to test out when they conduct this experiment are the effects of the following.

Water—*Do seeds germinate faster if the towel is damp or very soggy?*

What is necessary for seed germination?

Sunlight—*Do seeds germinate faster in the sunlight or in the dark?*

Seeds—*Do some seed varieties sprout faster than others?*

Temperature—*Will a boiled seed germinate? Will a frozen seed germinate? Will seeds germinate in the refrigerator?*

Whole or broken seeds—*Will incomplete or broken seeds germinate?*
(Broken or incomplete seeds may germinate, but they will most likely suffer stunted growth.)

Note: As children experiment with the seeds and the conditions for growing, they will notice that seeds without water or those kept in the refrigerator or some other cold place will usually not sprout and that warmth and moisture are necessary for germination.* Light or lack of light does not affect whether germination occurs. As long as seeds are kept warm and moist they will sprout whether there is light or not. However, seeds do germinate faster without light.

3. How Germinated Seeds Grow

Materials Germinated seeds growing in a moist paper towel; an empty clear plastic glass.

Procedure
• Have children observe the germinated seeds. Ask the following kinds of questions:

Which part of the seed grows first?
(The roots.)

What develops after the roots?
(The leaves.)

In which direction do the roots grow?
(Down.)

• Have a child place the seeds and the paper towel inside the clear plastic glass. Then have the child turn the seeds around in the glass so that the roots are facing up. Have children observe the seeds the next day to see if the roots are still growing up or if they have bent to grow downward again. (Roots have a tendency to curve downward no matter what position they are in.)

Note: This effect is caused by gravity and is called geotropism. The main stem of a plant shows negative geotropism and grows upwards toward sunlight and away from the roots.

4. The Conditions in Which Seedlings Grow Best

Materials Some healthy germinated seeds; 8 small containers (like empty milk cartons); soil to transplant the germinated seeds to.

*Some seeds such as apple, pear, peach, plum, cherry, dogwood, barberry, holly, and others need a period of cold and will not germinate without it. These kinds of trees grow in places where cold winters occur.

Procedure
• Have children transplant four germinated seeds to each of the eight small containers and plant them in some soil. Ask the children to think about what they think a seedling or plant needs to live a healthy life. Have the children set up some experimental conditions for the seedlings to see which conditions work best for the plants.
• Possible things or conditions children could experiment with might be the effect of the following:

Water or lack of water on the seedling.
Light or lack of light on the seedling. (Cover the plant with a paper bag or place it in a closet.)

5. Good Soil and No Soil (coffee grounds instead)

Materials Cups; soil; coffee grounds; beans; water; direction labels.

Procedure
• Explain to the children that in order to conduct such an experiment on the plants, eight seedlings need to be planted so that it is clear what conditions are best for the seedlings to grow. The following direction labels need to be made up for the seedlings by the children and the directions need to be followed by the children for a few days or until results occur.

Water, sunlight, good soil.
Water, sunlight, coffee grounds.
Water, no sunlight, good soil.
No water, sunlight, good soil.
No water, no sunlight, coffee grounds.
No water, no sunlight, good soil.
Water, no sunlight, coffee grounds.
No water, sunlight, coffee grounds.

See diagram on next page.

• Write up an experience chart with the children when the experiment with seedlings is finished. An experience chart might look like the one below.

We planted radish seeds and lima bean seeds in _____.
We found that:

1. Seeds that did not receive water did not grow.
2. Seeds that received water grew.
3. Seeds that received sun and water had green leaves.
4. Seeds that did not get sun did not develop green leaves.
5. Seeds receiving _____ did best.
6. Seeds planted in coffee grounds did not grow well.
7. Seeds need more than sun, water, and rich soil to grow well.

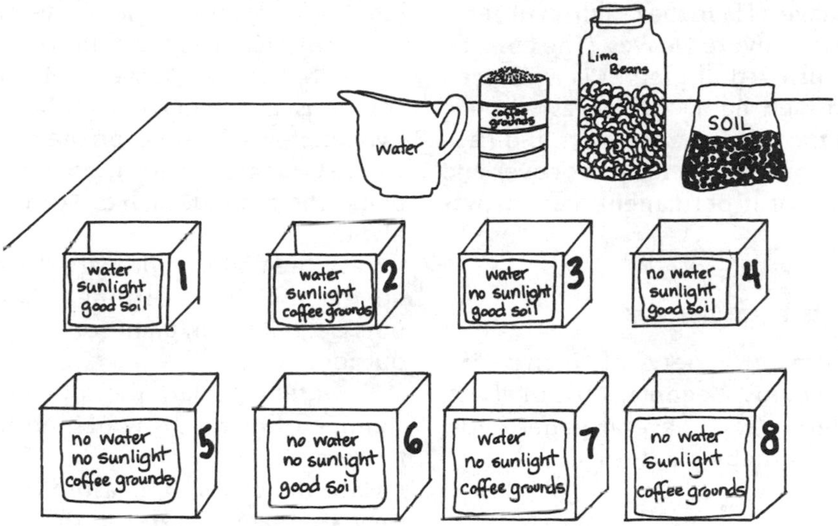

GERMINATING SEEDS IN DIFFERENT SOILS

VII. Experiments with Leaves and Stems

1. Leaves Give off Water

Materials A large leaf with a long leafstalk; four clear plastic glasses; a piece of cardboard; water.

Procedure

- Have a child fill two of the plastic glasses half full with water. Have another child cut a piece of cardboard into two pieces and cut a tiny hole in each piece of cardboard. Choose another child to put the cardboard on top of each of the plastic glasses filled with water. Add the leaf with a long leafstalk to one of the glasses and fit the leafstalk through the hole in the cardboard. Place an empty plastic glass on top of each of the glasses with water in them. Place each of the double cups in the sun.
- Explain to the children that this is an experiment to see if the leaf will give off water. The experiment has to sit in the sun as it is for several hours to see results. Ask the children what they think might happen. If leaves have water in them, what might happen inside the glass? Have the children check the experiment and see the results. (The glass with the leaf in it will have water vapor or tiny water droplets formed on the inside of the glass.) This process of leaves giving off moisture is called transpiration. The glasses without a leaf will not have moisture inside the inverted glass. Explain that leaves have tiny holes on their surface. When leaves become warm, tiny water droplets escape from the tiny holes into the air as water vapor. That is why it feels cooler to sit under a shade tree on a warm, sunny day. Not only does the tree block the sun, it also adds moisture to the air.

2. Leaves Need Sunshine

Materials A small, leafy plant like a geranium in a flower pot; a piece of tinfoil; a piece of black paper; a scissors; paper clips.

Procedure

- Show children the plant. Tell them you are going to cover one of the leaves with a piece of tinfoil, and another leaf on the plant with a piece of black paper. Cut a design in the black paper like a diamond shape, a circle, and a triangle. Attach the tinfoil and black paper to the leaf with paper clips. Ask the children what they think might happen to the leaves that are covered up with the tinfoil and the black paper mask. See diagram.
- Have the children check the covered leaves on the plant in a few days. Remove the tinfoil and the black

paper mask from the leaves. Have the children observe what has happened to the covered leaves. (The covered parts of the leaf will turn a dull green.) Leaves need sunshine. Without enough light, the leaves will die. Keep the plant out in the sun for a few days and have the children observe whether the leaves recover and turn bright green again or if permanent damage was done to the leaf.

3. Growing New Plants from Leaves

Materials Leaves from a variety of plants like geranium, jade plant, coleus, begonia, African violet, impatiens, and wandering jew; several paper cups; water; a spider plant with baby plants or shoots.

Procedure

• Explain to the children that some plants are capable of producing new plants if their leaves are placed in water. Roots start to form at the base of the leaf, and then a new plant can grow. Have children place each of the leaves into a small paper cup filled with water. Leave the paper cups on a sunny window for several weeks and check on them once a week. (Eventually small roots will be seen, and new leaves will begin to grow.)

• Have children observe the spider plant. Help them notice the shoots and the baby plants that are growing on the ends of the shoot. Have a child cut off one of the shoots and place it in water. The buds for roots are already on the baby plant. The water helps them grow longer.

4. Bulbs and Corms and Tubers

Materials Freshly picked tulips, daffodils and/or crocus or pictures of them; onions; daffodil bulbs; tulip bulbs; potatoes; crocus corms; a magnifying glass; a knife; a cutting board.

Procedure

• Show children the fresh flowers, or pictures of the flowers, and then explain that they did not grow from seeds. They grew from bulbs or corms.

• Show children the bulbs, corms, and tubers. Explain that they are underground stems. The scales that make up a bulb or a corm are leaves that are tightly packed. A bulb is a dormant plant. It can be dug up, stored, and replanted. Bulbs are usually planted in the fall and bloom in the spring. Bulbs need to be planted in a soil that has been prepared for them. After the bulb blooms, a new set of stems, leaves, and a bud are formed again in the bulb underground for the following year's bloom.

• Slice a potato, an onion, and a crocus corm open with a knife. Have the children observe how different they look on the inside. Have the children observe the center of each. There is a tiny plant inside the corm and the bulb. Bulbs are leaves that store food, and in their center is a flower bud. Tubers (like potatoes) are swollen stems. The eyes on the outside of the potato are where buds grow from. If a potato is cut up and planted under the ground, each eye can produce a new potato plant.

• Have the children prepare the ground by loosening up the soil. If it is spring, plant some potato eyes outside. If it is fall, plant some flower bulbs and corms outside.

Note: Preplan the planting so that the tall-stemmed flowers grow behind the shorter-stemmed flowers.

• Have the children measure the spring bulbs before they are planted. Later in the spring when the bulbs are blooming, have the children dig them up and re-measure them again. Then have the children replant them and measure them again in a few weeks, after they bloom.

5. Liquids Move Through Stems

Materials A freshly cut twig from a tree; celery stalks with leaves; a white carnation; a knife; a cutting board; cold water; food colors or colored inks; clear plastic glasses; a magnifying glass.

Procedure

• Have a child cut off the end of the celery stalk near the roots. Also cut off the end of the twig and the carnation stem. Place the celery stalks, the carnation, and the twig in cold water to freshen up and stiffen the tubes in the stems. Then place each of the stems into a separate clear plastic glass or jar with water. Have the children add different colors of food color or colored ink to the water of each stem specimen.

• Explain to the children that this is an experiment to see how stems of plants act as pipelines when they transport liquids. The celery stalks, the carnation, and the twig each have their stems in the colored water. Ask the children what they think might happen to the colored water if the stems are left in the colored water overnight or for a few days. (The water will travel up the stems to the leaves and the flowers. The leaves and the flowers will turn the color of the ink or food color. The color will be in the veins of the flower and the leaves.)

• In a day or two, if the color has reached the flowers and the leaves, have children take the stems out of the colored water and slice them off at the bottom to see the color inside of the stem. Have the children use a magnifying glass to look at the celery stalk. Each little colored dot is a vein that travels up and down the stalk. Ask the children to try to pull a vein out. A vein is like a string. Celery stalks are very stringy. Each string is a tube that carries liquids up and down the stalk to and from the leaves and to and from the roots. See diagram.

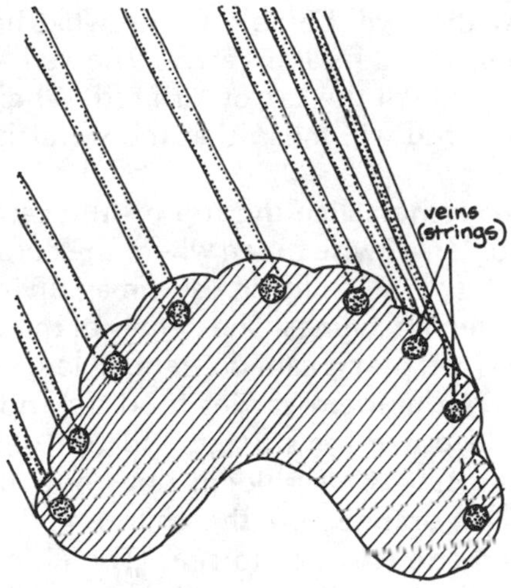

6. Growth Toward Light

Materials A sprouting potato planted in a small container; a shoebox with a lid; a knife; two pieces of cardboard; masking tape.

Procedure

- Place the seedling at one end of the shoebox. Cut a hole at the opposite end of the shoebox. Place two cardboard dividers inside of the box so that a maze is created inside the box. See diagram.
- Show the children the maze box with the sprouted potato. Tell them that you are going to keep the box covered. Explain to the children that this is an experiment to see whether stems and leaves of a plant grow toward sunlight. Ask the children what they think might happen as the potato continues to grow and sprout.
- Remember to have the children water the plant every day, and while the top is off the box, have the children observe how the potato plant's stems are growing.

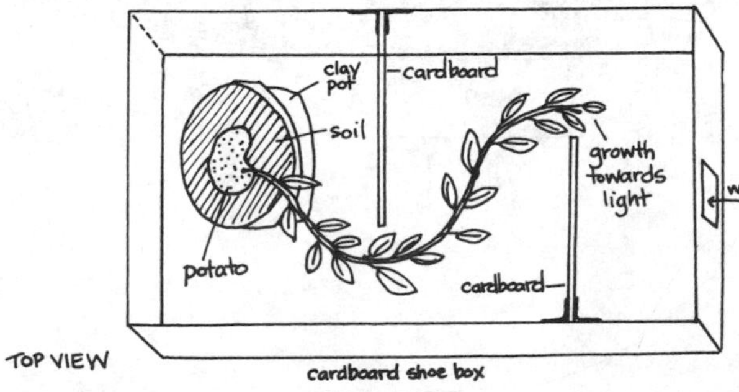

7. The Effect of Gravity on Stem Growth

Materials Three bean seedlings planted in pots; water; string; cardboard; a wire coat hanger.

Procedure

- Show the children the three bean seedlings planted in pots. Tell them you are going to conduct an experiment to see how stems want to grow. Place one plant on its side. Hang one plant upside-down. Leave one plant in a right-side-up position. Cover the plant that hangs upside-down with cardboard so the soil will not fall out. Water every day. See diagram.

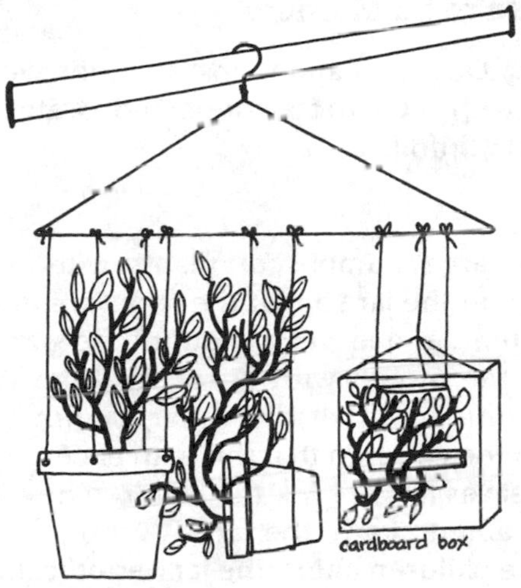

- Have the children observe what happens to the growth of the three plants. The three plants will all grow upwards. Leaves and stems of plants grow away from roots. Roots grow toward gravity.

8. Monocot and Dicot Stems

Materials Assorted leafy stems from various plants such as corn, bamboo, grass, a small tree, rose, forsythia.

Procedure

- Have the children observe the cross-section of the stems. Do they look alike? Are they hollow or woody inside? Do the leaves have a vein pattern that is parallel to the midrib or do the leaves have a netted vein pattern off the midrib? Have the children observe the solid yet scattered pattern of bundles of stringy tubes that run through the corn and the bamboo. Have them observe the distinct circles inside the cross-section of the stems of the small tree, the rose, and forsythia plant. Have them scrape the outside of each of the stems with their fingernail. (They will observe that the small tree and the rose and forsythia plants each have a bright green color underneath their epidermis or outer skin. This bright green layer is the cambium layer. The cambium layer is the layer that grows new xylem and phloem cells, which allows the plant's stem to increase in diameter. Monocots lack a cambium layer. Dicots can be either woody or hollow, but they all have a layer of cambium that can be seen if the outer layer on the stem is scraped off.)

• Have the children classify plants as monocots or as woody or hollow dicots.

VIII. Roots

1. Roots Take up Moisture

Materials Dug-up dandelions or other weeds from the grass with their roots connected; water; a small-necked jar; tinfoil.

Procedure

• Place a large number of plants with their roots connected in the jar so that the roots are in the water and the stems and leaves are out of the water. Fill the jar up to the mouth with water. Seal the top with a piece of tinfoil so that the water cannot evaporate. Explain to the children that this is an experiment to see if water leaves the jar. Ask the children how the water might be able to leave the jar.

• Have the children check the jar periodically over the next few days to see if the water level in the jar has gone down. If it has, it means that the water was absorbed by the roots of the plants.

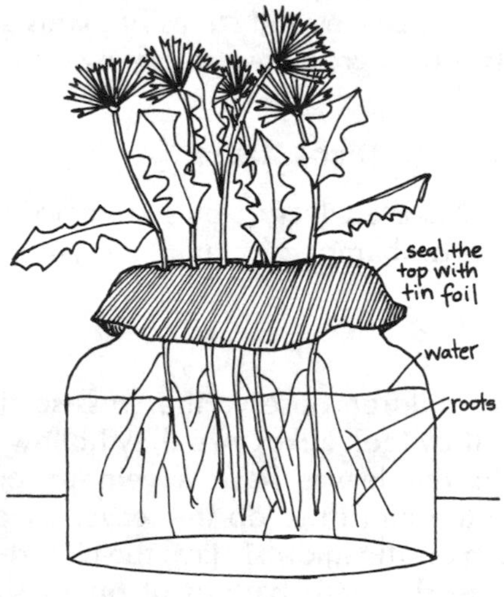

2. Dyeing a Carrot to Trace Moisture Absorption

Materials A carrot; red food color or red ink; water; a clear plastic glass; a knife; a magnifying glass.

Procedure

• Place the carrot in the colored water. Let it stay in the colored water overnight. Explain to the children that this is an experiment to see where the water goes when it enters the carrot. Ask the children if they know how they will be able to see what happens to water when it enters the carrot. The red water will make the inside of the carrot turn red. Wherever they can see, the red will mean that the water has passed through.

• Wait a day, then slice the top off the carrot. Make another cut lengthwise to see where the colored water has gone. Have the children use a magnifying glass to follow the red trace lines. The center of the carrot will be red. This red part is called xylem. Xylem tubes carry water up. The phloem carries food up and down. It carries food down for storage and up for the plant when it needs it. The phloem does not turn red. It remains light orange. Ask the children why coloring the water made it easier to see. (The colored water dyed or stained the inside of the carrot. Plain water just passes through and does not leave a trace mark.)

3. Growing a Root Garden

Materials A beet; a carrot; a parsnip; a radish; a sweet potato; an onion; a potato containing eyes; sand or gravel; water; a bowl; a magnifying glass.

Procedure

• Have a child pour the sand or gravel into the bowl. Place the various roots in the bowl with the gravel so that the root is in the gravel but the top where greens grow is above the gravel. Have another child pour some water into the bowl so that all of the roots touch the water. See diagram.

• Ask the children what they think might grow out of the top of the roots. Keep the water level high enough

ROOT GARDEN

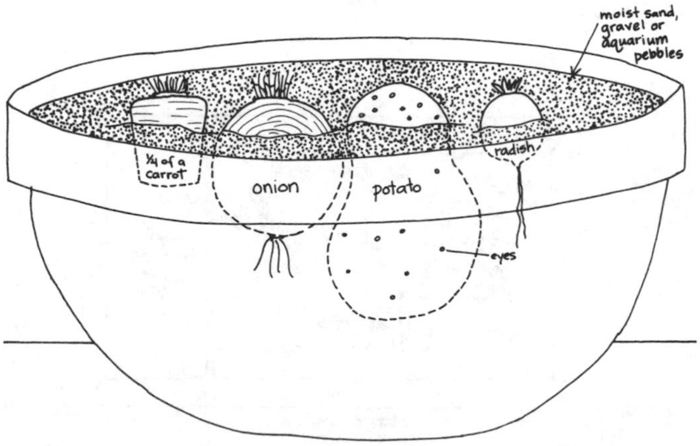

for the roots to reach the water. (After several days green stems and leaves will sprout from the water.) When the roots begin to grow toward the water, pull them out of the soil and observe the roots and root hairs under a magnifying glass.

4. The Effect of Moisture on Roots

Materials A basin; a clay flower pot; water; sprouted bean seeds; sawdust.

Procedure

• Have children spread some sawdust in a basin and place sprouted bean seeds on the sawdust and cover them up with more sawdust. Place a clay flower pot filled with water in the center of the basin. Tell the children this is an experiment to see if roots always grow down or if they can be made to grow sideways. Ask the children what they think will happen.

• In a few days, have a child dust away the sawdust from around the beans. The roots will most likely show a tendency to be growing sideways towards the clay flower pot filled with water rather than just down. See diagram.

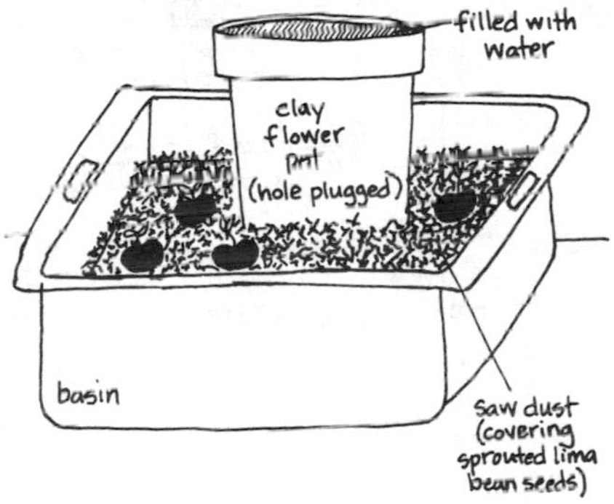

IX. Investigating Flowers and Fruits

1. How Flowers Are Different from Each Other

Materials Assorted fresh flowers like: rose, fuchsia, lily, columbine, dandelion, daffodil, crocus, daisy, violet, sunflower, aster, crysanthemum, or whatever flower is in season; a magnifying glass.

Procedure

• Have the children look at all of the flowers. Review the parts of a flower with them and how flowers are alike because they have the parts that make them flowers. Then discuss how each of the flowers is different. Ask the following kinds of questions:

Are any of the flowers the same color?

Do any of the flowers smell?

Do any of the flowers feel the same?

Are any of them the same size?

Do flowers have the same kinds of petals?
(Some flowers like violets have petals that have two different sizes on the same flower. Some flowers have petals that are joined together.)

Do all of the flowers have sepals?

Are the sepals green on all of the flowers?
(Fuchsia sometimes have brightly colored sepals. The daffodil sepals are the same color as the petals. There are three petals and three sepals. The sepals are on the outside of the petals.)

Do pistils always have one stigma?
(No. Some flowers like the crocus have a pistil with many stigma on the end.)

• Have the children tear a petal off a daisy or a dandelion. They will notice a tiny flower on the side of the petal. The petal is actually a long petal on the tiny flower. A daisy and a dandelion are made up of hundreds of flowers. They give the appearance that they are only one large flower. But each flower is composed of many clusters of tiny flowers. The tiny flowers are easier to see if the flower is pulled apart. Often there are two kinds of tiny flowers on the large flower. The flowers on the outside near the long petals are called ray flowers and are usually different from the flowers on the inside without the long petal. Have the children look at the tiny flowers through the magnifying glass. Help them find the sepal, the pistil with a split stigma, and the ovary on the tiny flowers. See diagram.

• Explain to the children that flowers that are composed of many flowers are called compound or composite flowers, and flowers with only a single

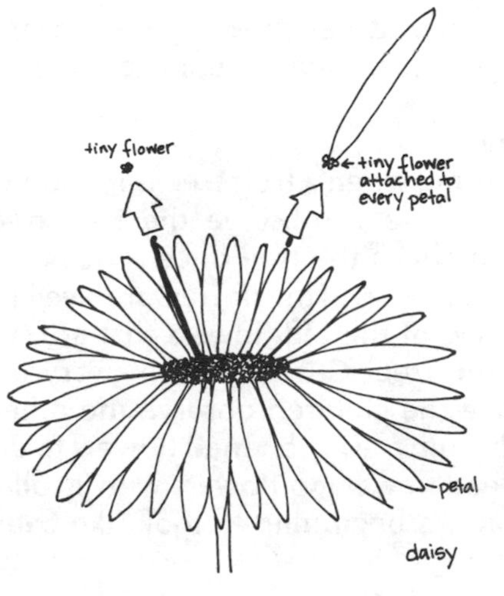

complete flower are called simple flowers. Have the children sort out the flowers according to whether they are simple or compound. See if they can tell by looking at the leaves attached to the stem on the flowers whether the flowers are from monocot or dicot plants. The daffodil and lily are monocots. The rose, columbine, and violet are dicots. The sunflower, aster, chrysanthemum, dandelion, and daisy are composite flowers.

Note: Explain to the children that monocot flowers usually have parts that grow in three and multiples of three. Like the daffodil, which has three sepals and three petals and six stamens, monocots usually have three or six stamens, and leaves with veins that run parallel to each other. Dicots have a netted vein pattern. The dicot flowers usually have parts that grow in fours and fives. Often the leaves of dicots have four or five lobes (look at a maple or sycamore leaf). Palm trees, lilies, and grasses are monocots. Otherwise, most flowering trees, shrubs, herbs and composite flowers are dicots.

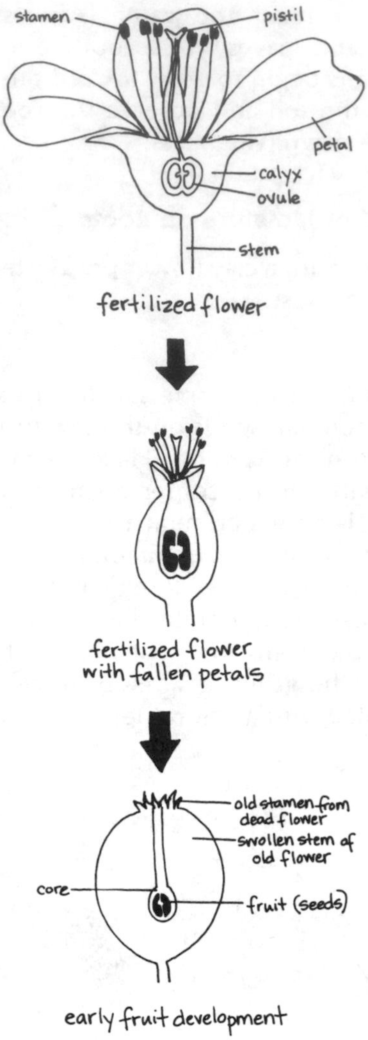

2. Pollen from Different Flowers

Materials A variety of several fresh flowers; a magnifying glass; black paper.

Procedure

- Have children shake each of the flowers onto a different part of the black paper. If pollen does not shake loose, then have them pull off the stamen from the inside of the individual flowers and rub the stamen on the black paper so that pollen grains can be seen.
- Have the children look at the pollen grains through the magnifying glass to see if all of the pollen grains look alike or to see if each flower has a different-looking kind of pollen.

3. Observing the Development of Fruit from a Blossom

Materials A fruit tree growing outside (apple or pear trees are ideal); pruning clipper; a knife.

Procedure

- In the spring when a fruit tree is in bloom, bring the children outside to observe the fruit tree growing. Have them check the tree once a week thereafter to see how the ovaries of the flowers are swelling into fruit.
- Take a few of the old flowers that are swelling into fruit off the tree. Cut a swollen ovary open with a knife. Have the children observe the different stages of growth from freshly opened flowers to dead flowers to very dead flowers to flowers with swollen fruits on them, that are beginning to look like baby fruit. See diagram.

Further Resources

Suggested Books for Children

Dewey Decimal Classification numbers: leaves-581; seeds-581.46; flowers-582.13; trees-582.16.

Adler, David A., *Redwoods Are the Tallest Trees in the World.* New York: Thomas Y. Crowell, 1978.

Aliki, *The Story of Johnny Appleseed.* Englewood Cliffs, New Jersey: Prentice-Hall, 1963.

Allen, Gertrude, *Everyday Trees.* Boston: Houghton Mifflin, 1968.

Baker, Laura, *A Tree Called Mosses* (a story about a giant sequoia tree). New York: Atheneum, 1966.

Bulla, Clyde, *A Tree Is a Plant.* New York: Thomas Y. Crowell, 1973.

Cole, Joanna, *Plants in Winter.* New York: Thomas Y. Crowell, 1973.

Cooper, Elizabeth, *Sweet and Delicious Fruits of Tree, Bush and Vine.* Chicago: Children's Press, 1973.

Cooper, Elizabeth, *A Tree Is Something Wonderful.* Chicago: Children's Press, 1972.

Earle, Olive L., and Michael Kantor, *Nuts.* New York: Morrow, 1976.

Gallab, Edward, *City Leaves, City Trees.* New York: Charles Scribner's Sons, 1972.

Garelick, Mary, *The Tremendous Tree Book.* New York: Scholastic Book Services, 1979.

Gutnik, Martin J., *How Plants Make Food.* Chicago: Children's Press, 1976.

Hammond, Winifred G., *The Riddle of Seeds.* New York: Coward-McCann, 1965.

Healy, Eleanor B., *Trees Are Forever, How They Grow from Seeds to Forests.* Hillside, New Jersey: Enslow, 1978.

Hogan, Paula, *Dandelion.* Milwaukee, Wisconsin: Raintree, 1979.

Hogan, Paula, *Oak Tree.* Milwaukee, Wisconsin: Raintree, 1979.

Jordan, Helene J., *How a Seed Grows.* New York: Thomas Y. Crowell, 1960.

Jordan, Helene J., *Seed by Wind and Water.* New York: Thomas Y. Crowell, 1960.

Kirkpatrick, Rena K., *Look at Leaves.* Milwaukee: Raintree Children's Books, 1978.

Ladyman, Phyliss, *Learning About Flowering Plants.* New York: Young Scott, 1970.

Mahy, Margaret, *Leaf Magic.* New York: Scholastic Book Services, 1977.

Rahn, Joan Elma, *Grocery Store Botany.* New York: Atheneum, 1975.

Rahn, Joan Elma, *How Plants Are Pollinated.* New York: Atheneum, 1975.

Rahn, Joan Elma, *How Plants Travel.* New York: Atheneum, 1973.

Rodgers, Matilda, *First Book of Tree Identification.* New York: Random House, 1951.

Selsam, Millicent E., and Joyce Hunt, *A First Look at Leaves.* New York: Scholastic Book Services, 1976.

Selsam, Millicent E., *The Apple and Other Fruits.* New York: Morrow, 1973.

Selsam, Millicent E., and Joyce Hunt, *A First Look at the World of Plants.* New York: Walker, 1978.

Selsam, Millicent E., *The Maple Tree.* New York: Morrow, 1953.

Selsam, Millicent E., *Seeds and More Seeds.* New York: Harper and Row, 1959.

Selsam, Millicent E., *Play with Trees.* New York: Morrow and Company, 1950.

Stropp, Martha and Charles, *Let's Find Out About Trees.* New York: Watts, 1970.

Tresselt, Alvin, *The Dead End Tree.* New York: Parents Magazine, 1972.

Resource Books for More Ideas

Blough, Glenn O., *Discovering Plants.* New York: McGraw-Hill, 1966.

Brockman, C. Frank, *Trees of North America.* New York: Golden Press, 1968.

Budlong, Ware, and Mark H. Fleitzer, *Experimenting with Seeds and Plants.* New York: Putnam, 1970.

Dowden, Ann O., *The Blossom on the Bough, A Book of Trees.* New York: Thomas Y. Crowell, 1975.

Dowden, Ann Ophelia, *Wild Green Things in the City.* New York: Thomas Y. Crowell, 1972.

Hutchins, Ross E., *The Amazing Seeds.* New York: Dodd, Mead, 1965.

Kieran, John, *An Introduction to Trees.* New York: Doubleday, 1966.

Petrides, George A., *A Field Guide to Trees and Shrubs.* Boston: Houghton, Mifflin, 1958.

Poling, James, *Leaves.* New York: Holt, 1971.

Shuttlesworth, Dorothy E., *The Hidden Magic of Seeds.* Emmaus, Pennsylvania: Rodale Press, 1976.

Zim, Herbert S., *Flowers.* New York: Simon & Schuster, 1950.

Zim, Herbert S., and A. C. Martin, *Trees* (a Golden Guide). Racine, Wisconsin: Western, 1956.

13

ECOLOGY

Objectives

• For children to become more aware of their environment.

• For children to become aware that living things grow and change and adapt to their environment.

• For children to develop an awareness that the Earth has many different biomes (large environments or regions), each of which has distinct characteristics that animals and plants have to adapt to in order to live in them and survive.

• For children to develop an awareness that animals depend on green plants for food and that green plants depend on the sun's energy.

• For children to develop an awareness that all living things are eventually food to other living things. (Even predators are "eaten" by decomposers when they die.)

• For children to develop an understanding of terms such as: predator, prey, food chain, consumer, producer, food web, balance of nature, environment, biome, pollution, poison.

• For children to develop an appreciation for life, its varieties, its delicate balance, and our responsibility as humans to care for the other living things with whom we share the planet.

General Background Information for Parents and Teachers

Ecology The study of relationships between animals and plants, and the relationships between organisms and their physical environment.

Organism Any living plant or animal.

Environment The surroundings of an organism. The physical conditions that affect and influence the growth and development of organisms.

Habitat The place where a particular species of a plant or an animal usually lives.

Niche The area within a habitat occupied by an organism.

Territory A specific area that one or more animals will defend.

Competition The striving or vying between animals for the things needed for survival.

Survive To remain alive or in existence.

Adaptation A characteristic which makes an organism particularly well suited for survival in its environment.

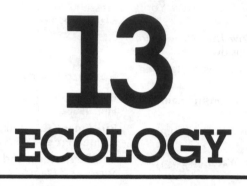

Protective adaptation Adaptation that organisms have developed to protect themselves. Examples are coloration, special anatomical features, very keen senses, speed, and agility.

Characteristic A distinguishing feature or attribute.

Ecosphere or biosphere The total environment of the Earth. It is the largest of the ecosystems. It includes all other ecosystems on Earth.

Biome A major community, covering a large area of the Earth. It contains several ecosystems within its territory.

Ecosystem A complete ecological community together with its physical environment. It is considered a unit that can be studied. An ecosystem consists of producers, consumers, and decomposers.

Producers Green plants that make their own food and release oxygen into the air through photosynthesis. Animals eat the food that producers produce. Producers are the first living things or link in a food chain.

Consumers Consumers are animals. Consumers eat producers. Consumers depend on producers or other organisms for their food.

Decomposers Many fungi, bacteria, and some animals (such as worms, crustaceans, and insects) are decomposers. A decomposer rids the ecosystem of dead producers and consumers by digesting them and breaking them up.

Fungi Yeasts, molds, and mushrooms that live on dead plants and animals or living organisms.

The major biomes on Earth Arctic—tundra; Taiga—evergreen forest, deciduous forest; Savannah—grassland, desert; Tropical Rain Forest—jungle.

Balance of nature Populations in an ecosystem are balanced. An equilibrium is established by the plant and animal populations within a given area.

Endangered species An animal or plant whose numbers are so small it could easily become extinct.

Food chain Consists of a series of animals that eat plants and other animals. It is a "picture" that shows the foods that producers produce and consumers consume.

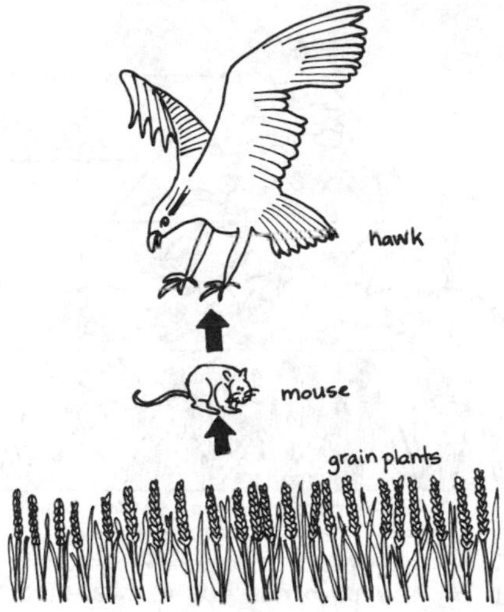

FOOD CHAIN

First order consumer Eats first animal in food chain.

Second order consumer Eats second animal in food chain.

Third order consumer Eats third animal in food chain.

Food web A food web consists of many food chains within an ecosystem. A food web is a "picture" of the food that is produced and consumed in an ecosystem. It shows how the numerous food chains are interwoven to form a weblike pattern.

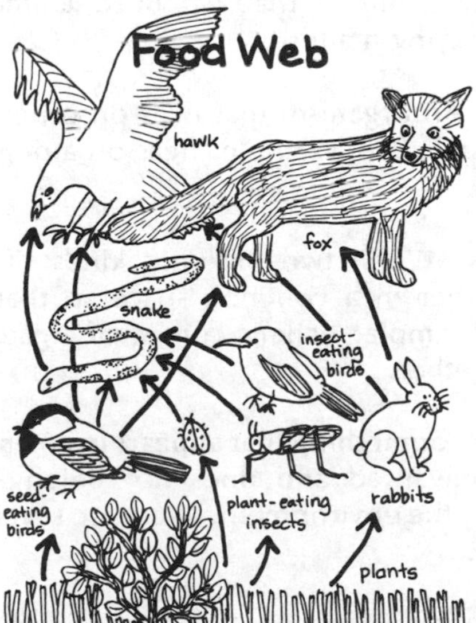

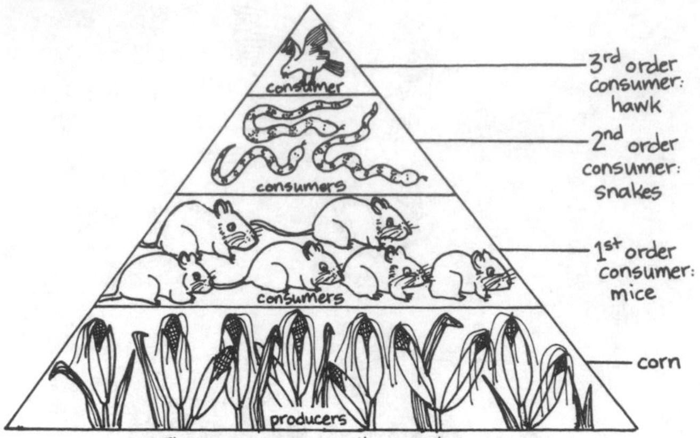
consumer
3rd order consumer: hawk
consumers
2nd order consumer: snakes
consumers
1st order consumer: mice
corn
producers
There are more mice than snakes.
There are more cornplants than mice.
The bottom of the pyramid has more in it.
The top of the pyramid has the least in it.

Food pyramid A broader "picture" that shows the transfer of food energy that takes place in every web and food chain. The pyramid shows the consumers, producers, and decomposers in an ecosystem. There are more decomposers than producers. There are more consumers than producers.

Predator Animals that eat other animals.

Prey Animals that get eaten by predators.

Herbivore Animals that eat only plants. They are often prey to predators.

Carnivore Animals that eat only meat. Carnivore animals are predators.

Omnivore Animals that eat both plants and animals.

Scavenger Animals that eat dead animal flesh or other decaying matter.

Parasite An organism that lives on other organisms that are still alive. Example: fleas on a dog, mistletoe on a tree.

Symbiosis When two different kinds of organisms live together in a common space so that each will benefit. Example: lichens consist of algae and fungi living together.

Pollution Something that appears in an environment that is unwanted and does not belong. It means "dirtying" the environment. There are several kinds of pollution.

Air pollution Air pollution sometimes results in smog. Dirty air caused from too many fuels being burned from factories, furnaces and cars. Sometimes layers of polluted air form that raindrops touch as they fall. The rain is then called acid rain. Some types of air pollution cause acid rain. Acid rain is detrimental to the environment, particularly bodies of water.

Water pollution Dirty water caused by detergents, insecticides, chemicals, oil spills, and sewage that is added to our rivers and streams. Water pollution can affect the ecosystem by poisoning food chains. It also may cause low oxygen content, which is generally harmful to aquatic animals.

Pesticides Kill insects but also add poisons to the atmosphere. The poisons seep into food chains. The food chains eventually affect some of the future consumers.

Solid waste Plastics, trash, junk and litter that are not biodegradeable. The solid waste is unpleasant to look at, and difficult to dispose of.

Noise pollution Too much noise. It is unpleasant to live near it because it drowns out all the natural sounds in nature.

Recycling Reusing materials that are normally thrown away. Recycling helps reduce solid waste and conserve or save some of our natural resources.

Conservation Using natural resources carefully and wisely.

Conservationist A person concerned that the Earth has limited resources and who believes that the resources should not be wasted or used needlessly.

Environmentalist A person who seeks to protect the natural environment from air and water pollution, wasteful use of resources, and excessive encroachments by humans.

Activities and Procedures

I. Observing Our Environment

1. Ecology

Materials The word "ecology" printed on a large word card.

Procedure

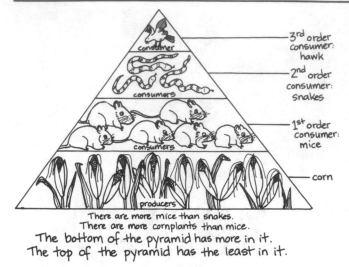

- Ask the children if they know what the word says and if they know what it means.
- Discuss what ecology means. "Eco" comes from the Greek word *oikos,* which means household. "Ology" means the study of something. Ecology is the study of households, or more precisely, the study of house-

holds in nature. Nature is our environment or our surroundings. Plants and animals are members of nature's households. Some of nature's households are very tiny and can live in a drop of pond water. Other households in nature are larger and are contained under a rock or a log; and some households include many households, like a large city. The biggest household in the world is the whole planet. Everyone, including all plants and animals, lives in the world together. Individual households, like the one you live in with your family, are called ecosystems. Ecosystems can be very tiny, or they can be very large and include the whole world. It is a little bit like living in an apartment building with your family. Your family has a space in the building, along with several other families in the building who have different spaces. You all live on the same block, on a space of the block. Several other families live on the block too in other buildings which occupy other spaces on the block. The block is one of many blocks that make up your community. Each building is made up of many possible ecosystems. Each building is like an ecosystem; so is each block, and so is the entire community like an ecosystem. An ecosystem can be as large or as small as you want it to be. An ecosystem includes the immediate environment or surroundings and the plants and animals that live in those surroundings. It must include plants that produce food, animals that consume food, and bacteria to destroy and eat dead and rotten things. We all share the earth together, and depend on each other. When we live in an apartment, we live in an incomplete ecosystem.

- Ask the children if they could survive by themselves in an apartment building with their families. Explain that their food comes from outside of their building and from outside of their block. They probably could not survive by themselves with their families. They depend on the farmers who grow food outside of their building and outside of their block. Even though their food can be purchased at a grocery store, it may have been shipped from far away, and it does not grow in large enough quantities on their block to feed everyone who lives in their apartment house.
- Explain that ecology is the study of the interdependency of households in nature. Ecologists are scientists who study the interdependency and relationships of nature's households to one another.

2. Nature Walks

Materials Paper bags.

Procedure

- Tell the children you are all going to go outside to observe the environment and to find plants and animals that live in the outside household. Explain that the environment means the surroundings. Discuss what the surroundings are like inside. There is a roof, a floor, walls, and windows. The temperature can be adjusted, the lights can be turned on or off, windows and doors can be opened or closed. Ask the children how the outside environment is different from the inside environment. Ask the children the following kinds of questions:

Can the temperature be adjusted outside?
(If you stand under a tree, it's cool. If you stand in the sun, it is warmer. But the temperature cannot be controlled.)

Can the lights be turned on and off?
(No, the sun comes up and the sun goes down, and clouds sometimes block the sunlight.)

Can breezes be let in or can doors be closed outside?
(No, the wind blows, but not always. Doors cannot be closed, but animals can hide under things like rocks and logs.)

Is there a roof or a floor outside?
(Yes, but a different kind of roof and floor. The ground is the floor and the sky or the thick trees are the roof.)

Are there any walls outside?
(Only natural walls. They do not look like walls. But a pond is like a wall. Animals that cannot swim cannot go into it. The pond becomes a natural barrier for some animals.)

If we lived outside, would we be comfortable?
(We would probably have to make some adjustments to adapt to living outside.)

- Take the children outside. Advise them to be quiet so that they can listen for sounds in the trees and in the grass. If they place their ears on the ground or on tree trunks, they may be able to hear sounds nearby. Help them to identify the sounds that they hear.
- Ask the children what other senses they can use on their walk. Ask them how many of nature's colors they can find. Pick some pine needles, some bark from the ground, an aromatic flower, and so on, and have the children smell the aroma of each. As you come across things on the walk, see if they have odors. Help the children label or identify the odors as earthy, or floral, or sweet, or putrid. As the children smell odors, have them use their hands to touch the different textures. Help them label or identify the things they feel as being something that feels: wet or dry, prickly, smooth or rough, sticky, warm or cool, moist or damp.
- Have the children look under rocks, leaves, and logs to see what lives underneath, and replace whatever they disturb or turn over, so that the animals that live under them will not be disturbed.
- If the walk is taken in the fall, have the children collect the colorful autumn leaves that have fallen on

the ground. Have them place the leaves in their paper bags. When they arrive back inside, have them sort the leaves by size, color, width, or length. Have them look for textures on the leaves or places on the surface of the leaves where insects took bites or caused other damage.

- Ask the children to collect small things that interest them on the walk. When the children are indoors again, have them make scrapbooks or collages of things they have gathered on their walk.

3. Watering the Soil

Materials Water; a water sprinkling can.

Procedure

- Take the children outside to a wooded area, where the foliage is very thick, and where a path is available so that they will not be walking through poison ivy. Ask the children what they think happens to the trees and the soil when it rains. Take a water-sprinkling can with you on the walk. Ask the children what they think happens to the trees and soil when it rains lightly. Stop in front of some foliage near the path. Tell the children you are going to pretend that it is raining. Explain that the sprinkling can is filled with water, and that you are going to choose a child to water the leaves on the tree so that they can see what happens to the rain water when it falls on the tree. Have the children observe what happens to the water after it comes out of the can. (The water will stick to the leaves and will run from one leaf to the next. Not everything will get wet. Chances are that unless there is a heavy downpour, the ground will receive only a little bit of moisture. The leaves will keep most of the water from reaching the ground.)
- Have a child water the soil directly and have the children observe what happens. (If the dead leaves are watered, the leaves will protect the soil. If the soil is watered directly, some of the soil may wash away.)
- Ask the following kinds of questions:

Does everything get wet?
(Some things get less wet than others. Trees protect some objects and things from getting as wet as those objects and things that are exposed to the rain without any protection.)

Does water get absorbed by the soil?
(Yes, the leaves on the surface help absorb some of the water and keep the soil from washing away.)

If the rain is very light, will water reach the soil?
(Some of it will, but most of the water will be caught by the leaves on the trees, and some of the moisture will be absorbed by the loose dead leaves on the ground.)

How do the dead leaves protect the soil?
(They help absorb moisture like a sponge, and they keep the water from washing away the soil.)

4. Seasonal Nature Walk

Materials Paper bags.

Procedure

- Take the same walk that you took in Activity I, Procedure 2 as the seasons change. Take the walk in the fall when the deciduous leaves begin to fall, and again in the middle of winter when everything appears to be asleep or dead, and again in the beginning of spring when the buds are opening up, and later when all of the buds have opened.
- Have the children observe some of the changes that are taking place as the seasons change. In the fall, many birds are migrating south. In the autumn, the plants are storing food, making and scattering seeds, losing their leaves, making and forming waxy coats on their buds. In the spring, the rains fall, the days become longer, the buds swell and sap begins to run through the trees, bulbs bloom, birds migrate north, and insects emerge.
- Have the children collect interesting materials in paper bags for nature collages or scrapbooks about their nature walk.

5. Adopt a Tree

Materials A deciduous tree.

Procedure

- Have the children adopt a tree outside and observe the seasonal changes that happen to it in the course of a year. What animals live in or off of the tree? What insects make their homes near or in the tree? Do birds nest in the tree or use its branches to perch on? What birds use the tree? What do the leaves look like? Where do the biggest leaves grow? Where do the smallest leaves grow? How much new growth took place on the branches? When are the seeds and fruits made by the tree? What happens to the seeds and fruits?
- Decorate the tree with seasonal decorations (such as paper pumpkins, hearts, or colored eggs). Take in the dead wood and leaves from the tree to observe.
- Force budded twigs from the tree to sprout in the winter by soaking them in water.

6. Seed-collecting Walk

Materials Paper bags.

Procedure

• In the fall, take the children on a seed-collecting walk. Try to identify the various seed cases and seeds, where they came from, and how they got where they got (by water, wind, animal, or by popping out of a pod and falling). Have the children collect seeds in paper bags.

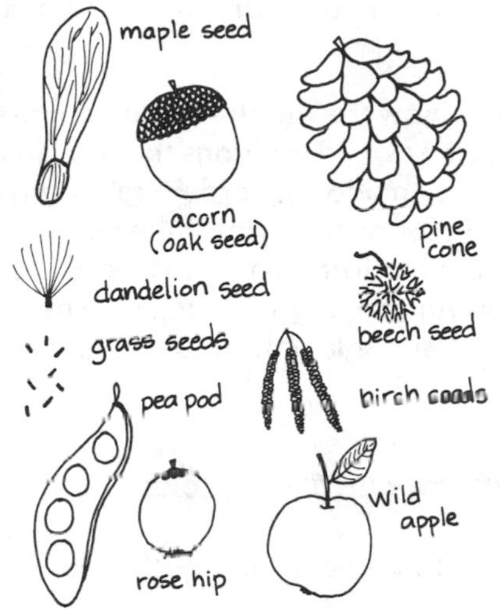

• Have children try to sprout them in moist soil inside. (Not all of them will sprout. Some need to be exposed to a cold winter before they sprout. See Germinating Seeds Procedure, page 183.) Discuss with the children why some seeds have a delayed sprouting. How does this help the plant? (If it sprouted before winter set in, it would die.)

7. Animal Track Walk

Materials None.

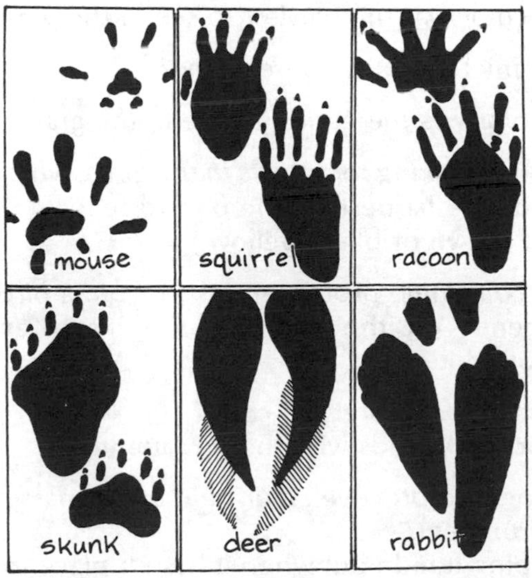

Procedure Take the children along a path that is frequented by animals, near a pond where there is mud, or on a field, or at the seashore. Have them look for animal footprints in the mud or along the sand, or in the snow if it snows. Help the children identify the animal that made the tracks.

II. Adaptations

1. Living Things Grow and Change

Materials Old photographs of children or their families.

Procedure

• Show children the old pictures of themselves or of their families. Discuss how the people in the pictures and they themselves have changed since the pictures were taken. They have probably grown up or changed since the pictures were taken. Discuss how they are not able to wear some of the same clothes they were wearing in the picture because their bodies have become larger, and they wear a different size now.

• Explain that all living things grow and change. When animals and plants change it is called adaptation. Adaptation means that a plant or an animal changes to fit into its environment so it can survive. If a plant or animal cannot change and adapt to its environment, it might mean that the plant or animal will die, and that it might become extinct as a species. The more versatile and flexible a plant or animal is with its growth, the more likely it is to survive.

2. Adaptability of Dandelions

Materials A cut lawn with dandelions and a field of tall grass with dandelions.

Procedure Have the children observe the dandelions growing in the two places—the lawn and the field of uncut grass. They will observe that the flower stalk is much longer on the dandelions in the tall grass than it is on the dandelions growing on the cut grass. In the cut grass, the dandelion grows with a very short flower stalk, and the leaves spread out flat. In the tall grass, the leaves grow upward towards the sun. Ask the children why a plant grows differently in different places. (Many plants like the dandelion are versatile or flexible and can adapt and change. Many plants can change their sizes and their forms as they grow.)

3. Specialized Body Parts for Protection

Materials Assorted pictures of animals with protective parts like claws, teeth, beaks, armor, feet with hooves (from wildlife magazines or picture books).

Procedure

- Show children the assorted pictures of the animals and discuss the special parts each animal has to protect itself from its enemies. Discuss the following: claws for scratching and climbing; feet with hooves for kicking and climbing rocks; armor or shells that protect animals like turtles and armadillos; teeth for digging, tearing, cutting, grinding, and puncturing other animals; horns for stabbing and digging.
- Have the children identify a part on each animal that helps protect it from other animals. Or you can describe to the children how each animal or set of animals protects itself from its enemies. For example:

This animal has a very sharp beak. What animal is it?

This animal gives off an unpleasant odor. What animal is it?

This animal has sharp teeth. What animal am I thinking of?
(Any carnivore.)

This animal can fly. What animals can do that?
(Many insects along with most birds and all bats.)

This animal has very sharp claws.

This animal swims very fast.

This animal has sharp spines.

This animal has horns.

This animal stays in large groups or herds of its own kind.

This animal has large and powerful legs.

This animal has tough, scaly skin.

This animal has eyes placed on the sides of its head so that it can see all around its body.
(Rabbit.)

These animals are hard to see because they blend into their surroundings.

This animal becomes very still when it senses an enemy is near.
(Rabbits, squirrels, snakes.)

This animal becomes very noisy when it senses an enemy is near.
(Monkeys, some birds, and rattlesnakes.)

- Have children create a make-believe animal and describe its parts and special adaptations.

4. Specialized Protective Survival Tricks and Habits

Materials Pictures of migrating birds in flight, of bears in caves hibernating, of animals that play dead like the opossum and hog nose snake, animals that mimic others like the viceroy and monarch butterfly or the coral snake and the king snake. (These kinds of pictures can usually be found in nature magazines.)

Procedure Show the pictures to the children. Discuss the special tricks or adaptations that the animals in the pictures have made in order to survive. Discuss mimicry of color or behavior, hibernation and migration for protection from extreme temperature changes, playing dead, and hiding in a shell as methods of protection and adaptation to the environment.

5. Camouflage and Toothpicks

Materials A box of colored toothpicks.

Procedure

- Have children sort out the toothpicks into different piles according to their color. Have them count each pile and record how many toothpicks are in each pile. Then have the children mix all of the toothpicks together again and toss them outside on a grassy area. Then collect them.
- Tell the children you are going to give them five minutes to find and collect as many toothpicks as they can find. After the five minutes are up tell the children to sort out the toothpicks they have found and to count each colored pile. Ask the following kinds of questions:

Which color was the hardest to see in the grass?

How many toothpicks were found?

What color was the easiest to see in the grass?

If birds are looking for insects in the grass, which color would be the hardest for the bird to see?
(Green, brown or black, yellow.)

Would color help protect an insect from a bird?
(It depends on the color of the insect and the background it is on.)

What color is a protective color?
(A color that blends with the surroundings.)

How does a protective color help an animal adapt to its environment?
(By helping it hide out when it has no place to hide.)

6. Beak and Feet Adaptations on Birds

Materials Pictures and models of various birds.

Procedure

- Have children observe pictures or models of birds. Have them notice the different kinds of beaks that birds have. Help the children see the differences between the kind of beak that a woodpecker has, and the kind of beak that a duck has. The woodpecker's beak is useful in trees for drilling to obtain insects in the wood, and the duck's beak is useful in the water as a shovel to find food in the mud. Have them look at a spoonbill on a flamingo, which is useful as a strainer to separate food from the mud, and at the short, strong beak on a sparrow, which is useful for cracking nuts and seeds.

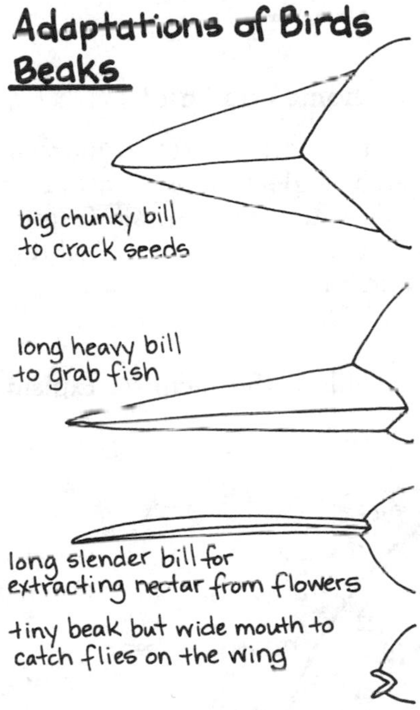

- Have children observe the different kinds of feet that birds have. Birds can have feet that are adapted for wading, climbing, perching, or grasping. Birds that live near water and swim like the duck have webbed feet. Birds that live in trees and need to perch on branches have feet with three toes in front and one long toe in back. Birds that climb trees like the woodpecker have two toes in front and two toes in back. Owls and hawks are animals of prey. They have clawlike talons on their feet for attacking animals that they eat. See diagram.

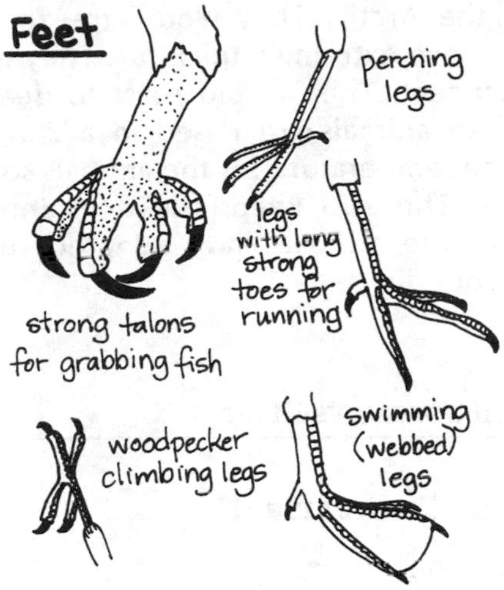

- Explain that birds can be divided into groups by the way their bodies look, or by their size, or by where they live, or by whether they migrate, or by what they eat. Some birds, like vultures, only eat dead animals. Others, like the hawk, eat other animals and small birds. Some birds, like the woodpecker, live on insects, and other birds, like sparrows, live on seeds. Some birds hunt fish with their spearlike beaks. Birds eat a wide variety of foods, and have many adaptations to survive. They can live in different climates by migrating when the temperature does not suit them. Most birds that migrate go to warmer places in the winter and migrate back to cooler places in the summer.

7. Adaptations for Extremes in Temperatures

Materials Pictures of animals that live in the desert and pictures of animals that live in the Arctic.

Procedure

- Have children compare the adaptations that plants and animals have to make in a desert with those that plants and animals would have to make in the Arctic. Discuss how the temperature in a desert is very hot and how the temperature in the Arctic is very cold. Ask the children how they themselves cope with a very hot day or with a very cold day. Discuss how their clothes in the middle of winter on a snowy day differ from the kinds of clothes they would wear if they were to go swimming.
- Explain that reptiles live in the desert and that they are cold-blooded animals. Having cold blood means that the animal's body temperature changes with its surroundings. These animals would not be able to

survive in the Arctic. They would freeze to death. Polar bears have extremely thick fur. They even have fur on their feet. They would roast to death in the desert. When animals are raised in a zoo, the zoo regulates the temperature for the animals so that they can survive. The zoo keeps the environment at a temperature the animals have adapted to in their natural surroundings.

III. How Environments Differ

1. What Is an Environment?

Materials None.

Procedure

• Explain to the children that an environment is all of the conditions that act on a plant or an animal. It is the physical conditions like the amount of water, sunlight, temperature, and condition of the soil. It is also things like population within the area and the communities of other living and nonliving things.

• Discuss with the children their environment at home, their environment at school, and the environment outside in the yard or inside of a car. Ask the children to think about how these environments differ and how they are alike. Remind children that plants and animals have adapted to certain environments. Ask the following kinds of questions:

How does our environment differ from the kind of environment other animals would experience, such as: an alligator, a whale, a frog, a penguin?

What are some of the conditions that keep all kinds of plants and animals from being able to live in your house, at school, outside, and in your car?
(Temperature, amount of water, sunlight, soil, space, your parents' consent.)

• Explain to the children that there are various kinds of environments. They differ from one another. Not all environments have the same temperature, rainfall, or sunlight. Biologists disagree as to how many different kinds of environments exist. But there are at least six. These large environments or regions are called biomes. A biome covers a large area or region of the earth and contains many communities with many populations. The amount of rain, the amount of sunlight, the temperature, and the soil are similar throughout most of a biome's territory, which makes it possible for certain specific animals and plants to live in them.

2. The Major Biomes on Land

Materials Pictures of: an Arctic–tundra area, a taiga–evergreen area, a deciduous forest, a grassland or savannah, a desert, a tropical rain forest; old nature magazines; paper; crayons; a physical relief globe of the Earth; a prism.

Procedure

• Show the children the pictures. Explain that these

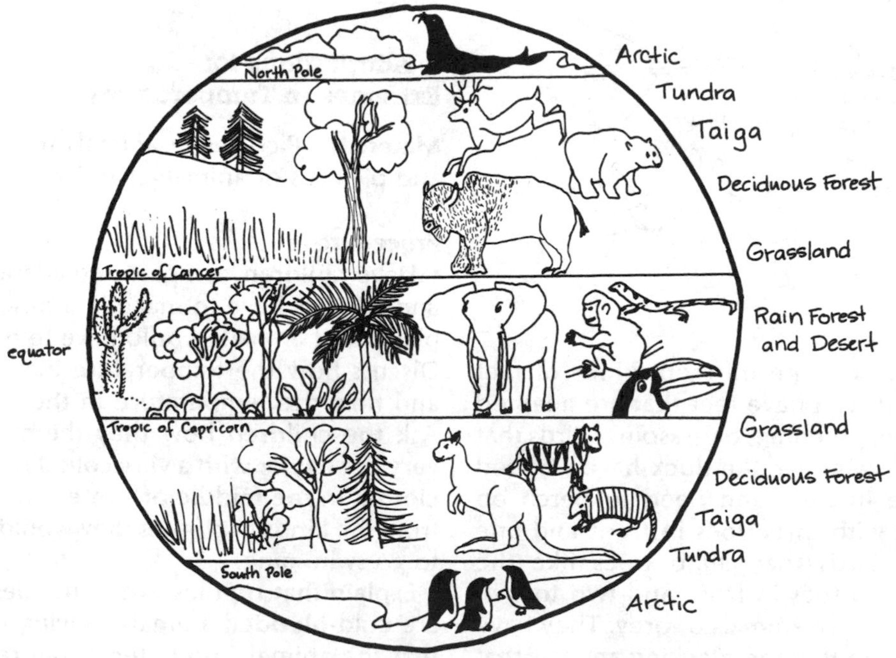

pictures represent the different environments on the Earth. Ask the children what kinds of animals would live in each of these environments. Have them draw pictures of some animals or cut animal pictures out of magazines. Have the children place their animal pictures on the appropriate environmental picture. Ask them which kind of environment probably has the most variety of living things. Which environment would be easiest for them to live in? Which kinds of plants and animals seems to live in the most environments (simple plants and animals like insects, algae, and moss).

• Show them the globe of the Earth. Explain that the globe is a model of the Earth. Show them the imaginary line that is called the Equator. It is very warm on and near the Equator. The ends of the Earth have ice caps and are called the North Pole and the South Pole. Explain that both poles of the earth are very cold. The environments of the Earth take up large areas on the Earth. Show them the deserts, and the oceans and lakes, and the mountainous areas of the Earth on the globe. Explain that the environments change gradually. They do not go from one extreme to another. Tropical rain forests and the Arctic poles are far away from each other. The environments in the different biomes change gradually. Some environments on the edges of two distinct areas blend together. Their boundaries intermesh so that it is hard to know when you have left one environment and entered another. The animals and plants that live in boundary areas are adapted to both environments. For example, ponds and woods often appear together, as do grasses and trees.

• Show the children the prism. Have a child catch a light beam with it. Explain that biomes are like a color spectrum made from a prism. The various colors appear side by side and though the colors may blend at the edges, each of the bands of color still has its distinct hue. The hues tend to be more intense in the center of the bands and become less intense on the edges. On the edges, the colors blend. Each hue is like a biome. At the edges of biomes, biomes blend together as the colors do in a spectrum. The rainbow or spectrum of colors consists of many bands or parts. Each color represents a part of the spectrum just as each biome represents a separate kind of environment on the Earth. All of the biomes are part of the whole. Each biome affects all of the other biomes.

3. The Tundra

Materials A globe of the Earth; pictures of Eskimos, caribou, lichen, huskies, polar bears, and other forms of Arctic life; ice; thermometer; fresh lichen on a rock or on a piece of bark.

Procedure

• Show children the globe. Ask them what they think the climate and environment would be like at the North Pole. Ask the following kinds of questions:

Would the snow and ice ever melt?
(Yes, briefly in the summer, but the soil that is six inches below the surface is permanently frozen.)

Would the summer be warm?
(The temperatures are still near freezing in the summer.)

How long would the summer last?
(Very briefly. Plants grow for two months all year.)

How cold would it get in winter?
(Extremely cold, below freezing.)

Is there a lot of food?
(Food is scarce because the soil is frozen most of the year.)

How do plants and animals survive in Arctic winter?
(Animals survive by migrating south to warmer climates, or by staying and growing a white fur for camouflage, and an extra thick coat of fur for protection from the extreme cold. Plants remain small. There are no trees in the tundra.)

What would human beings have to wear in the winter?
(Eskimo-like clothes or other warm outfits.)

• Pass the ice around for the children to feel. Place a thermometer in the ice so they can see how cold the temperature of ice is on the thermometer. Have them hold the ice until their fingers sting. Explain that when our skin is not protected in cold weather, we can get frostbite. Frostbite stings like a burn and numbs our sense of touch. Animals in the tundra have to adapt to the tundra to survive. Have the children study the photographs of animal and plant life in the tundra and discuss the adaptations that each has made to survive.

• Show the children the lichen. Explain that a lot of lichen grows in the tundra.

Note: Lichen is really two plants: an alga and a fungus growing together. The fungus holds water, but cannot make food. The alga can make food but has no roots. So the alga uses the water from the fungus. When two organisms live together and are useful to each other, they have a symbiotic relationship.

• Explain that very few trees can grow in the tundra. The ground is too frozen for roots to grow. Also explain that only a few birds live in the tundra, but many birds migrate to the Arctic from other biomes for the short summer.

4. The Taiga or Evergreen Forest

Materials Freshly cut twigs from spruce, pine, fir, and cedar trees, and their seed cones. Pictures of: moose, crossbill birds, red-backed salamander, porcupine, mink, wolverine, black bear, lynx, rabbit, beaver.

Procedure

• Show children the twigs from the freshly cut trees. Have them notice the differences in the needles of each kind of tree, and the differences in their seed cones. Have the children open up or shake a cone so they can see the seeds.

• Explain to the children that forests of evergreen trees border the tundra area. They are sometimes called coniferous forests because most of the trees grow their seeds in cones. The taiga area has very cold winters, and a small amount of underbrush that grows near the ground. As the needles of the trees fall to the ground, they form a layer of new soil. The needles make the soil very acidic. Evergreens grow well in the acidic soil. The evergreen trees are very narrow and grow very close to each other. They lose their bottom branches because the bottom branches do not receive much light. A canopy of leaves forms on top of the trees, which prevents most sunlight from reaching the ground. The largest animal that lives in this biome is the moose.

• Explain that there are different niches in the forest. A niche is a place an animal lives and feeds. Show children the pictures of animals as you talk about them. Some animals like the salamander live on the cool, damp ground. Other animals, like birds, divide the forest into vertical parts. Some of the species of birds live in the treetops, while other species of birds live on the mid-branches of the trees, and still other bird species live off the low scrubs. The crossbill birds have a beak designed for eating seeds from cones. Some animals come out only at night, while others come out only during the day. Some animals are herbivores and eat only plants or seeds, while other animals are carnivores and eat only other animals like insects, worms, and small mammals. Some of the animals are scavengers and eat only dead things that are left. Each population of animals has a different menu of food to eat. There are a great variety of animals that live in the taiga biome but they do not all compete with each other for the same food.

• Have children discuss any physical adaptations they may have noticed about the animals as they are discussed. Ask the children what makes it possible for these animals to adjust or to survive the winter (some of the animals migrate or hibernate).

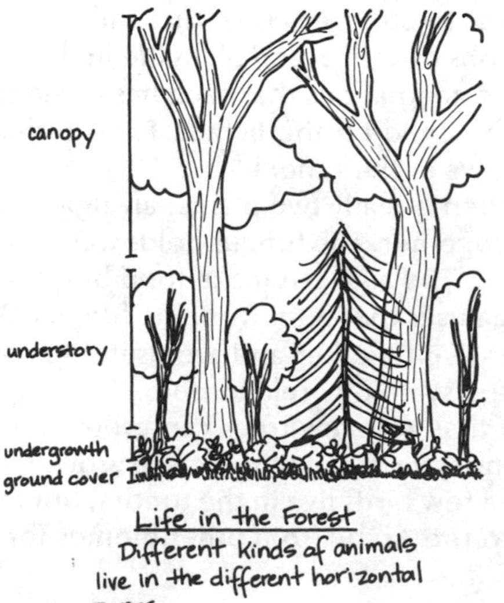

Life in the Forest
Different kinds of animals live in the different horizontal zones.

5. The Deciduous Forest

Materials Pictures of: deer, black bear, fox, racoon, mice, squirrel, chipmunk, opossum, turtle, toad, frog, owl, hawk, crow, bluejay, woodpecker, assorted insects, assorted decomposers on a log, the remains of a forest fire, a pond, a meadow.

Procedure

• Explain that deciduous forests are found in most of the eastern half of the United States. The temperature and the rainfall vary with the four seasons. However, the amount of rainfall is usually plentiful and a huge variety of plants and animals live in this biome. Deciduous forests are found between the evergreen forests and the grasslands or oceans. Most of the trees in a deciduous forest shed their leaves in the fall, and stay dormant and lifeless-looking all winter. Most of the animals in a deciduous forest live there all year, except for some of the birds that migrate to other biomes, and some of the animals that hibernate.

• Have the children think of all of the animals they can that live in a deciduous forest. Show them the pictures of animals that live in a deciduous forest. Then have them compare those animals with the ones that live in the tundra and in an evergreen forest. Talk about their differences.

• Explain to the children that there are a few evergreen trees that grow in the deciduous forest and a few deciduous trees that grow in the evergreen forest. Ask them if they can explain why this happens. (There is no clear line between biomes. There are a few hardy plants that can survive and adapt in an alien environment, but their population remains small. If the environment in a biome changes, they will either die out or they will be able to produce seeds for more of their own kind with the special adaptations they have.)

• Show the children a picture of a forest that caught on fire, and a large pond or swamp. Explain that a deciduous forest often starts out as a swamp or rebuilds

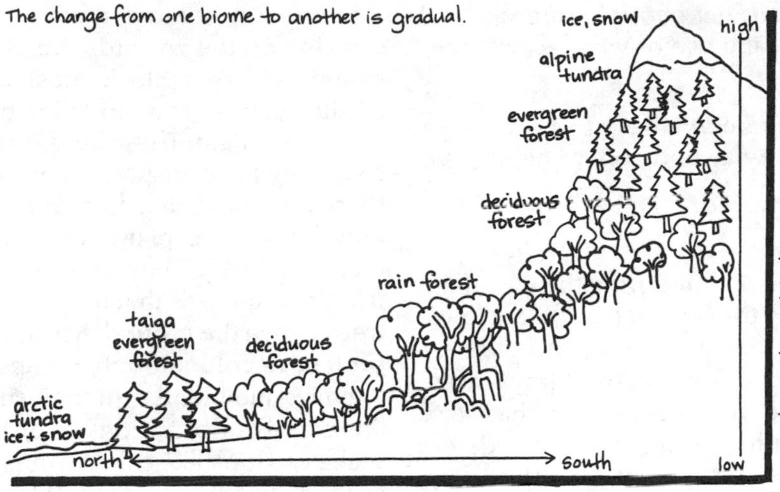

itself after a fire. Over time, the swamp evaporates and fills up with sediments and dead materials. Eventually the swamp becomes a meadow. Seeds blow in from nearby trees and the meadow becomes full of seedlings. Eventually, the trees become a forest. The whole process of change from burnt-out forest, swamp, or pond to forest takes place slowly and gradually over a long period of time, thousands and thousands of years. The process of change is slow and hard to see, but the surface of the Earth is constantly changing.

6. The Grasslands

Materials A physical relief globe of the Earth; pictures of animals that live in grasslands (mainly grazing animals, both wild and domestic); old nature magazines; paper and crayons; a hand trowel.

Procedure

• Show children the globe. Have the children locate the ice caps. Then show them the mountains and the grassland areas on the globe. Explain that the grasslands are usually located between deserts and forests. They are usually flat and have soil that can produce good grasses and few trees. Many farms are located in the Midwest grasslands of the United States. The area is called the Great Plains. Sometimes a grassland biome is called a prairie. Grasses help prevent erosion of soil. The roots of grasses help hold the earth in place. In Africa, the large grasslands are called the savannah. Many animals that graze on grasses live in the grassland biome.

• Ask the children what kinds of animals they think would live in the Great Plains of the United States and which kind of animals would live in the African savannahs. Explain that the Great Plains has a lot of farms, and that a lot of the African lands are still natural and wild. Have the children look at pictures of the kinds of animals that live in grasslands. Have them compare the differences between wild and domestic animals. Discuss the importance of animals living in herds for protection. Have the children cut out pictures of animals from magazines or draw pictures of animals that live in the American Great Plains and those that live in the African and Indian grasslands. Examples of animals that live in the grasslands are bison, antelope, deer, zebra, ostrich, elephant, giraffe, snake, termites, grasshoppers, ants, prairie dogs, gophers, mountain lions, coyotes, fox, weasel, lion, tiger, and domestic farm animals like horses, cows, and sheep that graze on the land.

• Take the children outside to a grassy area. Have them use a hand trowel to dig up some earth with grass and roots of grasses. Have them hold the grass and shake the earth loose. Have the children notice how the soil clings to the roots and how the roots help hold the soil together. Have the children examine the blades of grass. Ask them to observe whether or not all of the blades of grass have the same leaf, or whether there are a variety of grasses growing together. Also have the children observe whether any tiny animals are living in the soil under the grass in or near the roots of the grass, or on the grass.

7. The Desert

Materials Pictures of deserts and desert life; tiny cactus plants.

Procedure

• Show the children the pictures of the desert and of desert life. Ask the children how a desert is different from a forest or a grasslands or tundra biome. Ask the following kinds of questions:

How often do you think it rains in the desert?
(By definition, a desert receives less than 10 inches of rain a year.)

How do plants and animals get enough water to live?
(They have adapted to make use of what water there is.)

What is the temperature like in a desert?
(Extremely hot during the day and cool at night.)

What kind of soil is in a desert?
(Sandy and rocky soil.)

• Explain that because it is so hot during the day, most desert animals rest during the heat of the day and look for food in the evening or at twilight. Most desert plants store water in their stems and have tiny leaves. Some desert plants have very deep roots that seek water from deep beneath the ground. Most desert plants also have a tough waxy coat and thorns or prickly parts to help protect them from harm. Animals that live in the desert get most of their water from eating other plants or animals. The camel can store water in its hump. As it uses up its water, its hump becomes smaller.
• Show children the small cactus plants and have them observe the special adaptive features that the plants have for living in the desert.

8. The Rain Forest

Materials A globe; pictures of jungle life.

Procedure
• Show the children the globe. Explain to them that the area around the center of the Earth near the Equator has a very warm climate. When a region is very warm and receives a lot of rainfall, it is called a tropical rain forest. A tropical rain forest has a huge number of plants and animals. The climate is warm and moist and steamy every day of the year. Animals do not have to adapt to the extremes of temperatures as they do in other biomes. They just have to adapt to warmth and rain. The biome is like a giant greenhouse. *Note:* It is strongly recommended that you take the children on a field trip to a greenhouse that grows tropical plants and to a zoo or pet store that has tropical birds or fish. The rain forest biome is difficult to experience without feeling the temperature and humidity of the biome, and seeing how bright the colors of the animals are or how big the leaves are on some of the plants. It has such a lush and exotic biome that pictures alone are not enough.
• Show the children the pictures of jungles. Explain that life exists at lots of different vertical levels in the rain forest: on the ground, in the low bushes, in the lower and upper canopy of trees. A tropical rain forest has a larger variety of living things growing and living in it than any other biome. It is the most populated of all the biomes. It is fairly easy to walk on the ground in a rain forest because there is very little underbrush growing on the ground. The plants and vines and the canopy of trees block most of the sunlight. Some smaller plants grow on taller plants so that they can receive sunlight. These kinds of plants never touch the soil. They have adapted to grow without soil because there is so much moisture, sunlight, and warmth in the rain forest. The plants in a rain forest grow to an enormous size. They compete for sunlight. Most of the larger animals that live in the rain forest live in the trees above the ground. Most of them have adopted a protective coloration that helps them hide from their enemies and blend with their surroundings. Often the limbs and tail of a monkey or the hanging body of a snake can look like a thick vine. The spots on a leopard can look like the shadows of leaves. Many insects look like twigs, flowers, or leaves.

IV. Food Chains and Webs

1. What Did You Eat Today?

Materials None.

Procedure
• Ask the children what they ate for breakfast and lunch, and what they think they will eat for supper. Discuss with them where their food came from. Have them trace where the food was before it arrived at their house or at the grocery store. If they ate a cereal for breakfast or a bread for lunch, talk about how the cereal or bread became cereal or bread. Ask the children the following kinds of questions:

Where did the flour come from?

How did the wheat or grain become flour?

Where did the wheat or grain come from before it became flour?

• Explain that green plants are called producers. Green plants are able to produce their own food supply from the sun's energy. Green plants provide food or energy for animals. Animals cannot produce their own food. Animals are consumers or users and choosers of food. Not all animals eat plants, but some animals do. Animals that eat other animals are eating animals that grew from eating plants. So all animals are dependent on plants even if they do not eat plants. If it were not for the green plants, the herbivores or plant-eating animals would not grow up to be food for the carnivores or meat-eating animals.
• Explain that meat-eating animals eat other animals for food. Ask the children if they eat meat. Discuss where the meat they eat comes from. Explain that

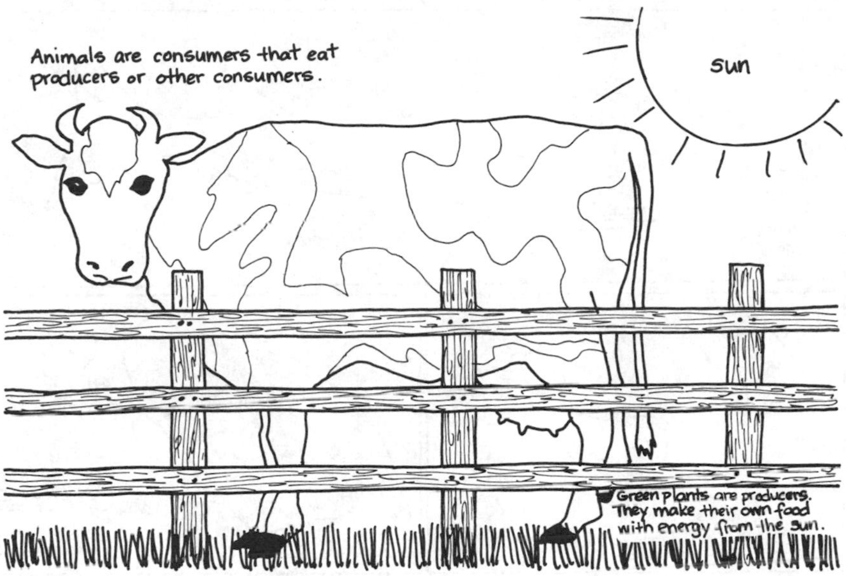

when we eat fish, chicken, lamb, pork, or beef, we are eating animals that have died. Ask the children what kinds of food chickens, sheep, and cattle eat. Explain that these animals eat plants. Ask what kinds of food fish eat. Most fish eat small plants, other fish, or small animals.

Animals are consumers that eat producers or other consumers.
sun
Green plants are producers. They make their own food with energy from the sun.

2. Food Preferences and Niches

Materials A fruitfly; a housefly; a jar; raw meat; a banana; a butterfly net

Procedure

• Catch a housefly and a fruitfly. Place them in a jar with a piece of raw meat and a banana. Have the children observe which fly prefers which food. Ask the following kinds of questions:

What do houseflies like to eat?
(Generally, garbage and putrid-smelling materials.)

What do fruitflies like to eat?
(Rotting fruit.)

Why are flies considered a nuisance?
(They tend to hand around garbage and land on rotting or dirty things. Most people consider them a nuisance because they believe that flies spread diseases.)

How do flies help the environment?
(They help clear away nature's garbage. They lay their eggs in decaying things like dead animals and when the eggs hatch the larvae eat the dead animal.)

• Explain that animals have their own niche or territory in an environment. A niche is a special place to live that belongs to a population of animals. The two flies are not in competition for the food supply in the jar. They each prefer eating a different kind of food. Explain that when there are a large variety of plants and animals living in a biome such as in a jungle, there tends to be less competition for food. The great diversity allows each animal to have its own niche or territory to live in. Animals in a jungle rarely need to compete for the exact same foods. There is a plentiful supply of food in a jungle or rain forest biome because of the immense diversity. In the Arctic or tundra where food is scarce in the winter, there is a lot of competition, but there are also fewer animals to compete with. Each healthy biome is balanced.

3. Predator and Prey

Materials Pictures of assorted animals that are eaten by other animals and of the animals that might eat them—for example: insect and frog, antelope and lion, bird and cat, toad and snake, snake and hawk, sheep and wolves, chickens and people, rabbit and fox.

Procedure

• Explain to children that all animals need food. Most living things eventually become food for other animals, or become food to bacteria and fungi when they rot. Show the children the pictures of the assorted animals. Ask the children if they can guess what kind of food they think each of the animals eats. Have them sort the pictures so that all of the animals that eat only plants are in one pile and all of the animals that eat only meat are in another pile. Then ask them if any of

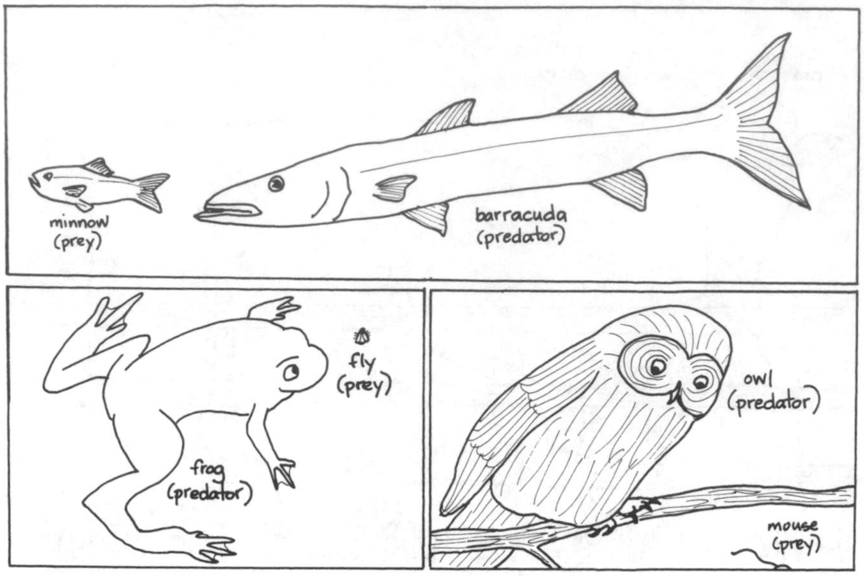

PREDATOR AND PREY

the animals from the meat-eaters group can also eat plants, and have them place those pictures into a separate pile. Explain that when an animal eats only meat, it is called a carnivore. Animals that can eat both plants and animals are called omnivores. Animals that can eat only plants are called herbivores. Ask the children the following kinds of questions:

Which animal group can eat the largest variety of foods?
(Omnivores.)

Which animal group probably has the best chance to adapt to foods in a new environment?
(Omnivores.)

What animal group do we as human beings belong to?
(Omnivore.)

• Have the children look at the sorted pictures and guess which of the carnivores would eat which of the herbivores. Help them become aware that the carnivores do not restrict themselves to just one kind of animal to eat. For example, foxes can eat rabbits, squirrels, mice, and birds, and so can hawks.
• Explain to the children that when an animal is eaten by another animal it is called the prey or the animal that gets caught and eaten. The animal that does the eating is called the predator. Predators attack other animals and help keep the population of the prey down. If foxes and hawks did not eat rabbits, there would be too many rabbits. The rabbits would destroy the balance of the biome by competing with each other and other animals for food. They might eat too many green plants so that other animals including themselves would not have enough food to eat.

4. Food Chains

Materials A picture of a grasshopper, frog, snake, hawk; paper; glue; a marking pen; old nature magazines; scissors.

Procedure
• Show the children the pictures. Explain that the grasshopper eats grass. It is a primary consumer. A primary consumer is the first animal in a food chain to eat a plant. Ask the children if they can think of other primary consumers. Explain to them that all herbivore animals are primary consumers. Explain that the other animals in the pictures listed in materials above can also eat grasshoppers. If these animals eat a grasshopper, they would be secondary consumers in a food chain. If the frog eats the grasshopper and is then eaten by a snake, the snake would be the third consumer in the food chain. The snake is a predator, but the snake has enemies. The hawk could eat the snake. The hawk would then be the fourth consumer in the food chain. The hawk has no enemies. It is at the top of the food chain. When the hawk dies, other animals eat it. The dead hawk eventually decays with the help of bacteria and fungi which help turn the remains of the dead hawk into soil. The soil then becomes rich in minerals and nutrients to grow new plants.
• Draw a picture of the food chain described above for the children so they can see how the arrows move from the first consumer to the fourth consumer. See diagram.
• Have the children cut out pictures from magazines that could make up a possible food chain. Ask them

what the first picture would have to be. Explain that all food chains start with the sun, and the first living thing in a food chain is a green plant. Then the consumers have to be added in. Have them arrange the cut pictures on a piece of paper before they glue them down and then add a pencil arrow mark to show the direction of the food chain, to show what eats what.

• Ask the children if they know what a food chain is. Explain that a food chain traces the chain of energy that transfers from plants that produce food to animals that consume food to other animals that consume other animals. Every time an animal eats food, energy is used. It takes energy for an animal to digest food, but the food gives the animal energy. Animals need food to keep their bodies working. Have the children jump up and down, blink their eyes, and feel their heart beating, and notice their ribs going up and down when they breathe. All of these activities that go on in

our bodies use energy. Food gives us the energy to keep going. Food is our fuel. As our bodies work and exercise, they use up or burn the fuel. The energy is consumed and charged. Food to animals is like gasoline for a car. Without energy from fuel, nothing can function.

• Ask the children to think back to the different kinds of animals that lived in the different biomes. Have the children think up various food chains for the different biomes discussed in Section IV of this chapter. They may want to use some of the reference books listed at the end of this chapter.

5. Food Webs

Materials A spider web; a toothpick; a diagram of a food web.

Procedure

• Take the children outside to look at a spider web. Have the children notice the pattern. Touch the web with a toothpick. Ask the following kinds of questions:

What happens when you shake the spider web?
(It bounces around, but stays together.)

What happens to the shape of the spider web if one small strand in the spider web breaks?
(The shape of the web changes slightly.)

What happens to the web if a major spike or thread breaks?
(The web is destroyed and needs to be repaired and rebuilt by the spider.)

• Explain to the children that a food web is like a spider's web. It is a complex system in which animals can be in more than one food chain. For example, rabbits, squirrels, and mice all eat plants. Rabbits are eaten by foxes, hawks, and mountain lions. Squirrels are eaten by foxes and hawks. Mice are eaten by snakes, foxes, and hawks. The food chains are interlocked and interwoven like a spider's web. See diagram.

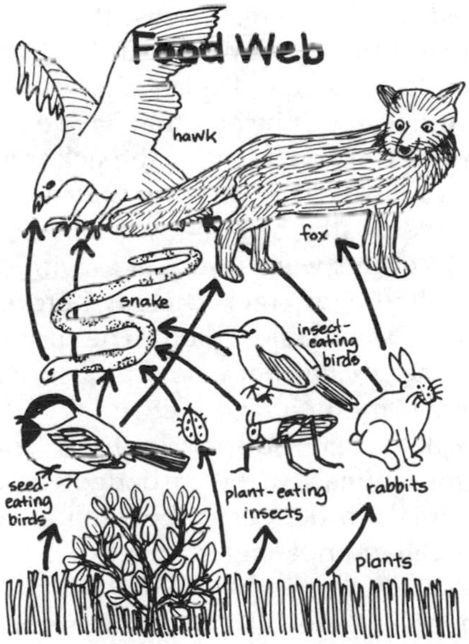

• Explain that many food chains make up a food web. Each biome has a food web that is as delicate as the spider's web. If one small chain in the food web breaks, not a lot of damage is done, but the shape of the web may change slightly. If a major part of the chain is broken, a lot of damage can occur. The whole food web could collapse. For example: If there were no mountain lions around to eat deer, the deer population would increase. There would be too many deer. The deer would eat all of the grasses and the soil would start to erode because there would be no more roots from the grasses to hold the soil in place. Eventually all of the deer would die of starvation because they would not have any food. All of these changes would take place gradually over many years.

• Explain that any change in a food web can bring about a disaster if it is not a balanced change. When foreign insects like the Japanese beetle arrived in our country, they caused much damage to plants because the Japanese beetles had no natural enemies and they were able to multiply. Farmers and gardeners used poisonous sprays like DDT to kill them, but the poisons began to get into the food chain and also poisoned parts of food webs, causing much harm and destruction. Eventually, when the effects of the poisons were understood, the spraying of some of the poisons was outlawed.

6. Poisons in a Food Chain

Materials Pictures of oil-soaked beaches, of polluted water and dead fish.

Procedure

• Show the pictures to the children and ask them whether or not the animals look healthy. Ask them what caused the problem. Discuss the pollution and how it affected the environment and the food chains and the whole food web. Explain that if birds eat fish from polluted water or insects that have eaten poison, the birds eat poison too by eating the sick animals. If the birds eat too many sick animals that are poisoned, the birds eventually become weak. Scientists discovered that eagles were laying eggs with thin shells. The thin-shelled eggs cracked easily before the birds hatched, and the babies died. The population of eagles became smaller because the birds were eating other animals in their food chain that had eaten poison. Explain that poisons in food chains have caused some animals to be in danger of becoming extinct. Animals in danger of becoming extinct as a species are called endangered species.

• Have the children find out what animals in their biome are endangered, and how these animals that are endangered are important to the food web. Information about endangered species can be gotten from: Fish and Wildlife Service, U.S. Department of the Interior, Washington, D.C. 20240.

Further Resources

Suggested Books for Children

Dewey Decimal Classification Number for ecology is: 574.

Amos, William H., *Life in Ponds and Streams.* Washington, D.C.: National Geographic Society, 1981. (Large color photos.)

Behnke, Frances L., *What We Find When We Look Under Rocks.* New York: McGraw-Hill, 1971. (Nature walk.)

Bendick, Jeanne, *Ecology, Science Experiences.* New York: Franklin Watts, 1975.

Berger, Melvin and Gilda, *Fitting in, Animals in Their Habitats.* New York: Coward-McCann, 1976. (How animals adapt to environment.)

Bolognese, Don, *All Upon a Stone.* New York: Thomas Y. Crowell, 1971. (Nature walk.)

Buck, Margaret, *In Yards and Gardens.* New York: Abingdon Press, 1952. (Beautiful small sketches to help observation skills.)

Busch, Phyllis, *Exploring as You Walk in the City.* Philadelphia: Lippincott, 1922. (Nature walk.)

Chargin, Claudia, *It's Your World, A Basic Ecology Guide and Project Book.* San Francisco: Troubadour Press, 1971.

Childcraft, the 1974 Childcraft Annual, *Animals in Danger.* Chicago: Field Enterprises Educational Corporation, 1974.

Clarkson, Jan Nagel, *Tricks Animals Play.* Washington, D.C.: National Geographic Society, 1978.

Cole, Joanna, and Jerome Wexler, *Find the Hidden Insect.* New York: Morrow, 1979.

Constant, Anne-Marie, *Waste Not, Want Not, Food.* London: Burke, 1977. (About conserving food resources and food chains.)

Coptesi, Wendy W., *Explore a Spooky Swamp.* Washington, D.C.: National Geographic Society, 1978. (Large color photos.)

Environmental Protection Agency, *Fun with the Environment.* Washington, D.C.: EPA, 1977.

Environmental Protection Agency, *Our Endangered World, ABC's of Human Ecology.* Washington, D.C.: EPA, 1976.

Environmental Protection Agency, *Resource Recovery and You.* Washington, D.C.: EPA, 1976.

Farb, Peter, *Life, Nature Library Ecology.* New York: Time, 1970.

Fisher, Aileen, *Once We Went on a Picnic.* New York: Thomas Y. Crowell, 1975. (Nature walk.)

Fisher, Ronald M., *A Day in the Woods.* Washington, D.C.: National Geographic Society, 1975. (Large color photos.)

Goldstein, Philip, *Animals and Plants that Trap.* New York: Holiday House, 1974.

Howell, Ruth, *A Crack in the Pavement.* New York: Atheneum, 1970. (Nature walk.)

Miles, Betty, *Save the Environment: An Ecology Handbook for Kids.* New York: Knopf, 1974.

National Geographic Society, *Secrets of Animal Survival.* Washington, D.C.: National Geographic Society, 1983. (Large color photos.)

Pringle, Laurence, *Into the Woods.* New York: Macmillan, 1973.

Selberg, Ingrid, *Our Changing World, A Revolving Picture Book.* New York: Putnam, 1982.

Selsam, Millicent, and Ezra Jack Keats, *How to Be Nature's Detective.* New York: Harper and Row, 1963.

Showers, Paul, *The Listening Walk.* New York: Thomas Y. Crowell, 1961. (Nature walk.)

Tresselt, Alvin, *The Dead Tree.* New York: Parent's Magazine Press, 1972. (About the organisms in a dead tree that decompose it.)

Van Soelen, Philip, *Cricket in the Grass and Other Stories.* New York: Sierra Club Books/Scribner's, 1979. (Stories told in pictures of food chains in a field. No words.)

Resource Books for More Ideas

Bendick, Jeanne, *Adaptation.* New York: Franklin Watts, 1971.

Berrill, Jacquelyn, *Wonders of Animal Migration.* New York: Dodd, Mead, 1964.

Billington, Elizabeth, *Understanding Ecology.* New York: Fredrick Warne and Co., 1968.

Blaustein, Rose and Elliott, *Investigating Ecology.* New York: Arco Publishing Co., 1978.

Bowan, John S., *On Guard: Living Things Defend Themselves.* Garden City, New York: Doubleday, 1969. (Animal adaptation and defense.)

Brennan, Matthew, *The Environment and You, How and Why Wonder Book.* New York: Grosset and Dunlap, 1974.

Cooper, Elizabeth, *Science in Your Own Backyard.* New York: Harcourt Brace, 1960.

Friendly, Natalie, *Miraculous Web—The Balance of Life.* Englewood Cliffs, New Jersey: Prentice-Hall, 1968.

Frith, Michael, *Some of Us Walk, Some Fly, Some Swim.* New York: Random House, 1971. (Animal adaptation and defense.)

Gutnick, Martin, *The Science of Classification.* New York: Franklin Watts, 1980.

Kalina, Sigmund, *Air, the Invisible Ocean.* New York: Lothrop, Lee and Shepard Co., 1973. (About air and air pollution.)

Pringle, Laurence, and Jan Adkins, *Chains, Webs, and Pyramids, The Flow of Energy in Nature.* New York: Thomas Y. Crowell, 1975.

Pringle, Laurence, *Natural Fire, Its Ecology in Forests.* New York: Morrow, 1979.

Reidman, Sarah, *Biological Clocks.* New York: Thomas Y. Crowell, 1982.

Shuttlesworth, Dorothy, *Natural Partnerships.* Garden City, New York: Doubleday, 1969.

Simon, Seymour, *Science in a Vacant Lot.* New York: Viking Press, 1970.

Simon, Seymour, *Science Projects in Ecology.* New York: Holiday House, 1972.

Simon, Seymour, *The Secret Clocks, Time Senses of Living Things.* New York: Viking Press, 1974.

Sterling, *Fall Is Here.* Garden City, New York: Doubleday, 1966. (How an ecosystem gets ready for winter.)

Tongren, Sally, *What's for Lunch, Animal Feeding at the Zoo.* New York: GMG, 1981.

BIBLIOGRAPHY

The American Heritage Dictionary of the English Language, Morris William, ed. Boston: Houghton Mifflin, 1976.

Arkady, Leokum, *It's Amazing*. New York: Scholastic Book Services, 1958.

Belth, Marc, *Education as a Discipline*. Boston: Allyn & Bacon, 1965. (See especially Chapter 3, "Inference is Shaped by Models," and Chapter 4, "Thinking: Models, Methods and Techniques.")

Blackwelder, Sheila Kyser, *Science for All Seasons*. Englewood Cliffs, New Jersey: Prentice-Hall, 1980.

Blough, Glenn, and Julius Schwartz, *Elementary School Science and How to Teach It*, 5th edition. New York: Holt, Rinehart & Winston, 1974.

Brown, Ed, *Bubbles, Rainbows and Worms, Science Experiments for Preschool Children*. Mt. Rainier, Maryland: Gryphon House, 1981.

Bruner, J. S., *The Process of Education*. Cambridge, Massachusetts: Harvard University Press, 1960. (See especially Chapter 2, "The Importance of Structure," and Chapter 3, "Readiness for Learning.")

Butts, David P., "The Degree to Which Children Conceptualize from Science Experiences," *Journal of Research in Science Teaching* 1:135–43, June 1963.

Children's Television Workshop, *3, 2, 1, Contact*. Educational Television Series. Various dates.

Cobb, Vicki, and Kathy Darling, *Bet You Can! Science Possibilities to Fool You*. New York: Avon Books, 1983.

Cobb, Vicki, and Kathy Darling, *Bet You Can't! Science Impossibilities to Fool You*. New York: Avon Books, 1983.

Coble, Charles, Elaine Murray, and Dale Rice, *Earth Science*. Englewood Cliffs, New Jersey: Prentice-Hall, 1981.

Fee, Sally, *A Child's Real World–Developing Science Within the Program*. A workshop presented in Washington, D.C. at the National Association for the Education of Young Children (NAEYC), Washington, D.C.: November, 1982.

Feravolo, Rocco, *Easy Physics Projects: Air, Water and Heat*. Englewood Cliffs, New Jersey: Prentice-Hall, 1969.

Forte, Imogene, and Joy Mackenzie, *Creative Science Experiences for the Young Child*. Nashville, Tennessee: Incentive Publications, 1983.

Fuller, Harry, *General Botany*. New York: Barnes and Noble, 1955.

Gagné, Robert M., *The Conditions of Learning*. New York: Holt, Rinehart, and Winston, 1965.

Godman, Arthur, *Barnes and Noble Thesaurus of Science*. New York: Harper and Row, 1981.

Goldstein-Jackson, Kevin, Norman Rudnick, and Ronald Hymen, *Experiments with Everyday Objects: Science Activities for Children, Parents and Teachers*. Englewood Cliffs, New Jersey: Prentice-Hall, 1978.

Good, Ronald, G., *How Children Learn Science*. New York: Macmillan, 1977.

Hadary, Doris E., *Laboratory Science and Art for Blind, Deaf, and Emotionally Disturbed Children, A Mainstreaming Approach*. Baltimore, Maryland: University Park Press, 1978.

Harlan, Jean Durgin, *Science Experiments for the Early Childhood Years*. Columbus, Ohio: Merrill, 1976.

Herbert, Don, *Mr. Wizard's Super Market Science*. New York: Random House, 1980.

Herrick, Virgil E., *Strategies of Curriculum Development*. Columbus, Ohio: Merrill, 1965.

Hewitt, Paul G., *Conceptual Physics, A New Introduction to Your Environment*. Boston: Little, Brown & Co., 1974.

Hoffman, James and Voris, *Second Grade Creative Units*. Minneapolis: T. S. Denison, 1963.

Holt, Bess-Gene, *Science with Young Children*. Washington, D.C.: National Association for the Education of Young Children, 1977.

Kamii, Constance, and Rheta DeVries, *Physical Knowledge in Preschool Education, Implications of Piaget's Theory.* Englewood Cliffs, New Jersey: Prentice-Hall, 1978.

Kirtland, Susanne, *Easy Answers to Hard Questions.* New York: Grosset and Dunlap, 1979.

Mandell, Muriel, *Physics Experiments for Children.* New York: Dover, 1968.

McCoy, Elin, *The Incredible Year-Round Playbook: Fun with Sun, Sand, Water, Wind and Snow.* New York: Random House, 1979.

Nelson, Leslie, and George Lorbeer, *Science Activities.* Dubuque, Iowa: William C. Brown, 1967.

New Unesco Source Book for Science Teachers. Paris: Unesco Press, 1973.

Nicklesburg, Janet, *Nature Activities for Early Childhood.* Reading, Massachusetts: Addison-Wesley, 1976.

Rosen, Seymour, *Earth Science Workshop, Understanding the Atmospheres and Oceans.* New York: Globe Book Co., 1978.

Rosen, Seymour, *Physics Workshop, Understanding Forces.* New York: Globe Book Co., 1978.

Russell, Helen Ross, *Ten-Minute Field Trips, Using the School Grounds for Environmental Studies.* Chicago: Ferguson, 1973.

Schneider, Herman and Nina, *Got a Minute?* New York: Scholastic Book Services, 1975.

Simon, Seymour, *Pets in a Jar.* New York: Penguin Books, 1979.

Sisson, Edith A., *Nature with Children of All Ages.* Englewood Cliffs, New Jersey: Prentice-Hall, 1982.

Skolnick, Joan, Carol Langbort, and Lucille Day, *How to Encourage Girls in Math and Science.* Englewood Cliffs, New Jersey: Prentice-Hall, 1982.

Stein, Sara, *The Science Book.* New York: Workman Publishing, 1979.

Stetten, Mary, *Let's Play Science.* New York: Harper and Row, 1979.

Tryon, Bette, *Science, A Practical Approach.* A workshop presented in Washington, D.C., at the National Conference of the National Association for the Education of Young Children (NAEYC), Washington, D.C., November, 1982.

Viorst, Judith, *150 Science Experiments Step by Step.* New York: Bantam, 1963.

Williams, David, *"Science" for Young Children—Gathering Experiences.* 16th Annual Conference sponsored by the Maryland Council of Parent Participation Nursery Schools, Montgomery College, Rockville, Maryland, March 7, 1984.

World Book Encyclopedia, 1979 ed. Chicago: World Book-Childcraft, 1979. (See especially: Sound, Light, Color, Air, Water, Weather, Volcanoes, Atoms, Animals, Plants, Leaves, Flowers, Ecology.)

Wyler, Rose, *Prove It!* New York: Harper and Row, 1963.

Wyler, Rose, *What Happens If?* New York: Scholastic Book Services, 1974.

Series

Doubleday Nature Guides. New York: Doubleday (various dates).

Golden Guides. Racine, Wisconsin: Western (various dates).

How and Why Wonder Books. New York: Grosset and Dunlap (various dates)

Ladybird Natural History Books. London: Ladybird Books (various dates).

Life Nature Library. New York: Time-Life (various dates).

National Geographic, Books for World Explorers. Washington, D.C.: National Geographic Society (various dates).

Peterson Field Guides. Boston: Houghton Mifflin (various dates).

Science 5/13 Series. MacDonald Education, London and New York, distributed from Milwaukee, Wisconsin: Raintree, 1976.

Spotter's Guides. London: Usborne (various dates).

Zim, H., et al., *Golden Nature Guides.* Racine, Wisconsin: Golden Press (various dates).

Teachers' Editions of Textbooks in Science Series

Anderson, Norris, et al., *Biological Science, An Ecological Approach* (3rd edition). New York: Rand McNally, 1973.

Blecha, Milo, Peter Gega, and Muriel Green, *Exploring Science* (K–6). River Forest, Illinois: Laidlaw, 1979.

Brandwein, Paul, Elizabeth Cooper, Paul Blackwood, Elizabeth Hone, *Concepts in Science* (3rd edition, K–6). New York: Harcourt Brace, 1972.

Brewer, A. C., Nell Garland, et al. *ESLI—Elementary Science, Learning by Investigation, Grades One Through Six.* New York: Rand McNally, 1973.

Brown, F. Martin, Grace H. Kemper, and John H. Lewis, *Earth Science.* Morristown, New Jersey: Silver Burdett, 1970.

Carter, Joseph, et al., *Life Science, A Problem-Solving Approach* (teachers' edition). Lexington, Massachusetts: Ginn, 1979.

Fischler, Abraham F., Laurence F. Lowery, and Sam Blanc, *Science, A Modern Approach, Preschool Through Grade Six.* New York: Holt, Rinehart and Winston, 1966.

Harris, Miles F., Dale T. Hesser, et al., *Investigating the Earth* (teachers' edition). Boston: Houghton Mifflin, 1973.

Heimler, Charles, *Principals of Science* (Book One, 4th edition—teacher's edition). Columbus, Ohio: Charles Merrill, 1979.

Holmes, Neal, John Leake, et al., *Science People, Concepts Processes.* New York: McGraw-Hill, 1974.

Mallinson, George and Jacqueline, et al., *Science (Level 2).* Morristown, New Jersey: Silver Burdett, 1968.

Navarra, John, and Joseph Safforoni, *Today's Basic Science (K–8).* New York: Harper and Row, 1963.

Renner, John W., Don Stafford, and Vivian Coulter, *Learning Science—Grades One Through Six—Things, Change, Systems, Variation, Action, Models.* Encino, California: Glencoe, 1977.

Rockcastle, Veiere, Frank Salamon, Victor Schmidt, and Betty McKnight, *STEM Science (Space, Time, Energy, Matter, K–6).* Reading, Massachusetts: Addison-Wesley, 1977.

Schneider, Herman and Nina, *Science for Here and Now* (3rd edition, 2–6). Boston: D. C.. Heath, 1965.

Smallwood, William L., *Challenges to Science, Life Science* (teachers' edition). New York: McGraw-Hill, 1973.

Sund, Robert, Donald Adams, and Jay Hackett, *Accent on Science (Levels 4–6).* Columbus, Ohio: Charles Merrill, 1980.

Thurber, Walter, et al., *Exploring Life Science.* Boston: Allyn & Bacon, 1975.

INDEX